'... deserve[s] space on the shelves of true movie buffs. ...
insightful'
Raymond Seitz, *The Times*

' ... what is so attractive about *The Crowded Prairie* is the way
Coyne takes a whole slew of westerns from 1939 to 1976, analyses
them in detail and places them within the context and concerns of
the period. ... few if any have matched the authority or scope
of Coyne's book.'
Brian Pendreigh, *The Scotsman*

' ... a bracing analysis of ... the golden age of Hollywood
Westerns ... For all academic film collections.'
Kim R. Holston, *Library Journal*

' ... an informative addition to an undergraduate reading list.'
Sight and Sound

Cinema and Society Series
General Editor: Jeffrey Richards

Published and forthcoming:

Best of British: Cinema and Society, 1930 to the Present
Anthony Aldgate and Jeffrey Richards
Second, revised edition

The British at War: Cinema, State and Propaganda, 1939–1945
James Chapman

British Cinema and the Cold War
Tony Shaw

British Film Noir: Shadows are my Friends
Robert Murphy

The Crowded Prairie: American National Identity in the Hollywood Western
Michael Coyne

Distorted Images: Film and National Identity in Britain, 1919–1939
Kenton Bamford

Film Propaganda: Soviet Russia and Nazi Germany
Richard Taylor
Second, revised edition

License to Thrill: A Cultural History of the James Bond Films
James Chapman

Somewhere in England: British Cinema and Exile
Kevin Gough-Yates

Spaghetti Westerns: From Karl May to Sergio Leone
Christopher Frayling
Second, revised edition

The Unknown 1930s: An Alternative History of the British Cinema, 1929–1939
Edited by Jeffrey Richards

The Crowded Prairie: American National Identity in the Hollywood Western

M ICHAEL C OYNE

I.B.Tauris Publishers
LONDON · NEW YORK

Paperback edition published in 1998 by I.B.Tauris & Co Ltd
Victoria House, Bloomsbury Square, London WC1B 4DZ
175 Fifth Avenue, New York NY 10010

In the United States and Canada distributed by St Martin's Press,
175 Fifth Avenue, New York NY 10010

First published in 1997 by I.B.Tauris & Co Ltd

ISBN 1 86064 259 4

A full CIP record for this book is available from the British Library
A full CIP record for this book is available from the Library of Congress

Library of Congress catalog card: available

Set in Berthold Baskerville by Ewan Smith, London
Printed and bound in Great Britain by WBC Ltd, Bridgend

Contents

List of Plates   vii

Preface   ix

Acknowledgements   x

Author's Note   xi

Introduction   1

1   Mirror for Prewar America: *Stagecoach* and the Western, 1939–1941   16

2   Puritan Paradigms: *My Darling Clementine* and *Duel in the Sun*   31

3   "The Lonely Crowd", Catholicism and Consensus on the Prairie: *Red River*, *Fort Apache* and *She Wore a Yellow Ribbon*   48

4   Dysfunctional Family Structures in Classic Westerns, 1950–1961: *The Gunfighter*, *Shane*, *The Searchers* and *The Last Sunset*   66

5   Politics and Codes of Masculinity in Late 1950s Star Westerns: *The Big Country* and *Warlock*   84

6   "No More West to Win": *How the West Was Won* and the Elegiac Westerns of 1962   105

7   A Genre in Flux, A Nation in Turmoil: The Vietnamization of the Western in Mid-1960s America   120

8   Receding Frontiers, Narrowing Options: *The Wild Bunch* and the Western in Richard Nixon's America   142

9   Legends Revisited, Legends Revised in "Bicentennial Westerns": *Buffalo Bill and the Indians*, *The Outlaw Josey Wales* and *The Shootist*   166

Conclusion   184

Notes   193

Filmography   212

Bibliography   220

Index   234

List of Plates

1. *Stagecoach* (United Artists, 1939), directed by John Ford
2. *My Darling Clementine* (20th Century-Fox, 1946), directed by John Ford
3. *Duel in the Sun* (Selznick Releasing Organization, 1946), directed by King Vidor
4. *Red River* (United Artists, 1948), directed by Howard Hawks
5. *The Gunfighter* (20th Century-Fox, 1950), directed by Henry King
6. *Shane* (Paramount, 1953), directed by George Stevens
7. *The Searchers* (Warner Brothers, 1956), directed by John Ford
8. *The Big Country* (United Artists, 1958), directed by William Wyler
9. *Warlock* (20th Century-Fox, 1959), directed by Edward Dmytryk
10. *The Man Who Shot Liberty Valance* (Paramount, 1962), directed by John Ford
11. *Ride the High Country* (Metro-Goldwyn-Mayer, 1962), directed by Sam Peckinpah
12. *How the West Was Won* (Metro-Goldwyn-Mayer & Cinerama, 1962), directed by Henry Hathaway, John Ford and George Marshall
13. *The Professionals* (Columbia, 1966), directed by Richard Brooks
14. *The Wild Bunch* (Warner Brothers-Seven Arts, 1969), directed by Sam Peckinpah
15. *Buffalo Bill and the Indians or Sitting Bull's History Lesson* (United Artists, 1976), directed by Robert Altman
16. *The Outlaw Josey Wales* (Warner Brothers, 1976), directed by Clint Eastwood

All stills courtesy of The Joel Finler Collection.

Dedicated:
May 26 1907 – June 11 1979,
To The Life and
The Memory

Preface

NATIONAL identity is one of the major current preoccupations of cultural historians. From its earliest days the cinema has been one of the most potent means of articulating and promoting concepts of national identity. For the United States, the Western film and the national identity have been inextricably linked. The cowboy has been recognized world-wide as one of the most potent and enduring symbols of America. Each generation has rewritten and refilmed the great Western myths and myth-figures to fit its own preoccupations and perceptions. At some point in their careers, most of the great Hollywood stars have saddled up and headed west, even such apparently unlikely figures as Humphrey Bogart and Errol Flynn. In his resonantly titled *The Crowded Prairie*, Michael Coyne sets out to explore the ways in which the Western has presented America's national identity from the end of the Depression to the Bicentennial in 1976. The Western has been approached from a variety of critical perspectives over the years. Coyne acknowledges them all while treading his own distinctive path. Armed with an encyclopedic knowledge of the genre, acute critical perception and an infectious enthusiasm, Michael Coyne examines and reinterprets a range of old favourites such as *Stagecoach* and *Shane*, but also revalues and explores neglected classics like *Warlock* and *The Big Country*. He examines the iconography of the great Western stars and the approaches of the great directors. As befits a trained historian, he carefully locates the films in their historic, cinematic and cultural contexts. He analyses both contemporary critical reactions to the films and retrospective judgements. He traces the impact upon the genre of such key historical events as World War II, McCarthyism, the Civil Rights movement, Vietnam and Watergate. He explores the changing attitudes within the genre to gender, race, violence, the family, the community and youth. Altogether, *The Crowded Prairie* adds up to an invigorating and enlightening study which enhances our knowledge and our understanding both of the Western and of American national identity.

Jeffrey Richards

Acknowledgements

I N the course of producing this study many people have been of help
in inestimable ways, for all of which I am grateful. Yet I would be
remiss indeed if I did not express my thanks to the following: Professor
Jeffrey Richards, who has encouraged this project at every stage of
development; Professor Michael J. Heale, my supervisor at Lancaster
University; and Mr Owen Dudley Edwards of the University of Edinburgh, who first gave my enthusiasm for American history and popular
culture a sense of substance and direction. I have learned much about
the craft of history and the craft of writing from these three gentlemen;
I am most thankful for their wisdom, their insight and their friendship.

I must also extend thanks to Philippa Brewster, my editor at I.B.
Tauris; Jim Dunnigan and the Edinburgh Film Guild; Mr Joel W. Finler
and The Joel Finler Collection, for much kind help in the matter of
illustrations; and, regarding this last, the film companies: Columbia,
Metro-Goldwyn-Mayer (now Turner Entertainment), Paramount, 20th
Century-Fox, United Artists and Warner Brothers.

In addition, several friends and colleagues were of great help in
many ways during the writing of this book. Many thanks to Desmond
and Pamela Coyne, my brother and sister-in-law; Dr Robert Bliss of
Lancaster University; John Gilhooly; Catherine and Jeremy de Satgé;
Jill Turner; John Beattie; James Chapman; Gregor Ewing; Gavin Forrest;
John Menzies; John McGinty; David Todd; Elizabeth McLellan; K. P.
Onn; Mr George Rehin of Sussex University; Roy Stewart; Lindsay
and Marion Wilson; and I must certainly extend special thanks to
Harry Ferguson, who introduced me to the wonderful world of Westerns
as soon as I could make sense of the flickering images on the screen.
Finally, my most lasting debt is to my mother and father, Elma and
Michael Coyne, for all their love, encouragement and support.

Author's Note

I N reporting on the commercial success of Westerns chosen for this study I have relied principally on a table of box office hits printed in David Pirie (ed.), *The Anatomy of the Movies* (Windward, London, 1981), which was originally compiled from rental figures reported in *Variety* and *The Motion Picture Almanac* and from the records of the film companies themselves. These figures apply only to the United States and Canada.

The figures quoted refer to a film's rental income from its initial release period. This is normally the most reliable indication of a film's success. The rental fee is the money the exhibitor pays the distributor to show a film, whereas the box office gross is the money the audience pays to see the film. Actual box office grosses are not easily accessible and, even if acquired, are difficult to interpret accurately. Thus, when I refer to a film's gross at the box office the figures I cite are normally predicated on gross rental income which, through offset costs, reflects the size of the audience for each film and adds up to approximately half the total box office gross, with the other half going to the exhibitors.

A further note is required regarding a particular use of language in this text. For most of the two decades immediately following World War II, the phrase "Native American" referred to American citizens born within the United States. As such, this phrase was a construct of the dominant, primarily *white* culture. However, in the wake of the raised racial and ethnic consciousness of the 1960s, the phrase "Native American" has been reclaimed by American Indians in reassertion of their own national and racial identity.

For much of the era under scrutiny in this book, in common parlance and certainly in the discourse of Hollywood Westerns, those indigenous inhabitants of North America prior to white settlement were referred to as "Indians". Thus, in accordance with historical accuracy, throughout the text today's Native Americans are referred to as "Indians", except when the focus is more specifically on a singular tribal identity, e.g., the Apache or Comanche Nations.

Introduction

ON November 22 1963 Fort Worth's Chamber of Commerce presented President Kennedy with a stetson. Amid some amusement, Kennedy decided not to don the hat and told the photographers he would wear it at the White House the following Monday. Kennedy had a noted disdain for strange headgear, and was probably conscious that the stetson might make him look ridiculous, as if he were pretending to be someone he clearly was not. On the last day of his life, John Kennedy refused to play cowboy. Perhaps this reluctance to embrace one of the nation's most potent symbols, reluctance long evident from his Eastern liberalism and urbane demeanour, accounted for some of the regional hostility toward him; many Southwesterners, with their fierce pride in frontier history and myth, could not identify this young man and his "New Frontier" with their particular concept of America.

By contrast, other presidents of the postwar era have been only too eager to include the cowboy in their constituency. In 1952 Dwight Eisenhower kept whistling the song from *High Noon*, which he could not get out of his head; for leisure he enjoyed the Western novels of Luke Short and Zane Grey; and in 1958 he was so impressed by William Wyler's sprawling pacifist Western *The Big Country* that he sat through four successive screenings at the White House.[1] Native Texan Lyndon Johnson sported a stetson and galloped on horseback in his 1964 campaign against Arizona's Barry Goldwater, thus using frontier iconography to help forestall his fellow Westerner's attempt to depict him as a creature of Washington. Richard Nixon spoke publicly of his admiration for the Western and numbered among his friends John Wayne and James Stewart. On Wayne's death from cancer in 1979, Gerald Ford and Jimmy Carter each paid fulsome tribute.

Most remarkable was Ronald Reagan's capitalization on his mediocre claim to sagebrush stardom, based mainly on his stint as host of the television show *Death Valley Days*. Only six of his fifty-four films were Westerns, but he artfully cultivated the image, ceaselessly posing in

I

Western garb and on horseback at his ranch and fudging in rhetoric the divide between U.S. history and the nation's collective memory as filtered through Hollywood. One 1980 campaign button even featured Reagan posed before a drawing of John Wayne, with the caption "Carry on for The Duke". Liberal intellectuals meant to disparage Reagan by calling him a cowboy actor, but in this respect he outflanked his detractors, perceiving in that epithet a durable appeal to Main Street. George Bush, despite his years as a Texas oilman, never entirely shook the aura of an effete, elitist Easterner, though he tried hard, even to the pitiable extent of asserting his Texan identity in 1992's election by showing voters in his adopted State his cowboy boots. Even Bill Clinton, despite his posturing as John Kennedy's heir, has gone on record declaring *High Noon* his favourite film. This was a shrewd choice: by selecting a Western Clinton touched base with the conservative heartland; naming *High Noon*, with its celebrated anti-McCarthy subtext, enabled him to re-emphasize his liberal credentials.

So, aside from Kennedy's distancing gesture, presidents of the last four decades have either consciously engaged with the Western or at least employed Western trappings to deepen their own sense of national identity and also, vitally, to reinforce their relationship with the American people. As purveyors of a national image and as consumers of popular culture, presidents both realized and responded to the Western's pull on America's imagination. Whether for personal pleasure or public display, a president's demonstration of affinity for the Western proved to voters that, at heart, he was just plain folks. Tennessee's Estes Kefauver, wearing a coonskin cap during the presidential race of 1952, understood this ploy; Adlai Stevenson did not.

As the quintessentially American melodrama, the Western's lure has been phenomenal. From Jamestown in 1607 to statehood for New Mexico and Arizona in 1912, three hundred years of the nation's history chronicled westward movement, settlement and development; and, as the journey to a new homeland was part of Americans' own or ancestral experience, Westerns appealed both to national identity and to individual heritage. I will define national identity herein as characteristic of, or pertaining to, the history, culture, political philosophy, social experience, myths, traditions and common origin of United States citizens.

Westerns were also ideologically seductive, and not simply with obvious regard to constructs of white male primacy. Just as Frederick Jackson Turner defined the frontier as "a gate of escape from the bondage of the past", Hollywood Westerns have furnished spiritual respite from the complexities of twentieth-century society, simultaneously soothing, feeding and thriving on romantic frustrations.[2] The revisionism of the 1960s and 1970s notwithstanding, the Western's overall thrust sanctified territorial expansion, justified dispossession of the Indians, fuelled nostalgia for a largely mythicized past, exalted self-reliance and posited violence as the main solution to personal and societal problems. Thus, alongside celebration of national aggrandizement and implicit acceptance of racism, the Western was fraught with philosophical and psychological pitfalls for modern society. Taken to extremes, nostalgia for an idealized, simpler age flirts with both reactionary and asocial impulses; the cult of individualism – also potentially asocial – might lead to rapacity among winners or feelings of inadequacy among strivers who did not win; and, despite wide thematic reverence for law and order, Westerns ultimately glorified and assuredly glamorized bloodshed as the genre's chief *raison d'être*.

This glorification of violence is one key to the Western's multi-faceted appeal, and also to an ideological dilemma which American society has never fully settled: the final vesting of responsibility, if not power, in the state or the individual. Throughout its popularity, the Western held its authoritarian and libertarian components in productive tension, infusing its narratives with social/political subtexts without alienating large groups of its potential audience, and playing both sides of the street by balancing subjugation of Indians or a law and order platform with distrust of capitalists (e.g., John Ford's *Stagecoach* (1939) and Fred Zinnemann's *High Noon* (1952)).

During the nineteenth century, the Leatherstocking saga of James Fenimore Cooper, newspapers, magazines, dime novels and Buffalo Bill's Wild West Show all whetted America's enthusiasm for the adventure of the frontier.[3] Television brought this romance into American homes, eventually familiarizing Westerns to the point of contempt. Yet, in between these phenomena, for a generation and more, while the United States grew accustomed to unprecedented global responsibility and domestic affluence, it was Hollywood's vision of the West which held the nation in thrall. Quality Westerns (i.e., with lavish production values) enjoyed a brief vogue from 1939 to 1941, subsided during World War II, then flourished for twenty-five years till the genre's sharp decline in the early 1970s. There is considerable irony in a prosperous, technologically sophisticated society forging an idealized self-image from a spartan past; but it was partly a reminder of American fortitude and partly, in the spirit of predestination, a justification for present opulence. Furthermore, if life in America failed to match its promise, Westerns implied past and – often, but not always – future greatness.

Westerns therefore focused on dreams frustrated and dreams fulfilled in virtually equal measure. Yet, overwhelmingly, the strand of American identity Westerns addressed and constructed was white and male. "Cowboy heroes", wrote Garry Wills, "ride on the little-boy imaginings of men in the audience".[4] In perpetuating this cult of the cowboy for mid-twentieth-century Americans, John Wayne and his confrères eulogized and promoted standards of masculinity which were fundamentally at odds with a regulated society. At the very start of the genre's heyday, in Michael Curtiz's *Dodge City* (1939), Errol Flynn's sidekick observes that the town Flynn is cleaning up is now too "sissy" for his liking.[5] This was primarily a comic aside, but it articulated a concern which would assume crucial import within the genre by the early 1960s. Essentially, such is the problem Kirk Douglas's doomed modern cowboy confronts in David Miller's *Lonely Are the Brave* (1962). The crisis was more psychological than social, and seldom stated in overtly sexual terms. Howard Hawks's *Red River* (1948) and Ford's *The Searchers* (1956) rebuke their chief protagonists as too macho for society's (and their own) good but, from Henry King's *The Gunfighter* (1950) on, the genre often reproached civilization's inability to accommodate such men, rather than the individual for his failure to adapt.

Moral culpability in elegiac Westerns lay not so much with man's savagery as with society's pliability. Within the genre the cult of masculinity and the ethos of individualism merged, effectively becoming indistinguishable. As such, the Western's hyperbolic concept of virility suggested, as did its nostalgic and individualistic strains, that the true mark of a man might ultimately lie in self-styled social alienation. Yet Westerns at least highlighted heroic man's exclusion from society; the genre predominantly marginalized women from the outset. While the stereotypical antithesis of schoolmarm and whore certainly oversimplifies women's participation in the Hollywood Western, significantly, the most individualistic heroines in the entire genre – Jennifer Jones in King Vidor's *Duel in the Sun* (1946) and Joan Crawford in Nicholas Ray's *Johnny Guitar* (1954) – embodied masculine traits, each finally resolving her problems through gunplay.[6]

The Western's habitual representation of American identity was white as well as male. Numerous Westerns either implicitly advanced or explicitly assailed depictions of white supremacy. What the genre actually reinforced was not white *supremacy* but white *centrality*. Jon Tuska's *The American West in Film* (1985) excoriated several celebrated directors because their Westerns marginalized the Indian.[7] His contention that the Western has done little to restore the Indian's dignity (or centrality within America's most enduring national epic) is undoubtedly a fair point, but Tuska gave no credence to the reason for this cultural development: Westerns marginalized the Indian because they were only marginally *about* the Indian. Equally, there are very few Blacks in the Western, and fewer Black heroes.[8] Some 1940s Westerns featured Blacks as faithful, usually comic retainers. Throughout the 1950s their presence was negligible. At last, in the 1960s, a handful of Black performers portrayed heroic figures as the genre thrived during the decade of Civil Rights' sharpest upsurge. Yet, as before, the Western remained a creature and a reflection of white America.

Thus Westerns typically enforced white centrality. Various Westerns had a Civil Rights agenda, but above all we must bear in mind that the genre customarily posited such narratives as problems for white America to solve. This centrality dictates the principal focus of the present undertaking. I will engage with questions of race and ethnicity in relation to particular films, but the general thrust of my study is an examination of white American identity within the Western.

Of the years from 1945 to 1960, William L. O'Neill wrote: "The American High was not based on arrogance or smugness – though both existed – so much as on a deep faith in America's possibilities".[9] Similarly, the American identity Westerns constructed – and dissected – in a roughly contemporaneous time-frame was not wholly the preserve of Manifest Destiny and American Exceptionalism, but these ideological conceits easily found a home in the genre. Westerns were commonly, though not exclusively, set west of the Mississippi between 1865 and 1900 – an era sharing sundry cultural components with U.S. society after World War II. In each case, the nation had just emerged from four years of war which had concluded with the death of a controversial yet beloved, patriarchal president; veterans had returned to an America of steadily growing corporate influence and changing social status for Blacks; and a distant war waged against a primitive, non-Caucasian people would soon preoccupy Washington. Through the 1960s, as the Vietnam War increasingly dominated American politics, the Western effortlessly absorbed this issue, reworking aspects of the conflict on the cinematic frontier.

The golden age of Hollywood Westerns spanned thirty years, from the release of *Stagecoach* in 1939 to Sam Peckinpah's *The Wild Bunch* (1969). Over those three decades, the Western hero gradually drifted from social commitment to estrangement. Certainly the most remarkable year of all in this respect was 1962, due to the striking thematic convergence of four classic films released then: *Lonely Are the Brave,*

Peckinpah's *Ride the High Country*, Ford's *The Man Who Shot Liberty Valance* and even the apparently celebratory *How the West Was Won* dealt with the end of the frontier and various adverse effects of the triumph of civilization. Thus by 1962 the heroic individual's alienation from modern American society was already evident, though still mainly implicit. In 1893 Frederick Jackson Turner finished his most famous essay by stating, "the frontier has gone, and with its going has closed the first period of American history"; in 1962 Hollywood declared the frontier gone, so ending the first major period of the sound era Western.[10] Yet for this book, it is appropriate to conclude in 1976, America's Bicentennial, when the waning genre offered three character studies of self-consciously mythic figures (*Buffalo Bill and the Indians*, *The Outlaw Josey Wales* and *The Shootist*) to address the nature of legend in America's past. I take little account of the success of *Dances With Wolves* (1990) or *Unforgiven* (1992), both filmed long after the Western ceased to be a vital force in American culture. Even should their box office takings dislodge George Stevens's *Shane* (1953) as the third top-grossing Western (after inflation-adjustment in 1981), this does not detract from *Shane*'s own impact, success or historical significance.[11]

Especially in the last generation, interpretive literature on the Hollywood Western has raised the genre's critical stock and emphasized its political and sociological import. A single incontrovertible schematization can scarcely do justice to so versatile an entertainment. Yet, in truth, there is a hitherto unspecified *dual* classification which embraces the majority of Hollywood Westerns while retaining express outlines of myth.

With very few exceptions (e.g., Custer bio-pics), Westerns are likely to revolve around either a community, essentially a social construct, or an odyssey, which is primarily a literary device.[12] Ironies, not to mention complexities, abounded in the Western's deployment of this schematization. Westerns with a community setting, despite their smaller geographical scale, were better suited to celebrate or criticize contemporary U.S. politics, values and national identity, while odyssey Westerns – though frequently ranging wide over the frontier terrain – tended to favour narratives of personal obsession. *Dodge City* and Edward Dmytryk's *Warlock* (1959), both thinly fictionalized versions of the Wyatt Earp legend, were as much discourses on the American psyche in their respective eras of production as they were town-taming sagas, whereas the grim quests of James Stewart in Anthony Mann's 1950s Westerns and Randolph Scott in Budd Boetticher's span far across America's outdoors but have little to contribute to observations on contemporary political affairs or national as opposed to personal identity within the United States.[13] Community Westerns – largely conforming to the narrative structure Will Wright labelled the "classical plot", i.e., featuring a skilful, self-assured hero ultimately driven to violence to defend a community he will subsequently consider home – spotlight a locality substituting for America (or, alternatively, the world, with the hero *as* America).[14] Odyssey Westerns, above all the Mann–Stewart cycle, equate the rugged landscapes with the individualist's tortured soul.[15]

Community Westerns are predisposed to reflect national and societal concerns. Odyssey Westerns accentuate personal traits and neuroses. The hero of the community Western is supremely possessed of self-knowledge, saves America and discovers a new home; the hero of the odyssey Western may discover America and redeem his soul but, often, he is too unstable to find a true home for himself. Whereas the community Western extols social adjustment, the odyssey Western is charitably disposed toward a strain of self-styled alienation. At its most grandiose, the community Western is a national epic while the odyssey Western is at heart a psychological epic. In the genre's relationship to national identity, the community Western often reflects the tension between *citizen* and *society*, while the odyssey Western customarily includes this conflict only to transcend it – and centres thereafter on interplay between *psyche* and *landscape*.

This dichotomy between community and odyssey narratives is an apposite methodology for classifying a majority of Westerns yet retaining both the essence and the semblance of myth. The community Western, Wright's "classical plot", may be America's foremost myth; the odyssey Western is descended from classical myth. The division between community and odyssey narratives is not always clear-cut, and a Western might effortlessly contain elements of each. However, this categorization is in essence identical to David Potter's definition of a dual "relationship between man alone, and man in society – man constantly straining against the compulsion imposed by the group, and man continuously driven by need for identity with the group".[16] Finally, besides offering a system of classification embracing the majority of Westerns, division into community and odyssey narratives has an advantage over previous studies of the genre supporting mythic contextualization: such writings have seldom been chiefly concerned with strands of U.S. identity inherent in the Western myth.

Broadly speaking, major interpretations of the Western have tended to fall within one of the following categories: 1. Mythic; 2. Auteurist; 3. Structuralist; and 4. Political/Allegorical.

1. The mythic approach

Chronologically first, during the 1950s, the Western was interpreted in predominantly mythic terms. Nowhere in American cinema has the myth of America received more potent treatment than in the Western itself, most memorably articulated in the oft-quoted line from *Liberty Valance*: "When the legend becomes fact, print the legend."[17] A decade later John Huston's *The Life and Times of Judge Roy Bean* (1972) opened with a preface: " ... Maybe this isn't the way it was ... it's the way it should have been."[18] This glib "higher truth" has been the primary rationalization for distortions of America's frontier past. Whether for profit or political motives, the Hollywood Western has posited for Americans a quasi-historical saga which does not merely supplement but threatens to supplant the reality of national development in the popular consciousness. "The way it should have been" elevates the ideal over the authentic and implies that America's heritage best reflects the essence of truth within the contours of myth.

Given American popular culture's propensity for national narcissism, it is perhaps ironic that the first major critical appreciation of the Hollywood Western should come from Europe. French film theorist André Bazin, in attempting to divine the Western's universal appeal, acknowledged that the genre was at least *temporally* rooted in U.S. history, although a number of critically acclaimed productions had little to offer by way of historicity.[19] Bazin's focus centred on the genre's global appeal, which transcended nuances of national identity. Thus he delineated correlations between narrative components of the Western and both ancient myth and medieval legendry.[20] Yet, even though such comparisons helped to establish the Western's mythic credentials, adding an aura of artistic respectability, they recast a quintessentially American phenomenon in European terms – European, as opposed to American, and also as opposed to universal. Classifying the cowboy as a transposed knight or Greek hero is itself an exercise in cultural imperialism – an intrinsically European rationalization of an American mystique – justifying European attention to the genre by virtue of its respectable (read "European") cultural antecedents.[21] While the lineal descent from Greek legend through medieval romance to the Western is incontrovertible, regarding the genre as a whole, especially as concerns its interplay with U.S. national identity, myths of other lands and other eras are of secondary importance.

The point here is that a Eurocentric interpretation of the Western must inevitably be a limited one. The Western is above all an American artifact, focused equally on the aesthetics of the nation's past and the ethics of contemporary America.

In 1970 John Cawelti wrote of the "epic moment", a (mostly fictitious) confrontation between the trailblazers of law and civilization and the agents of evil, violence and savagery at a crucial if localized juncture of American history.[22] Thus a generation of U.S. moviegoers were consistently offered and consistently responsive to a continually reworked re-enactment of a decisive Manichaean conflict between societal factions on the nineteenth-century frontier. The proposition implicit in the narrative unfolding on the screen was that had this event (or a likeness thereof) not occurred in the nation's idealized past, the United States would not have become a society truly dedicated to progress or, indeed, the great world power of the audience's own era. This foundation myth suggests the *Republic* was conceived in Philadelphia in 1776; the *United States* was finally born of the Civil War; but *America*, creature of mythic heritage, came of age amid flying lead on countless dusty Main Streets. Here was America's mythic turning point. Indians who needed no reason to attack settlers were edged off the map for the glory of civilization. Money-worshipping overreachers were exposed and prevented from wielding power in a society which valued people over profit. Outlaws died from bullets fired in the name of justice, freedom and democracy. Never were so many serpents banished from so many Edens in so restricted a time-frame.

Cawelti's definition of the Western myth helped illuminate the genre's narrative structure, but his discussion of textual components bore little relation to those thirty-plus years of American history, politics and culture in which Western movies enjoyed their greatest popularity. Furthermore, during those decades, the genre proved too pliable to submit to one single overriding schematization. The key to the Western's durability was its very tractability.

2. The auteurist approach

Auteurism, which advances a film's director as its primary influence and asserts a film may best be understood within the larger corpus of its director's *oeuvre*, first came to fruition in France before American critics embraced the concept. In the United States in the early 1960s Andrew Sarris, the homegrown champion of auteurism, was a solitary voice, at odds with much of America's critical establishment in his enthusiasm for John Ford.[23]

Auteurist interpretations of the Western rest largely – though not wholly – on attention paid to Ford. Several other directors (notably Hawks, Mann, Boetticher, Raoul Walsh, Henry Hathaway, Delmer Daves, John Sturges and Peckinpah) turned to the West with comparable frequency or aptitude, but none among them offered so complete and consistent yet so complex, subtly shifting a vision of America's history and society as Ford's.

Ford's Westerns, for example, are germane here insofar as they touch on a social or political strain related to American national identity. Whereas auteurist discourse may concentrate on the interrelationship between several Ford films, this book examines the intertextuality between significant Ford Westerns and others revealing similar themes or variant representations in a roughly contemporaneous time-frame. Only thereby shall we discern how truly the ethos was part of the era; otherwise, my study would simply chart Ford's *perception* of American history rather than the genre's *interaction* with history.

3. The structuralist approach

If the 1950s was the boom era for mythicists and the 1960s the heyday of the auteurists, the 1970s was, for literature on the Hollywood Western, the decade of the structuralists. John G. Cawelti's *The Six-Gun Mystique* (1970) and Will Wright's *Six Guns and Society* (1975) both located the essence of the genre via detailed analyses of structural components. These writers were primarily concerned with the Western as a crystallization of myth. Yet, while they were rigorous in their discussion of genre ingredients, they were nebulous in their connection of Westerns to American social culture. Cawelti maintained that the Western, like other formulaic narratives, fulfilled a deep cultural vacuum within American society; engaging with Oedipal conflict, Puritan constructs and a national preoccupation with masculinity, there was also extensive psychological rumination on the genre's distinctive appeal to adults and children.[24] *The Six-Gun Mystique* scrutinized the Western punctiliously but the culture which fed it remained ill-defined. In effect, the formula became the reality, while contemporary America waited in the wings.

Will Wright's book at least delivered the engagement with American society promised in his title, but his diagnosis of the genre's abiding mythic resonance and its popularity with American audiences from the late 1930s to the early 1970s was primarily socio-economic. Wright not only asserted the change from a market society to the postwar corporate economy was the "most significant development in American institutions in the last forty years"; he also identified this transition as the principal, albeit hidden, social dynamic dictating the Western formulae most favoured in those respective eras of market and corporate economies.[25] Certainly, there can be no doubt of the demarcation, in era as well as structure, between Wright's "classical plot" and the "professional plot" of the late 1950s and 1960s.[26] Wright's thesis, relating predominant Western plot to prevalent economic structure, is an ingenious one, but the contention that this correlation is central to the genre's development is intrinsically specious. In substance, the only economics film-makers regularly aspired to reflect through the Western were healthy box office receipts. More than any other genre, the Western was a paean to individualism, a consummate fantasy of freedom of movement and limitless horizons, lacking most social constraints, especially those governing the use of violence. No Western movie hero ever sidestepped a showdown because he was worried about job security, mortgage payments or how the courts might judge him for taking the law into his own hands. The Western helped keep alive faith in individualism as a national creed, but Wright could scarcely have chosen a more impersonal, implicitly anti-individualistic rationale for its success. He dealt comprehensively with the heroic individual, but his overview of the Western's function was so thoroughly grounded in an economic reading of postwar American society as to infer greater affinity for his theory than for the genre in its own right.[27]

Six Guns and Society is primarily a sociological tract. It makes no claim to be an historical study. It is essentially a science-oriented dissection of an artistic property; and while concentration on box office successes connotes a certain basis of objectivity, this is neither a barometer of significant developments within the Western nor an infallible guide to the genre's interaction with the social and political realities of twentieth-century America. The only logical *modus operandi* for my own study is a convergence between critical and commercial successes, with specific Westerns chosen for detailed analysis according to three principal factors:

1. A narrative or thematic engagement with issues pertinent to U.S. national identity: this may take various forms, ranging from depictions of race, gender and class in the Western to representations of contemporary political conflicts transposed to the mythicized, implicitly uncontroversial frontier past;
2. A measure of commercial success with American audiences: while it is virtually impossible to gauge a single Western's social impact, box office takings are at least some indication of appeal, and we may reasonably assume scrutiny of a popular hit – seen by more people

and thus likely to stay longer in more memories – would yield more than study of a little seen and largely forgotten failure. Yet certain key commercial misfires (e.g., *Warlock*, Robert Aldrich's *The Last Sunset* (1961)) are too important in the present context to be ignored; and

3. Awareness of these Westerns' critical reputations: this may require a fresh interpretation of a lauded yet seldom analysed classic (*Shane*) or reappraisal of the genre's most critically neglected money-spinner (*How the West Was Won*), but above all it will entail studying a select cluster of films to highlight interaction with U.S. national identity hitherto underexplored in previous critical literature.

Relationship to a strain of American identity is the most important qualification for a film's inclusion herein, and my study will apply a mythicist, auteurist or structural approach where germane. Yet my central thrust of interpretation will follow the political/allegorical school of Western analysis.

4. The political/allegorical approach

This mode of interpretation, relating the genre's narrative conflicts and thematic tensions to corresponding issues in twentieth-century U.S. society, hit its stride just before the structural approach peaked. Philip French's *Westerns* (1973) appeared two years before *Six Guns and Society*, but French began by forestalling precisely the style of argument Wright later employed, declaring his own approach "largely a social, aesthetic and moral one".[28] Thus French's perceptions and interpretations were principally socio-political rather than socio-economic.

In large part, French's book delineated the recurrence of major themes and iconic associations within Westerns. Probably its most distinctive facet, however, was his categorization of key 1950s and 1960s Westerns as either extensions or artistic representations of the ideological postures diversely adopted by John Kennedy, Barry Goldwater, Lyndon Johnson and William Buckley.[29] Significantly, all those films French listed as "Goldwater Westerns" starred John Wayne, one of the Senator's most vocal champions in Hollywood. Within French's framework, this implicitly posited a very political star as the principal *auteur* of an ideological construct.

French's specific politicization of Westerns runs the same risk as Wright's categorization of plot varieties: one man's schematization may become another's parlour game. Still, even though he ventured to connect the dynamics of the Western to a limited, disparate and ultimately ephemeral assemblage of U.S. politicians, French paved the way for a reading of the genre which explicitly accepted the fundamental correlation between Hollywood's romantic reconstruction of a vanished past and the social and political environment of twentieth-century America.

John H. Lenihan's *Showdown* (1980) extended this argument, drawing direct parallels between the West depicted on screen and the society which produced the films. The present study undoubtedly shares a strong kinship with Lenihan's in premise and approach, but my book differs fundamentally from Lenihan's in its focus. In his Introduction to *Showdown* Lenihan wrote:

> More important than any single Western is the totality of Westerns that reflect significant formula variations. *The Gunfighter* (1950) had negligible popularity, but its handling of individual alienation and social weakness characterized many subsequent Westerns of the decade. The significance of an individual film, in terms of either artistic merit or popularity, matters less than the recurrent pattern of themes and ideas in other Westerns. Popular films are naturally more important in determining acceptable filming ideas and assumptions, but here also the single film must be set against the larger body of Westerns. *Shane* (1953) and *How the West Was Won* (1962) drew large audiences, yet the same brand of classic optimism was much less evident in most other Westerns – popular or not – of the period. Only by treating Westerns collectively can what was unusual and passing be distinguished from what was common and pervasive.[30]

This study opts for a middle ground between the polarities of Lenihan's assertion and Will Wright's diametrically opposed contention that the Western's relationship to U.S. society may best be divined by confining analysis to box office successes. In direct opposition to Lenihan's rationale, atypical "classic optimism" notwithstanding, I will focus principally on a small number of individual Westerns for an in-depth appraisal of the crucial relationship between era and artifact. The main thrust of each chapter will be interpretive analysis of the social or political message underlying selected prestigious Westerns.

Despite dealing in detail with a relatively small group of films, my preparation has entailed viewing as many Westerns as possible. It is not clear that Wright, for example, embarked on such a task prior to writing *Six Guns and Society*, but this saturation is necessary to comprehend the Hollywood Western in an historical context. Thanks to the popularization of video cassette, a wealth of movie material is now accessible. Dozens of Westerns brim with socio-political significance. Literature on this cultural phenomenon has boomed in the last generation. All of these factors have transformed this field of study from a sparsely inhabited wilderness to a crowded prairie.

In 1992, while my own study was under way as a thesis, the prairie became significantly more crowded with the publication of Richard Slotkin's *Gunfighter Nation*, completing his mammoth trilogy on the mythology of the American frontier.[31] I only became aware of this book's existence after the bulk of my own had been written, and on reading Slotkin I have discovered we share several parallel insights, independently achieved. This is no cause for embarrassment. *Gunfighter Nation* is certainly a magnificent, monumental achievement, dazzling in both scope and depth, an epic landmark in studies of the Western; but the debate on the Western's significance for American identity and society continues, and will never truly be concluded. Parallel insights aside, this book differs fundamentally from Slotkin's in many crucial areas of method, selection, interpretation and ultimate socio-political concern. Whereas Slotkin has devoted scant attention to contemporary reviews, my analysis embraces such critical reception. Admittedly, perhaps inevitably, there is a degree of overlap in the films chosen for scrutiny. Yet I have, to cite one example, grouped *The Gunfighter*, *Shane* and *The Searchers* together to construct an interpretation markedly different from Slotkin's readings of the same films. Moreover, at least half of the Westerns foregrounded here receive little or no detailed consideration from Slotkin. Although both books offer a political reading of the Western, we have, in essence, adopted different approaches, bearing in mind different central preoccupations, to reach different ends. Slotkin has advanced a grandiose master-narrative, establishing the frontier and its various mythologies as the principal dynamic shaping America's history, culture and ideology, culminating in the tragedy of Vietnam. However, the paramount focus of my own examination of American identity within the Western will vary from chapter to chapter. Even our respective titles suggest a crucial thematic divergence: *Gunfighter Nation* is explicitly macropolitical; by contrast, *The Crowded Prairie*, as concerned with dysfunctional family structures and individual alienation as with national hubris, is implicitly micropolitical. Moreover, even a work as ambitious and formidable as *Gunfighter Nation* leaves room for dispute, as when Slotkin remarks on the dearth of interventionist Westerns before Pearl Harbor.[32] I have detected distinct interventionist subtexts in several big budget prewar Westerns, as I will demonstrate in Chapter 1.

To gauge the genre's impact on twentieth-century America's culture and consciousness, I must take account of contemporary critical reactions. In a country as vast as the United States, with a myriad of publications offering opinions on hundreds of Westerns, such examination must necessarily be selective. The first specification was that, as this is an in-depth appraisal of American identity in a quintessentially American artifact, the sources chosen should be exclusively American; I could not resist including a couple of particularly telling observations from the British magazine *Films and Filming* and one offering from Russia's *Pravda* but, otherwise, in my text I engage solely with the response of American critics.

For the most part I have focused on seven core sources. The *New York Times* is, of course, one of America's most prominent, most prestigious daily newspapers, whereas *TIME* magazine is an unfailing barometer of Middle America's mood-swings, its mores and its affinity for popular culture frequently balancing the magazine's innate conservatism with a glib, lively journalese. Through the 1940s, 1950s and 1960s, *The New Republic* and *The Nation* were staunchly liberal publications, although evidently the latter had little affection for the Western. The *Nation*'s input here is more qualitative than quantitative, for overall it tended to review highbrow and foreign offerings rather than Westerns; but for present purposes its inclusion among my core sources serves to offset *TIME* in temperament as well as taste. *The Hollywood Reporter, Motion Picture Herald* and *Variety* are all Hollywood trade papers and as such more concerned with a movie's box office potential rather than any underlying ideological import; yet each is frequently prone to flashes of socio-political insight. By choosing these seven publications, I have embraced a diversity of popular, intellectual and trade pronouncements *and* ranged across America's political spectrum, while keeping the logistical requirements of this study within manageable limits.

The Hollywood Western codified American identity as mainly white and male, largely accepted racial supremacy as a given, romanticized aggressive masculinity and, ultimately, eulogized resistance to regulated society as the truest mark of manhood. The story of the Western from its heyday to the "Bicentennial Westerns" of 1976 is basically one of loss of faith in America. In truth, one film and one year stand out as the only logical choices to begin this study of the Western's interrelationship with U.S. national identity. The genre, like the frontier past it idealized, abounded with its own legends, and the weight of critical consensus has decreed that the golden age for classic Hollywood Westerns began in 1939 with John Ford's *Stagecoach*. My analysis must do likewise.

CHAPTER I

Mirror for Prewar America: *Stagecoach* and the Western, 1939–1941

F OR Americans, 1939 was a respite between cataclysms. The nation had weathered the worst of the Great Depression and, though many citizens were increasingly anxious over events in Europe, Pearl Harbor was still two years away. Two-ocean security enabled the United States to regard Nazi expansionism as less than an imminent, direct threat. Far more than other nationalities, Americans could afford to relax.

Moviegoing ranked high on the list of American leisure activities in 1939. There were approximately 17,800 cinemas in the United States, and sixty million Americans attended every week at an average admission price of twenty-three cents.[1] That year, box office receipts totalled $659,000,000 – only 0.98% of consumer expenditure, but 19.1% of recreation expenditure, and 80.3% of all spectating expenditure.[2]

Whether Americans flocked to the silver screen to lose themselves or to find themselves, in 1939 there was much to lure them. Generally recognized as the pinnacle of Hollywood's golden age, 1939 witnessed an output of unprecedented quality. For their twenty-three cents, patrons were regaled with sagas of courageous Caucasians defeating dark-skinned infidels (*Beau Geste*, *Gunga Din*); celebrations of America's democratic spirit (*Young Mr. Lincoln*, *Mr. Smith Goes to Washington*); a paean to the American heartland (*The Wizard of Oz*); an implicit defence of free enterprise masquerading as a satirical love story (*Ninotchka*); and, above all others, various strands of white supremacy, American history, affinity to the soil, business machinations and tempestuous romance all served up in the most phenomenal of the year's releases, *Gone With the Wind*. With such narrative and ideological ingredients prominent among the era's box office successes, the time was evidently ripe for the Western to take its place as a major Hollywood genre.[3]

Prior to 1939, "A" Westerns of the sound era were few and far between. Andrew Bergman has observed that the celebratory implications of the genre reduced its popularity during the Depression, but the fact remains that the *quality* Western, as opposed to the multitude of "B" productions, was not yet a firmly established staple of Hollywood fare.[4] Westerns flowed steadily from the major studios throughout the 1930s, but epics such as *The Big Trail* (1930), *Cimarron* (1931) and *The Plainsman* (1936) were exceptions to the low-budget rule. A tabulation of "A" Westerns released by the eight majors from 1930 to 1941, weighed against the total Western output and the studios' total output, amply illustrates the genre's mediocre qualitative contribution to American cinema before 1939 (Table 1.1).

Table 1.1 Output of eight major studios, 1930–41[5]

Year	"A" Westerns	Total of Westerns	Total output
1930	9	42	350
1931	5	30	309
1932	2	43	308
1933	1	38	339
1934	0	18	359
1935	4	40	351
1936	7	54	366
1937	3	57	411
1938	4	58	363
1939	9	48	387
1940	13	60	370
1941	9	59	383

Bergman's diagnosis of the Western's limited appeal during the Depression has some validity, but during those years the genre consisted largely of second-rate productions, satisfying as cheap, instantly forgettable entertainment but unlikely to provide citizens with a subtle, complex, engaging reflection of their society and themselves. Yet in 1939 the Western began to rebel against its inferior status. Between January 1939 and November 1941, big-budget Westerns streamed from Hollywood as never before, and Americans could choose from those listed (in chronological order) in Table 1.2.

Only because the "A" Western subsequently became a central component of American cinema do we notice such a dearth of the product before 1939, when the genre's momentum truly began. By early March

Table 1.2 "A" Westerns, 1939–41

1939	*	*Jesse James* (20th Century-Fox)
		Stagecoach (United Artists)
		The Oklahoma Kid (Warner Brothers)
	*	*Dodge City* (Warner Brothers)
	*	*Man of Conquest* (Republic)
	*	*Union Pacific* (Paramount)
	*	*Frontier Marshal* (20th Century-Fox)
	*	*Drums Along the Mohawk* (20th Century-Fox)
	*	*Allegheny Uprising* (R-K-O)
		Destry Rides Again (Universal)
1940	*	*Geronimo* (Paramount)
	*	*Northwest Passage* (Metro-Goldwyn-Mayer)
	*	*Virginia City* (Warner Brothers)
	*	*Dark Command* (Republic)
	*	*The Return of Frank James* (20th Century-Fox)
	*	*When the Daltons Rode* (Universal)
	*	*Brigham Young – Frontiersman* (20th Century-Fox)
	*	*The Westerner* (United Artists)
	*	*North West Mounted Police* (Paramount)
	*	*Kit Carson* (United Artists)
	*	*Santa Fe Trail* (Warner Brothers)
1941	*	*Western Union* (20th Century-Fox)
	*	*Arizona* (Columbia)
	*	*Billy the Kid* (Metro-Goldwyn-Mayer)
		Shepherd of the Hills (Paramount)
	*	*Bad Men of Missouri* (Warner Brothers)
		Honky Tonk (Metro-Goldwyn-Mayer)
		Texas (Columbia)
	*	*Belle Starr* (20th Century-Fox)
	*	*They Died With Their Boots On* (Warner Brothers)

Note: * denotes historical theme

of that year the genre already had its paradigm in John Ford's *Stagecoach*.

The union between history and legend is essentially a marriage of convenience. Filtered through legend, the past is defined not by facts but by an iconic moment, which best reflects the truth. Thus America began at Plymouth Rock, not Jamestown; thus, since 1945, the indelible image of victory at Iwo Jima has been the photograph of the *second* flag-raising. Likewise, 1939's first successful Western was not *Stagecoach* but Henry King's *Jesse James*. Yet it was *Stagecoach* which revitalized the genre and redefined the contours of the myth. The good outlaw, the whore with a heart of gold, the Madonna/Magdalene dichotomy between opposing female leads, the drunken philosopher, the last-minute cavalry rescue, the lonely walk down Main Street – all became stereotypes from *Stagecoach*'s archetypes.[6] *Stagecoach* quickly became the model against which other "A" Westerns would be measured. Franz Hoellering's entire review for another 1939 epic read: "*Union Pacific* (Paramount), directed by Cecil B. de Mille [*sic*], employs every possible and impossible cliché so crudely that it makes one long to see *Stagecoach* again".[7] In 1941, *New York Times* reviewer Bosley Crowther praised Fritz Lang's *Western Union*, citing among its virtues "a climactic pistol duel quite as suspenseful as the memorable conclusion of *Stagecoach*".[8] These two notices, one damning and the other enthusiastic, demonstrate how swiftly *Stagecoach* was accepted as shorthand for excellence within the genre.

In Ford's classic, a cross-section of frontier and Eastern characters (prostitute, drunken doctor, gambler, lawman riding shotgun, Southern gentlewoman, whiskey drummer and embezzling banker) take a stage from Tonto to Lordsburg, joined *en route* by an escaped outlaw, the Ringo Kid (John Wayne). During the journey, crisis exposes the passengers' true selves: Ringo, the prostitute Dallas (Claire Trevor) and drunkard Doc Boone (Thomas Mitchell) emerge as brave and altruistic, whereas the "respectable" Easterners are actually snobs and hypocrites. Finally, the cavalry rescues the stage from Geronimo's Apaches and the survivors reach Lordsburg, where Ringo avenges the murder of his family and then, with the sheriff's connivance, rides away with Dallas to begin a new life in Mexico.

The narrative is straightforward and, along with its oft-acknowledged debt to de Maupassant's *Boule de Suif* and Bret Harte's *The Outcasts of Poker Flat*, is incontrovertibly rooted in Victorian melodrama.[9] As cinema, however, *Stagecoach* was electrifying. Critic Frank S. Nugent, later screenwriter for some of Ford's finest films, wrote: "In one superbly expansive gesture ... John Ford has swept aside ten years of artifice and talkie compromise and has made a motion picture that sings a song of camera. ... Here ... is a movie of the grand old school, a genuine rib-thumper and a beautiful sight to see".[10] Such was typical of *Stagecoach*'s instant, widespread acclaim.[11] Yet if prewar America embraced *Stagecoach* as a cultural asset, what representation of that society did Ford's film offer?

"What is most interesting about *Stagecoach*", wrote Andrew Sarris, "is that it does not seem to be about anything by 1939 standards".[12] What is most astonishing about Sarris's observation is that one of Ford's most astute interpreters did not recognize the clearly identifiable contemporary subtext in one of the director's most lauded films. *Stagecoach* is at its most resonant as a parable of 1939 America.

Like the United States in that year, the film is caught between the aftermath of the Depression and the crisis looming in Europe. The latter is only slightly apparent. The murderous Plummers, whom Ringo faces in Lordsburg, are roughly equivalent to Nazi thugs. They had killed Ringo's father and brother and subverted the judicial process to ensure the innocent Ringo's imprisonment. The Plummers flout society's accepted legal and moral conventions and are the lords of misrule in the dark, squalid world of Lordsburg.

Stagecoach's principal frame of socio-political reference, however, is the Depression. The most explicit parallel is the characterization of Gatewood, the embezzling banker (played by ex-union leader Berton Churchill).[13] Looking uncannily like a cross between Warren Harding and Herbert Hoover, Churchill's Gatewood epitomized the corruption, selfishness and hypocrisy which had wrought havoc on America over the last decade. Americans of the Roosevelt years could thus recognize Gatewood as a scoundrel of their own era. He absconds with the payroll from Tonto's "Miners' & Cattlemen's Bank", robbing working *and* business classes; he is a fair-weather patriot, first praising the cavalry but soon demanding that they make his protection their priority (isolationism reduced to its most unpleasant level); and he subjects his fellow passengers to a tirade of reactionary clichés: "America for Americans! [Given its 1939 context, Gatewood's xenophobia is implicitly isolationist.] The government must not meddle with business! Reduce taxes! ... What this country needs is a businessman for President!".[14] By putting such sentiments in Gatewood's mouth rather than, say, the sympathetic and cultured Doc Boone's, Ford and *Stagecoach* symbolically validated Franklin Roosevelt and the New Deal.

Businessmen have frequently received short shrift in the Western, and within the 1939–1941 period venal entrepreneurs also featured in *Jesse James, Union Pacific* and *They Died With Their Boots On*. Within the genre, a desk-bound capitalist was simply not the stuff of heroic myth. If not a villain, he was at best the visionary whose nation-building dream depended on the hero's physical authority (in Michael Curtiz's *Dodge City, Union Pacific*). The real American – the real *man* – whom the Western celebrated was a man of action, not vision, accustomed to rough living in a harsh environment and confident of his capabilities should violence become necessary. Businessmen in the Western were frequently greedy and cowardly – and thus, according to the code of the genre, guilty of both unAmerican and unmasculine traits. To audiences of the 1930s especially, the grasping entrepreneur presented the unacceptable face of the American Dream (*vide* the films of Frank Capra).

Also, this figure represented all the heroic Westerner was not – effete, selfish, outwardly respectable, his eyes turned forever toward the East. Moreover, by virtue of antinomy, this negative image of businessmen reinforced the cowboy's status among America's most potent and congenial symbols. Perhaps the Hollywood front office perceived such self-flagellation as a safety valve, for it was consistently a tenet of U.S. populist cinema that power and wealth were ultimately subject to democratic reproach. Furthermore, the WASPish plutocrat was arguably an appropriate *bête noire* for most of Hollywood's Eastern European Jewish moguls who had, figuratively, stormed the citadels to wrest their share of financial power from the Gatewoods of twentieth-century America.

Gatewood functioned, therefore, as a catch-all villain, emblematic of a culturally unpopular, implicitly anti-populist profession. By contrast, Ringo and Dallas are social outcasts through force of circumstances, not inherent immorality. Both are honest, brave and egalitarian, and they project idealized national and gender images for Americans of 1939.

Dallas personifies dignity's triumph over degradation. Her parents were killed by Indians and she took to prostitution to survive. Similarly, the Depression had shaken untold thousands of young men and women loose from secure foundations of family life, compelling them to keep body and soul together by means they might never have contemplated otherwise. Dallas and Ringo are in fact victims of involuntary moral dislocation, and 1939 audiences could easily relate to their early exchange:

RINGO: I used to be a good cowhand, but – things happen.
DALLAS: Yeah, that's it. Things happen.[15]

In this context Dallas's reward of a fresh start, complete with home and marriage, has a contemporary significance. It is essentially reassurance that, the Depression notwithstanding, in America, if nowhere else during the beleaguered 1930s, it was still possible to find some measure of personal security, tranquillity and hope.

Just as Dallas, nurturing Mrs Mallory's baby, represents both a feminine ideal and American generosity of spirit, Ringo is a suitable masculine icon for America in 1939. Dallas is an incarnation of the spirit which endured the Depression; Ringo, on the other hand, more resembles America on the eve of global conflict – a perfect fusion of right and might. His climactic escape, engineered by the sheriff and Doc Boone, equally has a political subtext for the 1930s: the individual worth of a good man takes priority over the literal application of an impersonal law.[16] Contrast with the totalitarian societies of Hitler's Germany and Stalin's Russia could not be clearer.

Stagecoach offered American audiences Dallas and Ringo as paradigm citizens in a harsh society. Like many of John Ford's later Westerns, *Stagecoach* effectively portrayed U.S. frontier society as a tree necessarily pruned of all feeble branches so that the reinvigorated corpus may flourish anew, its survival guaranteed. Hence the ineffectual whiskey drummer and coach driver are wounded, John Carradine's ideologically outmoded Southerner perishes, Gatewood is arrested, and the Plummers die. Thus there is no room for the timid, the unhealthily ancient, the corrupt or the malignant. *Stagecoach*'s narrative, then, despite a democratic patina, had at its kernel a strong moral affinity with Social Darwinism.

Yet the film presented no societal ideal. The passengers (Gatewood excepted) band together to help Mrs Mallory give birth and again to ward off attacking Apaches, but once these crises have passed the coalition fragments. The only frontier communities in *Stagecoach* are two diametrically opposed but equally nightmarish environments, the oppressively puritanical Tonto and the seamy, anarchic Lordsburg. The young lovers' new life involves their escape across the border into Mexico – as Doc says, "saved from the blessings of civilization".[17] The film which revived the genre's potential and appeal, directed by a man who would become America's chief cinematic celebrant, implicitly posited salvation in flight from America. It was as anti-American a conclusion as any major Western reached before the Vietnam era, far more so than the "unAmerican" closure of *High Noon*, which John Wayne found repugnant in the 1950s.[18]

In summary, the American *character* which *Stagecoach* exalts is at its best (Ringo, Dallas, Doc) brave, decent, democratic. Yet its American *society* is prey to the narrow-minded (Tonto's prohibitionist ladies), the venal and hypocritical (Gatewood) and tyrannical thugs (the Plummers).[19] America's best hope, according to *Stagecoach*, was that inherently noble citizens be in control of a society which possessed morally debilitating tendencies. The film thus extolled individual human virtue but denied the premise of a special national destiny, and its coda opted for voluntary exile over commitment to corrupt society. If *Stagecoach* were a paean to American Exceptionalism, Ringo and Dallas would not seek their Eden south of the Rio Grande.

What is truly striking about *Stagecoach* is that it is *like no other Western by prewar standards*. It was without doubt the progenitor of the genre as it evolved after World War II, but it was very much the odd man out among major Westerns of 1939–1941. Although it swiftly became the bench mark for subsequent Westerns, it was not the narrative or thematic archetype for other Westerns of that era. Many of these others, taken as a group, contain a marked degree of intertextuality. They relate to each other and to non-genre works by directors (Cecil B. DeMille, Michael Curtiz) or stars (Errol Flynn, Tyrone Power), to the virtual exclusion of *Stagecoach*.

A glance at the titles cited in Table 1.2 (p. 18) highlights the marked thematic and stylistic dichotomies between prewar and postwar Westerns. The fundamental difference is that the majority of prewar productions are historical epics in Western guise. Of the thirty Westerns listed, twenty-four (asterisked) were quasi-historical representations which focused on various factual heroes, villains and events. The majority belonged to one of two categories: the biographical reconstruction and the nation-building epic. Some lionized lawmen (Flynn's Earp-type hero in *Dodge City*, *Frontier Marshal*) or pioneer-statesmen (*Man of Conquest*, *Brigham Young – Frontiersman*), while others sanitized legendary outlaws (*Jesse James*, *The Return of Frank James*, *Billy the Kid*). Some chronicled the great technological nation-linking endeavours (*Union Pacific*, *Western Union*). Some took their cue from historical novels (*Drums Along the Mohawk*, *Northwest Passage*). Others played fast and loose with history in depicting extremist threats to the national consensus (*Dark Command*, *Santa Fe Trail*). A few ambitious films held narrative components of the bio-pic and nation-building epic in fruitful tension (*The Westerner*, *They Died With Their Boots On*).

Community and odyssey structures certainly existed in many of these Westerns. *Drums Along the Mohawk*, for example, was an archetypal community narrative, whereas *Northwest Passage* was an odyssey saga. *Stagecoach* itself was a critique of community within an odysseyan framework. However, the community–odyssey dichotomy previously outlined became a dominant feature of the Western *after* World War II. In the prewar period the prevalent structure was either bio-pic or nation-building epic, because in this era the genre's central theme was historic rather than mythic. Before Pearl Harbor most major Westerns celebrated how Americans had won the West. After Hiroshima, the genre became more concerned with preserving – and defining – the essence of that achievement.

Stagecoach aside, the Westerns of 1939–1941 were first and foremost historical pageants. They purported to illuminate the American past, but their qualitative contribution to the genre was negligible. In retrospect several of the Flynn and DeMille epics, Henry Hathaway's *Brigham*

Young – *Frontiersman* and King Vidor's *Northwest Passage* all seem unbearably turgid. Even on their release, some critics observed that many of these grand-scale adventures were actually plodding bores. *New York Times* reviewers gave lukewarm notices to *Dodge City*, *Virginia City*, *The Westerner*, *Santa Fe Trail* and *Billy the Kid*; panned *The Return of Frank James*, *Brigham Young* and *Belle Starr*; and sounded small notes of discord even in their generally favourable appraisals of *Union Pacific*, *Northwest Passage*, *North West Mounted Police* and the celebratory Custer epic *They Died With Their Boots On*.[20] Of this last, fifteenth on the 1981 inflation-adjusted chart of successful Westerns, *New York Times* reviewer Thomas Pryor wrote that director Raoul Walsh "would have had a more compact and compelling entertainment had he whittled a half hour or so out of the script".[21]

Thus, while a sudden surge of prestige productions revived the Western's box office appeal, few of those epics rank among the genre's finest. Yet their ideological underpinnings reveal unabashed faith in the course of American history and affirm U.S. society's prewar *status quo*.

Besides inordinate running time and/or leaden pace, many of these films featured passages of inflated, pompous rhetoric which the laconic tendency of postwar Westerns would eschew. Unctuous patriotic speeches were frequently delivered by bewhiskered, citified plutocrats and politicians in whose name lean, raw frontier heroes dispensed justice (*Dodge City*, *Union Pacific*, *Western Union*). Such scenes depict a normally benevolent Gilded Age oligarchy gifted with vision but devoid of the hardiness required to impose their ideal of America's future on a savage wilderness. They supplied grandiose dreams and capital; the Western hero supplied the muscle.

What Americans were witnessing in these narratives was the transition from financial to physical power, whose true source was not so much legal as moral authority. Errol Flynn's marshal in *Dodge City*, Joel McCrea's railroad troubleshooter in *Union Pacific* and Randolph Scott's reformed outlaw in *Western Union* were all champions of authority – inherently different heroes from Wayne's Ringo in *Stagecoach*, and who defended an entirely different society. The nation-building epics were essentially paeans to a perfectible society. *Stagecoach* was more cynical about U.S. civilization's ultimate worth. The Flynn and McCrea heroes owe allegiance to the political and economic *status quo* (significantly, each is an ex-Army officer, possibly deepening his Establishment sympathies). These men represent the strong arm of legitimate business and government interests, and they actively lay the foundations of a new societal order. Ringo's motivation, conversely, is purely personal.

Revenge spurs him to kill the Plummers. The social benefits accruing from their deaths are virtually incidental.

The moral infrastructure of the nation-building narratives was thus directly opposed to *Stagecoach*'s. Their heroes stood foursquare beside existing power elites, in contrast to Ringo. Thirty years later such characters would be represented as the agents of capitalist corruption in Sergio Leone's *Once Upon a Time in the West* (1968) and Sam Peckinpah's *The Wild Bunch* (1969). From Flynn's Wade Hatton in *Dodge City* and McCrea's Jeff Butler in *Union Pacific* to Henry Fonda's evil Frank in Leone's film and Robert Ryan's Deke Thornton in *The Wild Bunch* constitutes a huge moral leap but a small ideological step.

The 1939–1941 nation-building epics extolled great business enterprises of the West as paradigms of human achievement. Such self-congratulation befitted a nation which had weathered the Depression with its economic and political systems intact. Americans of the 1930s could take pride in their survival of this crisis, and in the screen representations of community foundation (*Drums Along the Mohawk*, *The Westerner*, *Brigham Young*) and pioneer ordeal (*Northwest Passage*, *Virginia City*) they could see a reflection of their own recent endeavours. In both theme and tone these films affirmed a Puritan work ethic, worship of God and the centrality of capitalism and community.

The prewar Western could celebrate national achievement in the wake of the Depression precisely because America triumphed over adversity. A crisis of confidence may be conquered and the event revered thereafter; hence the Westerns of 1939–1941. A moral crisis, however, may lead instead to self-excoriation; hence the Westerns of the late 1960s and early 1970s. In 1969, both the top-grossing Western (*Butch Cassidy and the Sundance Kid*) and the most controversial (*The Wild Bunch*) were blatant anti-Establishment fantasies, in which outlaw heroes possess a moral purity presumed beyond the plutocrats they rob. Those faceless corporations are lineal descendants not of the nation-building Westerns' visionaries, but of Gatewood.

Thus *Stagecoach* has more in common with postwar Westerns than with its contemporaries. *Stagecoach* romanticized the *fictitious* outlaw hero; the nation-building epics embraced the Establishment hero.[22] While *Stagecoach*, through its heroic outcasts, applauded the pioneer *spirit* from the bottom up, the epics celebrated the pioneer *achievement* from the top down (*Union Pacific*, *Virginia City* and *Western Union* all invoked Lincoln). *Stagecoach*, like *Jesse James* and *The Return of Frank James*, put no trust in plutocrats, satirizing their pompous rhetoric; the epics lionized such figures and solemnized their rhetoric. *Stagecoach* stressed the personal over the historic, foregrounding human drama over national progress. Above all, *Stagecoach* was implicitly critical of American society whereas the epics were explicitly triumphalist.

Yet if the epics were devoid of *Stagecoach*'s multi-layered nuances, some were just as replete with their own contemporary subtexts. Again the primary issues were the Depression and the approach of war. Significantly, the Depression subtext is most apparent in 1939–1940 productions, while Westerns of 1940–1941 reflect the drift toward war.

Dodge City shares *Stagecoach*'s affinity for the New Deal. Its hero is essentially a moral crusader who imposes new taxes and restrictions on firearms, thus curbing the individualistic excesses of a pre-regulated society; its villain (Bruce Cabot) is a crooked gambler and cattle speculator who pays off honest business rivals in lead; and its ideological message is simple and commonplace within the genre: America is not the exclusive preserve of power-entrenched opportunists.

John Lenihan has indicated parallels between *Jesse James* and Depression America; *Union Pacific*, the sound era successor to Ford's *The Iron Horse* (1924), is clearly a hymn to American industrial endeavour; and Henry Fonda's farmer in Ford's *Drums Along the Mohawk* has his crops burned by Iroquois, prefiguring the natural devastation endured by the Okies in the next Ford–Fonda project, *The Grapes of Wrath* (1940).[23] In 1940, three epics – *Northwest Passage*, Curtiz's *Virginia City* and *Brigham Young* – featured starvation subplots, recalling the rigours of the previous decade.

Yet two of the 1940 films were transitional, incorporating references to the European war as well as to the Depression. *Northwest Passage*, a Colonial era epic, focused on a punitive raid on an Indian stronghold in the wilderness. *Virginia City* centred on a Southern gold shipment which Rebels and Yankees finally join forces to protect from marauding Mexicans. These films were not so much odysseys as convoy dramas with prairies substituting for the Atlantic – and transparent subtexts. The climax of *Northwest Passage* has Rogers' Rangers at a deserted fort, starving, exhausted, bereft of hope, near death. As in *Stagecoach*, help arrives at the last minute. Here the saviours of the frontier are not the U.S. cavalry but British redcoats, carrying bounteous provisions. Clearly, in a 1940 context, the inference was that once the British had saved heroic Americans and the time had come to repay the debt. *Virginia City*'s moral was equally pointed: Americans must bury political differences in the face of foreign menace. *Virginia City* substituted Union and Confederate for interventionists and isolationists respectively, underlined in this exchange between Northerner Kerry Bradford (Errol Flynn) and a Southern boy:

BRADFORD: You don't like Yankees much, do you?

BOY: No, I don't.

BRADFORD: Well, I think I know how you feel. When I was a boy in Ireland I felt pretty much the same way about Englishmen. But you can change.[24]

The debate on the merits of aiding Britain against Hitler was touched on obliquely via an exchange between Gary Cooper's Texas Ranger Dusty Rivers and Canadian Mounties in that year's DeMille epic *North West Mounted Police*:

RIVERS: I was countin' on bein' home by the Fourth of July.

1st MOUNTIE [*scowling*]: Your birthday?

RIVERS: No – ma Uncle Sam's.

2nd MOUNTIE: It's an American holiday.

RIVERS: Yeah, the States sort of set up housekeepin' for themselves.

3rd MOUNTIE: After being hatched, and protected for a hundred and fifty years.

1st MOUNTIE: Don't mind him. He reads a lot.

3rd MOUNTIE: We stuck to our mother, that's all.

RIVERS: Well, it's a wise child that knows its own mother.

1st MOUNTIE: And a wiser one that appreciates her. Goodnight, sheriff [*extends his hand*].

RIVERS: [*shaking hands*]: Goodnight. But I still want to be home by the Fourth of July.[25]

Such dialogue reminded Americans of a kinship with Britain without violating their own national identity. Cooper's Ranger can join in common cause with Canadians (read British) and yet "be home by the Fourth of July". Anglo-American cooperation was thus wholly compatible with patriotism.

Cooper also undermined the frontier totalitarianism of Roy Bean ("*I'm* the government here") in William Wyler's *The Westerner*, and Walter Brennan's tyrannical judge was but one of the quasi-fascistic demagogues who stalked the Westerns of 1940 (Humphrey Bogart's Mexican bandit in *Virginia City*, Brian Donlevy's dissident Mormon in *Brigham Young*, Walter Pidgeon's Quantrill (renamed Cantrell) in *Dark Command*, Louis Riel in *North West Mounted Police* and Raymond Massey's John Brown in *Santa Fe Trail*).[26]

In 1940 anti-fascism in the epic Western peaked, although David Miller's romanticized *Billy the Kid* (1941) featured an urbane English rancher (Ian Hunter) and a kindly journalist (Henry O'Neill) who each made explicitly anti-fascist remarks. 1941 saw the genre's epic cycle slump, with only *Western Union* and *They Died With Their Boots On* of any real significance. Of the latter, *Variety*'s review, dated November 19, concluded: "*Boots* is surefire western, an escape from bombers, tanks and Gestapo. It's American to the last man".[27] Apparently, the reviewer had paid little attention to a scene, just before the Battle of the Little Big Horn, in which Custer (Errol Flynn) tried to send his English adjutant "Queen's Own" Butler to safety with a dispatch:

BUTLER: Why are you asking me to go back with it?

CUSTER: Well, for one thing, you're an Englishman, not an American.

BUTLER: Not an American? What do you Yankees think *you* are? The only real Americans in this merry old parish are on the other side of the hill, with feathers in their hair.

CUSTER: You're probably right about that. But there's six thousand of them, and less than six hundred of us. The regiment's being sacrificed, Butler. I wouldn't want to see a foreigner butchered in a dirty deal like this.

BUTLER: Sporting of you to think of it that way – and I'll remind you, sir, I'm a member of the mess of the Seventh U.S. Cavalry. Fancy walking into the Service Club in Piccadilly if the regiment ... Get somebody else to post your blinking letter!

CUSTER: Thanks, Queen's Own. Just so long as you know. I'll get someone else.[28]

According to this scene, an English ally stood firm beside an American hero at a crucial moment in the nation's history; now, as with *Northwest Passage*'s food-bearing redcoats, it was time to return the favour. Custer's adjutant, though nicknamed "Queen's Own", was actually a Canadian named Cooke; his change in nationality simply accentuated the film's interventionist subtext. Max Steiner's background music for the scene further reinforced this message. "My Country 'Tis Of Thee", which shares the same tune as the British national anthem, featured on the soundtrack – as it did for the endings of *Northwest Passage*, *Virginia City* and 1939's more ambiguous *Drums Along the Mohawk*.[29] Hollywood's prewar epics thus habitually identified America's pioneer endeavours with the British war effort.

They Died With Their Boots On was the last epic Western of the prewar era. Seventeen days after its New York opening, the question of intervention versus isolation became academic, and neither America nor the

Western were ever the same again. "The promised land" which Gary Cooper hailed wondrously at the end of *The Westerner* was suddenly, symbolically violated.[30] Americans flocked to defend their Eden from foreign aggressors and, in the rush, the Western was trampled.

Hollywood was as crucial a barometer and a succour as before, and through four years of war the nation retained its zeal for its image in the movies. America needed Hollywood's comforting myths in time of crisis – perhaps even more so than in time of repose. Yet, for that particular crisis, America did not need the Western. Until the mid-1960s, the genre essentially dramatized a series of Manichaean conflicts imbued with white supremacist implications; but between 1942 and 1945, in Hollywood's moral framework for World War II, the Nazis effectively supplanted frontier thugs and land-grabbers while the Japanese functioned as racial bogeymen, so there was no need for savage redskins. Movies reconstructed battles torn from the headlines, and over the war years the genre's quantitative output of "A" features dropped significantly, with four prestige productions each for 1942 and 1943 and only two apiece for 1944 and 1945 (Table 1.3).

Table 1.3 "A" Westerns, 1942–45

1942	*American Empire* (United Artists)
	The Great Man's Lady (Paramount)
	The Spoilers (Universal)
	Tombstone, the Town Too Tough to Die (United Artists)
1943	*The Desperadoes* (Columbia)
	The Kansan (United Artists)
	The Outlaw (United Artists/R-K-O)
	The Ox-Bow Incident (20th Century-Fox)
1944	*Buffalo Bill* (20th Century-Fox)
	Tall in the Saddle (R-K-O)
1945	*Along Came Jones* (R-K-O)
	San Antonio (Warner Brothers)

"Self-reflexivity is the death of any movement in the arts ... because the moment you become totally conscious of what you're doing you start tripping over your own ideas and you begin to produce parodies or pomposity. What killed the Western was that it became self-reflexive."[31] Howard Suber addressed these remarks to the genre's increasing irrelevance after *The Wild Bunch*, but his observation would have been equally valid at the end of 1945. Through America's war years Hollywood's steady flow of "A" Westerns trickled out, and all the genre had to offer besides the existing pomposity of the historical epics was one bleak, powerful, commercial failure (William Wellman's *The Ox-Bow Incident*), parody in *Along Came Jones* and the brazen silliness of Howard Hughes's *The Outlaw*.

In 1945 the Western was dead on its feet, yet the genre became an enduring staple of America's postwar culture. The historical epics of 1939–1941 thus appear in retrospect as virtually a self-enclosed subgenre while the classic artifacts of the postwar era seem clearly the children of *Stagecoach*. If 1939 was the year the Western gained respectability, 1946 was the year it asserted its primacy. After 1946, the Western was a vital feature of America's cultural landscape. As before the war, the genre limned the contours of U.S. national identity, reflecting the tensions and tribulations of American society. In 1946, however, it actually helped to set social guidelines. Two otherwise unconnected films, one a critical favourite, the other a huge commercial success, jointly established a ruling social and sexual moral framework for Westerns of the ensuing generation. It is to those two films we must turn now.

CHAPTER 2

Puritan Paradigms: *My Darling Clementine* and *Duel in the Sun*

H AVING won a war they could no longer avoid, in 1945 Americans beheld a world they could no longer ignore. The United States was transformed, within five years, from a nation historically dependent on isolationist security to the foremost proponent of peace via collective strength. Pearl Harbor had punctured America's faith in isolationism; Hiroshima wholly invalidated the proposition. Despite her nuclear monopoly, the U.S. could not blithely retreat from international affairs as after 1918. The American mainland stood unscathed while war ravaged Europe and Asia, but the birth of atomic weapons meant the inevitable death of two-ocean security. Furthermore, without American aid and friendship, the Soviet Union might seek to fill the power vacuum on those devastated continents. America had no choice but to embrace the postwar world. If, in 1939, she alone could afford a degree of complacency, by 1945 no other nation could match her new-found, terrible power – power glossed with U.S. leaders' idealistic proposals for the dawning era. As the sole possessor of nuclear weaponry and host to the United Nations, the United States now held unparalleled, unprecedented global responsibilities.

At home, wartime had revitalized the economy, obliterating the last vestiges of the Depression. The G.I. Bill, passed in 1944, facilitated upward mobility for thousands of returning servicemen. Yet the nation's triumph in war had sown seeds of racial and sexual tensions which would ultimately challenge the complacency of a predominantly white male power structure. Black G.I.s had fought, ostensibly for freedom and democracy, against racially based totalitarianism. They could not then be content to return to effective second-class citizenship in a society which could not even guarantee their right to vote. Equally, U.S. women faced a new socio-psychological limitation at war's end: after their crucial contribution to the wartime work force and the resultant increase in financial and social independence, many found they could not placidly return to a world no bigger than four walls. In 1946, WAVE director and ex-principal of Wellesley College Mildred MacAffee Horton predicted of the women who had served in the U.S. armed forces that "[t]heir changed estimate of themselves may make problems for themselves and their communities, but I prophesy that they will be the problems of individuals rather than of women veterans as a group".[1] For women working on the home front, too, the postwar readjustment in status, economic opportunity and social freedom was primarily a source of personal rather than societal dislocation. Nevertheless, like the Black G.I.s, participation in the war effort had introduced women to wider, richer avenues of experience. Understandably, both groups now wanted more from life than American society had traditionally offered them.

The war also wrought subtle discord in the intimate sphere of sex and marriage. If the threat of death invested liaisons with a sense of immediacy, the coming of peace was a time for the survivors to seize their long-postponed security – or to disengage themselves from relationships they now perceived, in the cool light of peace, as mistakes. Table 2.1, showing births, divorces, marriages and illegitimate births per thousand head of U.S. population, illustrates a marked upsurge, in 1946, of births, marriages and divorces, with only a slight tapering off from the 1945 figure for illegitimate births; and while the birth rate continued to rise in 1947, the statistics for both marriage and divorce show a significant falling-off from the previous year.

Table 2.1 U.S. births, divorces and marriages per thousand head of population, 1940–47[2]

Year	Births	Divorces	Marriages	Illegitimate births (%)
1940	19.40	2.00	12.10	4.03
1941	20.30	2.20	12.70	3.80
1942	22.20	2.40	13.20	3.80
1943	22.70	2.60	11.70	3.90
1944	21.20	2.90	10.90	4.30
1945	20.40	3.50	12.20	5.00
1946	24.10	4.30	16.40	4.90
1947	26.60	3.40	13.90	4.60

Thus soldiers came home, changed by the war, to a changed America, in which global affairs, social harmony and the realm of the personal were all in a state of flux. Moviemakers such as John Ford, Frank Capra, John Huston and George Stevens had all taken their cameras to war and then returned with darkened sensibilities.[3] Even those cinema-goers who had never left America had seen the newsreels of Auschwitz. Neither Hollywood nor its audience could be content with simple reversion to the bland optimism of 1939. The madcap comedies so beloved in the 1930s, for example, never regained their prewar favour; the frivolity of zany heiresses and playboy suitors was archaic in a world which could produce concentration camps and atom bombs – incontrovertible proof that love did not, as in the movies, conquer all.

In this serious new world, Americans still savoured their entertainments, and in 1946 the country had 18,700 four-wall cinemas (nine hundred more than in 1939) and approximately 300 drive-ins.[4] Eighty-two million Americans attended per week at an average admission price of forty cents, including seven cents admission tax.[5] That year was the box office's most phenomenal throughout Hollywood's golden age: takings totalled an unprecedented $1,692,000,000 – $1,033,000,000 more than in 1939 and, even without inflation-adjustment, a sum unsurpassed until 1974.[6] These receipts accounted for 1.18% of 1946's consumer expenditure, 19.8% of recreational expenditure and 81.9% of all spectating expenditure.[7]

A nation confronted with new complexities at all levels of postwar society could not find easy reassurance in celebratory narratives of the prewar type. After World War II, the Western could conceivably have become – like the screwball comedy – a relic of a simpler, more innocent past. Instead, it became a vital medium for reflecting and articulating crucial issues of modern American society. Westerns which addressed contemporary socio-political concerns could hardly be deemed irrelevant or old hat. Frontier dramas peopled by grim, often tragic heroes could scarcely be dismissed as puerile. While the Western was implicitly bound up with pride in the American experience, it could also be used with impunity to reproach twentieth-century political realities. The genre functioned as both a contained indictment and a reaffirmation of America, past and present. In short, the Western was a safe vessel, its red-blooded Americanism beyond question.

In another sense, too, the Western posited a safe national self-image. Westerns depicted the justified use of controlled physical prowess. After 1945 the representation of a powerful, righteous America via six-guns sidestepped the moral ambiguity of the A-bomb. Westerns offered U.S.

audiences the acceptable face of the sleeping giant – slow to anger, but terrifying in his wrath. Above all, as Blacks and women began to reassess their status in American society, the Western film became a preserve and propagating agent of white male primacy.

The genre's narrative contours made the Western naturally receptive to inherent constructs of white male superiority. A formula which repeatedly celebrated national progress via the subjugation of the Indian and marginalization of a "feminized" concept of negotiable coexistence already had its own specific ideological bedrock. Two 1946 Westerns reinforced this racial and sexual hegemony, entrenching such assumptions in the genre throughout its heyday – and positing an image of U.S. society which sat comfortably with a white male power structure.

John Ford's *My Darling Clementine* (20th Century-Fox) was a poetic, consciously mythic retelling of the Wyatt Earp legend, culminating at the O.K. Corral. *Clementine* recast an odysseyan premise as the genre's most explicit paean to community: Henry Fonda's Earp becomes marshal to find his brother's killers. By picture's end he has not only avenged his kinsman but, by his very presence in Tombstone, has ushered the town from darkness into light. Recalling the oppressive townships of *Stagecoach*, Tombstone is initially as grimy and anarchic as Lordsburg, but comes to resemble Tonto without the stranglehold of excessive virtue. The key scene depicting Tombstone as a model frontier community is, of course, the famed church-dance sequence which enshrines Earp and the Eastern Clementine Carter (Cathy Downs) at its hub. Here is a perfect (though primarily asexual) union between the best elements of West and East: the lawman's cool, controlled masculinity complements this Boston lady's delicate yet spirited nature. The film ends with Wyatt's gentle goodbye to Clementine, as he prepares to take his slain brothers home for burial and she tells him she will remain in Tombstone to teach school. The fact that Clementine functions as both nurse *and* schoolmarm is an over-schematic contrivance to present her as the agent and the essence of civilization. The church-dance sequence stands as the apogee of American citizenship, and the final scene guarantees the civilizing process will continue.

My Darling Clementine is today considered a genre classic, but it evoked a mixed critical response on its release. *TIME*, unwittingly echoing *The Hollywood Reporter*'s verdict on *Stagecoach*, pronounced *Clementine* "horse opera for the carriage trade" and enthused, "Director Ford has accomplished more than an intelligent retelling of a hoary yarn".[8] Ray Lanning of the *Motion Picture Herald* termed the film "quiet, leisurely, almost plot-bare" but "remarkable for its imaginative handling of raw and sometimes

brutal material to create a moody, almost poetic, picture".[9] Richard
Griffith was perhaps the most appreciative of contemporary American
critics. His review in *New Movies* praised *Clementine* as not only "a
jimdandy Western" but "also a sustained and complex work of the
imagination. ... It is a mixed portrait, half-truth, half folklore, but fact
or fancy, it is the West as Americans still feel it in their bones. ... Of
all our accomplished players, Mr. Fonda best understands and imagines
the Western American. ... Mr. Fonda is as surely the conscious interpreter of a vanished temperament as though he were a historian or
psychologist."[10] However, Griffith conceded that "[t]he ladies fare not so
well, because their roles are too much bound up with plot contrivances
to seem real".[11] The *New York Times* voted *Clementine* among the year's
"Ten Best", but Bosley Crowther's generally favourable review acknowledged *Clementine* was "a little too burdened with conventions of
Western fiction to place it on a par [with *Stagecoach*]. Too obvious a
definition of heroes and villains is observed, and the standardized aspect
of romance is too neatly and respectably entwined."[12] *Variety*'s review
began: "Sentimental saga of the western plains ... loaded with enough
marquee voltage to insure it heavy play at the box-office in all situations",
but went on to observe that "[a]t several points, the pic comes to a dead
stop to let Ford go gunning for some arty effect", and credited Fonda
as Wyatt Earp with "charging the role and the pic with more excitement
than it really has".[13] Yet if these were basically positive notices tempered
by judicious highlighting of *Clementine*'s flaws, two contemporary critics
pulled no punches. Herb Sterne remarked: "The plot, unfortunately, is
no better than the film's title, and *My Darling Clementine* is something
that Republic should have annexed for Roy Rogers if the studio had
really been on its toes."[14] Manny Farber's comments for *The New Republic*
were equally disdainful – and even more acerbic: "a dazzling example
of how to ruin some wonderful Western history with pompous movie
making ... in the new tradition of cowboy films: instead of hell-for-
leather action there is concentration on civic-mindedness, gags, folk art.
This one goes in for slow, heavy, character-defining shots."[15] All the
above reviews made mention, whether laudatory or pejorative, of
Clementine's self-conscious pictorial splendour. Yet only Farber's glancing
reference to "civic-mindedness" hinted at identification of an ideological
subtext, and even this completely missed the moral and racial elitism
which, we shall see, is at the film's core.

King Vidor's *Duel in the Sun*, producer David O. Selznick's Western
equivalent of his *Gone With the Wind*, focused on Pearl Chavez (Jennifer
Jones), a tempestuous half-breed who comes to live with the powerful

McCanles family after her aristocratic father is hanged for killing his faithless Indian wife and her lover.[16] Pearl endures the racist gibes of the autocratic Senator McCanles (Lionel Barrymore), but is befriended by his gentle wife, Laura Belle (Lillian Gish), and their elder son, the decent, cultured Jesse (Joseph Cotten). Her arrival at the McCanles ranch coincides with the Senator's last stand against the encroaching railroad and homesteaders. What counts in this changing nation is not the lord of the prairie but the will of the people. Yet the central thrust of *Duel* is neither pioneer achievement nor dynastic hubris, but the all-consuming passion of Pearl and Lewt McCanles (Gregory Peck), a spoiled, ruthless miscreant given to rape, murder and derailing trains. The film climaxes with Pearl and Lewt shooting each other then dying in one another's arms among the sun-baked rocks.

If *My Darling Clementine*'s cardinal thematic preoccupation was civilization, *Duel in the Sun*'s was sex. *TIME* termed *Duel* "a knowing blend of oats and aphrodisiac".[17] *Motion Picture Herald* critic William Weaver focused on *Duel*'s marketability, labelling it "star-studded as an exploitation man's dream and scenically beautiful as a sunset over the Grand Canyon; and ... very, very hot stuff", and alluding rather neutrally to its controversial rape scene as "the most forthright display of virility illicitly triumphant an American camera has looked upon in years".[18] Bosley Crowther adjudged Selznick's epic "a spectacularly disappointing job", assuming the producer was "more anxious to emphasize the clash of love and lust than to seek some illumination of a complex of arrogance and greed. ... [I]f only the dramatics were up to the technical style!"[19] Two reviewers expressed their displeasure with stylish albeit condescending wit. Herb Sterne, *Clementine*'s old nemesis, proclaimed *Duel* "a gamey celluloid memorial to the techniques of the defunct David Belasco and the artistically defunct Cecil B. DeMille"; targeting producer as well as picture, Sterne continued: "in recent years Selznick has come to confuse extravagance with quality[.] ... [H]e is not interested in filming any story that does not permit him, one way or another, to burn down the city of Atlanta."[20] His sign-off was equally punchy: "By reason of its cheap sensationalism, *Duel in the Sun* will probably net several millions above its exorbitant budget. However, to give it critical recommendation would be as ridiculous as if a Nobel Prize were to be bestowed upon the *Police Gazette*."[21] Jesse Zunser was equally glib, calling *Duel* "[t]he biggest and emptiest thing since the Grand Canyon[.] ... The whole absurdly overblown emotional steam bath is frequently and comically reminiscent of the 1890 school of panting passion and asthmatic melodrama. Its pop-eyed, hard-breathing innuendoes are aimed directly and without subterfuge at the peanut-munching, gum-chewing level of moviegoers."[22] *Variety* classed *Duel* as "raw, sex-laden, western pulp-fiction[.] … It's daring, even though all who love, when and where they can find it, meet production code punishment in the end."[23] Yet *Duel*'s puritan pay-off, also noted by *TIME* and Bosley Crowther, did not assuage indignant churchmen or right-wing congressmen John Rankin and Everett Dirksen.[24] *Motion Picture Herald* publisher Martin Quigley told Selznick that *Duel* was "capable … of creating a wave of political censorship throughout this country and seriously imperiling American prestige throughout the world".[25] *The Nation* perceived a different danger lurking in the fury over *Duel*: "The important issue here is not whether Selznick has a moral picture or an offensive picture, but whether a small segment of the population is to impose its standards on all the rest – whether one group has the right to decide for everyone what is right or wrong."[26]

No two Westerns could appear less similar. *Clementine* is leisurely and restrained, and venerates virtue; *Duel* sprawls frantically, and luxuriates in vice. *Clementine* is intimate, gentle, austere, romantic, and in stark black and white. *Duel* is epic, harsh, lavish, erotic, in opulent Technicolor. Yet close analysis of their narrative schematizations demonstrates that they share identical mythic and moral frameworks.

Both films feature a reasonable and intelligent man as the proponent of law and civilization (Earp, Jesse), each clashing with a tyrannical father figure (*Clementine*'s Old Man Clanton (Walter Brennan), McCanles) and vanquishing his authority to ensure a balanced, harmonious society. Both are concerned with the disintegration of families: *Clementine* ends with two Earps dead and the entire Clanton brood wiped out; *Duel* traces the internal disruption of one family which houses polarities of good and evil, civic spirit and greed, restraint and passion.

Both films assert frontier primacy over the East in terms of vigour: each features an Eastern character plagued by poor health (*Clementine*'s Doc Holliday (Victor Mature), Laura Belle McCanles), leading to their deaths. Each reveres the "Eastern" principles of peace, law and religion, identifying such values with a genteel lady (Clementine, Laura Belle). However, each advocates violence as the only way to remove extra-consensual threats to civic harmony (the Clantons, Lewt). Above all, each enforces dominant cultural concepts of race, class and gender.

This becomes instantly evident from the briefest glance at the sources on which these Westerns were based. *Clementine* was based partly on Stuart N. Lake's lionizing biography of Wyatt Earp and partly on John Ford's recollection of the O.K. Corral shoot-out as recounted by Earp early in Ford's career.[27] In spite of Ford's claim of historical accuracy, his re-enactment of the fight – even regarding the identity of participants – is at variance with the facts.[28] We should not be surprised that a consummate myth-weaver and sentimentalist, working from the oral and printed reminiscences of a self-promoted legend, would feel free to embroider his material. Yet Doc Holliday's death during the showdown is utter fabrication and, as such, fraught with social and moral import. Clementine has come West to find the consumptive Doc, her fiancé, who fled the East for Arizona's healthier climate. When she meets him in Tombstone, he spurns her in favour of his lover, saloon singer Chihuahua (Linda Darnell), who is either Mexican or Indian. Her ancestry is unclear, and Wyatt Earp's disparaging remarks imply he sees no difference between the two. The film features an intricate romantic moral hierarchy: characters face a choice between two possible lovers and consistently opt for the morally inferior of the two. Earp can only court Clementine on the rebound, for she loves Doc, who prefers Chihuahua, who cheats on him with Billy Clanton (John Ireland). Billy shoots Chihuahua after she has implicated him in the murder of Wyatt's brother. Doc then operates, attempting to save her life. His effort is seemingly successful, yet when Doc next appears just before the gunfight he informs Wyatt tersely (and with obvious self-disgust) that Chihuahua is dead. Thus Holliday seeks vengeance and oblivion equally, and he secures both at the O.K. Corral. Shot during a coughing fit, he guns down one of the Clantons before he dies.

Why, then, must *Clementine*'s Holliday perish in the battle which, historically, he survived? Why, for that matter, must Chihuahua die after her apparently successful operation? Here Ford's film is not simply mythic but deeply moralistic. It is not so much social construction as social engineering. Doc and Chihuahua die precisely because they are morally unworthy to participate in the ideal frontier community which Ford depicts in *Clementine*. Both demonstrate this essential impropriety via hostility toward Clementine, the exemplar of civilized society (Doc disrupts the decent citizens' meal after the church-dance to order her out of town; Chihuahua tries to pack her bags and eject her from the hotel). Such characters can never be recast as members of polite society, but rude behaviour is emblematic of what the film represents as moral dysfunction. Their true sin is the sexual violation of racial barriers; and, for good measure, their affair also contravenes canons of class. Doc is the son of a well-to-do Eastern family while his paramour is a grafting saloon-girl (read prostitute) of dusky hue. Chihuahua is from the wrong side of every track. Moreover, unlike Pearl in *Duel in the Sun*, she is treacherous, petulant and devoid of redeeming qualities. She dies primarily because, according to the "moral" precepts of 1940s Hollywood narrative structures, she cannot be allowed to survive.[29] Holliday follows suit, so sullied by his relations with Chihuahua that he is forever unworthy of Clementine. His death is a Manichaean mopping-up device which conveniently leaves Clementine free as a possible mate for Wyatt, her social and moral equal.

Clementine capsized Ford's previous representation of the Madonna/Magdalene dichotomy in *Stagecoach*. He had announced gleefully that *Stagecoach* "violates all the censorial canons"; *Clementine* reaffirms them with a vengeance.[30] *Stagecoach* celebrated a whore's innate decency and criticized a high-born Southern lady's frosty refusal of her friendship; *Clementine*, filmed seven years later, looks like the archetype *Stagecoach* might have set out to subvert, venerating the Eastern lady and vilifying the sensuous half-breed prostitute. The outlaw hero of *Stagecoach* is consistently chivalrous toward Dallas, while *Clementine*'s lawman hero is utterly contemptuous of Chihuahua, dunking her in a horse trough and threatening to "run you back to the Apache reservation where you belong".[31] Earp is the narrative's moral arbiter and, as such, his behaviour toward Chihuahua clearly suggests she deserves no respect or courtesy whatsoever.

This same Wyatt Earp first attains profile in Tombstone by subduing a drunken rampaging Indian, which he does by knocking the offender on the head, indignantly demanding, "What kind of a town is this anyway, sellin' liquor to Indians!", planting a kick on the transgressor's rear and ordering him, "Indian, get out of town and stay out!"[32] *Clementine* passes no judgement on Earp for his rough handling of Chihuahua or Indian Charlie. Earp's sense of morality contains an element of racial purity which the film, abstaining from reproach, appears to endorse. Granted, Earp is equally anxious to dissuade a white cardsharp from settling in Tombstone. Yet the excerpts of dialogue cited above clearly indicate how quickly and how instinctively Earp invokes race as an underlying justification for expelling non-white "undesirables".

In his quiet manner, Fonda's Earp is at heart as racist as John Carradine's Hatfield, defending white Southern womanhood even unto death in *Stagecoach*, and John Wayne's pathological Ethan Edwards in Ford's later *The Searchers* (1956). Yet unlike these other characters, his racism is comparatively muted, and only one component of his identity; for Earp, it never becomes an all-consuming ideological motivation. His controlled racism is never depicted as irrational or dysfunctional, and bears no adverse narrative consequences. He suffers neither Hatfield's death nor Ethan's social alienation. Indeed, Ford presents him as a model Western hero of impeccable virtue.

Clementine's status as a racist parable is reinforced by a brief glance at the narratives of a few other Ford Westerns. In *Fort Apache* (1948), the climactic massacre is caused not by Cochise but by a stubborn Custer-style martinet (Fonda again); John Wayne's even-tempered Captain York articulates the film's moral viewpoint, which is essentially one of sympathy for the Indian confronted with white corruption, treachery and greed. The protagonist of *The Searchers* is a disturbed, driven racist who embarks on an epic quest to retrieve his young niece from her Comanche captors. By the time he finds her she is an adult and the chief's squaw, and her uncle concludes the only way to redress racial purity and family honour is with a bullet. Yet he ultimately puts kinship above personal obsession, restoring her unharmed to a stable white family environment which he can neither provide nor share. *Cheyenne Autumn* (1964) dramatizes the Cheyenne nation's arduous 1,500–mile trek from an Oklahoma reservation to their homeland in 1878, recasting *Fort Apache*'s subordinate theme of white venality and Indian nobility as the narrative's central thrust.

In each of these films Ford accorded the Indian an innate dignity – a respect for his heritage, identity and legitimate grievances against the rapacious excesses of white America. In none of these films did Ford conceptualize white civilization *über alles*. Yet, albeit subtly, this was precisely what he did in *My Darling Clementine*. Certainly its tone is gentle whereas *The Searchers* is savage; however, *Clementine* is ideologically simplistic, and devoid of the later film's profound social and moral ambiguity. *Clementine* celebrates the West and America as a perfectible society, but true citizenship therein is morally and racially exclusionist.

This interpretation of *My Darling Clementine* presents an ideological conundrum in the *oeuvre* of a director who venerated Abraham Lincoln throughout his career; who, fiercely proud of his Irish Catholic heritage, identified emotionally with the downtrodden and disfranchised in his adaptations of *The Informer* (1935), *The Grapes of Wrath* (1940) and *How Green Was My Valley* (1941); and who, four years after *Clementine*, would deal the death blow to Cecil B. DeMille's attempted right-wing takeover of the Directors' Guild. Granted, John Ford was also an unabashed militarist, a naval officer in World War II, intimate of admirals and generals (among them William Donovan, founder of the Office of Strategic Services, forerunner of the Central Intelligence Agency). Following his war service, Ford became cinema's foremost celebrant of the U.S. cavalry. Thus several factors in John Ford's personality and experience disposed him toward an authority-friendly, top-down idyll of U.S. society, just as sympathy for the common man prompted his comparatively left-wing representation of frontier America in *Stagecoach*. Liberal critics who have excoriated Ford for the conservative, implicitly supremacist ethos of his Westerns centring on white conflict with Indians have often predicated their judgements on narrative *contours* at the expense of narrative *content*.[33] Ford's films are about the advance of white American society, but they are also about the moral erosion, hypocrisy and loss inherent in that advance. In this context, *Clementine*, devoid of John Ford's customary complexity, is his most authoritarian Western.

Ford was a sentimentalist, not an ideologue, and an artist may easily gain fresh inspiration by inverting the conventions he has helped estab-lish. However, the populist/authoritarian dichotomy which *Clementine* brings to his *oeuvre* stems directly from a fissure in Ford's own sense of national identity. As an Irish Catholic American patriot he was prone to both emotional kinship with disadvantaged ethnic groups *and* a touch of status anxiety. In those other films mentioned above, Ford exhibited a degree of affinity, whether partial or wholehearted, with U.S. society's least privileged citizens. In *My Darling Clementine*, he actively distanced himself from life among the lowly. Both Catholic and puritan, Ford's lack of empathy for Chihuahua may have owed more to sexual than to racial snobbery. Of his boyhood in Portland, Maine, he recalled: "Our next-door neighbors were black. There was no difference, no racial feeling, no prejudice."[34] After release of his final film, *Seven Women* (1966), he would write a future biographer: "Hollywood now is run by Wall St. + Madison Ave who demand 'Sex + Violence'. This is against my conscience, + religion."[35] Taking these statements together, Chihuahua and Doc are not so much social outcasts as moral outlaws – in a way *Stagecoach*'s Dallas and Ringo never were – most likely because they have violated the film's latent yet central taboo, miscegenation.

The same sensational (for 1946) issue is openly at the core of *Duel in the Sun*, and again the film drives its ideological message home by killing off a character whom white society – and propriety – might rather not accommodate. Niven Busch's novel ended with Pearl killing Lewt but surviving to marry the upright Jesse.[36] On screen, however, Jesse personifies the moral code to which Pearl aspires, but he is only temporarily cast as her potential suitor. Halfway through *Duel* he acquires a WASP fiancée of placid disposition and impeccable bloodline. The narrative clearly implies she should be his ideal partner. Pearl, on the other hand, is a caricature of wanton sexuality, too passionate to marginalize and too tempestuous to rest easy within wedded tranquillity.

Duel's climactic *Liebestod* was the frosting on its melodramatic and erotic appeal, and audiences responded eagerly. *Duel in the Sun* became the highest-grossing Western of the 1940s, ranking second only to *The Best Years of Our Lives* (1946) as the decade's box office champion; furthermore, after inflation-adjustment in 1981, *Duel* emerged as the greatest Western money-spinner of all time.[37]

If *Clementine*'s moral tone was essentially prudish, *Duel*'s was prurient. Besides attempting to outgross his own *Gone With the Wind*, David Selznick was determined to outdo *Duel*'s erotic Western forerunner, Howard Hughes's *The Outlaw* (1943), and to elevate his inamorata, Jennifer Jones, to love goddess status. While failing to topple *GWTW*, *Duel* was a visual and narrative feast of opulent sensuality unequalled by anything else in the genre. *TIME* proclaimed newly released *Duel* "the costliest, the most lushly Technicolored, the most lavishly cast, the loudest ballyhooed, and the sexiest horse opera ever made".[38] *How the West Was Won* (1962) and *Heaven's Gate* (1980) have since surpassed *Duel* in cast and cost respectively but, almost fifty years later, *TIME*'s last pronouncement still holds true. With hindsight, *Duel*'s full-blown, defiant, unrestrained passion is as much a metaphor for postwar American affluence, freedom and indulgence as David Lean's *Brief Encounter* (1945) stands as an allegory of sacrifice and repression in Britain's ration-book era. Contemporary American church leaders, however, were not disposed to such cultural interpretations. Los Angeles's Roman Catholic Archbishop John Cantwell told his co-religionists they could not "with a free conscience" see the "morally offensive and spiritually depressing" *Duel in the Sun*; further criticism came from L.A.'s Federation of Protestant Churches, which held that the film depicted wrongdoing as persistently triumphant, and the Catholic publication *Tidings*, which deemed its heroine "unduly if not indecently exposed".[39] Thus *Duel* attracted a furore which *Clementine* escaped, despite similarities in theme and characterization. *Clementine* is basically a puritan fable about America's civilization, with Doc and Chihuahua depicted as morally unfit to belong. *Duel*, by contrast, turns the world on its head: *Liebestod* implies the world isn't good enough for lovers who choose to die together. While Doc and Chihuahua are arguably little more than *Clementine*'s seamy subplot, Lewt and especially Pearl are *Duel*'s central focus, and their climactic bloody embrace is both consummation and celebration of illicit passion. To compound the watchdogs' discomfort, Jennifer Jones and Gregory Peck, the stars of this outrageous love-fest, were Catholics who first attained stardom as sainted nun and priest in *The Song of Bernadette* (1943) and *The Keys of the Kingdom* (1945) respectively (ironically,

Linda Darnell – *Clementine*'s "Magdalene" – appeared in *Bernadette* as the Virgin Mary); and as though rape, lewd dances and semi-nudity were not enough, religious groups were further incensed by Walter Huston's "Sin Killer", a sagebrush "preacher" who leers repulsively at Pearl while attempting to tame her semi-nude flesh through prayer.

Clementine unequivocally bolstered delicate sensibilities, whereas *Duel* joyously flouted them under its scanty narrative cover of retribution at fade-out. Selznick had even attempted to persuade the nun who was Jennifer Jones's spiritual adviser that "the story preaches a very moral lesson ... 'the wages of sin are death'".[40] This argument failed to convince *TIME*'s reviewer, who wrote: "The audience eventually learns ... that Illicit Love doesn't really pay in the long run, but for about 134 minutes it has appeared to be loads of fun".[41] *TIME*'s final verdict was unsympathetic, concluding: "[t]he picture adds nothing to his reputation as a producer of quality entertainment, ... because Mr. Selznick's profit motive is showing. All costly films ... are manufactured for profit, but the successful works generally keep pointing winningly to their warm hearts and remain sentimental about their subjects ... or their characters ... or their audiences. ... With no pretense at all to having a heart, big, beautiful, humorless *Duel* remains shrewdly cynical about both itself and its sensation-hungry public."[42]

Three weeks earlier, *TIME* had wound up its review of James Edward Grant's pacifist Western *Angel and the Badman* (1947) by observing: "in a season when horse operas are going stridently sexy, it is nice to see the great open spaces filled with something a little more edifying than heaving, half-bared bosoms".[43] The pejorative reference to the unnamed *Duel* was obvious. Likewise, Bosley Crowther's review for the *New York Times* bemoaned "the ultimate banality of the story and its juvenile slobbering over sex".[44] Yet, of course, the sexual content which church-men deemed offensive and critics dismissed as distasteful was the very magnet which drew the crowds, who happily paid roadshow prices of $1.20, three times the average admission fee. During 1962–1963, the audiences flocking to *How the West Was Won* paid to see a romanticized epic of the making of Americans. The appeal of *Duel*'s first-run was far simpler.

Although *Duel* gloried in sex, its ideological postures on race, class and gender were ultraconservative. Selznick's plea to Jones's spiritual adviser not to prejudge the film till its "very moral lesson" became evident was certainly meretricious but nonetheless accurate. In *Duel*, the wages of sin *are* death; unbridled sexuality *is* punished; and no character who indulges in its most exotic strain herein – miscegenation – survives.

Pearl, child of a dignified yet weak aristocrat and a sluttish Indian mother, is clearly depicted as the slave of conflicting hereditary impulses. When she succumbs to Lewt's advances, she is yielding to her "bad blood". *Duel* therefore not only infers racial inferiority but equates this with moral laxity; and the film's depiction of Blacks is limited to Butterfly McQueen as Vashti, Laura Belle's languid, addle-headed servant girl – in effect identical to her role as Prissy in *Gone With the Wind*.

Similarly, class in *Duel* is defined primarily by behaviour rather than by economic circumstances. Pearl tells the genteel Laura Belle she is "a good girl" and wishes to be a fine lady like her mentor; but after becoming Lewt's lover she proclaims herself "trash, like my Ma".[45] Social acceptability is, as with race, closely tied to sexual comportment. Significantly, Jesse tells Pearl his fiancée wants to be her friend; just as, in Ford's film, Clementine helped Doc in the operation to save Chihuahua's life, a WASP Madonna's lack of exuberant sexuality is supplemented by noble character. Moreover, Jesse's Eastern lady serves as assurance that feminine purity will flourish in the West even after Laura Belle's death.

More than any other Western, *Duel* is overtly obsessed with sex, and many of the above observations have already addressed the film's treatment of gender. Two additional points apply in this respect. First, *Duel* implicitly endorses the intellectual repression of women in a remarkable throwaway line during this exchange between Pearl and Jesse:

PEARL: I want to learn, Jesse. Will you learn me? Your Ma says you're a lawyer. I wanna be a lady and know everything, like her.
JESSE: I wonder if learning ever made Mother any happier.[46]

Education is not the only prerogative *Duel* would deny women. Pearl is physically attracted to Lewt but emotionally repelled by his ungallant manner. Her self-enslavement is a consequence of rape. Only after Lewt has forced himself on Pearl does she give herself to him totally – certainly an unhealthy image of romantic passion by any standards. Another throwaway comment reinforces the same point, albeit less brutally, when a cowboy at the McCanles fiesta observes of dancing, "Females shouldn't be allowed no choice. It ain't decent".[47] *Duel* thus stakes intellectual advancement and sexual initiatives as essentially masculine preserves.

Secondly, since Pearl is the film's central protagonist, the Madonna/Magdalene dichotomy evident in many classic Westerns is effectively transferred to the McCanles brothers who appeal to the contradictory facets of her character – environment or heredity, culture or nature, sex or respectability, passion or repression. The amorous alternatives confronting Pearl in *Duel* are identical to those Clementine and Chihuahua pose Doc.

The dark, wanton goddesses, fatal affairs and promiscuity-oriented narratives of *Clementine* and *Duel* in a sense function as exhortations to sexual responsibility. Incidence of venereal disease in the U.S. population actually *rose* in that first year of peace, from 2.54 per thousand head in 1945 to 2.73 – and this after a dip from the 1943–1944 figures.[48]

Yet, of course, racy plot lines, particularly *Duel*'s, were first and foremost designed to boost box office receipts. *Duel* grossed over $10,000,000 while *Clementine* took $2,750,000 and rated, after inflation-adjustment in 1981, as the thirty-first most successful Western.[49] Even though *Clementine* was only moderately profitable, along with *Duel* it was a qualitative standout in a year of otherwise lacklustre Western fare. In 1946, Hollywood's eight major studios produced a total of two hundred and forty feature films, thirty-two of which (13.33%) were Westerns (Table 2.2).

Table 2.2 Westerns/total output of Hollywood majors in 1946[50]

Company	Total of Westerns	Total output
Columbia	17	51
Metro-Goldwyn-Mayer	1	26
Paramount	2	19
R-K-O	2	34
20th Century-Fox	1	32
United Artists	3	19
Universal	6	37
Warner Brothers	0	22

These figures do not include *Duel in the Sun*; the Selznick Releasing Organization was formed specifically for that epic's distribution. *My Darling Clementine* was Fox's sole entry among 1946's Westerns. Low-budget cowboy sagas constituted one-third of Columbia's entire output, so undoubtedly there was a market for Westerns, regardless of quality. Perhaps strangest of all, Warner Brothers, who reaped handsome prewar dividends with the epic *They Died With Their Boots On* and who would later release several of the most critically acclaimed Westerns ever filmed, never ventured West at all that year.

Thus in 1946 the Western was still, to borrow from its own

mythology, largely open territory, inhabited by clichés rather than overt ideology. Between them, *My Darling Clementine* and *Duel in the Sun* drove their stakes deep into ground which had lain fallow since the prewar epics and claimed the genre for white male supremacy. No matter how America changed over the ensuing generation, the Western continued to assure the white male citizen that America was his.

Despite an occasional inversion of sexual roles, hinted at in *Duel* and the explicit theme of Nicholas Ray's *Johnny Guitar* (1954), the Western remained under masculine dominion. Racial inroads were more frequent and more assimilable. Hollywood had lambasted anti-Semitism in 1947 (*Gentleman's Agreement, Crossfire*), and 1949 had witnessed a cycle of films focusing on the problems of Black Americans (*Pinky, Intruder in the Dust, Lost Boundaries* and *Home of the Brave*). Pro-Indian Westerns became fashionable in 1950 with the release of Delmer Daves's *Broken Arrow* and Anthony Mann's *Devil's Doorway* – so much so that in December that year *TIME*, which had blithely praised *Clementine* as "a rattling good movie full of gusto, gunplay and romance", slammed Ford's "shoddy taste in material" concerning his anti-Indian *Rio Grande*.[51]

While the Western managed to accommodate racial minorities from 1950 onwards, its real power struggles were waged between whites. Pearl's climactic trek across the desert to rendezvous with Lewt technically qualified *Duel* as an odyssey Western. In substance, the film paid no more than lip-service to the ideal of community through Jesse and Harry Carey's honest lawyer. *Duel's* political conflict was shown from the viewpoint of the autocratic Senator McCanles rather than the incoming homesteaders. *Duel in the Sun* was about the passions which destroy a dynasty, not community aspirations. Yet this conflict was in effect identical to that at the heart of *My Darling Clementine* and many of the films to be scrutinized in future chapters. It was a clash between charismatic authority and the popular will which later pervaded such diverse sagas as *Fort Apache* and *Red River* (both 1948), *Shane* (1953), *The Big Country* (1958), *Warlock* (1959) and *The Man Who Shot Liberty Valance* (1962).

The prewar epics gave Americans icons who were charismatic *and* embodiments of the popular will, whether these were lawmen (Errol Flynn in *Dodge City*) or outlaws (Tyrone Power in *Jesse James*, John Wayne in *Stagecoach*). Yet they were Depression-era figures, when the most charismatic American hero of all was Franklin Roosevelt. World War II had demonstrated the downside of charisma, and therefore many of the charismatic figures in postwar Westerns were crypto-fascists resisting a transference of authority to the democratic majority. The postwar Westerns of the 1940s and 1950s centred on individual hubris as eagerly as Westerns of the late 1960s and 1970s targeted such national manifestations. The distinction I outlined previously, between prewar epics which celebrated the conquest of the West and the postwar Westerns which concentrate on the struggle to preserve what has been won, conforms to the same division Leo Lowenthal noted in his 1943 study of articles on celebrities in American magazines before or after 1940.[52] Prewar Westerns, produced with the Depression still fresh in memory as the nation geared for war, were narratives linked to a production-based society. In those films, men of goodwill banded together against common enemies. In postwar Westerns, they were more likely to quarrel among themselves for a bigger piece of the pie. Westerns after World War II, alternately lavish, sensual, nostalgic, violent, neurotic, solipsistic or any combination thereof, were clearly artifacts of a consumption-oriented, pluralistic culture. For example, compare *Duel* with King Vidor's 1940 Colonial Western, *Northwest Passage*. Although each adheres to a puritan vision, *Northwest Passage*'s puritanism is of the endeavour-sacrifice–achievement variety whereas *Duel*, more moralistic than morale-boosting, affects to deplore the sexual indulgence it lovingly depicts.

Duel in the Sun's interest-group conflict is resolved, in contrast to its erotic finale, without bloodshed. The Senator leads his ranch-hands to the wire which the railroad workers, homesteaders and coolies are preparing to cut. Promising them a massacre if they invade his land, he baulks when the cavalry arrives, declaring in the film's most poignant moment, "I once fought for that flag. I'll not fire on it."[53] Patriotism is thus the limitation McCanles imposes on his own hubris.

Another despotic cattle baron and a stubborn martinet were to dominate the genre in 1948. Recognizing no restrictions of popular will or patriotism, these men set pride above all else and incur disastrous consequences. The next chapter will focus on these two Westerns, plus one featuring a gentler patriarch, and thence the social, intellectual and political threads of contemporary American society with which they connected.

CHAPTER 3

"The Lonely Crowd", Catholicism and Consensus on the Prairie: *Red River, Fort Apache* and *She Wore a Yellow Ribbon*

A FTER 1946, the Hollywood Western became increasingly adult in theme and sophisticated in style. In 1947 the Freudian Western arrived with Raoul Walsh's *Pursued*, featuring Robert Mitchum as a cowboy plagued by a childhood trauma. From a script by Niven Busch, author of *Duel in the Sun*, *Pursued* was a commercially successful blend of fatalistic melodrama, laden with dark psychological undercurrents, in a Western setting. *Pursued* owed as much to the concurrently popular genre of *film noir* as to the Western, and similar hybrids followed in its wake – André de Toth's *Ramrod* (1947), Robert Wise's *Blood on the Moon* (1948), Raoul Walsh's *Colorado Territory* (1949) and, again from Niven Busch, Anthony Mann's *The Furies* (1950).

Significantly, each film is indebted to *Duel in the Sun* – *Colorado Territory* stylistically, the others thematically. The narrative content of "A" Westerns from 1947 to 1950 therefore suggests it was David Selznick's overwrought epic, rather than John Ford's *My Darling Clementine*, which gave the genre a much needed kick-start after the fallow years of the war. *Colorado Territory*, a Western remake of Walsh's *High Sierra* (1941), had a fatalistic climax especially evocative of *Duel*, as Virginia Mayo's sensual half-breed perished with her outlaw lover (Joel McCrea) among the rocks.[1] If the genre offered Americans an escape from the problems of their own age, 1940s *noir* Westerns afforded their protagonists no such refuge. In an increasingly complex world, the Western forsook easy narrative certainties. Its heroes were now most likely haunted, obsessed, arrogant or doomed. In this vein, one critical success at the edge of the genre, John Huston's *The Treasure of the Sierra Madre* (1948), spawned a cycle of gold-lust melodramas (*Yellow Sky* and *Silver River* (both 1948), *Lust for Gold* and *The Walking Hills* (both 1949)). These films demonstrated the inefficacy of collective security when self-interest reared its head. Reviewing *Sierra Madre* for the *New York Times*, Bosley Crowther indeed suggested director Huston "has filmed an intentional comment here upon the irony of avarice in individuals and in nations today".[2]

Though nation-building sagas had not regained their prewar predominance, these remained popular at the box office. The top-grossing Western of 1947 (*Duel in the Sun* excepted) was Cecil B. DeMille's Colonial era epic, *Unconquered* (Paramount) – second most profitable Western of the decade and, inflation-adjusted, the fifth biggest money-spinner in the genre.[3] *Unconquered* features an English heroine with the quintessentially American name Abigail Martha Hale (recalling the first two presidential wives, Martha Washington and Abigail Adams, and Revolutionary martyr Nathan Hale). After accidentally killing a soldier, she is deported to Colonial America as a bond slave. Aboard ship, Abby (portrayed by New York-born Paulette Goddard) arouses the interest of a courageous, patriotic Virginian militiaman (Gary Cooper) and an unscrupulous merchant (Howard Da Silva) intent on provoking Indian unrest for personal aggrandizement. A very turgid two hours and twenty-seven minutes later, Abby and her gallant Virginian have averted an Indian massacre at Fort Pitt and foiled the arms-running fifth columnist, retiring for the standard fade-out embrace behind a door bearing a quotation on liberty from Benjamin Franklin. *Unconquered* was, in both its Colonial setting and its plodding pace, more reminiscent of the prewar historical epics than typical of late 1940s Western trends; and even its bodice-ripping histrionics (in grandest DeMille tradition) pale beside the passion of *Duel in the Sun*. However, the film merits brief attention in the present study, because its casting was curiously prophetic of the political drama which was about to engulf Hollywood and divide American society.

Come 1950, as mentioned earlier, DeMille would be the driving force behind a right-wing attempt to unseat Joseph L. Mankiewicz as president of the Screen Directors' Guild; and he had previously proposed directors should, in effect, spy on their co-workers, alerting the Guild to whatever they learned about the politics of their associates on a movie, especially the actors and writers.[4] Certainly, DeMille had McCarthyite sympathies; and *Unconquered* offered audiences an alarmist saga of patriotic Americans besieged by barbaric, property-wrecking redskins (read communists). DeMille's stalwart heroes in this flag-waving endeavour were Cooper, who appeared as a friendly witness before the House UnAmerican Activities Committee less than two weeks after *Unconquered*'s New York opening, and Ward Bond, such a vehement anti-communist that he later flew his American flag at half-mast to protest Nikita Khrushchev's tour of Hollywood.[5] The villain was played by Howard Da Silva, soon to be a victim and one of the most vociferous critics of the Hollywood blacklist. Paulette Goddard's screen deportation as an undesirable is deeply ironic, considering her ex-husband Charlie Chaplin was labelled a communist sympathizer that year and denied re-entry to the United States five years later.

Perhaps *Unconquered*'s contemporary parallels touched areas some reviewers preferred to avoid in a political climate which eschewed nuances in favour of moral absolutes. *TIME* called the film "DeMille's florid, $5,000,000, Technicolored celebration of Gary Cooper's virility, Paulette Goddard's femininity and the American Frontier Spirit. ... Patriot Cooper wants peace and a strong frontier (he is the stuff that the unborn U.S. is to be made of)."[6] Bosley Crowther described *Unconquered* as "adventure drama of the sort that we got in silent films", and acknowledged DeMille was "[w]inking broadly at history".[7] The film was effectively reinforcing the mid-twentieth century conservative sentiment "better dead than Red" in a Colonial era context. Proportionately, virulent anti-Indian sentiment is much more pronounced in Colonial era epics (*Drums Along the Mohawk*, *Northwest Passage* and *Unconquered*) than in Westerns dealing with the Indian Wars.[8]

Yet most "A" Westerns of the late 1940s, whether including contemporary political undercurrents or not, had a post-Civil War setting rather than a pre-Revolutionary time-frame. Moviegoers evidently approved, and the Western flourished in an era of some crisis for the American cinema – a crisis which was economic as well as political. Between 1946 and 1950, American cinema audiences plummeted by one-third, from eighty-two to fifty-five million per week, while admission prices rose from forty to forty-eight cents, over twice the price of admission in 1939.[9] Over these five years, box office receipts fell from $1,692,000,000 to $1,376,000,000, and movie attendance as a percentage of consumer, recreation and spectator expenditure declined steadily from 1.18% to 0.72%, from 19.8% to 12.3% and from 81.9% to 77.3% respectively.[10] Production of Westerns, however, was a staple and an asset in the midst of Hollywood's changing fortune, as the genre's proportion of the eight major studios' total 1947–1950 output demonstrates (Table 3.1; for 1946, see Table 2.2 on p. 45 in the previous chapter).

Admittedly Columbia's Western output, while quantitatively phenomenal (37.19% of the studio's product), was virtually all "B" material; and though Western figures for Metro, Paramount, Fox and Warners were hardly spectacular, in 1947 these studios released a combined total of

Table 3.1 Westerns/total output of Hollywood majors, 1947–1950[11]

Company	Total of Westerns	Total output
Columbia	74	199
Metro-Goldwyn-Mayer	7	124
Paramount	11	100
R-K-O	30	138
20th Century-Fox	9	135
United Artists	22	82
Universal	15	95
Warner Brothers	11	96

three Westerns – whereas by 1950 this figure had risen to twenty-two. Moreover, as a proportion of all features produced in those years from 1947 to 1950, the Western accounted for 26%, 30%, 27% and 34% respectively.[12] Movie exhibitors polled in 1949 reported they had "never had a first-class western that was a box-office failure".[13] A list of the forty highest-grossing Westerns, compiled in 1981, includes thirteen from 1946 to 1950.[14] The filmic West was booming.

John Ford, whom posterity has crowned the genre's master, helmed fourteen full-length sound era Westerns from *Stagecoach* (1939) to *Cheyenne Autumn* (1964). Between 1948 and 1950 alone, he directed five. Four of these featured the same leading man. The most significant occurrence within the Western of the late 1940s was this individual's emergence as the genre's principal star.

John Wayne's first crack at stardom in an "A" Western had come at the age of twenty-three in Raoul Walsh's *The Big Trail* (1930). Thereafter, his career had settled into the rut of "B" features until Ford brought him to prominence as the Ringo Kid in *Stagecoach*. Still his career languished, and prior to 1948 the bulk of his output had been mediocre. Yet in 1950 and 1951 he was America's top box office draw – a position he retained overall throughout the 1950s and 1960s; moreover, a cumulative tabulation of box office favourites between 1932 and 1980, one year after his death from cancer, shows Wayne the indisputable champion.[15] His star image is forever associated with the Western, and three released between 1948 and 1949 were chiefly responsible for transforming this amiable veteran of scores of undistinguished oaters into the greatest of all Western icons.

Even in the first of the three, Ford's *Fort Apache* (R-K-O, 1948), despite top-billing Wayne actually played second fiddle to Henry Fonda. The film which really boosted his career – so much that even a batch of dreadful movies in the 1950s made no dent in his popularity – was Howard Hawks's *Red River* (United Artists, 1948), in which his portrayal of a tyrannical cattle baron impressed his mentor, John Ford, who remarked, "I didn't know that big sonofabitch could act".[16] *Stagecoach* made John Wayne a star; *Red River* made him a superstar. Ford thus acquired new respect for his protégé's capabilities and cast him as the ageing soldier of *She Wore a Yellow Ribbon* (R-K-O, 1949). In *Red River*, Wayne was imperious and unyielding. In *She Wore a Yellow Ribbon* he was dignified, honourable and humane. For the next twenty-seven years he would draw on these opposing traits – frequently within one characterization, as in *The Searchers* (1956) or Mark Rydell's impressive elegy *The Cowboys* (1972) – hence symbolizing power and benevolence in equal measure, like the American eagle, endowed with both arrows and olive branch. Yet if these Westerns marked the elevation of John Wayne as an American icon, what did they offer audiences about late 1940s America? Close examination suggests a relationship to several strands of contemporary American culture, intellectual, social and political.

Fort Apache and *Red River* each represented a fusion of two late 1940s trends in the genre. Both featured arrogant, driven protagonists akin, in compulsion if not in temperament, to the heroes of *noir* Westerns; yet each was also in the celebratory, nation-building, quasi-historical tradition, like *Unconquered*. *Fort Apache* and *Red River* successfully merge often conflicting *noir* and epic strains within the Western. Although *Fort Apache* opened first, its close relationship to *Yellow Ribbon* suggests they merit analysis together, so I will focus initially on *Red River*.

If *My Darling Clementine* was a hymn to community and *Duel in the Sun* a celebration of sex, *Red River*'s primary theme was work – hard, sweat-drenching, soul-killing work. It straddled the prewar nation-building epic and the postwar interest group conflict, housing both struggles within its narrative. In 1851 Tom Dunson (John Wayne) and his sidekick Nadine Groot (Walter Brennan) quit a California-bound wagon train to raise cattle in Texas. Dunson leaves the woman he loves with the settlers, who are massacred by Indians. Only one survives: a boy named Matthew Garth. Dunson's bull and Matt's cow are the beginnings of the Red River D (for Dunson) herd, which will become the greatest cattle empire in Texas. After the Civil War, however, Dunson has no money and no market in the Southwest for his massive herd. He decides to drive them to Missouri, aided by Matt (Montgomery Clift), now grown and a Civil War veteran, Groot and his ranch hands, whom he assures: "Every man who signs on for this drive agrees to finish it. There'll be no quittin' along the way – not by me and not by you".[17] On the trail, rumour comes of an easier way to market – the railhead at Abilene in Kansas. Unconvinced this railhead exists, Dunson holds to his original plan, ignoring the cowhands' growing discontent, pushing them harder on short rations, shooting three would-be quitters and humiliating a cowboy who accidentally causes a stampede and a co-worker's death. Several times Matt and Groot try to steer him toward a more rational, humane approach; but he grows ever more tyrannical, refusing to sleep and seeking solace in drink until he alienates them by vowing to hang two deserters. Matt rebels and assumes leadership of the drive, now destined for Abilene. Dunson, betrayed by his adoptive son, promises he'll catch up and kill him. A contrived romantic subplot has Matt fall in love with Tess Millay (Joanne Dru), a girl on a wagon train obviously meant to remind us of Dunson's lost love. Tess subsequently meets Dunson and accompanies him to Abilene. Matt completes the drive, his success vindicated by the presence of the railhead and the gratitude of Abilene's citizens, who had been suffering from a beef shortage. At the climax, Matt faces Dunson but refuses to draw on him. A brutal fistfight ensues, ending only when Tess shoots between them and lectures them – frantically – that they love each other and have no intention of killing one another. The film ends with Dunson promising to add an M (for Matt) to the Red River D, thus making Matt a full partner.

Red River focuses on a cattle baron's alienation from the community he leads; it ends with the herd's arrival in Abilene, boosting a community hungry for beef. Yet, though the film's commitment to community values is more pronounced than *Duel in the Sun*'s, primary emphasis remains on the autocratic rancher. *Red River* is actually the archetypal odyssey Western, and 1948 audiences lapped it up, paying over $4,000,000, making it the year's number three grosser and, after inflation-adjustment in 1981, the tenth most lucrative Western.[18] Critics were, for once, equally enthusiastic. "Up to a point ... one of the best cowboy pictures ever made", asserted Bosley Crowther, who went on to praise "a withering job of acting a boss-wrangler done by Mr. Wayne. This consistently able portrayer of two-fisted, two-gunned outdoor men surpasses himself. ... We wouldn't want to tangle with him."[19] *TIME* declared *Red River* "a rattling good outdoor adventure movie. ... Hawks obviously likes and understands men, grand enterprise, hardship, courage and magnificent landscape. The greatest satisfaction of this picture is ... the constancy with which all outdoors, and all human endurance of it and effort to conquer it, keeps bulging the screen full of honest and beautiful vitality."[20] *The New Republic*'s review noted contemporary critics' surprise at their own enthusiasm for *Red River*, explaining their discovery of "unexpected innocence in themselves" thus: "A workmanlike Western (and *Red River* is that) is a specimen of thoroughly disciplined folk spectacle and ... about the only pure motion picture, outside the newsreels, that we now get."[21] The *Motion Picture Herald* praised it as "a rousing tale ... told with hard-bitten realism in the heroic tradition of those epics of the West which have brought credit to the screen and profits to exhibitors since *The Covered Wagon*".[22] *Variety* predicted Hawks's film would "take its place among the other big ... western epics that have come from Hollywood over the years. It's a spectacle of sweeping grandeur, as rugged and hard as the men and the times with which it deals. ... A money film from any angle ... almost unlimited grossing potential ... slotted for important playdates and bigtime returns. ... The staging of physical conflict is deadly, equalling anything yet seen on the screen. Picture realistically depicts trail hard-ships."[23]

Variety and especially *TIME* made much of the fact that *Red River* was Montgomery Clift's film debut. One element reviewers found irksome was, unsurprisingly, the Matt–Tess romantic subplot, which today still seems contrived and out of place. The *Motion Picture Herald* conceded, "Its one weakness, perhaps, is in the romance department."[24] *TIME*, terming *Red River* "essentially ... about men, and for men", acknowledged that "Hawks gives even the relatively silly episodes with the girl a kind of roughness and candor which make them believable and entertaining".[25] Crowther, however, was scathing, lamenting this subplot as the point at which "the cowboys – and the picture – run smack into 'Hollywood' in the form of a glamorized female[.] ... she is the typical charmer ... and the havoc she plays with the hero – and with the contents – is almost complete. The characters turn into actors and the story turns into old stuff. It ends with the two tenacious cowboys kissing and making up."[26]

The extensive critical literature on *Red River* has engaged with constructs of masculinity, patriarchy and transition from charismatic authoritarianism to democratic egalitarianism, and this study must do likewise. However, previous interpretations have neglected one aspect of *Red River*'s resonance for postwar America: Dunson's promise to flood the nation with "good beef for hungry people" had special significance for audiences who, only two years before, had endured a meat famine.[27] If we recall the citizens' delight as Dunson's herd invades Abilene, *Red River* is clearly an epic of both achievement *and* salvation – consumers, as well as producers, have endured, and in this regard the film is as much a celebration of American spirit in 1946 as in 1866. Further, in the wake of auto, steel, coal and rail strikes over 1945–1946 and the Republican Congress's passage of the conservative Taft-Hartley Act over President Truman's veto in 1947, *Red River* presented Americans with both a dysfunctional (Dunson's) and an ideal (Matt's) approach to management–labour relations.

Red River is the archetypal generation-gap Western. Matt's ultimate revolt against Dunson's tyranny prefigures the edgy, occasionally neurotic youth-rebels of iconoclastic Westerns in the 1950s and early 1960s. The genre not only celebrated white male primacy. It especially validated white male maturity. The leading men most associated with the Western are self-evident proof of this (Wayne, Gary Cooper, James Stewart, Henry Fonda, Randolph Scott, Joel McCrea).

Bearing this tendency in mind, the characters portrayed by James Dean in George Stevens's *Giant* (1956), John Cassavettes in Robert Parrish's *Saddle the Wind* (1958), Marlon Brando in his own *One-Eyed Jacks* (1961) and Paul Newman in Arthur Penn's *The Left-Handed Gun* (1958) and Martin Ritt's *Hud* (1963) ranked among the genre's most confrontational. These were essentially anti-Western anti-heroes who frequently mocked the assumptions of the genre, the national past from which Westerns sprang and the culture in which they flourished. Above all, such figures challenged the complacency of Eisenhower's America, which they damned as flaccid, inert and implicitly hypocritical. Clift's Matt Garth was the spiritual progenitor of youth-rebels in the 1950s Westerns. *Duel in the Sun* had exposed the arrogance of a pioneer patriarch, but Lionel Barrymore's irascible McCanles was a secondary figure, whereas Dunson was *Red River*'s central character. Despite unassailable status as a celebratory epic, *Red River* was the film which punctured the moral authority of the mature Western hero, daring to suggest a potentially fatal discrepancy between age and wisdom. At the heart of the genre which exalted patriarchy, *Red River*, like *Duel in the Sun* and *Fort Apache*, posited the subversive notion that father may not always know best.

The degree to which *Red River* undercuts the mature Western protagonist becomes apparent when contrasted with a resolution of generational conflicts within the contemporaneous successes under scrutiny. In *Duel in the Sun*, the liberal and community-minded lawyer Jesse (Joseph Cotten) defies his despotic father and sides with the homesteaders. They will be reconciled (off-screen) after Jesse is wounded and the Senator has recognized his error of hubris. In *Fort Apache*, Henry Fonda's headstrong martinet dismisses Wayne's cautious advice and his respect for the Apache and provokes a massacre, subsequently leaving Wayne – a cooler, more humane figure – in command of the regiment. The arrogant hotheads of each are displaced by calm, rational, mature but not ossified, steady leaders who, under a patina of progressive philosophy, are safely conservative: Joseph Cotten and John Wayne, lawyer and military hero, are still creatures of the power structure, the stuff of which nineteenth-century presidents were made. *She Wore a Yellow Ribbon* is unequivocal in its adulation of the older generation. Here crisis lies not in the encrusted obduracy of age but in the uneasy transfer of power to callow youths who might finally be unable to preserve peace on the frontier. Thus the problem is not old men who are unwilling to relinquish power but a society which thanklessly discards those who have wielded it wisely. Next to such films, Clift's defiance of Wayne in *Red River* is a frontal assault on patriarchal hegemony, and one in which androgyny gets the drop on monolithic masculinity.

Superficially, then, *Red River* criticizes Dunson's austere brand of masculinity. Yet, at the film's core, his fierce male posturing is the absolute against which other men are measured – and frequently found wanting. Dunson humiliates the cowboy who caused the stampede by knocking over pots while trying to filch sugar, not merely because he has jeopardized the group's endeavour and violated his own professionalism (the worst sin any Hawks character can commit) but because his foible offends Dunson's stringent concepts of property, maturity and manhood. "Stealin' sugar like a kid!" he rebukes the hapless trail-hand as he prepares to whip him.[28] It is not just the theft, but the gratification of appetite (frowned on by ascetics) to feed a craving largely associated with children, which Dunson finds so distasteful – because he considers it so unmanly. Although the film condemns his sadistic solution, it never suggests his moral disapproval is unwarranted. Similarly, the film's happy ending has Dunson telling Matthew he has earned his initial on the brand – not because he realizes he has been wrong-headed, but because Matt has proved himself a real man by defying him, by leading the herd successfully to Abilene and by standing up to him in a fight. *Red River* focuses equally on Matt's rite of passage and Dunson's tyranny, but Matt's graduation to manhood is complete only when Dunson acknowledges it. Thus, in giving Dunson the last word, *Red River* actually identifies his rigid standard of masculinity as exemplary.

Red River's principal male characters conformed closely to three U.S. social types delineated in a study which was being written while Hawks's epic played to American moviegoers. David Riesman's *The Lonely Crowd* outlined postwar shifts in American national identity via disparate socio-personal constructs: the "tradition-directed", "inner-directed" and "other-directed" man.[29] Riesman contended that America's success had largely been shaped by individualistic personalities obeying their own internal imperatives ("inner-directed men") with single-minded determination and ambition beyond the capacity of the settled, non-innovative, sometimes preliterate types content with their station in life ("tradition-directed men"); yet inner-directed man was gradually being supplanted by a new figure in American life, whose attitudes, actions and aspirations were subject to peer-group approbation ("other-directed man").[30] Later, in his preface to the 1961 edition, Riesman cited the cowboy as a paradigm of inner-direction.[31] Riesman's thesis thus proposed a sociological variation on the recurring Western theme of charisma yielding to consensus, which received its most explicit genre treatment in *Red River*.

Peter Biskind's *Seeing Is Believing* (1983) identified a power struggle between inner- and other-directed men in Hawks's narrative, but the parallels between Riesman's character types and those in *Red River* were more striking and more fundamental than previously perceived.[32] Certainly, Dunson carries his inner-direction – and his *machismo* – to obsessive extremes. He stands as a dysfunctional exemplar, and his speech patterns – "*I*'m the law", "Nothing you can say or do ... ", his hatred of "quitters" and his promise to kill Matt – all indicate his singular sense of purpose has become wrong-headed for its own sake.[33] Matt is relatively placid, more attuned to his co-workers, their rights, grievances and sense of morality. He is a manager, whereas Dunson is a dictator. However, what finally provokes Matt's rebellion is not the other cowboys' discontent but his own revulsion as Dunson plans to hang the deserters – and he balks without gauging the reaction of his fellow trail-hands. He has simply had enough.

Such a plot development is a staple of the genre. At this juncture a skilled yet aloof protagonist finds he can tolerate abuses no longer and plunges into the conflict he had hoped to avoid. On an international political level, this is evidently an interventionist parable, as when Gary Cooper faced frontier fascist Judge Roy Bean (Walter Brennan) in William Wyler's *The Westerner* (United Artists, 1940). It is also fundamentally the outline of what Will Wright termed the "classical plot" in his *Six Guns and Society* (1975).[34] Yet in societal terms, this marks the cowboy's transition from inner- to other-direction. Here the hero forsakes the most selfish brand of individualism for enlightened self-interest, which is actually social interdependency. By the late 1950s and early 1960s, Western heroes who could not fully make this commitment were likely doomed to alienation or death; but in 1948 the genre presented no tragic ambiguity in societal involvement or allegiance. *Red River*'s resolution actually nudged interdependency a shade too far, as even Dunson converts to enlightened self-interest and thus, by inference, might eventually evolve into an other-directed man.

As *Red River* focuses chiefly on the "inner" versus "other" conflict, analysts have tended to neglect Brennan's Groot. Yet he is a model of tradition-directed man. Dunson's loyal friend (and probably dogsbody) for fifteen years, he is even prepared to continue this subservience when the other cowboys mutiny:

GROOT: You was wrong, Mr. Dunson. I've been with you a lot o'years, and up till now, right or wrong, I always done like you said. Got to be kind of a habit with me, I guess, 'cause that's why I'm stayin' with you.
DUNSON [*contemptuously*]: Go on with 'em!
GROOT: Thanks. Thanks for makin' it easy on me.[35]

Groot is so tradition-directed he asks Dunson's permission to desert him. As an early scene humorously establishes, he is also preliterate, as are some of Riesman's tradition-directed types.[36] Furthermore, Riesman noted the tradition-, inner- and other-directed types were susceptible to shame, guilt and anxiety respectively.[37] These same three restraints surface in *Red River*'s corresponding characters. Matt's anxiety stems from Dunson's threat to catch up with the herd and kill him. Groot himself has no reason to feel shame, but he functions as Dunson's conscience with "You was wrong" and in one scene with wordless yet obvious rebuke. A scene between Dunson and Tess suggests he feels some guilt over leaving his own woman to die with the settlers fifteen years before, but his sense of guilt also surfaces when he whips the cowboy who caused the stampede and again when he shoots the quitters. Each time, he restores his absolute *physical* authority; each time, however, he loses *moral* ground, and the knowledge that he has gone too far shows in his face. When he challenges Groot to tell him he was wrong he is effectively suppressing his own moral uncertainty; for a moment, he looks almost afraid.

If Wayne's autocratic cattle baron in *Red River* threatened frontier harmony, in *Fort Apache* he was its foremost champion. In his interpretation of social and political undercurrents of Hollywood films from late 1940s to early 1960s, Biskind recast *Fort Apache*'s Wayne–Fonda conflict as one between conservative and corporate liberal respectively, yet this is specious.[38] Here Biskind's schematization is contorted to fit the overall screen images of Wayne and Fonda, and also takes cognizance of these actors' personal political beliefs. Granted, Fonda was a liberal Democrat who carved a niche in America's consciousness with his portrayals of honest, idealistic heroes in and beyond the Western (*Young Mr. Lincoln, The Grapes of Wrath, The Ox-Bow Incident, My Darling Clementine*). Wayne was a right-wing Republican whose screen persona ultimately embodied benevolent authoritarianism, yet this trait became most pronounced in the films he made *after Fort Apache*. Wayne's York is considerably to the left of Fonda's Colonel Thursday on issues of race and class. Less concerned with dress codes and discipline, York is far more pragmatic and diplomatic in dealing with Cochise. Thursday is not merely a martinet but a racist, an elitist, a reactionary, his name partly reminiscent of 1948's Dixiecratic candidate, South Carolina's Strom Thurmond. Kirby York is the consummate organization man, a true corporate liberal.[39] We can identify Riesman's three social types in *Fort Apache*: Owen Thursday is another inner-directed man gone tragically haywire and York the placid other-directed mediator who tries to check both his impulses and his excesses, with the fort's sergeants (Ward Bond reading his Bible, Pedro Armendariz and Victor McLaglen still nurturing allegiances to the Confederacy and Ireland respectively) as tradition-directed figures.

Fort Apache was a thinly fictionalized version of Custer's Last Stand, substituting Apaches for Cheyenne and Sioux, and Arizona for the Dakotas. Colonel Thursday assumes his frontier command with contempt for the assignment and also for the War Department which withdrew him from duty in Europe, voicing his resentment with an unAmerican "Better there than here".[40] He quickly proves inimical to the outpost's relaxed, familial environment, alienating his officers with his high-handedness, dismissing the formidable Apaches as "cowardly digger Indians" and forbidding young Lieutenant O'Rourke (John Agar) to court his daughter Philadelphia (Shirley Temple), clearly on grounds of class and ethnicity.[41] York, sympathetic to the Apaches defrauded by the Indian Ring, secures Thursday's permission to meet with Cochise and persuade him to return to American soil. York and Cochise, both honourable men, reach agreement. When York takes this news to the fort, however, Thursday orders the entire regiment into the field. Intending all along to trick Cochise and use his capture for his own glory, Thursday finds his cavalry outnumbered by the Apaches. During a parley with Cochise, Thursday ignores York's advice and insults the chief, provoking a pitched battle. Thursday is wounded. York rescues him, but Thursday insists on rejoining the remaining troops on the battlefield, and he perishes with them. The coda has York, now commander of Fort Apache, attesting to Thursday's heroism. Thursday's last-minute bravery atones for his wrong-headedness – in an exact reversal of the "coward" legend which climaxed the gangster classic *Angels with Dirty Faces* (1938). The army closes ranks behind the official story, the nation gains a new hero, and history and legend merge beyond refutation.

Fort Apache was the first of Ford's valentines to the U.S. cavalry, his microcosmic exemplar of American society through which he venerated his own sacred trinity of family, community and nation. His cavalry trilogy, filmed between 1948 and 1950, centred in turn on the various strata of the frontier military environment. *Fort Apache* dealt with the problems of command; *She Wore a Yellow Ribbon* lionized a gallant line officer; and *Rio Grande* (Republic, 1950), despite Wayne's top-billing as fort commander, focused largely on the adventures of enlisted men.

Fort Apache grossed $3,000,000 domestic in 1948 and, after inflation-adjustment in the early 1980s, ranked as the genre's twenty-third biggest earner.[42] Reviews were mixed. Bosley Crowther applauded the film's "new and maturing viewpoint upon one aspect of the American Indian wars" and John Ford's "new comprehension of frontier history".[43] "This One Has It" trumpeted the *Motion Picture Herald*, praising Ford's "superior and careful craftsmanship" in making *Fort Apache* "one of his best".[44] *Variety* termed it "super action entertainment" and "socko" in "seat-edge attention".[45] *The New Republic* was decidedly unimpressed, stating that "the movies used to do ... Custer's Last Stand ... remarkably well. On the evidence of *Fort Apache* they've lost the knack. ... as dull a massacre as ever you've seen. ... The Indians are presented not as heathen devils but as a minority group with a grievance. That at least is a point worth noting. ... Postcards are supposed to be sent through the mail; flashed self-consciously on the screen, they look like Oscar bait."[46] *TIME* lamented the "many protracted and unrewarding views of domestic life around the post, and some of the bleakest Irish comedy and senti-mentality since the death of vaudeville".[47] In *The Nation*, James Agee fired off the most vicious observation: "Shirley Temple and her husband, John Agar, handle the love interest as if they were sharing a soda-fountain special, and there is enough Irish comedy to make me wish Cromwell had done a more thorough job."[48]

The distinctive Irish flavour actually renders *Fort Apache* unique among Ford's Westerns. In the previous chapter we saw how Ford, Yankee puritan and Irish Catholic both, presented *My Darling Clementine* as his puritan parable of frontier America. However, in *Fort Apache* Irish Catholicism becomes the dominant culture by default because Thursday, undoubtedly WASP, negates his status as natural patriarch of the fort's family-community by totally alienating his subordinates' affection and respect. One scene pinpoints the cession of Thursday's moral authority, and also his implicit recognition of that fact.

Lieutenant O'Rourke and Philadelphia witness the aftermath of an Indian atrocity while out riding, and a furious Thursday orders O'Rourke, both as father and commanding officer, to stay away from his daughter. O'Rourke reluctantly obeys, but Philadelphia does not realize why her young suitor is suddenly avoiding her, so she invites herself into the O'Rourke family quarters where he is dining with his parents (Irene Rich and Ward Bond, the fort's master sergeant). Thursday appears and demands that Philadelphia return home with him:

LT. O'ROURKE: Colonel Thursday, sir, I would like –
THURSDAY: Mr. O'Rourke, I want no words with you at this time.
LT. O'ROURKE: But, Colonel, sir –
THURSDAY: You heard me, sir. Now, get out of here before I say something I may regret!
SGT. O'ROURKE: This is *my* home, Colonel Owen Thursday, and in my home I will say who is to get out and who is to stay. And I will remind the colonel that his presence here, uninvited, is contrary to Army Regulations – not to mention the code of a well-mannered man![49]

This is the precise moment when Irish Catholicism becomes the dominant culture of Fort Apache; and although Thursday, in the face of the youngsters' instantaneous betrothal, tells his daughter, "this is not a proper or suitable marriage for you", and reminds Sergeant Major O'Rourke, "as a non-commissioned officer, you are well aware of the barrier between your class and mine", he departs on a genuinely dignified note, begging pardon for both his uninvited entry and his harsh words to the lieutenant.[50] Like Dunson shaming the sweet-toothed cowboy and shooting the quitters, Thursday's intrusion ends with his will still prevailing but a severe loss of both face and moral authority. Thursday's final acceptance of this is evident when he sends young O'Rourke to safety just prior to the massacre, and also in his exchange with the boy's father as he rejoins his depleted command:

THURSDAY: Sergeant Major O'Rourke – my apologies, sir.
O'ROURKE: You can save them, sir, for our grandchildren.[51]

Thus, just before dying, Thursday implicitly accepts his descendants will be O'Rourkes. The fort's new commander is the ethnically ambiguous but amiable Kirby York. Irish Catholicism is in the ascendancy here, and at film's end it is the ruling culture on the frontier. Its role in *Fort Apache*'s narrative is organic, whereas in *She Wore a Yellow Ribbon* and *Rio Grande* it appears extraneous and contrived. Moreover, just as we saw Ford's Irish Catholic status anxiety emerge in *Clementine* via Earp's contemptuous treatment of racial minority figures, in *Fort Apache* the other side of Ford's ethnic consciousness came to the fore, not only in celebration of Irish Catholicism but in York's sympathy for the Apaches. So Ford the Irish Catholic displayed emotional kinship with America's most marginalized ethnic group as surely as Ford the Yankee puritan had excluded them from his previous model frontier community in *Clementine*.

The Western abounded with religious imagery and themes; it had its own icons, desert ordeals and sagas of sacrifice and redemption. Even if its obsession with revenge and violence ultimately eschewed concepts of Christian charity, until the 1960s the genre acknowledged the centrality, however muted, of religion in its world. Yet the churches to which God-fearing, barn-raising, tax-paying frontier folk flocked on cinematic Sundays were invariably Protestant. In Westerns Catholicism is the religion of Mexicans, and Henry King's *The Bravados* (1958) – featuring a White Anglo-Saxon *Catholic* protagonist – was a rarity in the genre. Yet in 1948, Ford ended *Fort Apache* with his beloved Irish Catholicism at the heart of his romanticized America, and did so at the very time writer Paul Blanshard was sounding an alarm about the Catholic hierarchy's encroachments upon the U.S. democratic process.[52] The following year, the same exhibitors' poll which stressed the commercial guarantee of high-quality Westerns opined: "We have had a great deal of glorification of the Catholic and Jewish religions. We must not lose sight ... that the vast majority of our people, and our critics, are of the Protestant faith."[53]

Granted, a handful of prestigious productions in the 1940s focused on Catholics, Jews or the indignities each had endured (*The Song of Bernadette* (1943), *Going My Way* (1944), *The Keys of the Kingdom* and *The Bells of St. Mary's* (both 1945), *Crossfire*, *Gentleman's Agreement* and *Boomerang* (all 1947)); but, in view of WASP America's omnipresence on screen, the exhibitors' criticism appears churlish and even somewhat sinister. Yet we can certainly see how these same people took heart from the Western, which sanctified Protestantism as crucial to the U.S. frontier experience. Thus *Fort Apache* is unique among Westerns precisely because it deviates from a genre norm so established yet so rarely foregrounded that it existed as automatically as the horse and the six-gun.

No religious subtext infuses *She Wore a Yellow Ribbon*, but once again a cloying junior league romance fleshes out the proceedings. The film opens with news of the Custer massacre sweeping the West, and thereafter centres on the last few days of Captain Nathan Brittles (John Wayne) before his retirement from the cavalry. *Yellow Ribbon* is geared to sentiment rather than story, with Brittles visiting the graves of his wife and daughters, the boozing and brawling of Victor McLaglen's Irish sergeant, and the squabbling of two lieutenants, Cohill (John Agar) and Pennell (Harry Carey, Jr.), over the pretty Easterner Olivia Dandridge (Joanne Dru). Yet there is a plot, of sorts: the Indian tribes are banding together after Custer's defeat, the young brave Red Shirt (Noble Johnson) is whipping up anti-white fervour, Brittles appeals to his friend Pony-That-Walks (Chief John Big Tree) to help him avert the impending conflict but finds the old chief effectively displaced. After his own retirement ceremony, Brittles rides off to rejoin his men and spends his last hour of military service dispersing the Indian ponies, bringing the threat of war to a bloodless close. As he rides into the sunset, Southerner Sergeant Tyree (Ben Johnson) catches up to deliver a dispatch confirming his appointment as chief of scouts – endorsed by Grant, Sheridan and Sherman. He agrees good-naturedly when Tyree wishes Robert E. Lee had been among his sponsors. They return to the fort, where a dance is being held in Brittles's honour, and he learns that Olivia and Cohill are engaged. The film ends with the cavalry riding past as an off-screen narrator eulogizes them in language similar to York's tribute to the fallen troopers of *Fort Apache*.[54]

Yellow Ribbon, like *Fort Apache*, is a community Western depicting and celebrating the cavalry as a paradigm community. Unlike the gritty monochrome of its predecessor and *Red River*, it was filmed in Oscar-winning Technicolor. In 1949 it grossed $2,700,000 domestically and, after inflation-adjustment, stood thirty-second on the early 1980s tabulation of most profitable Westerns.[55] *The Hollywood Reporter* hailed *Yellow Ribbon* as "the finest outdoor picture produced in Hollywood for a very long time. ... John Wayne achieves the best performance of his long career, for he makes the hard-bitten old regular army officer, courageous, wise in the ways of their Indian foes, unfailing in his sense of duty, but kind and sentimental underneath, into a real person whom the spectator admires and loves."[56] *Variety* termed it "a real moneymaker. ... done in the best John Ford manner. ... Much of the outdoor color photography is awe-inspiring", but conceded, "Picture really has five climaxes, and any one of the last two or three could have been eliminated without hurting."[57] Bosley Crowther called *Yellow Ribbon* "a dilly of a cavalry picture", declaring: "Ford has superbly achieved a vast and composite illustration of all the legends of the frontier cavalryman. ... His action is crisp and electric. ... No one could make a troop of soldiers riding across the western plains look more exciting and romantic than this great director does. No one could get more emotion out of a thundering cavalry charge or an old soldier's farewell ... than he."[58]

She Wore a Yellow Ribbon reveres the ideal of service. Two details recall George Washington: Brittles, donning spectacles to read the inscription on his retirement gift, has eyes grown old in the service of his country; and Olivia's surname is the same as Martha Washington's maiden name (Dandridge). If it is the tale of a soldier whose legacy is peace and benevolence, it nonetheless strikes a chord of unease apropos the situation confronting Americans in 1949. The film opens with an ominous narration announcing the Custer débâcle and continuing: "The Sioux and Cheyenne are on the warpath ... one more such defeat as Custer's, and it would be a hundred years before another wagon train dared to cross the Plains. And from the Canadian border to the Rio Bravo, ten thousand Indians – Kiowa, Comanche, Arapaho, Sioux and Apache – under Sitting Bull and Crazy Horse, Gall and Crow King, are uniting in a common war against the United States Cavalry."[59]

A mere hiccup in westward expansion's inexorable sweep was presented in almost apocalyptic terms. Why? The answer lies in the enumeration of tribes gathering against the U.S. military: it is the frontier equivalent of a Comintern or a Warsaw Pact. *She Wore a Yellow Ribbon* premièred in 1949, a year in which Americans had seen government officials Alger Hiss and Judith Coplon accused of treachery, mainland China fall to communism, Soviet Russia attain nuclear capability and eleven communists convicted under the Smith Act of conspiring to advocate the overthrow of the American government through violence. *Yellow Ribbon* thus began with the prospect of carnage and closed on a roseate note of peace. However, its Cold War prologue stands as the bridge between the conciliatory tone of *Fort Apache* and the hawkish *Rio Grande*.[60]

Yet, on the whole, *Yellow Ribbon* is a hymn to consensus. In 1948, Richard Hofstadter had published his ground-breaking *The American Political Tradition*, stressing common threads in the national past rather than the themes of turmoil previously emphasized by Progressive historians.[61] The same transition from conflict to consensus is mirrored in a comparison between narrative components of *Fort Apache* and *Yellow*

Ribbon. Fort Apache ends in massacre, *Yellow Ribbon* with bloodshed avoided. Thursday is a racial, ethnic and class bigot who stands in the way of true love, Brittles a tolerant egalitarian who tacitly approves of the youngsters' romance. Thursday is motivated by self-advancement, Brittles by duty. Thursday's dream is one of conquest, Brittles's is of coexistence. Thursday never learns appreciation of the fort as family unit, which comes naturally to Brittles. Thursday makes pejorative remarks about Robert E. Lee and Jeb Stuart, whereas Brittles participates respectfully in the Confederate burial of a trooper who had been a Southern general; even Sergeant Tyree's disparaging quips about Yankees are essentially good-humoured, as Brittles realizes. Thursday constantly provokes discord while Brittles encourages harmony. Finally, *Yellow Ribbon* also features an upper-class figure who tries to thwart the young lovers, but Ross Pennell is a rival suitor, not an enraged father. In truth, his is no threat at all; and after some benevolent instruction by Captain Brittles and acceptance that he has lost Olivia, Pennell acquiesces and remains securely within the military's extended family, as the obstructionist Colonel Owen Thursday never truly could.

This chapter has identified and examined the emergence of certain intellectual, political, social and cultural trends of the late 1940s in three classic Westerns released in that era. We have seen the hubris of inner-directed patriarchs result in negation of their charismatic authority: each brings about his own downfall. Yet both Tom Dunson and Owen Thursday undergo a last-minute change of heart, and Nathan Brittles presides over a community whose primary impulse is harmonious. In Dunson's reconciliation with Matt, Thursday sending Lieutenant O'Rourke to safety and the Army recalling Brittles as chief of scouts, each narrative ended by reassuring audiences that, conflict over, happy families prevailed on the frontier (and from such stock sprang modern Americans). As the 1950s progressed, the myth of happy families became increasingly difficult to maintain within the Western. The next chapter will scrutinize four films made over eleven years, all by different studios and directors and featuring different stars, which in essence contain recurring plot elements and, if interpreted together, an ever-darkening representation of the nuclear family in 1950s America.

CHAPTER 4

Dysfunctional Family Structures in Classic Westerns, 1950–1961: *The Gunfighter, Shane, The Searchers* and *The Last Sunset*

THE nation-building Westerns of the late 1940s were, like the prewar historical epics, at heart reverential toward America's past and optimistic about her future. Before 1950, the Western focused largely on the march of civilization. After 1950, the genre dwelt increasingly on roads not taken. Over the ensuing decade, the Western's principal theme veered from the glory of the pioneer achievement to its awful cost. Prior to 1950, John Ford's *Stagecoach* excepted, Westerns represented U.S. society as a benevolent ideal and membership therein as the aspiration of all well-adjusted, law-abiding citizens. *Fort Apache*'s Owen Thursday was a disruptive autocrat unable to adapt to frontier realities, but his *legend* could be accommodated. The personal crisis confronting Thursday, like Dunson in *Red River* and Ross Pennell in *She Wore a Yellow Ribbon*, centred not on conforming but on belonging. Alienation was essentially the individual's fault. Frequently, in the 1950s, this adversarial relationship deepened – but, as often as not, the culpability shifted.

In the 1950s Western heroes need not be as arrogant, reckless or dictatorial as Thursday and Dunson to find themselves at odds with their fellows. Social assimilation was no longer an automatic reward at fade-out for lone Westerners. Sometimes it was not even a desirable option. Now society had to prove itself worthy of the hero and, often, society was found wanting.

Perhaps the uncertainty of the late 1940s, with the threat of growing communist influence overseas and shortages, strikes and spy scandals at home, necessitated the celebratory strains of *Red River, Fort Apache* and *Yellow Ribbon*. The beleaguered nation could gain inspiration from its

66

romanticized heritage. Yet if adversity encouraged fervour, similarly, the increasing affluence of 1950s America afforded pause for reflection and anxiety. Faced with the prospect of global conflict, Americans could not linger over their doubts and flaws. Once the urgency of the late 1940s had abated, however, the Western's principal thematic concern was not struggle for survival but the quality of life in U.S. society. Affluence harboured its own ills, and the genre avidly encoded these within a frontier setting.

Raoul Walsh's Freudian *Pursued* had been a novelty in 1947. Through the 1950s, however, psychological Westerns flourished, becoming a major staple of the genre. The four Westerns to be examined in depth here – *The Gunfighter, Shane, The Searchers* and *The Last Sunset* – are each, to some degree, psychological dramas. Others included Anthony Mann's *The Naked Spur* (1953), Richard Brooks's *The Last Hunt* and Delmer Daves's *Jubal* (both 1956), Daves's *3:10 to Yuma* (1957) and, finest of all, Edward Dmytryk's *Warlock* (1959).

Glenn Ford had portrayed a psychotic judge in *The Man from Colorado* in 1948, but the real deluge began in the mid-1950s. Suddenly, stars who had built careers as genial, clean-cut, All-American personae took turns playing dishevelled, mentally unbalanced racists (Robert Taylor in *The Last Hunt*, John Wayne in *The Searchers*, Joel McCrea in *Fort Massacre* (1958)) or vengeance fanatics, whether neurotic (James Stewart in Anthony Mann's films) or stoic (Randolph Scott in Budd Boetticher's).

Westerns from the 1950s also cast stars as neo-fascists (Charlton Heston in Charles Marquis Warren's *Arrowhead* (1953), Richard Widmark in Daves's *The Last Wagon* (1956)); sadists (William Holden in John Sturges's *Escape from Fort Bravo* (1953), James Cagney in *Tribute to a Bad Man* (1956)); psychopaths (Jeff Chandler in *Two Flags West* (1950), Alan Ladd in *One Foot in Hell* (released 1960)); cowards (Frank Sinatra in *Johnny Concho* (1956), Gary Cooper in *They Came to Cordura* (1959)); drunkards (Dean Martin in Howard Hawks's *Rio Bravo* (1959)); and even, in this most masculine of genres, as latent homosexuals (Burt Lancaster and Kirk Douglas in Sturges's *Gunfight at the O.K. Corral* (1957), Paul Newman in Arthur Penn's *The Left-Handed Gun* (1958), Richard Widmark in Sturges's *The Law and Jake Wade* (1958), and Anthony Quinn in *Warlock*).[1] Psychoses, traumas and forbidden ideological and sexual impulses thus plagued the protagonists of 1950s Westerns with unprecedented frequency and severity.

Certain contemporary problems permeated the 1950s Western. Juvenile delinquency featured prominently as theme or subplot. The genre was still weighted heavily in favour of older men as the repositories of virtue and benign authority; ergo, despite their occasional forays into bizarre characterization, mature leading men remained the Western's foremost symbols of moral guardianship and true Americanism.

Sometimes the generational interplay was chiefly didactic, as in Anthony Mann's *The Tin Star* (1957). Sometimes the plot hinged on a youth's gradual realization that his gunman father was not the villain he had believed (*The Lonely Man, Gun Glory* (both 1957)). *The Proud Ones* (1956) was a hybrid between the first strain and a variation of the second. Occasionally a young man attempted to restrain the excesses of a cruel patriarch (*The Searchers, Tribute to a Bad Man*). If the youth was a tearaway, however, the 1950s Western ultimately offered a simple choice: listen to older, wiser men, or end face down.

The choice was thoroughly authoritarian. As a rule, so was the resolution. The odd ruffian might reform (*Johnny Concho*); but more commonly, they perished (Nicholas Ray's *Run for Cover* (1955), *Gunfight at the O.K. Corral, The Left-Handed Gun*, Budd Boetticher's *The Tall T* (1957), *Saddle the Wind, Gunman's Walk* (both 1958), *Warlock*). The genre absorbed contemporary issues, recasting these within its own inherent ideological framework. Juvenile delinquents in stetsons might flout the sensibilities of Eisenhower's America, but 1950s Westerns essentially reduced this generational defiance to token gestures, for time and again the older hero's triumph implicitly reasserted the hegemony of the existing power structure. Clearly, in terms of production *and* plot outcomes, the Western was still primarily the preserve of mature white males.

Throughout the 1950s the genre returned continually to two contemporary political issues which, if regularly addressed in their twentieth-century context, would have invoked right-wing wrath. Hollywood was still reeling from the House Committee on UnAmerican Activities' investigation (begun 1947) of communist influence in the film capital, and films which were liberal on racial equality or critical of McCarthyite witch-hunters ran a risk of being labelled pink. Yet, by disguising such dramas as Westerns, Hollywood liberals could convey social and political messages relatively free from restraint and reproach. Westerns were set safely in the past, so their sources of conflict were implicitly closed issues and, moreover, the genre was already replete with its own inherently patriotic nuances. It was thus virtually the last place conservative watchdogs would think to look.

This strategy backfired memorably with the release of Fred Zinnemann's controversial *High Noon* (1952), which screenwriter Carl Foreman penned as an allegory of the witch-hunts, with Gary Cooper's marshal a lone man of courage (read conscience) deserted by his cowardly townspeople (the Hollywood community) when a gang of killers (McCarthyite thugs) threaten. *High Noon* aroused the ire of Hollywood rightists such as John Wayne, culminating in Foreman leaving America for Britain.

High Noon was also, along with 1950's *The Gunfighter*, the inspiration for the decade's town-bound, "law and order" cycle which often contrasted the heroism and integrity of a solitary lawman or gunman with the avarice, cowardice and hypocrisy of their communities (e.g., *The Proud Ones*, *The Tin Star*). In the 1930s and 1940s, town Westerns had been nation-building sagas and paeans to community endeavour (*Dodge City*, *My Darling Clementine*). Yet during the 1950s, Westerns grew increasingly sceptical of American society's intrinsic merits, most evident in scathing depictions of frontier communities as timid or petty, motivated by greed (*High Noon*) or mob hysteria (Nicholas Ray's *Johnny Guitar* (1954)). Sometimes the craven community scenario had explicit anti-McCarthy overtones (*High Noon*, *Johnny Guitar*, *Silver Lode* (1954), *A Man Alone* (1955)). Sometimes the target was not specifically political but simply the moral flab of a self-interested society (*At Gunpoint* (1955), *The Proud Ones*, *The Tin Star*, *3:10 to Yuma*, Sturges's *Last Train from Gun Hill* (1959)). Decent yet weak communities sometimes peopled 1950s Westerns (*Shane*, Mann's *Bend of the River* (alternately titled *Where the River Bends*, 1952) and his *The Far Country* (1955)), but as the decade wore on the genre heightened its criticism of complacency in domestic politics by depicting American frontier communities mainly composed of witchhunters and/or money-grabbers and, as such, an ideal scarcely worth defending.

The other contemporary charge 1950s Westerns customarily levelled against Main Street past and present was racism. Two 1950 productions – Delmer Daves's *Broken Arrow* and Anthony Mann's *Devil's Doorway* – paved the way for a cluster of pro-Indian Westerns in the 1950s. These were not the first films to deplore white America's marginalization of the Indian. Several silent Westerns (e.g., various versions of *The Squaw Man* and *Ramona*, *The Vanishing American* (1925)) and one big-budget "B" Western, *End of the Trail* (1932), were sympathetic to the red man's plight. The white heroes of three 1940s epics (Errol Flynn in Raoul Walsh's *They Died With Their Boots On*, Joel McCrea in William A. Wellman's *Buffalo Bill* (1944), John Wayne in *Fort Apache*) also condemned white perfidy against the Indian, but did so from their secure positions within the existing power structure. However, *Broken Arrow* and *Devil's Doorway* were historically important as the first major postwar Westerns which attempted to view the white/Indian frontier conflict primarily from the red man's perspective.

As in Ford's *My Darling Clementine* and King Vidor's *Duel in the Sun*, miscegenation was still punishable by death, at least for Indians (but not their white paramours), whether the affair had been consummated (*Broken Arrow*) or merely tentative (*Devil's Doorway*). The two groundbreaking pro-Indian Westerns thus balanced racial liberalism with social conservatism and, significantly, were subject to sexual double standards. *Broken Arrow*'s consummated affair involved a white man and an Apache maiden, while the ultimately impossible romance in *Devil's Doorway* featured a Shoshone warrior and a white woman. Evidently, even the thought of miscegenation was, within a 1950 movie's moral framework, enough to sign an Indian's death warrant.

In 1948, two years before *Broken Arrow* and *Devil's Doorway* were released, British anthropologist Geoffrey Gorer published *The Americans: A Study in National Character*, observing: "The position of minorities in America can only be understood if it is remembered ... only the fully American can be considered fully human."[2] The issue of miscegenation in Westerns was based on a similar premise, focusing on racial interaction at the most intimate level as the truest test of tolerance. Just as full humanity is equated with full Americanism, full social integration finally depended, according to 1950s Westerns, on white willingness to welcome racial minorities into the family unit. It is not so much a question of accommodation as one of assimilation: either they *belong*, or they don't.

Previous studies on the Western have amply demonstrated the relationship between pro-Indian Westerns and the Civil Rights struggle in the decade which saw the Supreme Court's historic 1954 decision *Brown v. Board of Education of Topeka* outlawing segregation, bus boycotts in the South and the 1957 crisis at Little Rock. Equally pertinent is the contention that, just as red protagonists in the 1950s pro-Indian Western were actually surrogates for Black Americans, the blood-crazed insurgents of anti-Indian Westerns (Ford's *Rio Grande* (1950), *Arrowhead*) were scantily disguised frontier equivalents of the communist threat. Without a doubt, *Arrowhead* was as vehemently racist as *Broken Arrow* was integrationist, but the Western's enduring appeal was predicated on violent resolution rather than racial harmony and peaceful coexistence; while *Broken Arrow* was a box office hit (grossing $3,500,000) and tremendously influential in reshaping Hollywood's representation of the Indian, a genre which thrived on violence could reap only limited rewards from a pacifist premise.[3] Yet, aside from the bleak fatalism of

Devil's Doorway, the dewy-eyed idealism of *Broken Arrow* and such re-workings as the painfully tedious *White Feather* (1955), countered by the rousing, barbaric *Arrowhead* and *The Charge at Feather River* (1953), in that decade there emerged three films which subtly probed the frontier clash between red and white. These featured ideologically divergent but similarly alienated protagonists, each at war with the dominant culture, each with his own fiercely cherished racial pride and personal identity, none of whom aim to make peace with society. Burt Lancaster's last renegade Indian defying white America in Robert Aldrich's *Apache* (1954), John Wayne's Indian-hating, irreconcilable Confederate in *The Searchers* and Rod Steiger's equally implacable Rebel who chooses to join the Sioux rather than swear allegiance to the Stars and Stripes in Samuel Fuller's *Run of the Arrow* (1957) represented various tenacious racial–national loyalties which could not tranquilly be absorbed in consensual society. In essence, these characters were symbolic reminders that America's racial problems would not go away.

Thus Hollywood cloaked its reproof of 1950s America within Westerns, but for U.S. moviegoers the genre retained its basic appeal. The 1981 inflation-adjusted table of forty top Western box office hits lists thirteen released during the 1950s.[4] Nevertheless, between 1950 and 1961 the major studios' Western output and the genre's percentage of all feature productions, box office receipts, cinemas in operation, audience attendance and related consumer expenditure all declined sharply. In 1950 the eight majors released a total of fifty-eight Westerns; in 1961, the surviving seven made sixteen.[5] In 1950, Westerns constituted 34% of all features produced; by 1961, this figure had plummeted to 17%.[6] Box office receipts in 1950 totalled $1,376,000,000 and accounted for 0.72%, 12.3% and 77.3% of consumer, recreation and spectator expenditures respectively; 1961 yielded $921,000,000 (the lowest takings since 1941), and resulted in 0.27% of consumer, 4.7% of recreation and 56.7% of spectator expenditure.[7] In 1950, 16,900 four-wall cinemas and 2,200 drive-ins operated within the United States; by 1961 drive-ins numbered 4,700, while traditional movie theatres had dwindled to 12,000.[8] In those eleven years, average weekly audiences plunged from fifty-five to twenty-seven million, and ticket prices rose from forty-eight to sixty-seven cents.[9] If Hollywood's quantitative preoccupation with the Western was gradually declining through the 1950s, qualitatively the genre flourished. That decade, the Western formula received an added boost in popularity – ironically, from the medium which would finally familiarize the genre to the point of ennui. The high-water mark was 1959, with forty-eight Western series airing on television, including eight of TV's ten top-rated shows.[10]

My previous chapters have focused on the social, political and cultural import of selected thematically related Westerns, each group produced within a relatively brief time-frame. The remainder of this chapter centres on four films, each released several years apart, by four different studios, helmed by four separate directors, with no overlap of stars and superficially diverse narratives. However, close examination of these films in chronological conjunction with one another reveals an ever-darkening portrait of the lone Westerner and his dysfunctional impact on both the nuclear family and American society.

Jimmy Ringo (Gregory Peck), hero of *The Gunfighter* (1950), is an infamous gunman, tired of his rootless notoriety and the constant challenges of aggressive young hotheads each eager to make a name as his killer. The film opens with one such scene, in which Ringo is forced to shoot a pushy youth and leave town to avoid a further confrontation with the dead man's brothers. Ringo rides to Cayenne, where his wife teaches school under an assumed name, his small son is oblivious of his father's true identity and idolizes Wyatt Earp, and his ex-outlaw companion Mark Strett (Millard Mitchell) is marshal. Ringo's presence in town causes consternation. Schoolboys cut class to peer in the saloon where the legendary badman is magisterially ensconced, moralistic matrons demand the sheriff take action against him, and the inevitable punk, Hunt Bromley (Skip Homeier), attempts to provoke Ringo into a showdown. Yet Ringo wants only peace, rest, a home. Eventually he persuades his wife to agree that, if he stays out of trouble for a year, she will return to him and they will live together as a family. Without divulging his true relationship, Ringo also advises his son never to tangle with Strett, whom he calls "the toughest man *I* ever met".[11] Thus Ringo, who is contemptuous of Earp, points his son toward an unassuming, genuinely heroic lawman rather than a confected legend. Just as Ringo rides off, Bromley leaps from hiding and shoots him down. As Ringo lies dying, he tells Strett he wants people to believe Bromley killed him in a fair fight – so his murderer will never know peace, plagued throughout his life by other gunmen eager to make a reputation against *him*. The film ends with Ringo's funeral service in Cayenne, his wife and son openly declaring themselves, and his spirit riding across the skyline into the desert.

Directed by Henry King at 20th Century-Fox, *The Gunfighter* was a critical success but a commercial flop. *Variety* classed the film "a sock melodrama of the old west. It can sell itself to those who usually pass up westerns and is a cinch to please the genuine oater fan. It is grade 'A' entertainment, told in terse, well-stated terms with relentless pace and intense suspense. ... The scenes and the characters have a vivid, earnest life, constantly hitting at the emotions."[12] Bosley Crowther's *New York Times* review praised the script, direction and performances, found the reluctant gunman scenario unusual and refreshing, and termed *The Gunfighter* "one of the tautest and most stimulating Westerns of the year" and "an intriguing film which actually says ... something about the strangeness of the vainglory of man".[13] *TIME* admitted "the movie makes every shot count, manages to fill a barroom interior with more suspense than most horse operas get from all outdoors", yet concluded: "like its outlaw hero, it comes to a bad end. Its plausible air lasts until the final scenes; then the hero goes out of character and the picture goes off on a ... sentimental jag to treat him like a tin god."[14]

The Gunfighter heralded the advent of true maturity within the classic Western. *Stagecoach* had proved Westerns could be sold to adult audiences. *My Darling Clementine* and *Duel in the Sun* re-established the genre's prominence after World War II by introducing adult themes of sex and race. Yet *The Gunfighter* broke new ground by infusing its narrative with a strong sense of inescapable tragedy. Granted, *The Gunfighter* owed some debt to *noir* movies of the late 1940s; but it was also the first in a generation of Westerns, threading through the 1950s to Sam Peckinpah's *Ride the High Country* (1962) to Don Siegel's *The Shootist* (1976), which presented their protagonists – and, by extension, their audiences – with a profound consciousness of their own mortality. *The Gunfighter* was filmed in black and white and ran eighty-four minutes (the three later films under analysis here are all in colour and approximately two hours in length), but similar presentation was no box office hindrance to *High Noon*. 20th Century-Fox supremos Darryl F. Zanuck and Spyros Skouras felt the moustache Peck sported as Ringo worked against his star image and lost the movie a million dollars at the box office. However, the true reason for *The Gunfighter*'s commercial failure was much simpler: the hero died. Audiences were not yet ready to accept so bleak a view of the frontier, and in this respect clung to a Turnerian interpretation of the West as a land of second chances and new beginnings. Yet, in truth, audiences never did become overly responsive to tragic-elegiac Westerns. The inflation-adjusted table of commercially successful Westerns lists very few of this strain. Those which do rank high are *covertly* elegiac. For example, *Shane* and *The Searchers* each depict the social marginalization of a frontier hero who has outlived his time, but these at least ended with the illusion of his survival. In 1969, Peckinpah's apocalyptic *The Wild Bunch* grossed $5,300,000, while *Butch Cassidy and the Sundance Kid* treated its heroes' deaths, in the spirit of the film, as a last cheerful lark – and grossed $29,200,000.[15] Considering the genre's pronounced pessimism, especially since the late 1960s, the trend toward tragedy and elegy helped kill the Western's commercial appeal. American popular culture has traditionally venerated winners. Conversely, the tumult of the 1960s led many white middle-class citizens to reject triumphal representations of America's past. Together, these apparently conflicting impulses meant 1970s movie-goers grew progressively less sympathetic to films about old-timers of a waning culture fighting rearguard actions against encroaching civilization. Elegiac Westerns made for superior cinema but poor box office. *The Gunfighter* therefore stood not only as an illustration of the heroic Westerner's mortality and an uneasy reminder of the audience's own. Its high quality narrative contained a seed of the genre's ultimate undoing.

Alan Ladd starred as the eponymous hero of George Stevens's *Shane* (Paramount, 1953), a buckskin-clad drifter who alights at the small Wyoming homestead of Joe and Marian Starrett (Van Heflin and Jean Arthur), becomes their hired hand and the idol of their son Joey (Brandon de Wilde), and finally defends them against the grasping rancher Rufe Ryker (Emile Meyer) and evil gunslinger Wilson (Jack Palance). *Shane*, like *The Gunfighter*, focused on a lonely, Odyssean hero's stopover in a community. Yet *Shane* represented the culmination of the classic community Western just as *The Gunfighter* inspired the alienated hero who gradually assumed centrality within the genre. *The Gunfighter* looked somewhat askance at the township buzzing excitedly over the famed outlaw's presence, whereas *Shane* retained a romantic optimism in the value of community. The sod-busters in *Shane* are family men and no match for Ryker's strong-arm tactics, as Wilson proves via a brutal murder. Shane's personal tragedy – his ultimate inability to hang up his gun and settle among the homesteaders – lies mainly in the fact that the home he wants already has another man at its head. Shane's alienation stems from his own emotions rather than rejection or margin-alization by the community. The repressed love between Shane and Marian Starrett may be the subtlest and most poignant relationship in the genre; and when Marian tells the hero-worshipping Joey not to become too fond of Shane, she is really warning herself. In the climactic gunfight, Shane dispatches Wilson and the Ryker brothers but he too is wounded, perhaps fatally. He rides into the mountains as Joey, who witnessed the showdown, calls after him, begging him to come back: "Mother wants you! I *know* she does!"[16] Suddenly, a curious expression crosses the boy's face. He realizes the strangeness and the significance of what he has just said. In that moment, Joey loses both his boyhood hero and his childhood innocence. Shane continues riding away, slumping in the saddle as the screen goes dark.

Shane was a massive success with public and critics alike. It grossed $8,000,000 – thus by 1981 ranking after inflation-adjustment as the genre's third biggest money-spinner.[17] "A magnificent western filled with action, drama and offbeat, intriguingly developed characterizations," wrote *The Hollywood Reporter*'s correspondent, "George Stevens's *Shane* earns a place along with *High Noon* and *The Gunfighter* as one of the great tumbleweed sagas of the decade".[18] "It has sweep, suspense, authenticity, technical detail, powerful drama. It has Western flavor so real you can taste the dust. ... It has an incisive insight into the ... much lied about Western gunfighter. ... It is a Western in the classic tradition, ... which must rank among the greats", proclaimed the *Motion Picture Herald*, which immediately recognized Shane as a "white knight" and discerned in Stevens's narrative "the inevitability of the ancient Greek tragedy".[19] "Strong boxoffice possibilities accrue to this socko drama of the early west, which draws on sound plot and characters, solid directorial interpretation and fine playing to give it both class and mass appeal. ... Stevens handles the story and players in a manner that gives his production and direction a tremendous integrity", enthused *Variety*.[20] *TIME* declared *Shane* "high-styled ... almost rises above its stock material to become a ... celluloid symphony of six-shooters and the wide open spaces".[21] Bosley Crowther called *Shane* "a rich and dramatic mobile painting of the American frontier scene", especially lauding "a very wonderful understanding of the spirit of a little boy amid ... tensions and excitements and adventures of a frontier home"; that December, his end-of-year review numbered *Shane* among 1953's "Ten Best" films.[22]

Instantly hailed as a classic Western, *Shane* was a perfect distillation of chivalric myth: the blond, buckskin-clad Shane is the emissary of light and goodness, who alone has the power and skill to vanquish his evil counterpart, the dark, menacing Wilson. In killing Wilson, Shane is repressing the dark side of himself – the part of him which could disrupt the Starrett's marriage; for Shane has the potential to be either Galahad in Camelot or the serpent in Eden. The unspoken, unrequited love between Shane and Marian is essentially courtly romance transposed to the frontier; and Shane's final victory in battle and lonely departure, wounded, into the Tetons is suggestive of knightly sacrifice, of exile, and of Valhalla. Nevertheless, while the narrative contours of *Shane* owed as much to medieval legendry as to the Western, the film's ideological subtexts related directly to the social and political concerns of 1950s America. Shane's final decision to intervene on behalf of the Starretts against Ryker is another instance of the American hero who is keen to avoid trouble if possible but who ultimately finds he must resort to violence. Once more, the conflict is between democracy (the homesteaders) and charismatic authoritarianism (Ryker). Again, the protagonist's dilemma is one of isolationism versus interventionism. Though this dilemma is strictly formulaic – was there ever a Western hero who rode off, leaving the decent but defenceless to their own devices? – in *Shane*'s case the international connotations are unmistakable. Shane's reluctance to engage one of Ryker's thugs in a saloon brawl until goaded to the point of explosion was a frequent plot component of 1950s movies and a resonant national metaphor. Such a hero is, like the nation's idealized self-image, friendly, benevolent, peaceable and slow to anger; yet once roused to violence he establishes his moral authority with thorough and often terrible finality. John Wayne in John Ford's Irish comedy *The Quiet Man* (1952), which – given star, director and title – *sounds* like a Western, Spencer Tracy in John Sturges's *Bad Day at Black Rock* (1955), Kirk Douglas's Doc Holliday in *Gunfight at the O.K. Corral* and Gregory Peck in William Wyler's *The Big Country* (1958) stood with Ladd's Shane as personifications of the sleeping giant in the age of atomic weaponry. Each character was naturally inclined to negotiation and coexistence, but best not provoked too far.

In 1957 *TIME*, bastion of Middle America, categorized adult Westerns among "the dizzying spires of cinematic art".[23] Of all the Westerns released during the 1950s, *Shane*, along with *High Noon*, was generally considered the exemplar of the genre. Within the past generation critical consensus has shifted, and received wisdom now declares John Ford's *The Searchers* (Warner Brothers, 1956) the *ne plus ultra* of the genre. Several of the film's champions are modern directors, young moviegoers in the 1950s who later graduated from film school and peppered their own productions with homages to past masters. The concept of a "best-ever Western" is far from helpful. It attempts to impose a purportedly objective judgement derived from an assemblage of subjective opinions, and by now *The Searchers* has been perhaps over-analysed and certainly over-praised.

As self-consciously artistic as *Shane*, it is nevertheless impressive. Its photography is stunning, its complex narrative alternately poignant and gripping. In 1956 *The Searchers* took $4,900,000 at the box office, rating upon inflation-adjustment in 1981 as the sixteenth most successful Western film.[24] It was not hailed as an instant classic as *Shane* was, though they had several common narrative features. Unrepentant Confederate Ethan Edwards (John Wayne) arrives at his brother's Texas home in 1868, his first appearance there since going off to war. He and his brother's wife Martha (Dorothy Jordan) are clearly in love, though this is never verbalized. While Ethan is properly avuncular toward his nephew and two nieces, he is surly toward the Edwards's adopted son, Martin Pawley (Jeffrey Hunter), who is one-eighth Cherokee. Ethan is an unregenerate racist, and much of the stylish narrative focuses on the white supremacist demons gnawing at his soul. The morning after Ethan's arrival, he and Martin join a posse of Texas Rangers to pursue rustlers who have stolen a neighbour's cattle; but it is a trick. They have been lured away by Comanches, who raid the Edwards's ranch, rape and murder Martha, butcher her husband and son and abduct the two girls. Ethan vows to follow and find the girls. Early in his search he discovers the elder, violated and slain (this is undoubtedly Ford's most brutal Western, even though most of the violence occurs off-screen). The rest of the film details Ethan's quest as, accompanied by Martin, he scours the West in pursuit of his surviving niece, Debbie (Natalie Wood), and her captor-cum-husband, the Comanche chief Scar (Henry Brandon).

Gradually, Martin realizes Ethan aims to kill Debbie, whom he believes has tarnished familial and racial pride. One scene reveals a glaring inconsistency in this much-lauded narrative. Shortly after Ethan and Martin finally come face to face with Debbie in Scar's camp, she goes to the riverbank to meet them. Ethan draws his gun, preparing to kill her. Martin leaps in front of her, shielding her from Ethan. Ethan orders Martin to stand aside. Granted, Martin has been his companion for five years; but a man hell-bent on killing to preserve his demented notions of racial supremacy surely would not hesitate to shoot someone who is part-Indian. This inconsistency cannot be rationalized away by the film's champions; it is simply not mentioned. In narrative terms, the puzzle is sidestepped by a well-timed arrow which wounds Ethan, diverting his bullet. The two men flee from the attacking Comanches. Later, as Martin is about to cut the poison from Ethan's shoulder, Ethan renounces Debbie as his kin. In the ensuing argument, Martin throws down his knife; we never know if he actually cleanses the festering wound. When Scar's nomadic camp is again discovered, Ethan and Martin accompany the Texas Rangers on a punitive raid. Martin sneaks into the camp, finds Debbie and kills Scar. During the skirmish between Rangers and Comanches, Ethan scalps Scar then rides Debbie down. Yet, instead of killing her, he sweeps her up into his arms and takes her home. In the famous last scene, Ethan, Martin, Debbie and the Rangers ride to the neighbouring ranch where Debbie will find her new home. Her new substitute parents welcome her amid hugs and tears and usher her inside. Martin, in love with the daughter of the family, follows with his sweetheart. Ethan stands framed in the doorway, but there is no home, no hearth, no place in human society for him. He turns away, wandering back into the desert as the door closes, shutting him out forever.

The Searchers is an odyssey narrative cherishing community values which are alien to its hero; there lies much of Ethan's personal tragedy. Admittedly, it is profoundly moving, though overwrought. Yet, on release, it was not the critics' darling it has since become. Some were enthusiastic. *The Hollywood Reporter* declared it "undoubtedly one of the greatest Westerns ever made".[25] Likewise, *Motion Picture Herald* averred: "one of the greatest of the great pictures of the American West", and predicted it would "make economic as well as entertainment history".[26] Bosley Crowther's notice for the *New York Times* was generally favourable, praising the film as "a rip-snorting Western, as brashly entertaining as they come", and John Wayne as "uncommonly commanding ... magnificently uncontaminated by caution or sentiment"; but Crowther conceded that "Ford, once started, doesn't seem to know when to stop. Episode is piled upon episode, climax upon climax and corpse upon corpse until the whole thing appears to be taking a couple of turns around the course".[27] *Variety* acknowledged the film was "a western in the grand scale", yet found it "somewhat disappointing ... . it could have been so much more. Overlong and repetitious at 119 minutes there are subtleties in the basically simple story that are not adequately explained."[28] *TIME*'s review stated: "The lapses in logic and the general air of incoherence are only minor imperfections in a film as carefully contrived as a matchstick castle", but concluded that, in the climactic raid, "there is a flavour of buffoonery that suggests the actors may be kidding the pseudo realism of the earlier scenes. Even John Wayne seems to have done it once too often as he makes his standardized, end-of-film departure into the sunset."[29] The most vitriolic verdict was from *The Nation*'s Robert Hatch, who pronounced *The Searchers* "long on brutality and short on logic or responsible behavior" and "a picnic for sadists in very beautiful country".[30]

The drifter at the centre of the fourth and final Western scrutinized here is even more disturbed than Ethan Edwards. If Ethan is a sadistic racist, at least his demons are plainly in evidence. Kirk Douglas's Brendan O'Malley is a charming rogue, but fundamentally unbalanced. O'Malley is not the nominal hero of Robert Aldrich's *The Last Sunset*

(Universal, 1961), and the film is not widely considered a classic. It has suffered from critical neglect, and it does not feature on the tabulation of Western box office successes – though, with lavish production values and two of the era's top male stars (Douglas and Rock Hudson), Universal executives surely had good cause to believe they had a winner. However, *The Last Sunset* merits attention – certainly in the present context, and also because a study of this nature should not focus simply on films which previous literature has enshrined.

Black-clad Brendan O'Malley is pursued through Mexico by a trail boss-cum-lawman, Dana Stribling (Hudson), who intends to arrest him for killing a man in a gunfight. Stribling's motive is partly personal: the deceased was his sister's husband, and soon after the duel the grief-stricken widow hanged herself. O'Malley seeks haven at the ranch of John Breckenridge (Joseph Cotten), a dissipated Southern gentleman whose honour rests on falsified military glory, and his wife Belle (Dorothy Malone), O'Malley's former lover. Her sixteen-year-old daughter Missy (Carol Lynley) is fascinated by the stranger, who spins poetic fables of sea monsters. Stribling also arrives at the ranch, and he and O'Malley form an uneasy truce as they agree to help Breckenridge drive his cattle to Texas. O'Malley's terms are high: he wants a fifth of the herd – and Belle. Yet when, on the drive, Breckenridge is humiliated and killed in a cantina, Belle turns to Stribling for comfort. Later on the trail they encounter Indians, and O'Malley needlessly shoots one, not out of an Ethan Edwards-type racism, but out of pure recklessness. Stribling appeases the Indians by giving them O'Malley's fifth of the herd. The night before they arrive in Texas, they throw a fiesta where Missy, in love with O'Malley, captivates him by wearing a yellow dress Belle had worn years before. O'Malley falls in love with her and decides to take her away with him. Once in Texas, Stribling, who has grown to respect O'Malley, contemplates letting him ride free. O'Malley tells Belle that he and Missy are in love, but Belle shatters him by revealing Missy is the product of their youthful affair, which leads him to face Stribling with an unloaded gun. *The Last Sunset* closes with Missy cradling the dead O'Malley on her lap as Stribling and Belle gaze into each other's eyes.

In 1961 the *Motion Picture Herald* went against the tide by rating the film "Excellent", lauding its "well-written screenplay ... that builds to a shocking climax".[31] However, the general reaction was one of disappointment. Both *The Hollywood Reporter* and *Variety* judged the finished product inadequate in view of its prestigious line-up, respectively asserting "it is not an exciting picture" and "the selling angles ... are not matched on the screen".[32] Bosley Crowther's *New York Times* review was acrid: "Considering what is free on television, it is not worth paying a lot of money to see. ... The actors all go through their assignments as if they were weary and bored. We don't wonder. After only one hour's exposure to them, we were quite weary and bored, too."[33]

The Last Sunset was scripted by Dalton Trumbo, one of the Hollywood Ten convicted of communist affiliations in 1947, but the film contains no overt political message. It is in fact an odyssey narrative with no sense of community whatsoever. Like the other three films examined in depth here, *The Last Sunset* bears a strong kinship to classical myth. Featuring an impure protagonist brought low by incestuous tragedy, the film serves as a prairie variant of the Oedipus saga, involving father and daughter instead of mother and son.

What we can perceive by juxtaposing *The Gunfighter*, *Shane*, *The Searchers* and *The Last Sunset* is the increasingly perilous position of the American family in Hollywood Westerns between 1950 and 1961, plus an inexorable narrowing of opportunity for the lone Westerner's socialization. Granted, Stribling will no doubt settle down as Belle's new husband but, despite Hudson's top-billing in *The Last Sunset*, he is only a conventional foil for Douglas's flamboyant O'Malley.

Each film is a fatalistic tale of a loner who arrives in a pre-established social environment with some idea of finding a niche therein. Each wishes to belong, and to love an idealized woman; ultimately, they can neither belong nor enjoy the love they seek. Each is alienated and knows the pain of loss; for each is, essentially, a displaced patriarch. Ringo, unable to declare himself as head of his own family, must behave toward his son as a friendly stranger. Shane instantly recognizes his ideal, ready-made family environment when he sees it. However, he is too decent to try to usurp Joe Starrett's rightful place – even when Starrett is implicitly prepared to leave the way open for him by resolving to walk into Ryker's trap, telling his wife: "I know I'm kinda slow sometimes, Marian, but I see things – and I know that if – if anything happened to me that you'd be took care of."[34] Ethan not only loves his sister-in-law but his colourful presence effectively unseats his drab brother as familial leader. Ethan's nephew and nieces cluster round him, gravitating toward his charisma and away from their own father's natural, although nominal, authority. O'Malley is blatantly inimical to marital propriety. He aims to take Belle from her husband, and even tells Breckenridge so. If Ethan is truly asocial, O'Malley is at heart amoral. Yet this amorality has limits, as his guilt-inspired suicide surely demonstrates. Ringo, Shane and Ethan all suffer because they have missed the chance to be true fathers, and by the time they realize their mistakes it is too late. O'Malley's tragedy lies mainly in the fact that he *is* a father, but does not realize this till after he has begun his affair with Missy – for him, also, it is too late.

Thus, throughout the 1950s and into the early 1960s, in an era when many Americans commonly viewed marriage as a socially stabilizing factor which encouraged "responsibility, community spirit, respect for children and family life, reverence for a Supreme Being, humility, love of country", Westerns focused in large part on loners who could not assimilate, tormented souls to whom the contentment and security of family must forever be denied.[35] Shane is the only one who truly values community; he sides with Joe Starrett and the other homesteaders in their collective security stance against Ryker. O'Malley is the only one who is utterly, if latently, psychopathic. An early scene from *The Searchers* shows Ethan outside the family cabin as his brother and sister-in-law retire together. When the family dog approaches Ethan, he pats it gently. A scene early in *The Last Sunset* features O'Malley sitting outside Belle's cabin; again, a dog approaches. Yet this dog, sensing another feral spirit, growls viciously – and O'Malley grabs it by the throat, ready to kill if necessary.

Ringo, Shane, Ethan and O'Malley all disrupt the delicate, deficient familial balances which exist before they arrive. In each case, the tragic wanderer loves a woman who is ultimately unattainable. Ringo's appearance in Cayenne finally strips his wife of her cherished anonymity. Shane explicitly defends but, by his unvoiced love for Marian Starrett, implicitly threatens the stability of the family. Furthermore, since the Starretts' wedding anniversary is July 4, *Shane* skilfully identifies the institution of marriage as the essence of American society. In this context, the unrequited passion between Shane and Marian appears doubly hazardous. Ethan Edwards's muted desire for his sister-in-law poses a quasi-incestuous threat, positioning his emotional attachment halfway between Shane's for Marian and O'Malley's for Missy; besides this, he is resolved to kill his own niece. Ethan thus provides an extreme example of Geoffrey Gorer's equation of the fully human with the fully American: a white girl who is content to live among Indians, according to Ethan's reasoning, is no longer fit for family or American/human society and is better off dead. Finally, O'Malley tries to lure Belle into adultery and, when rebuffed, embarks on the most damaging emotional course within a family environment.

From Ringo's effort to regain his own family to O'Malley's disastrous intrusion into the family he does not know is his, these Westerns charted an ever-darkening representation of the nuclear family in the United States. In *The Gunfighter* Marshal Strett acts as surrogate father to Ringo's son; while he is an authoritative figure, he is also an upright citizen, devoid of Ringo's romantic aura. The conventional father figures of the other three films appear colourless and/or ineffectual next to the dashing strangers who ride up to the porch. Their wives are each in some measure tacitly dissatisfied, needful of more emotional fulfilment than their husbands can give; and in each film the children, perhaps sensing their mothers' frustration, are in awe of the glamorous loners who have brought excitement into their humdrum lives. The family structures delineated in these four Westerns were therefore remarkably similar, and an element of dysfunction existed even before a solitary horseman loomed on the horizon.

In each film the solitary horseman is as much catalyst as protagonist; in each film he pays dearly, both spiritually and physically. Ringo and O'Malley die; Shane rides away wounded, possibly dying; and Ethan may, for all we know, still carry an arrow's festering poison – hence my suggestion that *Shane* and *The Searchers* end with the *illusion* of their heroes' survival.

These Westerns offered the archetypal drifter neither home nor happy ending as earlier films had. Moreover, beneath their superficially satisfactory conclusions, each held the seeds of future familial or social turmoil. Ringo's wife and son cannot settle back into obscurity; the harmony of the Starrett family will be tenuous at best, considering all three are aware that Marian loved Shane; Debbie's return to white society does not guarantee complete social acceptance (which Ford emphasized in *Two Rode Together* (1961)); and since Belle is unlikely to tell Missy that her lover was her father, how is Missy to reconcile herself to living in the same house as the man who killed him? All these situations bode conflict, partially generational, on the eve of an era in which generational strife helped polarize U.S. society. Ringo's son, Joey Starrett, Debbie Edwards and Missy Breckenridge would grow up just in time to riot.

Shane's final ride into the mountains and Ethan's suddenly forlorn figure turning from the doorway of the replenished and reconstructed frontier family stand as two of the genre's most revered, enduring images, simultaneously heroic and poignant. Yet a lesser-known scene from *The Gunfighter* deserves to rival these, and its significance is all the greater for its lack of conscious stylization. Ringo is harassed by two arrogant hot-heads goading him into gunplay. He kills one at the beginning of the film; at the end, the other kills him. However, a third young man appears in this film, about an hour into the story. He enters the saloon, converses amiably with Ringo, buying him a drink without realizing who he is. Their exchange is brief and pleasant. The young man reveals he used to be a tearaway and a drinker till his wife tamed him; now he is working hard, making a success of their ranch. He politely refuses Ringo's offer of another drink; one is his agreed limit. As this young man leaves, Ringo wordlessly realizes he would have been happy with such a life, but now it is too late. Though Gregory Peck was intrigued by a character who "in other circumstances could have gone on to become a Senator", this was not the tragedy he conveyed in the aforementioned scene.[36] Ringo's tragedy is that he missed his chance to be ordinary. His meeting with the young rancher recalls that lost moment. This understated scene is as profound as any the genre has ever produced, for this is not just about the Western, nor just about America. It speaks to human experience around the globe through the ages with its quiet, relentless reminder of roads not travelled and precious opportunities lost, never to return.

This chapter has examined coded representations of 1950s America's social and political tensions within the Western and has focused especially on the personal alienation and familial discord permeating four ostensibly unrelated narratives filmed several years apart. The next case study centres specifically on the late 1950s, and the heroic individual's alienation from society is again a primary thematic concern. The two Westerns under scrutiny were each lavish, ambitious and star-laden, yet in the ensuing decades they have suffered unwarranted critical neglect. However, when we look closely at *The Big Country* and *Warlock*, we may discern grandiose reworkings of themes crucial to late 1950s U.S. foreign and domestic politics respectively, which engaged extensively with the nature of American manhood.

CHAPTER 5

Politics and Codes of Masculinity in Late 1950s Star Westerns: *The Big Country* and *Warlock*

B Y the mid-1950s, the United States faced new responsibilities and new realities in both domestic and foreign affairs. Along with (and mainly due to) mutations in the political arena, the temper of American society had also shifted perceptibly. The watershed year in domestic politics was 1954. On May 17 that year the Supreme Court, in its historic ruling on *Brown v. Board of Education of Topeka*, outlawed racial segregation in the public school system, thus providing the Civil Rights crusade with an irreversible impetus. Contemporaneously, Senator Joe McCarthy was fast losing public support and credibility as his whining, bullying demeanour was fully exposed and ultimately execrated in the nationally televised Army–McCarthy hearings. The Senate censured McCarthy by a vote of 67 to 22 that December, and two and a half years later he was dead. Yet, though 1954 saw Black aspirations boosted and the end of McCarthy's reign of terror, these were liberal triumphs in an inherently conservative era. The congenial war hero Dwight D. Eisenhower won the presidency for the Republicans in 1952, ending the Democrats' two-decade monopoly of the White House. Eisenhower was not an ideologue. Indeed, much of his political genius stemmed from his ability to appear aloof from the bitterest partisan wranglings. He was nonetheless essentially both an icon and a celebrant of Middle America, of Main Street, of "middle C" conservatism, devoid of ideological rancour; and in February of 1954, the very year of *Brown v. Board* and Senator McCarthy's downfall, Eisenhower had subtly reinvested the term "conservative" with respectability, urging a Lincoln Day audience, "And don't be afraid to use the word."[1]

In international affairs, too, Americans were beset by new complexities. The Korean War had ended in a truce in late July 1953, but

America's respite from disastrous involvement in an Asian land war would merely be temporary. The following year, the French lost their hold on Indochina with the fall of Dienbienphu, and the United States stepped up an ultimately tragic assumption of ever-increasing obligations to preserve the non-communist status of South Vietnam. One other matter of gravest political significance reached fruition in the early 1950s, as both America and Soviet Russia developed hydrogen bombs. John Foster Dulles, Eisenhower's fiercely Presbyterian Secretary of State, championed the concept of massive retaliation, by which America would be so formidably armed that the Soviets would be cowed into peace. Yet for millions of Americans, Ike included, any prospect of full-scale war was too terrible to contemplate with such a weapon in existence. Aside from other intricacies of Cold War diplomacy, this fact alone precluded U.S. military involvement in the crises of Suez and Hungary in 1956.

Little wonder, then, that mid-1950s America was becoming more insular – in mood, if not in official government policy. Confronted with the limitation of superpower status yet buoyed by the balm of affluence at home, gradually, after a decade of vigilance, contentment was replacing containment as a national priority. The past generation of Depression, World War II and the Cold War had been one of the most dramatic in the nation's history. Little Rock and Sputnik would each expose and shatter U.S. complacency in 1957 but, in large part, during the latter half of the 1950s, social and political life in America became less anxious. In effect, Middle America was settling down.

Symptomatic of this societal change was a 1956 film titled *The Man in the Gray Flannel Suit*, directed by Nunnally Johnson for 20th Century-Fox. Adapted from the popular novel by Sloan Wilson, this was a melodramatic tale of a World War II veteran striving to build a lucrative and satisfying career on Madison Avenue without sacrificing personal scruples or the primacy of family life. Of especial import here is the principal casting: the eponymous hero and his fretful but usually supportive wife were portrayed by Gregory Peck and Jennifer Jones, the illicit lovers of the infamous *Duel in the Sun* ten years previously. There could be no clearer filmic illustration of 1950s America maturing and settling down than the recasting of Lewt McCanles and Pearl Chavez as the essentially decent and respectable Mr and Mrs Middle America of 1956. The skyscrapers of Manhattan have replaced the deep canyons of Texas, and instead of *Duel*'s world-defying, self-destructive passion the modern saga offers middle-class angst. The sympathetic patriarchs of *Gray Flannel Suit* are plagued not by hubris or an incursion of homesteaders but by emblematic, mid-twentieth century ailments: Peck's boss (Fredric March) is beset by a bad heart, a ruined marriage and a spoiled daughter he doesn't understand; and Lee J. Cobb, who in the 1950s delivered a series of outstanding performances as dysfunctional, often demented patriarchs, appeared as a kindly but dyspeptic judge.[2] The film also featured a running gag stressing the prevalence, the banality and yet the fascination of Westerns within contemporary American culture. The same TV Western is blaring from the family parlour whenever Peck walks through; his children sit, transfixed, before the small-screen spectacle. At one point Peck, the sophisticated adult, gently chides them for watching such nonsense and he ushers them from the room. Immediately, he too is hypnotized by the flickering images of flying arrows and tumbling horses. For sophisticated adults, too, the Western still had resonance and an undeniable appeal.

The Western had managed to remain popular largely by being both thematically and stylistically responsive to the nation's ever-changing culture. Throughout the 1950s, from Henry King's *The Gunfighter* onwards, the primary *thematic* trend had been the Western hero's social alienation or marginalization, which had threaded through terse black and white classics to wide-screen Technicolor spectaculars. Perhaps the genre's chief *stylistic* transformation in the 1950s was this recasting of Westerns as epic tales. Hollywood countered television's encroachment with entertainment the box in the parlour could not match: all-star casts, wide-screen vistas and lavish production values adorned films frequently running over three hours. Biblical epics (*The Ten Commandments* (1956)) and World War II epics (*The Bridge on the River Kwai* (1957)) were huge box office successes, so why not accentuate the Western's inherent epic proportions? Thus, in the grand-scale tradition of King Vidor's *Duel in the Sun*, the two biggest, most sprawling Westerns of the 1950s centred on Texas dynasties. George Stevens followed his phenomenally successful *Shane* with *Giant* (Warner Brothers, 1956), primarily a modern era family saga addressing issues of gender, race and class, which skilfully embraced a liberal perspective within a celebratory framework. *Giant* may more truthfully be classed as a soap opera than as a Western, and its fame in cinema history lies not in the unwieldy narrative unfolding on the screen but as cult star James Dean's last film before his death. However, the second sprawling Texan epic is of far greater significance in the present context.

Heralded by perhaps the most expansive and evocative music ever to grace a Western movie, William Wyler's *The Big Country* (United Artists, 1958) opens with Baltimore sea captain James McKay (Gregory Peck) arriving in Texas to be reunited with his fiancée, Patricia Terrill (Carroll

Baker), daughter of wealthy cattle baron Major Henry Terrill (Charles Bickford). Jim McKay encounters hostility immediately from Terrill's foreman, Steve Leech (Charlton Heston), who obviously resents him for winning Patricia's affections. McKay is also, on his way to Terrill's ranch, roughed up by Buck Hannassey (Chuck Connors), cowardly, thuggish son of another rancher, Rufus Hannassey (Burl Ives), who is Major Terrill's sworn enemy. McKay, used to the rough-house behaviour of seamen, regards Buck's treatment as little more than boisterous horseplay. He is appalled when the Major, who considers the Hannasseys vermin, leads his men into Blanco Canyon on a punitive raid, laying waste to Hannassey property and beating up Buck's sidekicks in town.

It is worth noting that, even in embryonic form, *The Big Country* contains traces of earlier dynastic Westerns. Raymond Durgnat, in discussing King Vidor, has indicated a correlation between the Gregory Peck and Charlton Heston characterizations and those roles essayed by Joseph Cotten and Peck respectively in *Duel in the Sun*.[3] Yet Steve Leech's son-in-all-but-name relationship to Major Terrill is certainly very reminiscent of Montgomery Clift and John Wayne in *Red River*. Furthermore, as in Howard Hawks's 1948 classic, dialogue whets the appetite for a clash between two quick-tempered young men (Leech and Buck/Matt Garth (Clift) and Cherry Vallance (John Ireland)) which never actually occurs. Most striking of all, the relationship between the Major and his daughter is a watered-down variation of that between Walter Huston and Barbara Stanwyck in Anthony Mann's *The Furies* (1950). Whether Patricia Terrill realizes it or not, there is enough in her demeanour and in her utterances to suggest clearly that the great love of her life is not Jim McKay but her own father.

In any event, Patricia becomes progressively disenchanted with Jim precisely because he is so unlike her father. He does not feel humiliated by Buck's rough antics; and he declines to ride Old Thunder, Terrill's wildest horse, when Leech tries to set him up for a pratfall. No matter to McKay that everyone on the ranch thinks he is afraid to ride the horse; he prefers to master the animal in private. Later, when Leech tries to pick a fight with Jim in front of Patricia and the Major, Jim will not oblige him. For Patricia, this is the final degradation. She is convinced Jim is a coward. In truth, however, he simply refuses to prove his masculinity on aggressive Texan terms. He is just as inner-directed as the classic Western hero and just as much in conflict with his surrounding social environment as the protagonists of other 1950s Westerns. Yet here the hero is well-adjusted and, unusually for a Western, urbane. In this instance, the tension between individual and society stems not from the individual's alienation or unwillingness to adapt but from society's over-aggressive dysfunction. Atypically among Westerns, *The Big Country* appears to venerate "Eastern" values and character traits. John Ford, for example, in Westerns from *Stagecoach* (1939) to *The Man Who Shot Liberty Valance* (1962), celebrated the hearty, morally uncomplicated masculine virtues of the Westerner – courage, honesty, independence, unwavering resolve and, ultimately, selflessness. Against these romantic criteria, the genre's stereotypical Easterners were frequently found not merely lacking but actually enervating. Yet *The Big Country* features Gregory Peck (also the film's co-producer) as an Easterner who prefers reason to emotion and intelligence to violence. His is a triumph of instinct over environment and of culture over nature. Significantly, if uncharacteristically for the hero of a Western film, McKay never kills anyone. By contrast, the "Westerners" of *The Big Country* (Leech, Terrill, Rufus, Buck) are each, to varying degrees, stubborn, arrogant and brutish. *The Big Country* implicitly condemns Western *white macho* aggression. The only other wholly sympathetic man in the movie is the gentle Mexican, Ramon (Alfonso Bedoya), a Terrill ranch-hand who soon becomes McKay's sidekick.

An early exchange underscores McKay's commitment to a code of reasoned, intelligent pacifism after he has presented Major Terrill with a brace of duelling pistols:

TERRILL [*looking down barrel of pistol*]: They've been used.
MCKAY: Yes. They belonged to my father.
TERRILL: Oh. Jim, I know how proud you are of his memory.
MCKAY: We loved him, Major. We were just as proud of him when he was alive.
TERRILL: A man's honour and his good name ... are his finest possessions.
MCKAY: I agree, but his good name needed no defence, and his honour was beyond question. You know, no-one remembers exactly what that last duel was about.[4]

Only Julie Maragon (Jean Simmons), the local schoolteacher and Patricia's best friend, instinctively realizes Jim's quiet dignity is not cowardice but the truest mark of his integrity. However, Julie is also reluctantly caught in the middle of the Terrill–Hannassey feud. She is the owner of the Big Muddy, the spread from which neighbouring ranchers draw their water. Ever since the death of Julie's grandfather, both Major Terrill and Rufus Hannassey have been badgering her to sell the land. Each aims to control the region and deprive his enemy of all access to water. McKay journeys to the Big Muddy and persuades Julie to sell him the property, promising her that both the Terrills and the Hannasseys can continue to draw their water as before.

Tensions reach a flashpoint when Jim returns to Terrill's ranch before he has a chance to tell them he has purchased the Big Muddy. This is the juncture at which Steve Leech publicly issues his challenge, but McKay responds: "You aren't going to prove anything with me, Leech. Get this through your head: I'm not playing this game on your terms, not with horses, or guns – or fists."[5] Patricia feels shamed by McKay's refusal to fight Leech, and their engagement is off. She neither respects nor even understands his genuine sense of inner-direction:

PATRICIA: Don't you care what people think?
MCKAY: No, I'm not responsible for what people think. Only for what I am, Pat.
PATRICIA: Don't you care what *I* think? D'you like to have people think of you as a –
MCKAY: A coward. Why don't you say it? Are you afraid of the word? I'm not. And I'm not going to spend the rest of my life demonstrating how brave I am.
PATRICIA [*with brittle contempt*]: You've already demonstrated that quite fully enough![6]

Before leaving Major Terrill's ranch, McKay pays a call on Leech. Now, in private and in the darkness of night, the time has come for the fistfight Leech wanted. Such a confrontation between two of Hollywood's most prominent he-men was usually a sure-fire recipe for box office success, but *The Big Country*'s treatment of this scene is exceptional: here the film cheats, *and* delivers, *and* makes a striking moral and political point. The Peck–Heston punch-up cheats in that it is set in darkness, and filmed mostly in long-shot. This distancing device perhaps frustrates audience expectations, but it also deglamorizes the conflict effectively. The fight delivers inasmuch as it truly is an epic, protracted brawl, with the protagonists ultimately punching one another to a standstill. The use of extreme long-shot, which will recur in the climactic showdown, dramatically emphasizes the inconsequential, transitory quarrels of mortals as pathetic and ineffectual against the vast permanence of the unyielding Texan landscape. As the two men retire, bloody and exhausted, McKay has won his adversary's respect, but he asks, "Now, tell me, Leech – what did we prove?"[7]

The fight also seems to have given Leech a new perspective on the Major's obsessive feud with the Hannasseys. We next see Leech driving the Hannasseys' thirsty cattle away from the Big Muddy, following the Major's orders, but clearly unhappy about the task. Rufus Hannassey is furious, and orders Buck to bring Julie to their stronghold. Rufus resolves he will force her to sell the Big Muddy. When she arrives, he finds she has already sold the land to McKay. Rufus intends that Terrill and his men should ride to Julie's rescue – and straight into a Hannassey ambush. Yet he is still fundamentally a man of honour, and he forcibly prevents Buck from raping Julie, warning his son that one day he may have to kill him. Meanwhile, as Terrill and his men prepare to ride into Blanco Canyon, McKay arrives. He and Ramon are going in alone. Jim believes he can bring Julie back without violence, and even Leech is shocked when Terrill draws his gun to prevent McKay from entering the canyon. McKay tells him: "I'm going in. If you want to stop me, you'll have to use that. But if you shoot me down, let's have it clear, in front of all these men – you're not here to get Julie Maragon out. You're just using this for an excuse to start your own private war."[8] At the Hannassey spread, Jim is equally forthright when, despite the promise of continued access to water, Rufus remains obstinately committed to bloodshed:

RUFUS: You've got the looks of a man that means what he says. But this ain't just a matter of water! The Hannasseys'll have no peace till the bones of Henry Terrill is bleachin' in Blanco Canyon! Now, he started this blood-spillin', an' I aim to *finish* it – his way!

MCKAY: You had me fooled for quite a while, Mr. Hannassey, with your self-righteous talk. What's the difference between his way and your way? How many of those men out there know what this fight is *really* about? This isn't their war; this is nothing but a personal feud between two selfish, ruthless, vicious old men – Henry Terrill and you![9]

Rufus realizes that Jim and Julie are in love, even before they are aware of the fact themselves. When Julie attempts to protect Jim from Buck and receives a slap for her trouble, Jim loses his temper and lashes out with his fists. In the ensuing brawl, Buck pulls his six-shooter – but Rufus fires a warning shot. He will not permit Buck to shoot an unarmed man. Jim had his father's duelling pistols packed on his horse (returned by Patricia after their break-up); bearing these weapons in mind, Rufus wonders if Buck has the stomach for a gentleman's fight. He also asks

Jim, "What about you? Talk's cheap."[10] Even in this pacifist epic, the dominant ethos of the genre ultimately requires a measure of action for a satisfactory solution. Yet Jim's moral strength prevails even when he is compelled to use a gun. Buck disgraces himself by firing before the signal. His bullet creases Jim's forehead. Rufus is disgusted by his son's perfidy, but Jim reminds him he still has his shot to fire. As Jim takes aim, Buck whimpers with fear, drops to his knees and shields himself, then cowers behind a wagon-wheel. Rufus calls out for Jim to fire. Jim discharges his pistol into the dust, then tosses the weapon down. With this virtually contemptuous gesture, Jim rejects the path of wrong-headed patriarchy (both Rufus's indignation and the heritage of his own father's senselessly exaggerated concept of pride) once and for all. He does not need patriarchal approval, but he has finally demonstrated by example that to be a man on one's own terms is enough.

Rufus, now thoroughly ashamed of Buck, spits on him. Buck reacts by grabbing a gun, intending to kill Jim. Rufus has no option but to shoot his own son.[11] As Jim, Julie and Ramon leave the Hannassey spread, Terrill is leading his men into an ambush at Blanco Canyon, during which Leech is wounded. Rufus catches up with Jim and tells him he agrees the fight ought to be between him and Terrill alone. In their climactic showdown, the two old men wend their way through Blanco Canyon till they exchange gunfire. Both men perish, and are last seen sprawled together in long-shot – no bigger and no more impressive than two dead insects. As with Jim's father's last duel, the feud's origin remains a mystery. Jim and Leech regard each other over the bodies of the slain chieftains. In Leech's eyes there is a new respect for Jim and a regret which plainly suggests he has acquired a deeper sense of both maturity and responsibility – and, by implication, a more rational standard of masculinity. Leech alone among the aggressive Westerners has survived. Yet, as the film ends, the real victors are the trio who survey the vast expanse of Texas then gallop triumphantly through the Big Country (Jim McKay, Julie Maragon and Ramon): Eastern liberal, pragmatic educated woman and peaceful Mexican – inheritors of the Dream.

Filmed in Technicolor and Technirama and running for two-and-three-quarter hours, *The Big Country* is today perhaps best remembered for Jerome Moross's majestic music. The film grossed $5,000,000 on its release, and critical response was generally favourable.[12] *TIME* termed the movie "starkly beautiful" and worthy of comparison with *Shane*.[13] *Variety* adjudged Wyler's epic "massive in its pictorial splendor".[14] The same review made the astute point that *The Big Country* "perhaps represents how well a carefully-conceived theatrical sagebrush drama can overwhelm and render puny anything the western telepix producers can possibly place on a 21-inch screen", and it also noted: "The story carries some philosophic comments about the meaning of bravery and the value of a sane, peaceful approach to hot-headed issues."[15] *The Hollywood Reporter* proclaimed: "This lavishly expensive western has the boxoffice appeal of an all-star cast and the magic of William Wyler's directorial reputation to give it unusual marquee value."[16] The *Motion Picture Herald* was fulsomely appreciative: "It is big in every dimension and in every sense ... a work of art. ... [R]eplete with memorable scenes, each polished to gem-like perfection [.] ... All of it adds up to a production that will make box office and industry history."[17] Bosley Crowther, writing in the *New York Times*, struck the wittiest note: "the most bellicose hymn to peace ever seen. ... Out there in the wide open country, ... those verbal encounters and violent battles are like something on the windy plains of Troy. ... Iron-featured Mr Bickford and barrel-chested Mr Ives glare and roar at each other like a couple of fur-bearing gladiators. ... But for all this film's mighty pretensions, it does not get far beneath the skin of its conventional Western situation and its stock Western characters. It skims across standard complications and ends on a platitude. Peace is a pious precept but fightin' is more excitin'."[18] One British reviewer interpreted the film as an overtly political allegory. Peter G. Baker of *Films and Filming* observed: "Terrill runs his prosperous outfit like a Fascist dictator. Hannassey runs his less prosperous community like a Communist dictator. In between ... is the woman figure, Julie Maragon – the Marianne of France."[19]

Baker's interpretation has a degree of merit, but it is in large part a Eurocentric reading of an American saga. Granted, on one level Jim McKay might represent American common sense, bringing reason to the warring factions of the globe. Yet, by 1958, the principal lines of ideological contention were drawn not between communism and fascism but between Soviet communism and the West, led by the United States. I already mentioned in the Introduction that President Eisenhower was extremely taken with *The Big Country*, screening the film at the White House on four successive evenings. An instinctive centrist committed to world peace, it is not overly fanciful to suggest Eisenhower may have identified with Gregory Peck's Jim McKay. Ironically, *The Big Country* more accurately suggests its closest likeness to the former General is *Major* Henry Terrill, a self-satisfied patriarch of a prosperous empire. Philip French has termed *The Big Country* "William Wyler's United Nations hymn to peaceful coexistence".[20] John H. Lenihan has briefly remarked on the film's contemporary relevance and has also observed a thematic kinship to *The Man in the Gray Flannel Suit*.[21] Effectually, Gregory Peck's flawed yet principled executive in *Gray Flannel Suit* provides a crucial transitional link between his immoral, murderous Lewt McCanles in *Duel in the Sun* and his calm, self-assured Jim McKay in *The Big Country*. As such, with its man of quiet integrity resisting the demands of a powerful patriarch, *The Big Country* might easily be subtitled *The Man in the Gray Flannel Suit Goes West*, even down to the clothes McKay is wearing when he alights from the Eastern stage.

Besides its liberal/pacifist ideology, *The Big Country*'s most forceful engagement is with the issue of patriarchy. The film features strands of community and odyssey narratives. Jim McKay's cool reason is clearly at odds with the fiery-tempered *machismo* of his neighbours; and McKay's journey west, his trek to the Big Muddy and his ride into Blanco Canyon lend the film a tripartite odyssean structure. Yet these are plot components rather than prominent themes. Crucially, the film also adopts a tripartite approach to its treatment of patriarchy. *The Big Country* is actually a story of *three* patriarchs, if we include McKay's late father; and we must. Jim McKay's mature pacifism is in large part a rejection of his father's ultimately self-destructive code of honour. This tragedy is the formative mark of his own manhood; consequently, he will not blindly defer to either Major Terrill or Rufus Hannassey.

Yet if *The Big Country* is partly a story of three fathers, it is also the tale of three sons. Jim McKay is already secure in his identity and has no need of patriarchal approval. Steve Leech is Major Terrill's surrogate son, loyal but finally more judicious than the older man he respects. In the course of the film, he outgrows the need for the Major's approval. Only Buck Hannassey fails, much to Rufus's disgust, to be a better, wiser man than his father; and it is in the wake of the most extreme exhibition of his father's disapproval (Rufus spitting on him) that Buck provokes his own death. Thus one son begins as a man in his own right; another gradually acquires greater maturity; the third is thoroughly worthless and reprehensible, and dies.

Essentially, however, *The Big Country* is more star vehicle than morality play. If the betrothal of the upright, dignified McKay and the flighty, spoiled Patricia appears as incongruous as a liaison between George Washington and Scarlett O'Hara, no matter. It is a poorly contrived romantic schematization, and the briefest glance at the billing (Jean Simmons second, below Peck) indicates that Julie Maragon is the film's true heroine. Yet the most significant star teaming here is that of Peck and Charlton Heston. Increasingly through the late 1950s, Westerns frequently showcased two prominent male stars playing off one another. Westerns tended to be good box office and established American actors' rugged credentials. Thus, a Western featuring two such stars might, logically, prove doubly profitable. This gambit inspired several formidable marquee teamings, including Burt Lancaster and Kirk Douglas in John Sturges's *Gunfight at the O.K. Corral* (Paramount, 1957), John Wayne and Dean Martin in Howard Hawks's *Rio Bravo* (Warner Brothers, 1959), and Wayne and William Holden in John Ford's *The Horse Soldiers* (United Artists, 1959).

Edward Dmytryk's *Warlock* (20th Century-Fox, 1959) went one better, boasting three top male stars: Henry Fonda, Richard Widmark and Anthony Quinn. As with the three "sons" of *The Big Country*, one of *Warlock*'s three protagonists is an exemplar of manhood; another attains true manhood as the tale unfolds; and the third fails ignominiously, then provokes his own death.

Based on the novel by Oakley Hall, *Warlock* was a stylish, classic Western melodrama filmed in colour and CinemaScope and running for two hours. The last of a remarkable cycle of 1950s law-and-order Westerns which examined the nature of individual integrity contrasted with the hypocrisy and self-interest of a superficially respectable town, *Warlock* was a subtle variation on the Wyatt Earp/Doc Holliday legend. With its prestigious cast, opulent production values and a rich narrative, on paper *Warlock* had all the ingredients of a box office hit. Yet, like *The Last Sunset* two years later, it was not a popular success. Paradoxically, the key to *Warlock*'s commercial failure may lie in its most distinctive narrative strength, for *Warlock* is the finest psychological Western ever made.

Warlock is a mining and mercantile town plagued by lawless cowboys from the neighbouring San Pablo ranch. In despair, the town council hires legendary gunman Clay Blaisedell (Fonda) as an extra-legal marshal.[22] He arrives complete with heroic reputation, twin gold-handled Colts and a dark *alter ego*, Tom Morgan (Quinn), a club-footed gambler who is Blaisedell's best friend and his second gun in a showdown. Blaisedell also comes with the melancholy knowledge that the very people who welcome him as their saviour will eventually despise and dread him for the power he wields. Some townsfolk are already wary, such as Jessie Marlow (Dolores Michaels) – but she will grow to love Clay; the crippled Judge Holloway (Wallace Ford) is hostile to Blaisedell from the outset, but he is a self-righteous old man mouthing platitudes about the sanctity of the law. Blaisedell quickly establishes his authority in town, warning Abe McQuown (Tom Drake) and his San Pablo henchmen that any man who causes trouble will be posted out of town; if the offender returns to Warlock, he comes in against Blaisedell's gun. McQuown and his cohorts back down and leave town – for the time being.

One of the cowboys has had enough. Johnny Gannon (Widmark) is haunted by his part in the massacre of thirty-seven Mexican *vaqueros* and sickened by his friends' humiliation of Warlock's last deputy and the murder of the town barber. Now, realizing that McQuown aimed to have one of his cronies shoot Blaisedell in the back during their confrontation, Gannon breaks with the San Pablo gang and opts to remain in town. Later, the visiting sheriff appeals to the citizenry for a legal deputy in Warlock – and Gannon volunteers. Yet soon he finds himself powerless in the middle of a showdown between Blaisedell and some of the San Pabloites, among them his own younger brother. Gannon asks Blaisedell for a chance to talk to his brother, and Blaisedell agrees; but to no avail. Gannon's brother refuses to listen to reason, and Blaisedell finally has no alternative but to shoot him and another San Pabloite (*Warlock*'s equivalent of the gunfight at the O.K. Corral). Enraged by these killings, McQuown proclaims himself "Chief of Regulators" and issues a "Wanted" poster on Blaisedell.

Blaisedell has other worries. Lily Dollar (Dorothy Malone) has arrived in Warlock. A glamorous saloon queen who was once Morgan's lover, Lily left Tom for a man whom Blaisedell later killed in a gunfight. However, Lily knows what Blaisedell does not even suspect: Morgan engineered the killing by convincing Clay that the man was on the prod. Morgan gets word that Lily is headed for Warlock with the dead man's brother, planning to have him kill Clay. Morgan rides out to ambush the stage, only to see it intercepted for a hold-up by two San Pabloites. This enables Morgan to shoot Lily's companion then ride off unseen, laying the blame on the stagecoach robbers. So Lily arrives in Warlock, still intent on seeing Blaisedell killed. Blaisedell, however, remains unaware of Morgan's murderous duplicity, past and present.

Morgan poses another problem. Blaisedell and Jessie have fallen in love and plan to marry, but Morgan's devotion to his friend is beginning to look like homosexual fixation. Lily has long suspected this latent feeling in Morgan, which is why she wants Clay dead – to punish Morgan. Now Morgan starts making snide quips about Clay's engagement (just before the shoot-out with Gannon's brother: "thinkin' of weddings could lead to a funeral").[23] Clay gradually realizes Morgan's dependence on their friendship is unhealthily intense, and he advises him to move on to another wide-open town.

At this juncture, Gannon approaches to tell Blaisedell the threat implicit in McQuown's poster is *his* responsibility, as Warlock's legal deputy. The personal and moral motivations of the three protagonists are inherent in the ensuing exchange:

GANNON: I just want to tell you that ... this is my job – to keep the peace.

BLAISEDELL: How do you propose to do that, Sheriff?

GANNON: I'll tell McQuown he's not to come in.

BLAISEDELL: He'll come in, all right ... and when he does – you're not going to fight *my* fight, Deputy.

GANNON: I guess I'll have to, Mr. Blaisedell, 'cause this is the law's business, not yours. [*Passes Morgan, turns*] Nor *yours*, Mr. Morgan.

BLAISEDELL: Well, looks like our problem is solved, Morg. The law's takin' over.

MORGAN: Clay, y-you can't mean that.

BLAISEDELL: Why not? Let's see if Warlock's grown up enough to take care of itself.

MORGAN: Clay – Clay, i-i-if you're not the Marshal you're *nothin'*!

BLAISEDELL: Ah, maybe it's time. Maybe we've run out of towns. [*Rides off in the buggy with Jessie*].[24]

Gannon rides to the San Pablo spread and warns McQuown not to come into Warlock. An argument soon becomes a scuffle, and McQuown plunges a knife into Gannon's gun hand. The next day, as Gannon prepares for the showdown with McQuown's Regulators, Lily appeals to Blaisedell to help Gannon, whom she loves. The gunman drops by the deputy's office to offer his help. Some of the greatest Westerns feature a scene in which the experienced hero passes on his wisdom to a protégé via a shooting lesson. Yet *Warlock* dispenses with pyrotechnics in this instance. Clay sits down opposite Gannon and reveals the code he has evolved: "I remember when I first killed a man. It was clear and had to be done – though I went home afterwards and puked my insides out. I remember how clear it was. Afterwards nothing was ever clear again, 'cept for one thing. That's to hold strictly to the rules. S'only the rules that matter. Hold on to 'em like you were walkin' on eggs – so you know yourself you've played it as fair and as best you could."[25] Blaisedell promises he will back Gannon against the Regulators, but Morgan keeps Clay at gunpoint in his hotel room, figuring that if the Regulators kill Gannon the town will revert to Blaisedell's authoritarian rule. Morgan's scheme misfires when the townsfolk back Gannon, who kills McQuown. The Regulators are routed. Blaisedell feels shamed Morgan prevented him from helping in the showdown. The two men argue, and Blaisedell finally grasps the extent of his friend's past treachery.

Morgan now believes Gannon must die so that Blaisedell can be top dog in Warlock once again. That night he gets drunk and proceeds to shoot up the town, calling Gannon out. Blaisedell enters Gannon's office and locks him in his own jail, claiming Morgan is *his* responsibility. Blaisedell tells Morgan to leave town. Morgan begins to comply with this order; however, as the townsfolk jeer, he turns and goads Blaisedell into a gunfight. Blaisedell kills him but, distraught, takes Morgan's body into the saloon, harangues the townsmen, humiliates Judge Holloway, kicking his crutch away, and finally sets fire to the saloon, giving Morgan a Viking funeral as a thunderstorm rages. Gannon asks Blaisedell to leave Warlock, otherwise he must arrest him in the morning. Blaisedell, now all pride and fury, refuses to go and warns Gannon to "come shootin'".[26] He also realizes he can have no future with Jessie. She wants him to remain in Warlock and live as an ordinary, anonymous citizen. Clay wants her to accompany him to the next town in need of taming, where he can become marshal:

JESSIE: To another town, and another, and another ... ?
BLAISEDELL: Why not? It's the way I've lived, it's the way I'll always
    live. Times are changing, sure. But there'll be enough towns to last
    my lifetime.
JESSIE: I'm not Morgan. I can't back you. I can't even hold a Colt,
    much less fire one. Who'll kill the back-shooters in Porphyry City?
BLAISEDELL: Maybe I'll have to find another Morgan.[27]

Blaisedell and Gannon face one another the next morning. Blaisedell has lost everything save his heroic reputation. For this last gunfight, and for the first time in the film, we see him wearing the gold-handled Colts. Gannon, a well-intentioned amateur with a wounded gun hand, is no match for Blaisedell. Twice Blaisedell beats him to the draw – tossing each Colt in the dust. Having divested himself of the last vestiges of his charismatic authority, Blaisedell walks past a grateful Gannon and rides out of Warlock – into legend, and into oblivion.

Critical response to *Warlock* was generally favourable, if relatively low-key for so lavish a production. In his *New York Times* review, Bosley Crowther observed: "*Warlock* ... meets all the specifications for a supra-television Western film. ... [T]he major conflicts, while not unusual, are fundamental and raw, and a first-rate cast plays them to the limit under Edward Dmytryk's practiced hand. ... [W]hen the shooting commences and climax follows climax ... and strong men fight with their emotions, it is good, solid, gripping Western fare. ... *Warlock* is colorful and noisy. It should drag those Western fans out of their homes."[28] *Variety* proclaimed: "It is an 'adult' western in depth, and given a class production, it should be a strong box-office attraction. ... Fonda is particularly fine. It may not be a romantic conception, but Fonda gives his role great validity. It embodies the ... mock-chivalric disillusion that seems to have characterized some of ... the 19th Century 'lost generation', rootless and eventually aimless as the frontier outgrew them."[29] The *Motion Picture Herald* praised *Warlock* as "[a] big and well-produced Western with an unusual plot complication [.] ... It has pace and spirit and excited suspense, plus a full quota of action."[30] Bearing the subheading "Dmytryk Prod'n Rather Cerebral For Western Tale", *The Hollywood Reporter* opined: "the complicated storyline and the devious cross-currents of motivation ... demand such close intellectual attention that ... [spectators will] have little time left for emotional surrender to the happenings – unless they remain to see the film a second or third time".[31] *TIME* adopted a glib, joky approach, terming the film "a two-hour, $2,000,000 western with three major stars ... two main heroes, two main villains, three main plots, five subplots, eight cooling corpses, and nine major outbreaks of violence. ... In the end, with the villains all gone, the heroes have nothing left to do but answer the all-important questions: 1) Who is faster on the draw? 2) Who is slower on the drawl?"[32] The *Newsweek* review of April 20 1959 summed *Warlock* up as "The Jamesian West – Henry, not Jesse".[33] Peter John Dyer wrote a sharply discordant critique for *Films and Filming*: "*Warlock* is that miscalculated thing – a literate, highbrow Western. It is also ... much too long. ... Dmytryk has been impressed by the indigestible wealth of authentic detail in Oakley Hall's novel, and led astray by the Freudian trimmings and classical quotations of Robert Alan Aurthur's screenplay. The result, unfortunately, is merely silly, and by no means entertainingly silly. ... What a tragic decay of noble talents this film is. If this is what can happen to five artists of integrity [Henry Fonda, Aurthur, Dmytryk, Quinn and Widmark] every time someone breathes the name Freud, then the sooner the West is given back to the Indians the better."[34]

On the whole, retrospective critical appraisal has been no kinder than the initial response.[35] Despite its impeccable credentials, *Warlock* has never enjoyed the status it deserves. Frank McConnell, one of the few writers to scrutinize the film in depth, astutely remarked that "in the spate of cowboy films released every year, year after year, it is perhaps not too surprising that even a film as good as *Warlock* should have been lost temporarily in the crowd"; McConnell also noted that Edward Dmytryk has never been a darling of auteurists.[36] I would offer that hierarchical construct as one cardinal reason *Warlock* has often been consigned to limbo instead of enshrined in the pantheon of all-time great Western films. The auteurist school of interpretation certainly has considerable merit; but it also tends to focus on the same band of directors, and thus the same groups of films, time and again. Certainly, Dmytryk's contribution to the genre cannot be compared with John Ford's or Howard Hawks's, but it does not naturally follow that Ford's *Sergeant Rutledge* (1960) or Hawks's *Rio Lobo* (1970) are richer films than *Warlock*.

Of directors' approach to genre, Colin McArthur wrote in 1972: "If he is Nicholas Ray, he transcends the genre; if he is Edward Dmytryk, he makes just another Western."[37] This clearly illustrates a hierarchically structured and therefore blinkered evaluation. Other than the contemporary rodeo drama *The Lusty Men* (1952), Nicholas Ray's significant contribution to the Western actually boils down to one electrifying film – *Johnny Guitar* (Republic, 1954), a highly stylized exploration of sexual role reversal and McCarthyite hysteria. Ray's other Westerns (*Run for Cover* (1955), *The True Story of Jesse James* (1957)) were of little import. Equally, Dmytryk's other forays into the genre (*Broken Lance* (1954), *Alvarez Kelly* (1966) and *Shalako* (1968)) are starry but lacklustre affairs. Yet *Warlock* is far from "just another Western".

Indeed, *Warlock* is as comprehensive an engagement with the anti-communist witch-hunts of the 1940s and 1950s as are *Johnny Guitar* and Fred Zinnemann's *High Noon* (United Artists, 1952). Carl Foreman scripted *High Noon* as a left-wing parable damning Hollywood's moral cowardice in the face of the witch-hunters. Yet, as with William Golding's novel *Lord of the Flies* (1954), Zinnemann's film is inherently protean, subtly reinforcing the spectator's own convictions. Thus *High Noon* may be interpreted as an indictment of the witch-hunts or as a paean to patriotic vigilance; as a vindication of individualism, or socialism; or as a justification for internationalism, or isolationism.[38] *Warlock* has a far more complex narrative but, in one respect, its political intent is more nakedly evident than *High Noon*'s, for *Warlock* is Edward Dmytryk's *apologia pro vita sua*.

Dmytryk was a casualty of the Hollywood blacklist; *Warlock* screen-writer Robert Alan Aurthur was a *near*-casualty. The film depicts a witch-hunter (Blaisedell) hired to root undesirables out of the body politic, till he exceeds legitimate authority. When Blaisedell learns of the San Pablo cowboys' formation of "Regulators", one of McQuown's henchmen tells him: "You know, this could get to be quite a thing, Mr. Marshal. The town o' Warlock 'points a marshal, he comes in and kills a whole bunch of us cowboys, and we appoint Regulators, and we kill you, and the town gets another marshal, and he kills more cowboys, and we appoint – well, you can see how it'd go back and forth and forth and back for all time. Be kinda like – looking into two mirrors put face to face."[39] In effect, this subtly asserts that the far right (Blaisedell) and the far left (Abe McQuown) are at heart alike, equidistant from a consensual, law-abiding society.

John Gannon is *Warlock*'s pivotal *consensual* hero. The most commanding performance in *Warlock* is undoubtedly Henry Fonda's as Clay Blaisedell, yet Richard Widmark was given top billing. One credible explanation for favouring Widmark might simply be that Gannon is constructed as a frontier equivalent of Edward Dmytryk. Dmytryk was one of the infamous "Hollywood Ten", the directors and screenwriters who chose jail in 1947 rather than cooperate with the House Un-American Activities Committee. More pertinently, he was the only one of the Ten who later recanted and cooperated with HUAC – much to the disgust of many of his former associates. Against the opening credits of *Warlock*, we see nine cowboys riding toward town. Eight ride in a fairly close grouping, while the last (Widmark) hangs back, his heart clearly not in their venture. Widmark is alone in the frame as Dmytryk's screen credit appears. Thus, even before one word of dialogue is uttered, producer-director Dmytryk has established Gannon as a man of conscience, accompanying but *apart* from his confrères – literally, a reluctant fellow traveller. *Warlock* is, like Elia Kazan's *On the Waterfront* (1954), its director's rationalization of his cooperation with HUAC. Dmytryk returned to testify as a "friendly witness". Significantly, the one San Pablo cowboy who survives the O.K. Corral-type shoot-out with Blaisedell is called Friendly (as is the tyrannical union boss in Kazan's film). Gannon's progress in *Warlock* is identical to Marlon Brando's in *On the Waterfront*: at first tied to his old companions through his brother, he must ultimately oppose his former mentor. Brando is beaten to a pulp, Widmark's Gannon is stabbed in the hand, yet both remain resolute. The correlation between these characters is especially apt since Oakley Hall's book has no Gannon–McQuown shoot-out; this is the film-makers' construction. Equally intriguing are parallels between Gannon and Dmytryk himself. Gannon breaks with McQuown's gang just as Dmytryk broke with the rest of the Ten. He allies himself with the established political-legal structure (by becoming deputy) as Dmytryk did (by cooperating with HUAC). As Warlock's deputy Gannon earns the respect of decent citizens, just as Dmytryk's full reinstatement within the Hollywood community restored him to directorial prominence. Political pariahs are not assigned star-packed, big-budget films such as *The Caine Mutiny* (1954), *Raintree County* and *The Young Lions* (both 1958) and *Warlock*.

So Gannon, the rehabilitated outlaw caught between the San Pabloites' anarchy and Blaisedell's one-man rule, functions as Dmytryk's neo-centrist, neo-conformist spokesman, representing a truly moral and democratic authority as surely as Blaisedell embodies charismatic, intrinsically patriarchal authority. Yet Blaisedell, although a witch-hunter, is a supremely honourable man; and both the character's legendary reputation and Fonda's portrayal invest him with a dignity and integrity more akin to General Douglas MacArthur than Senator Joe McCarthy. In truth, Clay Blaisedell is a crucial but undervalued figure in Fonda's screen iconography. Not only is Blaisedell a complex variation on Fonda's Earp in Ford's *My Darling Clementine* (1946), but he also represents a consummate blend of righteousness and power, poised halfway between the actor's decent but powerless cowboy in William Wellman's *The Ox-Bow Incident* (1943) and his superfast but thoroughly vicious gunman in Sergio Leone's *Once Upon a Time in the West* (1968). Moreover, *Warlock* stands alongside *You Only Live Once* (1937), *Young Mr. Lincoln* (1939), *The Ox-Bow Incident*, Anthony Mann's *The Tin Star* and, implicitly, *Twelve Angry Men* (both 1957) in establishing Henry Fonda as America's foremost screen opponent of lynch-mob rule. A scene in *Warlock* features him single-handedly dispersing such a crowd with the admonition: "All of you, go home. And while you're doin' it, think how bein' in a lynch-mob is as low a thing as a man can do."[40] While admittedly the witch-hunter of *Warlock* (giving town and film title particular relevance for 1950s America), Blaisedell is certainly no frontier version of Joe McCarthy.

Tom Morgan, however, is as sinister a figure as McCarthy's chief aide, Roy Cohn; *Warlock* also infers Morgan is homosexual – as was Cohn. Yet this is possibly an over-simplification of Morgan's motivation. The actual crux of his anxiety is exposed when he tells Clay "if you're not the Marshal you're *nothin'*!" If Blaisedell becomes "nothin'", then what will Morgan be? The tragedy of both Blaisedell and Morgan is that they are trapped in their own legend. Their prowess with guns has made them all they are. As itinerant town-tamers, they have enjoyed a mythic status, living on a favoured edge between legend and legality.

Morgan realizes that will all end if Blaisedell marries Jessie and settles as an ordinary citizen in Warlock. At the root of Tom Morgan's violent and emotional excesses, therefore, is his compulsion to preserve his pitiful fragment of reflected glory rather than an overtly sexual desire for his friend. Morgan is also the blind spot in Blaisedell's intelligence. An otherwise worldly man, Clay naïvely assumes Tom is as decent and upright as himself. Blaisedell and Gannon have each, in the past, been duped into needless killing. Each later grasps the treacherous nature of a respected friend (Morgan, McQuown) he will finally be forced to kill. Yet Blaisedell is so honourable and Morgan so patently corrupt that, even eschewing any sexual subtext on Morgan's part, their friendship stretches plausibility. Morgan is the subject of a sensationalist account entitled "The Black Rattlesnake of Fort James"; but Blaisedell has accepted Morgan at face value for ten years, never seriously examining why his friend's reputation is as villainous as his own is heroic. The ultimate resolution is thematically identical to that of *Shane* and, later, *The Man Who Shot Liberty Valance*: the charismatic hero vanquishes the agent of darkness but his own authority is supplanted by a colourless "common man". Gannon represents the communitarian principles of democracy and civilization as Clay Blaisedell never can; and what is to become of the charismatic hero once he has served his purpose? Unlike the doomed hero of *The Gunfighter*, whose tragedy was that he missed his chance to be ordinary, Blaisedell never really wanted such a chance; his own tragedy is that, finally, even being a legend is no longer enough.

When Gary Cooper dropped his marshal's star in the dust at the climax of *High Noon*, he was condemning a community's moral cowardice; Burt Lancaster dropped his badge and gun at the end of *Gunfight at the O.K. Corral* in reaction against one killing too many; and Gregory Peck tossed his father's duelling pistol away in *The Big Country* as a rejection of wrong-headed notions of masculinity. Evidently, this discarding of frontier symbols of authority, power and manhood was a recurring motif in 1950s Westerns. Yet when Henry Fonda as Blaisedell throws his gold-handled Colts into the dust, this is above all an act of self-negation. Like many a grand gesture, behind the spectacle it is inherently self-destructive. Regarding the moral/thematic evolution of the genre, it is significant that the tin star is the principal symbol of power in 1952's *High Noon*. *O.K. Corral*, of 1957, whose hero discards badge *and* gun, is transitional. By 1959, however, the ultimate frontier status symbols are Clay's gold-handled Colts. Even though he is ultimately too decent to enforce his knowledge, Blaisedell realizes the gun is the true source of power.

The gun was to loom larger in American life in the ensuing decade, and during that era of escalating violence traditional faith in law and order was a related casualty. One instance of this trend is that very few 1960s Westerns foregrounded lawmen as heroes. Even when major stars worked for directors who had previously lionized the profession, lawmen were deromanticized as corrupt (James Stewart in Ford's *Two Rode Together* (1961)), vengeful (James Garner in Sturges's *Hour of the Gun* (1967)), or decrepit though valiant alcoholics (Robert Mitchum in Hawks's *El Dorado* (1967) and John Wayne in Henry Hathaway's *True Grit* (1969)). By the late 1960s issues of law and order had found a new home in the urban thriller, including Don Siegel's *Madigan* (1968), which again teamed Henry Fonda and Richard Widmark as lawmen with differing concepts of duty.

It is not too extravagant to suggest *Warlock* is the apogee of two quintessential 1950s constructs of the genre: the law and order, town-based Western, and the psychological Western. From *The Gunfighter* and *High Noon*, through Sturges's *Bad Day at Black Rock* (1955) and Delmer Daves's *3:10 to Yuma* (1957) to *Rio Bravo*, Westerns of the 1950s continually explored and reshaped themes of hypocrisy and/or responsibility in modern American society. *Warlock* was the last such Western of the decade, and also the genre's last and most complex statement on the witch-hunts. The pluralistic supporting cast of ranchers, miners and merchants adds another layer of socio-political (and economic) complexity. In its acknowledgement of special interest groups, as well as its division of narrative sympathy between a mythic and a prosaic hero, *Warlock* is an ambitious Western equivalent of postwar America's Consensus school of history. Furthermore, in the decade which saw the release of opulent and overwrought small-town melodramas (e.g., *East of Eden* (1955), *Peyton Place* (1957), *Some Came Running* (1959)), *Warlock* brought comparably stylized intensity to the town Western. Granted, Gannon's ill-fated younger brother is just a surly juvenile delinquent; and Dorothy Malone's Lily and Dolores Michaels's Jessie are no more than caricatures – respectively a glamorous Magdalene and an insipid Madonna. Yet these are minor stereotypical flaws in an exceptionally dexterous chronicle of labyrinthine motivations, subtle power shifts and raw emotions. *Warlock* is a masterpiece among Westerns, and deserves wider recognition as a classic.

In 1946, *My Darling Clementine* and *Duel in the Sun* revived the Western and endowed the genre with an implicit ideological subtext of white male primacy. A dozen years on, the principal male stars of these Westerns each returned to a superficially similar narrative for far more intricate analyses of masculine identity in virtually all-white frontier environments.

The Big Country climaxes with a gun duel in which both men die, yet its message is essentially optimistic. *Warlock* closes with a showdown which both men survive but, from the viewpoint of the mythic Western hero, it is a pessimistic film. Thus, as the 1950s drew to an end, the epic, star-laden Western was in ascendancy at the same time as (but usually separate from) the predominant image of the tragic Westerner steadily running out of options and time. The theme of personal alienation features prominently in the next case study, where the moral dignity of marginalized heroes contrasts with the compromise, ingratitude and hypocrisy of a society whose finest impulses are gradually being stifled by the onslaught of civilization. The heroes are no less tragic but, unlike Jimmy Ringo, Shane, Ethan Edwards and Clay Blaisedell, the roads not taken are U.S. society's. Four films form the basis of scrutiny – all, in a remarkable convergence of theme and time, released in 1962, the Western's most significant year.

CHAPTER 6

"No More West to Win":
How the West Was Won and the
Elegiac Westerns of 1962

As the United States entered the 1960s, the Hollywood Western and America's prestige were both still riding high. The launch of the Soviet space capsule *Sputnik* in 1957 shattered faith in the innate superiority of the U.S. educational system, and the U–2 incident of May 1960 proved internationally embarrassing; yet, on the whole, the nation embarked on the new decade with confidence. The Eisenhower era ended as the Democratic Senator John Kennedy of Massachusetts won 1960's presidential election by the narrowest of margins. The new president did not share Eisenhower's enthusiasm for paperback Westerns or his halting, unsophisticated verbal delivery. For leisure Kennedy preferred reading the adventures of superspy James Bond. In rhetoric, he affected a high-flown style complete with poetic and classical touches. The past John Kennedy attempted to evoke was the past of ancient Rome, of Shakespeare, of Lincoln. His much-stressed appreciation of Western civilization did not include a marked affinity for the Western film. Moreover, born in 1917 and thus significantly younger than many of the genre's reigning stars, Kennedy's youth and his continual emphasis on America's future development rather than her mythic past served to distance him further from the ethos of the Western.

Two major films of 1960 unwittingly portended the quagmire which would engulf and divide America later that decade. John Wayne's *The Alamo* and John Sturges's *The Magnificent Seven* both lionized brave Americans defending freedom and justice against Mexican tyrants. In each film, the American heroes are vastly outnumbered but fight to the bitter end. All the defenders of the Alamo and four of the Seven perish but, spiritually, their triumphs are complete and eternal. These narratives prefigured America's ideological commitment, as a redeemer nation, to the Vietnam conflict; but their plot resolutions were romanticized inversions of what ultimately transpired in Southeast Asia. In Vietnam, too, the Americans suffered heavy casualties against a non-Caucasian people. However, in Vietnam, the United States had military superiority and still could not prevail. Victory, both actual and spiritual, eluded them. Yet in the early 1960s, Vietnam was still a minor overseas commitment; and the radicalization of the Civil Rights crusade was, like the sexual revolution, still several years away. The Hollywood Western still constructed American national identity in white and male terms, and remained chiefly preoccupied with homegrown components of American experience. In his study of the Western, Philip French cited an unnamed French critic who claimed 1950, in which five prestigious Westerns were released within four months, was "a little like the 1789 of the genre's history".[1] As I indicated in the Introduction to this book, a Eurocentric interpretation of the Western partially obscures its significance in terms of American identity. If we must use historical analogies to explain the development of the Western then surely an American analogy may throw the best light on an American phenomenon. In that spirit, I suggest 1962 stands as the Western's most significant year, the genre's equivalent of 1893, when Frederick Jackson Turner's famed essay declared the frontier closed.[2] In 1962, Hollywood did likewise.

In output as well as theme, the Hollywood Western appeared to be nearing the sunset in 1962. The total number of Westerns released, fifteen including small independent productions, had never been so low; even Western television series nose-dived, with nineteen on the air, compared to thirty-six in 1961.[3] By 1962 only 11,000 four-wall cinemas were still operating in the United States, though the drive-in had reached its peak of 4,800; average weekly attendance fell to twenty-five million, while admission prices rose by six cents and stood at seventy-three cents (over three times the price of admission in 1939), in spite of which box office receipts continued their downward spiral, yielding only $903,000,000 that year.[4] Moviegoing now accounted for only 0.25% of consumer, 4.4% of recreation and 54.9% of spectator expenditure.[5]

The Western's quantitative decline, as delineated here and earlier in Chapter 4, runs exactly parallel to the gradual erosion of cinema as the centre of twentieth-century American popular culture. Yet, qualitatively, 1962 was the genre's most remarkable year. That summer, within little more than a month, three superb elegiac Westerns were released; and, furthermore, before 1962 was over, movie exhibitors gleefully anticipated a box office bonanza with the most ambitious, star-laden Western ever made.

First to appear was John Ford's *The Man Who Shot Liberty Valance* (Paramount), starring John Wayne and James Stewart. In the era of Technicolored wide-screen spectaculars Ford offered a black and white drama largely set indoors as his last major statement on white America's frontier civilization. Beneath a superficially clichéd narrative, Ford constructed his complex, poignant, relentlessly bleak coda to his sagas of celebration.

Senator Ransom Stoddard (Stewart) and his wife Hallie (Vera Miles) return to the town of Shinbone for the funeral of their old friend Tom Doniphon (Wayne). When the editor of the local newspaper presses Stoddard to reveal why a legendary political figure has come to bury an unknown old-timer who died a lonely pauper, via flashback the Senator discloses the true story of the famous gunfight which launched his public career.

Stoddard had come west as a young, idealistic lawyer. Outside Shinbone his stagecoach was robbed by a notorious outlaw, Liberty Valance (Lee Marvin), who whipped Stoddard and left him for dead. Doniphon, a local rancher, found Stoddard and took him to Hallie, his own girlfriend, who tended his injuries. Stoddard wanted Valance jailed; Doniphon told him the only way to settle problems out west was with a gun. Refusing to pack a gun, Stoddard stayed in Shinbone, helping in Hallie's parents' restaurant and carving his niche as a lawyer and schoolteacher – all the time growing closer and more precious to Hallie.

Election of delegates to the statehood convention brought events to a head. Liberty Valance's nomination was rejected. Stoddard and newspaper editor Dutton Peabody (Edmond O'Brien) were chosen as Shinbone's representatives. Valance was furious and vowed reprisals. That night, he and his two henchmen beat Peabody. Stoddard went to face Valance in the street. Contrary to all expectations, Valance was killed. Later, when Doniphon walked into the restaurant and saw Hallie embracing Stoddard, he realized how completely she had transferred her affections. Depressed, he got violently drunk and burned the extension he was building for Hallie on his ranch. In one night, Doniphon lost his girl, his property and his heroic stature within the community – yet it was he, in an alley across the street, who actually fired the fatal shot. Stoddard, hailed as a hero, was horrified at the prospect of building a political career on a killing, but Doniphon salved his conscience by telling him who really shot Liberty Valance.

Back in the present, as Ransom Stoddard finishes recounting his tale, the editor tears up the interview notes, declaring, "This is the West, sir. When the legend becomes fact, print the legend."[6] Stoddard and his wife leave Shinbone, their journey back to Washington tinged by melancholy and a wordless realization that Hallie still loves Doniphon, who twice saved and, ultimately, ruined Stoddard's life. Unable to live with a killing, Stoddard has lived for decades with a lie. Now in old age, the judgement of history refuses him absolution. The last line of dialogue in the film is grimly, grotesquely ironic. As Stoddard thanks a porter for the railroad's attentive service, the man replies: "You think nothing of it. Nothing's too good for the man who shot Liberty Valance."[7] The most shameful incident of his life is the one which guarantees immortality. All his subsequent public achievements will be buried with his bones.

The Man Who Shot Liberty Valance did respectable business at the box office, but critical reception was mixed. There was strong feeling, articulated in *Variety* and the *New York Times*, that *Liberty Valance* was too rudimentary to satisfy the tastes of 1962 audiences.[8] *Variety* termed the film "entertaining and emotionally involving", yet "ultimately ... fanciful and unconvincing. ... [T]he film's creators have refused to give the audience the benefit of the doubt. The picture concludes with 20 minutes of condescending, melodramatic, anti-climactic strokes."[9] A. H. Weiler, reviewing *Liberty Valance* for the *New York Times*, claimed that the "basically honest, rugged and mature saga has been sapped of a great deal of effect by an obvious, overlong and garrulous anticlimax", concluding, with reference to the film's most famous line: "In *Liberty Valance*, there is too much of a good legend."[10] The *Motion Picture Herald* asserted that Ford's film had "employed his remarkable talents to full advantage", predicting, "if any combination of basic ingredients would appear to guarantee top box office results, that of Ford directing a Wayne–Stewart starring duo should do it".[11] *The Hollywood Reporter* hailed the film as "John Ford's best picture in years", but opined that "straight narrative [rather than flashback] might better have pointed up the final irony of the principals and the story".[12]

Liberty Valance is a community Western, made by the master of community Westerns, in which the ideal of community darkens and sours irrevocably. What is the innate worth of a community which allows a decent and dignified man to die in poverty and obscurity? Previous analysts of the film have dealt with this issue and other social and ideological inferences extensively. John H. Lenihan, for example, has identified Tom Doniphon and the equally marginalized heroes of other early 1960s elegiac Westerns as the self-reliant remnants of a bygone age and code whose pride would be eroded by the welfare state socialization of the Kennedy and Johnson years.[13] Just as the genre showcased young stars as rebel figures in the relatively quiescent Eisenhower era, during the youthful, forward-looking Kennedy's administration the Western foregrounded ageing heroes resisting the inexorable tide of social change. Yet this is only part of the tragedy at the heart of *Liberty Valance*. Stoddard, too, is a tragic figure, a fundamentally decent man who is continually fated to lose his innocence. As a young idealist he is beaten by Valance on his arrival in the west and then befriended by a man who cheerfully recommends violence as a solution to social disputes. Both encounters connote a loss of innocence. Later, Doniphon humiliates him because he suspects Stoddard may have romantic designs on Hallie, yet Stoddard ingenuously indicates that he respects the fact Hallie is Tom's girl. It is Hallie who gravitates toward Stoddard, not he who takes her from Tom.

The relationship between Doniphon and Stoddard is complex. Doniphon despises Stoddard's brand of civilization, even as he respects his courage, stubbornness and integrity. On occasion, however, he takes delight in rupturing his dignity, especially in front of Hallie, because he instinctively recognizes him as someone to whom Hallie may be drawn. Better for Doniphon, the film suggests, if he had allowed Valance to kill Stoddard. Yet both the film and retrospective critical appraisals neglect a deeper irony: Stoddard *is* a genuine hero. He faced Valance of his own accord, with no idea that Doniphon was over the street with rifle poised; but that is not what the film stresses, and it is not what Stoddard remembers. So the layers of innocence are stripped away, one by one: the initial belief that he had killed a man, the knowledge that he married his mentor's girl, the knowledge that his distinguished career is built on a lie, have all combined to poison his soul. In the end, there is no escape from the manufactured myth – he is a hero to a society which *prefers* the romantic lie, and with that realization dies Ransom Stoddard's last illusion of hope and his last shred of innocence.

Liberty Valance is so disillusioned with civilization that it may almost, by default, resemble a paean to primitivism. In that very year, historian Richard Hofstadter was writing *Anti-Intellectualism in American Life*, which included the following observation:

> In various guises primitivism has been a constantly recurring force in Western history and in our own national experience. It is likely to become evident wherever men of the intellectual class itself are disappointed with or grow suspicious of the human yield of a rationally ordered life or when they seek to break away from the routine or apathy or refinement that arise with civilization. In America primitivism has affected the thinking of many men too educated and cultivated to run with the frontier

revivalists but sympathetic to their underlying distrust for civilized forms. ... It runs through the popular legend of frontier figures such as Daniel Boone and Davy Crockett down to the heroes of modern Western stories and detective fiction – embracing all those lonely adventurers whose cumulative mythology caused D. H. Lawrence to say ... the essential American soul is "hard, isolate, stoic, and a killer".[14]

The same sensibility lies beneath the surface of the era's elegiac Westerns. Most of the protagonists are not killers by nature, but to a man they are increasingly out of step and out of sympathy with modernization and the new social realities of corporate America.

Jack Burns (Kirk Douglas), hero of *Lonely Are the Brave* (Universal, 1962), is such a man. Directed by David Miller and scripted by the formerly blacklisted Dalton Trumbo, *Lonely Are the Brave* was the second in an unofficial trilogy of twentieth-century Westerns released in the early 1960s. Along with John Huston's *The Misfits* (1961), penned by Arthur Miller, starring Clark Gable and Marilyn Monroe in their last screen roles, and Martin Ritt's *Hud* (1963), starring Paul Newman, Patricia Neal, Melvyn Douglas and Brandon de Wilde, *Lonely Are the Brave* was the tale of a frontier individualist struggling to survive in a technologically sophisticated society which has passed him by. All three utilized black and white photography to portray life in the modern West as bleak and arid as the land. *Hud* was actually the last major Western filmed in black and white until Jim Jarmusch's *Dead Man* (1995). All the films scrutinized in subsequent chapters of this book were made in colour.

Burns is a far more amiable soul than the disturbed cowboy Trumbo had written for Kirk Douglas in the previous year's *The Last Sunset*, but he is no less alienated, no less an outcast. He arrives at the home of his best friend, Paul Bondi (Michael Kane), who is in jail for helping illegal Mexican immigrants. Paul's wife, Jerri (Gena Rowlands), tells him there is nothing he can do to help, but Burns contrives to have himself thrown into jail so they can escape together. However, Paul has other plans; he intends to serve his sentence and return placidly to married life. Burns decides to break out alone, only to find himself pursued by police jeeps, a military helicopter and a lawman (Walter Matthau) secretly sympathetic to the fugitive's plight. Burns takes to the mountains, heading for Mexico. He and his beautiful horse Whiskey evade capture but, on the last stretch of highway before the border, Whiskey becomes skittish in the rainy dark and they are hit by a truck transporting, of all things, lavatories (an ironic and perhaps unwitting take on King Vidor's *Man Without a Star* (1955), in which Kirk Douglas's free-spirited cowboy found great amusement in the novelty of indoor plumbing). Traffic stops, a crowd gathers, among them the pursuing sheriff and his deputy. The camera dwells on Burns's stunned, frightened features as he hears the shot which ends Whiskey's suffering, and the life visibly ebbs from him. As Burns is loaded on to an ambulance, the hapless truck driver asks, "He ain't gonna die, is he?"; the ambulance-man replies, "How do *I* know?"[15]

Lonely Are the Brave's theme of alienation and its plot of pursuit resulted in an odyssey narrative eulogizing a hero who is divorced from the modern community. Yet Burns does cherish a genuine sense of community, as he demonstrates to Jerri in a brief tirade against the erosion of traditional Western ways: "A Westerner likes open country. That means he's got to hate fences, and the more fences there are the more he hates 'em. ... Y'ever notice how many fences there're getting to be? And the signs they got on 'em: 'No Hunting', 'No Hiking', 'No Admission', 'No Trespass', 'Private Property', 'Closed Area', 'Start Moving', 'Go Away', 'Get Lost', 'Drop Dead'."[16] The film also contains a searing indictment of the heroic cowboy's inherent emotional imbalance, as Burns tells Jerri, with whom he was once romantically involved: "It's God's own blessing I didn't get you. ... I'm a loner, clear down deep to my very guts. Know what a loner is? He's a born cripple. He's crippled because the only person he can live with is himself. It's his life, the way he wants to live, it's all for *him*. God, I bet he'd kill a woman like you – 'cause he couldn't love you. Not the way you *are* loved."[17] Such painful self-knowledge was perhaps beyond Shane and Ethan Edwards, but Burns realizes his own emotional limitations from the beginning.

Whether too downbeat or too self-consciously allegorical in its conflict between natural man and modern technology, the film was not a commercial success. Critical response, however, was generally appreciative. "With a tiny cast, the simplest of story situations and a sure understanding of human behavior, this quietly penetrating film is a joy to watch", according to Howard Thompson of the *New York Times*.[18] *Variety* criticized the film from both sides, regretting its too obvious symbolism but declaring, "audiences will doubtless sympathize, but they are not likely to 'empathize'. Nor are they apt to discern the larger implications of all-but-vanished individualism in a highly organized society."[19] In a romantic vein, the *Motion Picture Herald* termed the film "unusual, moving and dramatic" in its depiction "of a wandering cowboy whose deep, almost obsessive desire for freedom and the open spaces of the west lead him into trouble, and finally to the ultimate freedom which is death itself".[20] Referring to that ironic demise, *The Hollywood Reporter* observed: "This ultimate indignity sums up what ... has happened in the age of H-bombs and rocketry to the cowboy, vestigial echo of a heroic saga of long ago. So *Brave* is a film with wry message, a sad commentary that sheds a tear for bold and honorable anachronisms."[21] The verdict from *TIME* was also tinged with philosophical rumination: "The symbolic question is clear: Is the untamed free spirit an outlaw that must learn to toe the white lines of the modern world or perish?"[22] The review concluded by congratulating *Lonely Are the Brave*'s major contributors, who had "fashioned a film of distinction and signed it with honor".[23]

Honour is a central theme of 1962's third elegiac Western, Sam Peckinpah's *Ride the High Country* (Metro-Goldwyn-Mayer), known in Britain as *Guns in the Afternoon*. Filmed, unlike the others, in autumnal colour, it contained elements of community *and* odyssey narratives as its heroes journeyed from a turn-of-the-century frontier town filled with street-corner policemen, Chinese restaurants and crooked fairground attractions, to a mining camp peopled by ruffians, prostitutes and a family of degenerate sociopaths. Yet it is primarily an odyssey of the soul, centring on the old age of two proud, dignified men who once were legendary town-tamers yet now must eke out a living in a society which neither remembers nor cares. *Ride the High Country* was only Peckinpah's second directorial credit, and it was a happy historical coincidence that the Western's greatest visionary talent since John Ford made his first authoritative statement on the moral and spiritual decay of frontier America in the same year the old master neared the close of his career with a virtually identical pronouncement. *Liberty Valance* and *Ride the High Country* intersect not only thematically but also stylistically. Like *Liberty Valance*, Peckinpah's film featured two top Western stars teamed for the first (and here the last) time. Two of Hollywood's richest men, Randolph Scott and Joel McCrea had each, since the end of World War II, starred almost exclusively in Westerns. In *Ride the High Country* each found a perfect swan song.[24]

Ex-lawman Steve Judd (McCrea) rides into a town, gratified to find the main street lined with cheering people. As he tips his hat appreciatively, a policeman orders him out of the way. The crowd has not gathered to greet him but to witness a camel racing against horses. Judd has come to town to work as a bank guard, transporting gold from the mining camp of Coarse Gold. Judd discovers his old friend Gil Westrum (Scott), another ex-lawman down on his luck, working as a carnival sharpshooter, and enlists his help and that of Westrum's protégé, the callow Heck Longtree (Ron Starr), in transporting the gold. Unknown to Judd, who has retained his personal code of honour even though the society he served has discarded him, Westrum, bitter about his similar fate, has turned larcenous in his old age. He and Heck aim to steal the gold, and Westrum hopes to persuade Judd to throw in with their plan. Reasoning that they are entitled to some remuneration for all their years of thankless service to society, Westrum subtly tries to plant the same thought in Judd's mind, but to no avail.

En route to Coarse Gold Judd, Westrum and Heck stop at the farm of Joshua Knudsen (R. G. Armstrong), a religious fanatic who rules his daughter Elsa (Mariette Hartley) with slaps and Scripture. Sick of Knudsen's tyranny, Elsa joins Judd's party on the trail, intending to marry her sweetheart Billy Hammond (James Drury) once they reach Coarse Gold. Billy Hammond is no more than a smooth-talking lout, but his four brothers are far worse. Disgusting in appearance and behaviour, evil and almost moronic, they fully expect to share Billy's new bride. Elsa's wedding, one of the most nightmarish ever filmed, is held in a brothel, with a drunken judge presiding, the madame as matron of honour and her whores as bridesmaids. When the groom passes out, two of his brothers attempt to rape Elsa. Judd and Heck hear her screams and rush to her rescue. Westrum persuades the judge to confess (falsely) that he has no legal authority to perform wedding ceremonies, so the marriage is annulled and Elsa starts back down the mountains with the two ex-lawmen and Heck, with whom she shares a mutual attraction. Westrum still plans to steal the gold but Heck, who has come to admire Judd, is reluctant to see the scheme through. When Westrum tries to abscond with the gold, Judd catches him in the act, slaps him and challenges him to a gunfight. Westrum refuses to draw his gun. Deeply hurt by his friend's betrayal, Judd ties Westrum up and vows to hand him over to the law when they get back to town. However, the Hammonds have learned of Westrum's trickery with the judge, and they ambush Judd's party. Judd agrees to give Heck a gun to help fight off the Hammonds, but he refuses to cut Westrum loose. The scar of betrayal runs too deep. Two Hammonds die in the skirmish. That night, Westrum escapes. The next day Judd, Heck and Elsa return to the Knudsen farm – but Elsa's father has been killed by the three remaining Hammonds, who again ambush them. Westrum, who has been following Judd, rides to the rescue, and the two old friends meet the Hammonds head-on. In the ensuing shoot-out, the Hammonds are dispatched but Judd is mortally wounded. Westrum promises he will see the gold is delivered to the bank, just as Judd would have done.

Judd tells him: "Hell, I know that. I always did. You just forgot it for a while, that's all."[25] At Judd's request, Westrum, Heck and Elsa leave him to face his death as he lived his life – alone, and with dignity. Tom Doniphon's off-screen death in *The Man Who Shot Liberty Valance* is ignominious; that of Jack Burns in *Lonely Are the Brave* is simultaneously ironic and pathetic. Yet the demise of Steve Judd in *Ride the High Country* is the most poignant, most beautiful in the genre.

Ride the High Country was not a commercial success on its release, but critics were instantly appreciative. The *New York Times* described it as "the most disarming little horse opera in months".[26] *The Hollywood Reporter* praised the film as "a real gutsy cinematic adventure that Hollywood could use more of".[27] *Motion Picture Herald* termed it "[a] refreshing and novel approach to the Western, without resort to the psychiatrist's couch".[28] *TIME*, reviewing *Ride the High Country* in the same issue as *Lonely Are the Brave*, stated: "This story could have been sheer slumgullion, but under Sam Peckinpah's tasteful direction it is a minor *chef-d'oeuvre* among westerns. ... *Ride the High Country* has a rare honesty of script, performance and theme – that goodness is not a gift but a quest."[29] *Variety*, however, sounded a discordant note which was unkind yet commercially astute: "The old saying 'you can't make a silk purse out of a sow's ear' rings true for Metro-Goldwyn-Mayer's artistic western *Ride the High Country*. It remains a standard story, albeit with an interesting gimmick and some excellent production values, but lies in the hard-to-sell area in between an expensive 'B' and a big one."[30] It might have experienced considerably less difficulty had it not been marketed as the second feature supporting a drab Italian-made epic, *The Tartars*.

An early scene in *Ride the High Country* shows Judd meeting the bankers for whom he will work. He is much older than they expected, and the cuffs of his shirt are noticeably frayed. He is, in a sense, a Western equivalent of Willy Loman in Arthur Miller's play *Death of a Salesman* (1949). After all, Judd is, like Willy, desperately trying to remain employable in a fast-buck society which cares nothing for past services. Later, at Knudsen's farm, Westrum offers a further clue to Judd's social dislocation when he mentions Sarah Truesdale, Judd's old love, whom everyone expected him to marry. Significantly, all three elegiac Westerns made in 1962 featured heroes whose failure to achieve complete social integration stemmed at least partially from the loss of the women they loved. Again, the Western here explored the question of roads not taken and, in the process, implicitly identified the institution of marriage as a crucial agent of socialization. Yet the most serious tragedy of these narratives was the road not taken by U.S. society. Unlike the outcasts at the heart of the Westerns examined in Chapter 4, Tom Doniphon, Jack Burns and Steve Judd have no overt anti-social status. Society is clearly adjudged at fault for marginalizing such men: it cannot accommodate them gracefully, it does not value their experience, it condemns their brand of individualism as outmoded. If their lonely lives are their own tragedies, their lonely deaths are society's; and perhaps the greatest tragedy of all is that society does not realize how much poorer it is for their passing.

Jack Nachbar wrote of 1962's elegiac Westerns: "With these three pictures, the Western film tradition formally called a halt to the celebration [of Frederick Jackson Turner's frontier thesis] and admitted that whether or not Turner had been correct in defining the American experience, he was certainly correct in announcing its demise – the frontier and the freedom that accompanied it were indeed no more."[31] Yet 1962 saw not only the release of three Westerns which declared the frontier closed but also the world première of Hollywood's most lavish celebration of the American West.

As its very title suggested, *How the West Was Won* aspired to be the definitive Western. The most successful Western of the early 1960s, *How the West Was Won* grossed $12,200,000 and, after inflation-adjustment in 1981, ranked fourth on the table of Western box office champions.[32] The first narrative film *produced* in Cinerama, it was the second *released* (after *The Wonderful World of the Brothers Grimm*). U.S. audiences did not actually see the film until 1963, but Hollywood's trade papers were able to give their advance verdicts in November 1962 from the film's world première in London.

Trade reviewers found themselves dealing in superlatives. The *Motion Picture Herald* proclaimed: "This screen show has the epic qualities of treating familiar material in a way that makes other tellings fade away. It depicts men and women of character struggling against formidable odds in a way which is both particular and symbolic of generations of pioneers. No one in the United States or abroad who sees this film – and untold millions ultimately will see it – can leave the theatre without a greater appreciation of the role the makers of the West played in building a great nation. ... [T]he world has a screen attraction for all time."[33]

The Hollywood Reporter called it "a cornucopia spilling over with romance, history, comedy, music and action[.] ... In historic show business terms, *How the West Was Won* is chautauqua at its best. ... Americans particularly, with their strong Puritan heritage, want not only entertainment for this kind of money, they want something 'worthwhile', in short, education. *How the West Was Won* fits this formula. ... There has never in history been anything quite like the winning of the west, and its magnitude and significance are given their due in *How the West Was Won*."[34]

Variety was similarly enthusiastic: "the blockbuster supreme, a magnificent and exciting spectacle[.] ... It will, undoubtedly, run for several years, and will become one of the industry's all-time top grossers. ... The courage and tenacity of the pioneers is effectively etched in James Webb's screenplay, but the narrative is no more than a peg for the magnificent action sequences, which nightly dominate the production. The story is never intended to be more than a slender thread. ... And the final scene, of the present day West, with its crowded highways, is a striking salute to the adventurous pioneers."[35]

How the West Was Won, inspired by a six-part series which ran in *LIFE* magazine from April 6 to May 11 1959, was released under the auspices of Metro-Goldwyn-Mayer in conjunction with the Cinerama corporation, whose three-camera travelogues on a giant curved screen had left 1950s audiences breathless. Thus, as an epic Western in Cinerama, *How the West Was Won* laid more emphasis on spectacle than on plot or character development. Three directors were assigned to helm the handsome Metrocolor narrative, which was actually composed of five segments, each depicting an episode from frontier history. Henry Hathaway was responsible for the bulk of the project, directing the first, second and fifth episodes – "The Rivers", "The Plains" and "The Outlaws" respectively – which together constituted most of the film's running time. John Ford directed the third part, "The Civil War", while George Marshall contributed the fourth segment, "The Railroad". Spencer Tracy, unseen, provided the narration linking the episodes together.

How the West Was Won is the chronicle of one family's role in the taming of the American frontier. Its first two episodes focus on pioneers moving westward; its final panel deals with a marshal's effort to bring an outlaw to justice, only to find himself hampered by legal niceties. So the film contains, but does not combine, elements of both an odyssey and a community narrative. One of *How the West Was Won*'s charms – and one of its flaws – is that it tries to have something for everyone.

One of the film's key strategies to attract the widest possible audience was its all-star cast. Debbie Reynolds and George Peppard portrayed the central characters. Through their eyes and their experiences a half-century of American history unfolded. Yet the supporting cast included actors who had been winning the filmic West for years: John Wayne,

Class and "moral" prejudice in John Ford's *Stagecoach* (United Artists, 1939) as prostitute and outlaw are ostracized by the hypocrites of "polite society" (*l.* to *r.*: Claire Trevor, John Wayne, Marga Ann Daighton, Louise Platt, John Carradine and Berton Churchill).

Class and "moral" prejudice endorsed in John Ford's *My Darling Clementine* (20th Century Fox, 1946): Henry Fonda's Wyatt Earp is contemptuous of the racially ambiguous prostitute Chihuahua (Linda Darnell).

Polar opposites of femininity in King Vidor's *Duel in the Sun* (Selznick Releasing Organization, 1946): Joan Tetzel as Jesse's genteel fiancée and Jennifer Jones as the sexual Pearl Chavez.

Polar opposites of masculinity in Howard Hawks' *Red River* (United Artists, 1948): monolithic *machismo* (John Wayne) versus androgynous youth (Montgomery Clift) in the climactic fistfight.

The mythic fast gun as tragic hero, I: Gregory Peck as Jimmy Ringo in Henry King's *The Gunfighter* (20th Century Fox, 1950).

The mythic fast gun as tragic hero, II: Alan Ladd as Shane and Brandon de Wilde as Joey, the small boy who idolizes him, in George Stevens' *Shane* (Paramount, 1953).

The loneliest man alive: John Wayne as Ethan Edwards in John Ford's *The Searchers* (Warner Brothers, 1956). Also pictured here are Jeffrey Hunter (sleeping in foreground) and Ward Bond (wearing top hat).

Burl Ives as the tenaciously proud patriarch Rufus Hannassey in William Wyler's *The Big Country* (United Artists, 1958). Rufus is the first to realize that Jim McKay (Gregory Peck) has come to rescue Julie Maragon (Jean Simmons, here next to Chuck Connors) because he is in love with her.

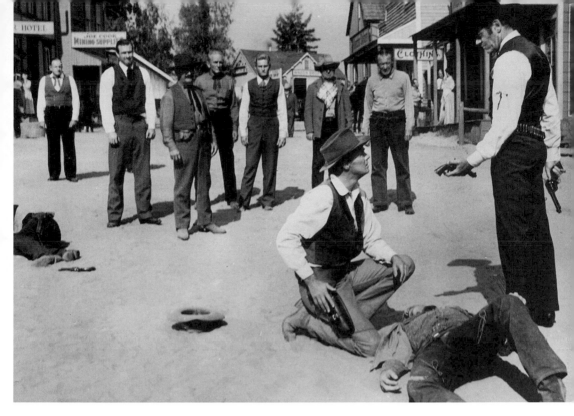

ABOVE: Clay Blaisedell (Henry Fonda)
offers Gannon (Richard Widmark) his slain
brother's gun and, implicitly, a chance to
avenge him in a ritualistic scene from
Edward Dmytryk's superb *Warlock*
(20th Century Fox, 1959).

LEFT: Tom Doniphon (John Wayne) advises
tenderfoot Ransom Stoddard (James
Stewart) that the gun is the only way to
deal with vicious thug Liberty Valance
(Lee Marvin) in John Ford's *The Man Who
Shot Liberty Valance* (Paramount, 1962).

Randoph Scott and Joel McCrea, down but not yet out as the old-time ex-lawmen nearing the end of their days in Sam Peckinpah's masterful *Ride the High Country* (released in the U.K. as *Guns in the Afternoon*, Metro-Goldwyn-Mayer, 1962).

This collage from the 1962 Metro-Goldwyn-Mayer and Cinerama epic *How the West Was Won* (directors: Henry Hathaway, John Ford and George Marshall) amply demonstrates the extent to which spectacle and especially the all-star cast were the film's major attractions.

Cynical opportunist (Burt Lancaster) and jaded yet honour-bound idealist (Lee Marvin): the two faces of American adventurism in Richard Brooks' *The Professionals* (Columbia, 1966).

The bloody death throes of American adventurism in Sam Peckinpah's *The Wild Bunch* (Warner Brothers–Seven Arts, 1969). During the climactic blood-bath, a Mexican woman shoots Pike Bishop (William Holden) in the back.

The Legend Maker (Burt Lancaster) and his confected Legend (Paul Newman) in Robert Altman's *Buffalo Bill and the Indians or Sitting Bull's History Lesson* (United Artists, 1976).

Josey Wales (Clint Eastwood) is purged of all hatred for post-Civil War America after killing his arch-enemy, the murderous Redleg Captain Terrill (Bill McKinney) in Eastwood's *The Outlaw Josey Wales* (Warner Brothers, 1976).

All Stills Courtesy of The Joel Finler Collection

James Stewart, Henry Fonda, Gregory Peck, Richard Widmark. Thirteen stars and ten co-stars featured, and the film's set-pieces (a raft-wreck on the Ohio River, an Indian attack on a wagon train, the battle of Shiloh, a buffalo stampede through a railroad camp, and a train robbery which soon becomes a train-wreck) were all spectacular. When *How the West Was Won* finally opened in the United States in 1963, its box office takings were equally spectacular.

However, if ticket sales vindicated the trade reviewers' extravagant praise, other critics were not so easily pleased. Stanley Kauffmann, writing for *The New Republic*, pronounced it "a historical stew of the sort that is usually defended at the last ditch as educational for children. Any cultivated parent who takes a child to this saccharine, distorted trash will regret it."[36] Bosley Crowther of the *New York Times* was just as disdainful: "a dutiful duplication of something you've already seen in anywhere from one to a thousand Western movies in the past 60 years. … All in all, an excellent opportunity to do a real historical drama of the West was wasted in this Hollywood-cured 'epic'. It should be called *How the West Was Done – to Death*."[37] *TIME*'s review was generally favourable but inclined more toward description than opinion, concluding: "As a final, visual commentary of its own, *West* offers an air view, not through an eagle's eye but a helicopter's, of what the winners won. Looking directly down on a field of Los Angeles cloverleafs, with speeding cars darting 30 ways into the smog, the camera asks a searching, unanswered question. Then the screen is filled with the silver-blue Pacific, there being no more West to win."[38]

How the West Was Won declared the frontier closed, but not in the manner of its elegiac contemporaries. Despite its grand design, the film is, compared to the other three examined here, thematically shallow. Films had moved on from the era of Cecil B. DeMille and, in an age of intelligent epics such as Stanley Kubrick's *Spartacus* (1960), Anthony Mann's *El Cid* (1961) and David Lean's *Lawrence of Arabia* (1962), cardboard characterization buttressed by awesome spectacle was no longer enough. Yet certain ideological inferences in *How the West Was Won* are worth noting. Spencer Tracy's opening narration marks the film as a saga of essentially benevolent conquest, which might more cynically be subtitled "*The Whiting of America*". The Prescott family have their own pioneering anthem, "Home in the Meadow", sung to the tune of "Greensleeves", which subtly underscores their indisputably WASP identity. The film plays the Indian question both ways by casting the red men as rampaging savages in "The Plains" episode but as the victim of white rapacity in "The Railroad". The film avoids either depiction or mention of Blacks, and Tracy's brief narration for "The Civil War" never alludes to slavery by name.

Yet, if *How the West Was Won* appears celebratory compared to *The Man Who Shot Liberty Valance*, *Lonely Are the Brave* and *Ride the High Country*, it nevertheless contains an element of ever-increasing disillusion for its central male character. Peppard's Zeb Rawlings starts out as a lanky farm boy keen to taste his share of glory in the Civil War. When we see him at Shiloh he is bloodied, confused and repulsed by what now seems senseless killing. Yet he remains in the army after the war, serving as a lieutenant guarding the construction of the railroad. He promises the Indians their hunting ground will remain sacred, only to find his pledge violated and his authority worthless as the territory fills up with buffalo hunters. He argues with the unscrupulous railroad boss Mike King (Richard Widmark), the unacceptable face of capitalism, and resigns his commission. In the final episode Zeb is a middle-aged marshal. He encounters an old enemy, outlaw Charlie Gant (Eli Wallach), whom he suspects is planning a train robbery. Gant lodges a complaint of harassment against Zeb, which another lawman (Lee J. Cobb) treats seriously. Zeb finds his friend and colleague prepared to take the word of a notorious thief and killer over his own. Zeb Rawlings is betrayed successively by the military establishment, corporate America and the judicial system. Thus *How the West Was Won* implies dissatisfaction with the nation's power structure but does not develop the theme, as *Lawrence of Arabia* did so superbly with the British Empire that same year.

The elegiac Westerns of 1962 lionized men who had outlived their time and stood poised at the edge of the sunset; but *How the West Was Won* ended with that literal image, which inferred that the genre had attained its pinnacle. If *How the West Was Won had* been acclaimed as the definitive Western, where could the genre go from there? If even Hollywood's mythic frontier was now closed, would it leave a void in the American identity which the Western had so lovingly constructed and reflected? Perhaps this was the "searching, unanswered question" the *TIME* reviewer detected in *How the West Was Won*'s climactic scene – just before finding the answer in the next sentence: "Then the screen is filled with the silver-blue Pacific, there being no more West to win". Across that ocean lay America's immediate, troubled future; and, far from dying with Tom Doniphon, Jack Burns and Steve Judd, the Western remained a vital contributor to American popular culture and national identity for another decade. During those years the Western would change along with U.S. society, so much so that *How the West Was Won*'s triumphal patriotism would soon appear tragically naïve, its edge of the sunset one of the last flickers of America's innocence. Such a film would have been hopelessly old-fashioned and irrelevant if released in the late 1960s, as some reviewers had dismissed *The Man Who Shot Liberty Valance* in 1962. After all, how could a film like *Liberty Valance* possibly touch the experience of modern audiences? That year's psycho-political thriller *The Manchurian Candidate* notwithstanding, who in the United States in 1962 would ever have believed that a lurking rifleman could alter the course of national destiny?

CHAPTER 7

A Genre in Flux, A Nation in Turmoil: The Vietnamization of the Western in Mid-1960s America

THE murder of John Kennedy shattered the myth of America as a perfectible society. Both the assassination in Dallas and the televised shooting of Lee Harvey Oswald that weekend presented an astonished global audience with two inescapable realities: an irredeemably virulent strain of frontier chauvinism and, of course, the prevalence of firearms in U.S. culture. Writing in the mid-1960s, gun control advocate Carl Bakal emphasized that an average of fifty-five Americans died from gunshot wounds every day.[1] The world's most affluent nation was one of the world's most violent. The essence of America's tragedy is that the nation most dedicated to freedom has frequently confused liberty with licence, and nowhere is this more clearly evident than in the national love affair with guns. The right to bear arms is enshrined in the Second Amendment to the Constitution; it is gravely irresponsible to suggest that gun *control* equals *abolition* of that right. Martin Luther King and Robert Kennedy were slain in 1968. A generation later, the United States is nowhere nearer a comprehensive response to the proliferation of ever more lethal firearms in a society hell-bent on further fragmentation.

Granted, the Western must bear its share of responsibility for the romanticization of a gun culture and the glamorization of violence. A steady diet of films stressing such themes was bound to have a degree of psychological or ideological impact. Yet in the five years after John Kennedy's death, the violence on American screens strained to keep pace with the violence on America's streets. Westerns merely reflected the turmoil which blighted 1960s America.

One romantic/elegiac legacy of Kennedy's assassination is the notion that America has never been the same since. This is heartfelt and symbolic in equal measure: a truth-based example of legend become fact. After all, 1950s America had also faced challenges to the U.S. democratic process, but those rested on issues of national security (fear of communism) and inequality (Civil Rights). In each case, the crisis confronting America's power structure and, by extension, dominant culture was partly one of assimilation. Even native-born communists were deemed unAmerican, whereas non-violent campaigners for racial justice were absorbed within the mainstream of national politics. The American consensus adjudged one group an alien influence while expanding to embrace the other. Yet, significantly, the kernel of that consensus itself remained unaltered. By the mid-1960s, however, polarization threatened to supersede consensus as the grand narrative of American society.

The first major challenge to consensus in the post-Kennedy era came from the right, with the presidential candidacy of Arizona's Republican Senator Barry Goldwater in 1964. A devout Constitutionalist, Goldwater was a scrupulously honourable man who ran for president on a fundamentally erroneous assumption: the notion that large, untapped numbers of the electorate were deeply conservative, disaffected by moderate Republicans' lack of ideological divergence from the Democrats, and thus effectively disenfranchised. Goldwater's candidacy was predicated on the wishful conviction that this untapped grass-roots fervour would be sufficiently strong and pervasive to sweep a genuine conservative into the White House. That illusion perished with the landslide victory of Lyndon Johnson, posturing as the very epitome of consensus.

Goldwater's rhetoric was that of the romantic reactionary, rooted in rugged individualism and Manichaean certitudes – in effect, no different from the morality underlying the films of John Wayne, an ardent Goldwater supporter. The response of the electorate affirmed the limitations of the national myth: life is not a Western movie. Adherence to the inner morality of the artifact could not solve the problems of the era. Yet once the far right had been routed, Lyndon Johnson's centrist coalition soon splintered over escalating racial tension at home and the American government's spiralling commitment to the conflict in Vietnam. Race riots scarred dozens of American cities between 1965 and 1967, while thousands of young men were being drafted to fight in a bloody jungle war, undeclared by Congress, for a country which many of them could not find on a map – and many of them would only be coming home in body bags. Over the next decade, the quagmire of Vietnam would gradually demolish faith in American invincibility. As reports of indiscriminate mayhem filtered back, Lyndon Johnson was denounced as a child-killer. Besides political assassinations, violent racial discord and a costly, brutal Asian war, the nation was rocked by a series of grotesque slayings – stranglings in Boston; a knife-wielding maniac in Chicago; another sniper in Texas; and, hiding out at an old Californian desert ranch once used for making Westerns, a hippie "family" whose murderous rampage in 1969 was designed expressly to ignite all-out racial war. In the 1960s America appeared to be drowning in blood. A culture cannot blithely produce a self-congratulatory pageant similar to *How the West Was Won* in the midst of obscenities, and it was hard to cling to concepts of American Exceptionalism and Manifest Destiny in the age of Manson and My Lai.

Television brought the unfolding horrors of race riots and Vietnam into American homes with the evening's entertainment. Yet, increasingly, television *was* the evening's entertainment, and this cultural centrality continued to take its toll on the fortunes of Hollywood. Between 1963 and 1968, both four-wall and drive-in cinemas declined in number, from 10,300 to 9,700 and from 4,500 to 3,700 respectively, while the average weekly attendance fell from twenty-two to nineteen million.[2] Movie admission prices during those years jumped significantly, from eighty-two cents to one dollar thirty-one cents, which perhaps accounted for the upswing in annual box office receipts, from $904,000,000 to $1,045,000,000; but as percentage of consumer, recreation and spectator expenditures, moviegoing continued to contract, from 0.24% to 0.20%, from 4.1% to 3.1%, and from 53.4% to 46.7% respectively.[3]

The number of Western television series on air between 1963 and 1968 fluctuated but was still substantial – seventeen in 1963, down to eleven the next year, as high as twenty in 1967, thirteen in 1968; thereafter, Western series dropped steadily from the television schedules.[4] By the mid-1970s, Americans were being served a staple diet of cops and robbers instead of cowboys and Indians. This boom in police dramas was partly in response to the success of similar big-screen narratives from the latter half of the 1960s, which themselves were largely a response to the violence, decay and hypocrisy infecting modern American society: The Crowded Sidewalk.

During the 1960s, Westerns remained a bulwark of the major studios' output: a paltry six in 1963, but seventeen in 1964, eighteen in both 1965 and 1966, and nineteen in 1967.[5] Yet, in a rapidly changing social and political culture, the genre had to adapt to the tastes of modern moviegoers. Although many fine Westerns were released during this era, in retrospect the mid-1960s appear as years of flux, as if the genre were unsure of its direction. In Westerns, too, patriotic certainties were on the wane – even among the old masters. John Ford made his last Western in 1964. *Cheyenne Autumn* (Warner Brothers) was a well-intentioned if sluggish epic of atonement for all the red men Ford had killed on screen. That same year Raoul Walsh, who had glorified Custer in *They Died With Their Boots On* (1941), bowed out with another cavalry and Indians saga for Warners, *A Distant Trumpet*. Significantly, in the wake of the shooting in Dallas, each film ended with bloodshed averted. Veteran critic Bosley Crowther blasted *A Distant Trumpet* as "a deadly bore", but termed Ford's film "a stark and eye-opening symbolization of a shameful tendency that has prevailed in our national life – the tendency to be unjust and heartless to weaker peoples who get in the way of manifest destiny".[6] Other reviewers were far cooler. "*Cheyenne Autumn* has everything it takes to make a great western epic, except greatness", proclaimed *TIME*, suggesting Ford perhaps "feels alien to Indians who don't come over the hill in war paint".[7] Under the unkind yet accurate heading "No Ford in Our Future", Stanley Kauffmann rated it "a pallid and straitened version of the best Ford, with no new visual ideas and ... fumbling use of the old ones[.] ... The acting is bad, the dialogue trite and predictable, the pace funereal, the structure fragmented, the climaxes puny."[8] Certainly, *Cheyenne Autumn* is not Ford's greatest achievement; and by far the gravest error is the James Stewart/Dodge City interlude. This vignette might have worked wonderfully in John Sturges's comic epic *The Hallelujah Trail* (1965) – the episode in itself is hilarious; but it irreparably violates the entire tone of an otherwise solemn narrative. Ford's habit of juxtaposing high tragedy and low, knock-about comedy was frequently among his films' least attractive traits (see the embarrassing antics of Pat Wayne in *The Searchers* and of O. Z. Whitehead in *The Man Who Shot Liberty Valance*).

Yet in several other respects *Cheyenne Autumn* is a Western of considerable merit. It is clearly a "Civil Rights" Western, which recasts the dispossessed Cheyenne trekking back to their Dakota homeland as nineteenth-century Freedom Marchers; and in this context, the film even evokes the recently slain Kennedy, as Secretary of the Interior Carl Schurz (Edward G. Robinson) gazes wistfully at a portrait of Lincoln and asks the martyred president, "Old friend – what would you do?".[9] Of special interest here is the fact that Ford's last Western contained a trenchant cautionary message for the younger generation on the eve of an era of inter-generational polarization.

In *Cheyenne Autumn* cavalry and Indians each harbour a hot-head eager for war against the other's race. Lieutenant Scott (Patrick Wayne) despises Indians because he lost his father in the Fetterman Massacre.[10]

For Red Shirt (Sal Mineo), hatred of the white man is wholly impersonal, and so more irrational. Scott's animosity toward Indians is rooted in family loyalty, whereas Red Shirt's desire for war is just one component of a dysfunctional, destructive personality: he not only fires the first shot of the conflict but flaunts his semi-incestuous adultery with his chief's youngest wife. Scott recalls Wayne's callow Lieutenant Greenhill in *The Searchers*; Red Shirt's name and costume evoke the identically clad, utterly irreconcilable hostiles of *She Wore a Yellow Ribbon* and *Two Rode Together*. In Ford's Westerns such Indians were beyond pacification, for red is the colour of danger, of unrestrained fury, of blood – and of communism. *Cheyenne Autumn*'s Red Shirt therefore functions, in effect, as a fellow traveller inciting Freedom Marchers to violence.

Both Scott and Red Shirt embody Ford's recurrent misgiving (evident in *Yellow Ribbon* and *The Last Hurrah* (1958)) that the younger generation lack the charismatic moral authority of the old guard. Yet by the end of *Cheyenne Autumn* Scott has matured through experience and hopes for a peaceful settlement of the Cheyenne grievances, while Red Shirt remains intent on war and even attempts to shoot the white negotiators. Scott ceases to perceive his private grudge as a priority, finding contentment within *Autumn*'s embryonic interracial consensus; but Red Shirt is still the sworn enemy of American society, devoid even of a redemptive regard for his own tribe. Scott survives; Red Shirt is shot by the cuckolded chief. The film thus ends with reason triumphing over passion, experience over blinkered ideology. A sense of narrative justice prevails while, like Ford's earlier *Sergeant Rutledge* (1960), still implicitly favouring the white power structure. In both films Ford eulogized America's downtrodden racial minorities, but the centrality of white heroes within these narratives inferred that the plight of Blacks and Indians was essentially a problem for white America to solve.

Despite its liberal intentions, *Cheyenne Autumn* was simply too plodding and old-fashioned to excite mid-1960s moviegoers. The new era demanded a new ethos if the Western were to remain popular with modern audiences. Chivalric Westerns such as *Fort Apache*, *She Wore a Yellow Ribbon* and *Shane* never returned to fashion. Nobility through service or sacrifice had no romantic allure for the "Me Generation". The highest-grossing Western of the mid-1960s was Elliot Silverstein's irreverent spoof *Cat Ballou* (1965), whose happy-go-lucky young outlaws would surely appeal to the emerging counterculture; similarly, in retrospect, Lee Marvin's drunken gunslinger comes over as a dazed remnant of the Beat Generation.[11] Yet, overall, mid-1960s Westerns were characterized by cynicism or pessimism and, increasingly, brutality.

Italian-made Westerns, particularly Sergio Leone's *"Dollar* trilogy", which catapulted Clint Eastwood to international stardom, were possibly the most influential factor in this new development. Leone and Eastwood created a grimy, violent West which eschewed concepts of both American national identity and Manichaean morality. However, American Westerns of the 1950s had already demonstrated a propensity for incidental sadistic violence, elliptically rather than graphically depicted (James Stewart shot through the hand in Anthony Mann's *The Man from Laramie* (1955), John Wayne shooting out a dead Comanche's eyes in Ford's *The Searchers*, Richard Widmark knifed in the hand in Edward Dmytryk's *Warlock*). Moreover, beyond Westerns the trend toward intensified violence in American films of the 1960s was apparent at decade's outset in Stanley Kubrick's *Spartacus* and Alfred Hitchcock's *Psycho*. So, leaving aside the impact of the "Spaghetti Westerns", an upsurge of violence in the homegrown product was probably inevitable. Audiences were now confronted directly with images of sadism which 1950s Westerns had merely inferred (Richard Widmark shooting off William Holden's finger in Dmytryk's *Alvarez Kelly* (1966), Donald Pleasence and "sons" viciously beating, stabbing and searing Charlton Heston in Tom Gries's *Will Penny* (1967)). Even these scenes were surpassed in savagery. Ellipsis was still used, only now this was reserved for grotesque extremes (Dennis Weaver's brains roasted over an Apache fire in Ralph Nelson's *Duel at Diablo*, Steve McQueen's Kiowa mother skinned to death in Henry Hathaway's *Nevada Smith* (both 1966)). The very inclusion of such atrocities in Western narratives illustrates the genre's complicity in accommodating and also in expanding those representations of violence deemed acceptable in mid-1960s American culture. The relationship was essentially symbiotic: brutality on screen reflected but also fostered the climate of violence in American society. In 1967, a year before the socio-cultural flashpoints of My Lai and the assassinations of Martin Luther King and Robert Kennedy, films were probing the nature of extreme violence and the psychology of its perpetrators in Arthur Penn's *Bonnie and Clyde*, Richard Brooks's *In Cold Blood* and Robert Aldrich's *The Dirty Dozen*. In the mid-1960s, violence became ensconced as a high-profile and hugely profitable cinematic theme, a cornerstone rather than a condiment.

Government-sanctioned violence in the escalating commitment to Vietnam lay at the heart of America's tumult. That conflict helped shape the contours of the Western in the mid-1960s. The town Western was a major casualty. In the 1930s and 1940s, the town Western had been a vehicle for patriotic celebration. The 1950s turned such idealized images of Main Street upside down. In the 1960s, the town Western lost its pre-eminence. As such, odyssey narratives attained even greater prominence within the genre as the ideal of community fragmented both on and off the screen. The town Western's principal concern during the 1950s had been the exigencies of U.S. *domestic* politics and society. During the 1960s, however, the Western focused increasingly on frontier parallels of the war in Vietnam. Town Westerns still appeared in the 1960s, but their cumulative ideological import diminished. Towns remained convenient settings for television series, A. C. Lyles's features for Paramount, certain indulgent star vehicles (Howard Hawks's *El Dorado* (1967), Burt Kennedy's *Support Your Local Sheriff* (1968)) and excessively downbeat melodramas (Kennedy's *Welcome to Hard Times* (a.k.a. *Killer on a Horse*, 1967), Vincent McEveety's *Firecreek* (1968)). Yet even John Sturges's *Hour of the Gun* (1967), a Wyatt Earp film, could not resist a foray into Mexico. The town Western, a mirror for 1950s America, declined in the 1960s, becoming a victim of the genre's Vietnamization.

As Vietnam assumed major significance, big-budget Westerns tended to highlight American military action against Indians (Sam Peckinpah's *Major Dundee*, Arnold Laven's *The Glory Guys* (both 1965), Robert Siodmak's Cinerama epic *Custer of the West* (1968)) or adventurism in Mexico (Gordon Douglas's *Rio Conchos* (1964), Richard Brooks's *The Professionals* (1966), Buzz Kulik's *Villa Rides!*, Tom Gries's *100 Rifles* and Andrew V. McLaglen's *Bandolero!* (all 1968), the second and third in *The Magnificent Seven* series (1966 and 1969), George Roy Hill's *Butch Cassidy and the Sundance Kid*, McLaglen's *The Undefeated* and, towering over its competitors in both vision and violence, Peckinpah's *The Wild Bunch* (all 1969)).[12]

By far the most ambitious of the era's cavalry and Indians sagas was *Major Dundee*. Amos Charles Dundee (Charlton Heston) is a Southernborn Union officer whose independent action at Gettysburg has earned the displeasure of the Washington brass, resulting in his assignment to the New Mexico territory as the commandant of a prison for Confederate soldiers. Late in 1864, after Apache chieftain Sierra Charriba (Michael Pate) and his warriors raid a neighbouring ranch and seize three small boys, Dundee calls for Confederate volunteers to join his expedition to retrieve the children – an expedition which will lead them over the border into Mexico and, eventually, into conflict with the Emperor Maximilian's French lancers.

Major Dundee is a handsome, fascinating, extremely complex Western, but it is ultimately too incoherent to be an exemplar of the genre.

Granted, *Major Dundee* was hampered by tortuous production problems, and the movie which Columbia released was not the penetrating saga Peckinpah had crafted.[13] Charlton Heston identified *Dundee*'s crucial problem even before filming started when he wrote, "We still haven't isolated exactly what this picture's *about*"; and his verdict on the finished product was equally astute: "the whole thing is somehow diffuse. The story is as it always was, too complicated. ... Looking back, I think we all wanted to make a different sort of film. Columbia wanted a cowboy and Indian story, I wanted a film that dealt with the basic issue of the Civil War, and Sam ... wanted the film he later got to make. Very few directors get two chances to make the same film. Sam did and the second time around, it turned out very well. It was called *The Wild Bunch*."[14]

Yet *Major Dundee* is far more than simply a dry run for *The Wild Bunch*. Above all, *Dundee* is a critique of both individual and imperial hubris, centring on a proud, wrong-headed authoritarian whose single-minded pursuit of the Apache provokes an international confrontation. Another Columbia release of 1965, James B. Harris's *The Bedford Incident*, starred Richard Widmark as an autocratic submarine commander whose dogged pursuit of a Soviet vessel accidentally triggers nuclear annihilation. Both Dundee and Widmark's Captain Finlander are unstable, obsessive line officers whose zeal, coupled with a *de facto* enjoyment of absolute power, goads them into exceeding their authority with tragic consequences. Ironically, *Major Dundee* preceded actual events. Though released in 1965, Peckinpah finished filming on April 30 1964, exactly three months before the Gulf of Tonkin incident inflamed American opinion and enlarged the commitment to win in Vietnam.

Furthermore, Dundee is also essentially a puritan, and his rhetoric is that of a righteous, vengeful patriarch: "I intend to smite the wicked, not save the heathen"; of his old friend, Confederate Captain Benjamin Tyreen (Richard Harris), now his sworn enemy: "He is corrupt, but I will save him"; of the men under his command: "I'm concerned with how they fight, not how they feel about me".[15]

Dundee's expeditionary force is emphatically heterogeneous. The film's most Fordian moment depicts the outfit leaving Fort Benlin: the Confederates sing "Dixie", the Union troopers sing "The Battle Hymn of the Republic", and assorted civilians sing "My Darling Clementine". Dundee's command is also racially and ethnically diverse, featuring Black Union soldiers, a Mexican sergeant, a Christian Apache, a preacher of Nordic extraction, an Irish immigrant leading the Confederate contingent. Captain Tyreen serves as Dundee's lieutenant against

Charriba. Most of all, however, he serves as Dundee's conscience. Cashiered out of the U.S. army prior to the Civil War after killing a fellow officer in a duel, Tyreen remains bitter toward Dundee, whose casting vote sealed the court's decision. Tyreen has promised Dundee he and his men will serve "until the Apache is taken or destroyed", after which he aims to lead his troops home to the South.[16] As much a cavalier as Dundee is a puritan, Tyreen is the film's centre of moral authority, often pitted directly against Dundee's charismatic/martial/ political authority. Yet, far from being the chief hope of mutineers, Tyreen is the best man in Dundee's command. Twice Dundee's unit threatens to degenerate into internecine violence. On each occasion, it is Tyreen who defuses a potentially explosive situation. When the Black trooper Aesop (Brock Peters) is insulted by the Southern racist Jimmy Lee Benteen (John Davis Chandler), Dundee remains impassive and even prevents another Union officer (Jim Hutton) from intervening. At this juncture Preacher Dahlstrom (R. G. Armstrong) steps in to give Benteen a thorough beating, but it is Tyreen who heals the breach with his quiet, dignified words to Aesop. The second time, when Dundee resolves to execute a Confederate deserter, Tyreen himself kills the man – the only way to preserve authority *and* hold Dundee's command together. In the climactic battle against French lancers, Tyreen rescues the American flag he had earlier damned and, mortally wounded, charges headlong into the midst of French reinforcements, thus allowing Dundee and his depleted troop to cross the Rio Grande and re-enter the United States.

Not content to be simply a cavalry and Indians narrative or a tale of American adventurers in Mexico, *Dundee* incorporates elements of both. As such, Peckinpah's film is top-heavy with political symbolism – and racially schizophrenic symbolism at that. An uneven mixture of pursuit drama and liberation saga, *Major Dundee* recasts the communist guerrillas of North Vietnam as *Apaches*, but its equivalent of the South Vietnamese are the *Mexican* villagers oppressed by the *French* – whose failure in Indochina precipitated American involvement there. Even though complexity may obscure the precise meaning, Peckinpah's intent to send a message is quite clear. The three abducted boys are retrieved after only forty-five minutes of screen time. Having dispensed with this narrative pretext, Amos Charles Dundee and David Samuel Peckinpah devote themselves to their respective obsessive quests. Dundee wishes to destroy Charriba once and for all, and thus restore himself to favour with his superiors in Washington. In the process, he provokes an international incident and gets a good number of his men killed. Peckinpah's epic chronicle of violence and hubris never reached the screen in the form he had envisaged. Columbia cut over forty minutes from *Dundee* before its release, the film flopped ignominiously at the box office, grossing only $1,600,000 within a year, and Peckinpah's career nose-dived – until 1969 and the film which would catapult him to new fame and notoriety.[17]

Critical reception was mixed. Rating the film "Excellent", the *Motion Picture Herald* proclaimed: "The production is big, strong, colorful, swift, violent in emotion and in action, realistic and completely credible."[18] Stanley Kauffmann of *The New Republic* thought the script "begins traditionally and therefore well. Later, when the troop has pursued the Apaches into Mexico and the authors feel that romance is overdue, the story gets wobbly and slow, and only belatedly recovers."[19] Kauffmann found Dundee's affair with a gorgeous Austrian widow (Senta Berger) an unlikely plot development, and observed that the Major's subsequent descent into drunkenness and self-pity "seems to have been filmed and retained by mistake"; nevertheless, his overall verdict was favourable: "most of the picture is dashingly done, with that always appealing combination of realistic detail and romantic sweep".[20]

Eugene Archer's lengthy review for the *New York Times* took a middle line, praising *and* criticizing Peckinpah's epic:

> *Major Dundee* has an interesting cast, a superior visual texture, unexpected bits of character revelation and a choppy continuity that finally negates its impact.
>
> ... This particular West is an ugly place, and the director's camera searches intractably for its grimmest aspects.
>
> ... [Peckinpah's] viewpoint may be a little too pessimistic, but his realistic method is a welcome departure for a Western adventure. Its drawbacks only emerge when the script veers into more conventional regions.
>
> ... Heston is solidly effective, as a Western hero ought to be. ... The intrusion of an alien love interest plays havoc with the realistic context, and Mr. Harris's role, as a Confederate prisoner who joins the major's regiment only to threaten a personal vendetta at the end of the quest, is merely another contrived bow to commercial clichés. Nothing could clash more stridently with Mr. Peckinpah's naturalistic approach.
>
> ... [S]ome choppy editing abruptly disposes of whole characters, leaving several plot lines dangling. By provoking more curiosity than it satisfies, *Major Dundee* ends as a big, lopsided melodrama, pleasant to watch but hardly a challenge to the eminence of the great Western folk director, John Ford.
>
> ... Action abounds, and the pace is lively. The outdoor vistas are better

than the intimate scenes, ... but Mr. Peckinpah does have an eye. He has a lot to learn, but his education should be worth paying for.[21]

TIME suggested the real key to the film was Heston's pre-established screen persona: "the writers of this long-winded, quasi-Biblical western apparently had fun filling their script with reminders that the star has previously played such roles as Ben-Hur, Moses and John the Baptist. With Old Testament wrath, he pursues Chief Sierra Charriba through the wilderness in A.D. 1865. But once Heston gets on Mexican soil, Director Sam Peckinpah ... lets *Dundee* ramble so freely that the Apaches are soon lost in subplots".[22] *Variety* was even more forthright: "Somewhere ... the central premise was sidetracked and a maze of little-meaning action substituted. What started out as a straight story-line (or at least, idea) ... devolves into a series of sub-plots and tedious, poorly-edited footage in which much of the continuity is lost."[23] One of the most damning notices of all, however, was *The Hollywood Reporter*'s: "*Major Dundee* is an ambitious effort with lavish action and spectacle, interesting characters, good acting. But something has gone wrong. It seldom happens so completely, but it has here. The film is stuck together with almost no continuity, so the spectator eventually has only the dimmest notion what is going on, and finally no notion and no interest. Character changes and development occur without explanation. Action has no motive or background. The Jerry Bresler production for Columbia is a bewildering, exasperating picture. Not in memory has a major film been such a confusing experience. Sam Peckinpah directed."[24]

The final three words clearly imply where the blame should lie, but blame is not the issue here. Simply from an aesthetic viewpoint, *Major Dundee* is an uneven film, with performances ranging from excellent (Heston, Harris, James Coburn's grizzly scout Sam Potts) to embarrassingly bad (Jim Hutton and Michael Anderson, Jr, consistently as poor as Ford's worst low-comedy relief). Furthermore, Dundee's vertiginous collapse into boozy debauchery is implausibly sudden for this starchy, puritanical autocrat. It is as if Henry Fonda's immaculate gunfighter from *Warlock* had transformed overnight into Dean Martin's pathetic drunkard from *Rio Bravo*. Whether betrayed by poor scripting or by excessive cutting, the true import of Peckinpah's truncated epic remains in its intent rather than its impact.

If Heston's Dundee is essentially as racist as his Indian-hating scout in *Arrowhead* (1953), this motivation is not fully developed. In genre terms, however, the film is successful as a gritty revision of Ford's cavalry trilogy. I suggested in an earlier chapter that *Fort Apache*, in focusing on a Custer-type martinet, was concerned with the responsibility of command; in *She Wore a Yellow Ribbon* the focus shifted to the gallant line officer; whereas much of *Rio Grande* dwelt on the enlisted men. *Major Dundee*'s emphasis on an illegal raid across the Mexican border recalls *Rio Grande*, yet *Dundee* reworks *Rio Grande* from the commander's viewpoint. Peckinpah's script for another 1965 cavalry versus Indians film, *The Glory Guys*, with its theme of raw recruits facing almost certain death for the greater glory of an egotistic general, has its own resonance for draftees in the Vietnam era. Thus *The Glory Guys* reworks *Fort Apache*, but from the viewpoints of a line officer and the enlisted men.

Major Dundee's command divided against itself is prophetic of the military intervention which was about to polarize American society, but even on the issue of war itself the film has no explicit ideological message. Neither pro-war nor anti-war, *Major Dundee* falls between two stools and, ultimately, is unsatisfying. Yet in its own oblique way it attempts to offer some comment on American hubris on the imperial stage, on U.S. vulnerability in the face of myriad small enemies around the globe and on the tragic futility of trying to wage war against an invisible, indigenous foe. The first arises after Dundee's men have fired on the French garrison and distributed food to the starving Mexicans. The grateful villagers throw a fiesta, and someone has painted "Viva Dundee" on a wall. Gesturing to this sign, Tyreen remarks, "You haven't got the temperament to be a liberator, Amos"; Dundee, partly redeemer, partly in need of redemption, responds with a self-assured "I *don't*?"[25]

American vulnerability in a hostile world is briefly highlighted in an exchange between Dundee and the bugler, Tim Ryan (Anderson) after the latter has killed Sierra Charriba:

RYAN: He looks so small now.
DUNDEE: He was big enough, son.[26]

That Ryan, not Dundee, kills Charriba itself de-emphasizes Dundee's heroic status. Yet, as diarist and narrator, Ryan has the most important line in the film when he wonders, "How can we catch the wind, or destroy an enemy we never see?"[27] In spring 1964 this was merely a poetic conundrum in an ambitious Western. A decade later, that unanswered question had wrought tragedy throughout the United States. Now those thirteen words would be appropriate in Washington, inscribed on black marble, beside the names of over 58,000 Americans, killed in Vietnam.

Major Dundee and Andrew V. McLaglen's *Shenandoah* were both released in spring 1965, coinciding with the centennial of the end of the Civil War, and this conflict, too, could be adapted to absorb contemporary misgivings about Vietnam. *Shenandoah*, beneath its churchy, right-wing platitudes and its distinction as the weepiest Western ever made, is profoundly pacifist. In *Journey to Shiloh* (1968) seven young Texans leave home to join the Confederate army, only to learn – at fatal cost to six – that war is not the glorious romp they had envisaged (just as Union recruit George Peppard had discovered at the same battle in *How the West Was Won*). However, besides cavalry and Indian sagas, the Western backdrop most suited to encode parallels of the Vietnam War was Mexico.

The 1960s began with an idealistic southward odyssey, John Sturges's *The Magnificent Seven*. The decade ended in the blood-drenched brutality of another Americans-in-Mexico Western, Sam Peckinpah's *The Wild Bunch*. The greatest commercial success in this subgenre, however, was Richard Brooks's *The Professionals* (Columbia, 1966), both temporally and thematically the halfway house between the altruism of the Seven and the harsh nihilism of the Bunch. Despite the *Dundee* débâcle, Columbia reaped huge dividends from the Western in the mid-1960s, releasing the two biggest money-makers of that era (the other being *Cat Ballou*). *The Professionals* grossed $8,800,000, ranking after inflation-adjustment in 1981 as the twentieth most successful Western of all time.[28]

The plot of *The Professionals* may be summarized concisely: boys are hired to rescue girl from bandit, boys discover girl loves bandit, boys give girl back to bandit. The film's appeal lay in its prestigious cast. As the four mercenaries, Brooks cast Burt Lancaster (at his most roguish), Lee Marvin (as the group's honour-bound leader), Robert Ryan (wasted in a colourless, thankless role) and Woody Strode (who, as a tracker and marksman with bow and arrow, is in effect presented as a Black Chingachgook). Ralph Bellamy featured as an American railroad tycoon whose beautiful young Mexican wife (Claudia Cardinale) has been kidnapped by a revolutionary (Jack Palance). In fact, the wife and the bandit have been lovers since long before her marriage, and she has connived in her own abduction to finance revolutionary activities with the ransom money. Lancaster and Marvin, themselves veterans of the Mexican struggle, send wife and bandit back over the border in a buggy at movie's end just as *Stagecoach*'s doctor and lawman sent Ringo and Dallas off to freedom south of the Rio Grande twenty-seven years earlier. In *The Professionals*, however, the escaping lovers are not merely saved from the blessings of civilization; they are also spared from the curses of corporate capitalism.

The Professionals was a Richard Brooks film with a Robert Aldrich cast (Lancaster, Marvin, Ryan, Palance). Its men-on-a-dangerous-mission scenario clearly recalls Columbia's previous heavyweight money-spinners *The Bridge on the River Kwai* (1957) and *The Guns of Navarone* (1961). One scene between Lancaster and his dying ex-lover (Marie Gomez), a busty revolutionary he has been forced to shoot, evokes nothing so much as the climax of *Duel in the Sun*. Yet, besides kinship to earlier box office champions, *The Professionals* proved hugely entertaining in its own right, and most of the critics responded enthusiastically.

The Hollywood Reporter hailed *The Professionals* as "a free-swinging, romance and adventure film that combines lush and lavish production values on a grand scale with intimate character portraits and a lusty sense of humor".[29] *Variety* shrewdly recognized the essence of Woody Strode's character as "Negro-Indian", and noted: "Exciting explosive sequences, good overall pacing and acting overcome a sometimes thin script. ... Undertones of the inevitable disenchantment of both idealists and freebooters, plus pithy observations on human nature, are interpolated into scripting. But emphasis is on action, mixed with adroit amounts of broad comedy."[30] The *Motion Picture Herald* observed: "What *The Professionals* does is to hark back to an honorable tradition in moviemaking that has become rare: The straightaway, uncomplicated action film that one can relax and enjoy without strain."[31] Pauline Kael was complimentary but clinical, comparing *The Professionals* to "the expertise of a cold old whore with practiced hands and no thoughts of love. There's something to be said for this kind of professionalism: the moviemakers know their business and they work us over. ... The buyer gets exactly what he expects and wants and pays for: manipulation for excitement. We use the movie and the movie uses us."[32] *TIME* proclaimed gleefully: "there hasn't been a livelier western whoop-up since Villain Palance bared fang and claw against *Shane*. ... Director Richard Brooks ... sets up a neat surprise or two and shows a marksman's instinct for knowing what to do with all that awesome western scenery – he pumps it full of high-gauge performances, guts, ingenuity, flaming arrows, dynamite and hot lead."[33] Bosley Crowther's *New York Times* review was less indulgent: "The scenery ... is clearly more profound than the script, and the sense of magnitude in the environment more engrossing than that in the plot. ... Take it for noisy adventure ... and you may throb to ... *The Professionals*. But don't expect anything else."[34]

Produced under the auspices of "Pax Enterprises", Brooks's film wore its facile liberal/revolutionary sentiments on its sleeve like insurrectionary *chic.* From the opening shot ("Viva Villa" scrawled on a wall) to the quartet's ultimate defiance of Bellamy's fat-cat plutocrat, *The Professionals* stood firmly on the side of the down-trodden against power-hungry tyrants. The film's intrinsic distrust of existing power structures and the deathless nature of this struggle are best articulated in the following exchange between Ehrengard (Ryan) and Dolworth (Lancaster):

EHRENGARD: What were Americans doing in a Mexican revolution, anyway?

DOLWORTH: Maybe there's only one revolution, since the beginning. The good guys against the bad guys. Question is: who are the good guys?[35]

Yet *The Professionals* also implies that America's years of jaunty interventionism are over, as when Fardan (Marvin) tells Maria (Cardinale), "It's not our war any more", and toward the end, when Dolworth tells Raza (Palance): "The revolution? When the shooting stops and the dead are buried and the politicians take over, it all adds up to one thing – a lost cause."[36] Jesus Raza is effectively a Ho Chi Minh figure, an indigenous revolutionary at whose side Dolworth and Fardan (America) once fought in a more idealistic conflict (World War II). Precisely because these men are so experienced in guerrilla warfare, they realize the disadvantages and dangers of this foreign terrain. There are echoes of Vietnam in Fardan's recognition of Raza's superior resilience and also in Dolworth's "Nothing's harmless in this desert unless it's dead".[37] Even Fardan's advice to Dolworth that he hold off their pursuers by a strategy of "Hit and run, stall and retreat" is more redolent of jungle warfare than of a desert shoot-out.[38]

The Professionals is at heart an exuberant caper movie, in which a group of seasoned tough guys plot to steal a beautiful woman rather than gold bullion. Essentially light-hearted, *The Professionals* was devoid of the tragedy which infused both *The Magnificent Seven* and, later, *The Wild Bunch*. All four heroes survive. The only sacrifice they make is a monetary one, when they each forfeit a $10,000 payment by sending Maria away with Raza. Thus the film inadvertently reinforces an idealized, if flippant, concept of American invincibility. The Professionals kill over two dozen Mexicans so they can seize Maria merely to give her back again, but the futility of their quest is not an issue here. Stated bluntly, there is no tragedy, because none of the Americans die. This foreign intervention is a limited, wholly successful escapade. Nevertheless, the script does have certain subtle allegorical inflections.

On one level *The Professionals* has a contorted Christian/Oedipal sub-text: *Maria* Grant flees from her husband *Joseph* to join her lover, a popular revolutionary named *Jesus*. This may seem overly fanciful, but the film is undeniably a critique of patriarchal oppression. Significantly, Grant is decades older than Maria; she only married him at her dying father's behest – itself an indictment of wrong-headed patriarchal instincts. Furthermore, Maria clearly symbolizes Mexico, whose purity has been sullied and ravaged by greedy foreign capitalists (Grant) but who truly belongs to her native people (Raza). While Ralph Bellamy is adequate as J. W. Grant, how much better the entire film would have been had Brooks dropped Robert Ryan's role and cast *him* as the ruthless yet pathetic railroad magnate.

Maria frankly informs her rescuers of her abiding love for Raza. By 1966 screen standards this is a forthright exposition of female sexuality. Perhaps yielding to racial sensitivities, one of the four is not around to hear these disclosures: Woody Strode's Jake Sharp. The film treats both actor and character in most ambiguous fashion. As the movie opens Strode is billed third, even preceding Burt Lancaster, the production's biggest name.[39] However, Strode was the only one of the seven stars whose name did not appear on publicity posters (nor on posters for Ford's *Sergeant Rutledge* (1960), in which he had portrayed the title role). Within the film itself, Strode's character is dependable but almost deferential, in essence as servile as his role as John Wayne's faithful retainer Pompey in *The Man Who Shot Liberty Valance*. *The Professionals* raises the subject of racial equality at the beginning, simultaneously making a low-key statement and dispensing with the matter to concentrate on the business at hand, and the film does this by showing its heroes doing exactly the same. There is no racial discord within the group. With typical insensitivity, it is Grant who asks Fardan – in Sharp's presence – if he has objections to working with a Negro. Fardan glances away and says nothing, clearly deeming the question unworthy of an intelligent answer. Neither he nor the others ever refer to Sharp's colour. Like them, the man is a Professional. Nothing else counts.

To be accepted as a professional was all a Black man could hope for in mid-1960s Westerns but, in fairness, this was also the apogee of white male experience in the genre. Major Black characters gained acceptance within white America primarily by asserting their physical authority on behalf of the prevailing power structure, hence the heroics of Black troops in *Sergeant Rutledge*, *Rio Conchos* and *Major Dundee*. There were a couple of striking exceptions. Sidney Poitier's ex-soldier turned horse-trader in *Duel at Diablo* is an ambitious, abrasive man chiefly concerned with his own profit. This character is at the centre of several heated exchanges, but at no point does anyone refer to the colour of his skin. Both selfish *and* heroic, he acquits himself through sheer force of personality. In this instance, colour truly does become irrelevant. By contrast, race is very much at the forefront of the dialogue in Sydney Pollack's *The Scalphunters* (1968), which features Ossie Davis's runaway slave using his ingenuity to prove himself equal to Burt Lancaster's inherently supremacist fur-trapper. *The Scalphunters* concluded with Lancaster and Davis sharing the same horse – an explicit image and message of racial cooperation which modern audiences could not fail to grasp. However, this was still essentially a plea for Black acceptance within America's ruling consensus. Confrontational alternatives were effectively marginalized. In Tom Gries's *100 Rifles*, for example, Black star Jim Brown is at once a sheriff and a revolutionary – but the insurrection he spearheads is in Mexico, thus displacing any direct threat to American society.

Two rather backhanded critiques of America's racial record came from white stars cast in non-Caucasian roles (Yul Brynner as the quick-draw Creole of *Invitation to a Gunfighter* (1964), and Paul Newman as an Indian-raised white killed defending the society which despises him in Martin Ritt's *Hombre* (1966)). As before, however, the Western was largely the psychic territory of white males. Now, more than ever, it became the preserve of *mature* white males. Moreover, the ageing process itself became a central theme of the genre in the 1960s.

Gary Cooper had died at age sixty in 1961. Randolph Scott and Joel McCrea had each retired in 1962, bowing out together with Peckinpah's marvellous study of ex-lawmen outliving their time, *Ride the High Country*. John Wayne, Henry Fonda and James Stewart all entered their sixties during that decade and, aged fifty-seven in 1964, Wayne had his first battle with cancer. Burt Lancaster, Kirk Douglas, Gregory Peck, Dean Martin, Glenn Ford, William Holden and Richard Widmark reached their fifties in the 1960s. As the genre's most prominent stars grew older, Westerns inevitably absorbed that fact of life and reshaped it as a narrative theme. By far the finest such film of this era was Tom Gries's *Will Penny* (Paramount, 1967), starring Charlton Heston as an illiterate cowhand past his prime. Like Gregory Peck's notorious Jimmy Ringo in *The Gunfighter*, Will realizes his life has been empty and unfulfilling. Yet his has been an uneventful life of drudgery riding the range, not a chronicle of heroic exploits gone sour and hollow. Will survives torture and torments from a family of trashy frontier degenerates akin to *My Darling Clementine*'s Clantons, *Wagon Master*'s Cleggs and

Ride the High Country's Hammonds, but ultimately he cannot overcome his own limitations and make a life with the woman he has grown to love (Joan Hackett). Heston's decent, lonely Will has none of the arrogance the actor purposely brought to his portrayals of the racist Ed Bannon in *Arrowhead*, aggressive Steve Leech in *The Big Country* and the high and mighty Major Dundee. A gentle, simple man, Will sums up his prosaic life as "a case o' too soon old and too late smart".[40] *Duel in the Sun* ends with its tempestuous lovers dying together triumphantly; it is essentially a happy ending. *Will Penny* closes with its lovers alive but parting forever – and there are few more heartbreaking endings in the history of cinema.

Nevertheless, many star Westerns of the mid-1960s remained largely superficial entertainments. John Wayne's *oeuvre* merits particular attention here. Between two highly political forays into directing (*The Alamo* (1960) and *The Green Berets* (1968)), aside from *The Man Who Shot Liberty Valance*, virtually Wayne's whole output for this troubled era eschewed significant social commentary. In 1959 Wayne had headed the cast of Howard Hawks's *Rio Bravo*, the director's paradigm paean to professionalism in a tightknit male group. Throughout the 1960s and early 1970s, Wayne's films, Westerns and non-Westerns, reprised *Rio Bravo*'s basic character structure with almost religious frequency, and with only minor subtle variations and adjustments: John Wayne; second lead (often another formidable star, e.g., Dean Martin, Robert Mitchum, Kirk Douglas); eager youth; crusty old-timer. In addition, *Rio Bravo*'s elementary conflict of Wayne and pals versus a ruthless land baron recurred in five films within six years (*The Sons of Katie Elder* (1965), *El Dorado* and *The War Wagon* (both 1967), *Chisum* and *Rio Lobo* (both 1970)). Even *The Green Berets*, Wayne's fervent defence of American intervention in Vietnam, was in reality little more than an updated cavalry epic in jungle garb, with Wayne's heroic Americans protecting tame Indians from their savage neighbours.[41] This knee-jerk dependence on tried and tested movie formulae was commercially safe, politically conservative and artistically unadventurous. While Wayne's 1960s Westerns were spectacular entertainment in their own right, with hindsight they suggest his reluctance to engage with fundamental cultural shifts and an ever-spiralling violence all around him in American film and American society. Instead, prior to grisly bursts of blood-letting in *True Grit* (1969), *Big Jake* (1971) and *The Cowboys* (1972), John Wayne was the foremost symbol of a glamorized West in a sanitized world. His benevolent superhuman cowboy dealt devastating blows which left no bruises, villains died quickly and cleanly, and heroes triumphed unequivocally.

Even more than Barry Goldwater, Wayne was a monument of Manichaean certitude in an age of ambiguity.

John Wayne Westerns were usually good box office during the 1960s. Yet, overall, the genre remained dynamic and profitable by incorporating vital thematic and stylistic innovations. Not even a trio of top Western stars (Kirk Douglas, Robert Mitchum and Richard Widmark) could rescue Andrew V. McLaglen's *The Way West* (1967) from box office oblivion. Douglas was magnificent as the autocratic visionary (worthy to rank with Henry Fonda's Blaisedell in *Warlock* and Charlton Heston's Major Dundee), the film itself an informal reworking of *The Ten Commandments*; but the final product was, despite its soap opera excesses, simply too traditional – too *celebratory* – to find favour with 1967 audiences.[42]

If the patriotic platitudes of *The Way West* already seemed outmoded in 1967, they were utterly obliterated by the events of 1968. Early that year, the Tet Offensive rocked the nation. From that point on, America's previously ever-imminent victory in South Vietnam receded further and further. In mid-March of the year *The Green Berets* was released, American troops killed several hundred inhabitants of a Vietnamese hamlet known as My Lai, and this atrocity remained secret for a year. On April 4 1968 an assassin cut down Martin Luther King. Two months later another bullet claimed the life of Robert Kennedy. That August, mayhem erupted between policemen and anti-war demonstrators in Chicago, right outside the Democratic National Convention.

Little wonder, then, that a genre buttressed by assumptions of American invincibility, innate righteousness and God-guided national destiny lost its appeal as those cherished concepts turned to bile on the nightly news. Whereas 1969 was a watershed year for the Western, 1968 was a pivotal one and was the last year in which traditional-style Westerns such as *Firecreek* and Henry Hathaway's *5 Card Stud* were viable entertainments. Even in 1968 these were threadbare narratives whose principal value lay in their star teamings (James Stewart and Henry Fonda, and Dean Martin and Robert Mitchum respectively). In 1969 the most noteworthy Westerns were by turns elegiac, parodic and, in the most significant of all, supremely, awesomely violent.

Yet one Western of 1968 summed up various mid-1960s trends of the genre and, to a degree, preceded the most controversial Western ever made. In *Shenandoah*, Andrew V. McLaglen examined America's involvement in Vietnam obliquely, by foregrounding a family who wished to remain aloof from national conflict. In *The Way West* he marginalized the issue completely. However, in *Bandolero!* (20th Century-Fox, 1968), McLaglen's representation of carnage had terrifying and unwittingly ironic resonance for 1968 America. *Bandolero!* is a "house divided" tragedy as well as an Americans-in-Mexico Western. In the Texan border town of Val Verde in 1867, Dee Bishop (Dean Martin) and his associates await the noose for robbery and murder. The hangman is waylaid by a stranger (James Stewart), who turns out to be Dee's elder brother, Mace. Posing as the hangman, Mace springs Dee and his gang. While lawman July Johnson (George Kennedy) and his posse pursue the escaping prisoners, Mace calmly walks into the town bank and instructs the teller to fill his saddlebag with cash. When Mace meets up with Dee's gang he finds they have seized a hostage, Maria Stoner (Raquel Welch), the lovely Mexican widow of a rancher killed in the gang's abortive hold-up. The Bishop brothers had fought on opposite sides during the Civil War – Mace with Sherman, Dee with Quantrill. Mace is disgusted with the loathsome members of Dee's gang and begins to persuade his brother to quit outlawry for a new life on a ranch in Montana, without mentioning he has stolen the money which will finance this dream. With both their parents dead, each is now the only family the other has. The idea has added appeal for Dee as he and Maria are falling in love, and she would be a part of that new future.

Maria has another admirer – the solid, colourless Sheriff Johnson (intriguingly, sharing his surname with the incumbent presidents of both 1867 and 1968). Johnson's posse has crossed the border in dogged pursuit, where even greater danger lurks. They have unwittingly entered *bandolero* country, where several of the posse fall prey to the vicious machete-wielding bandits who pounce unseen from the rocks, the fiercest force of nature and a blood-curdling embodiment of the treacherous savagery of Vietnam's jungle warfare (*Bandolero!* was scripted by James Lee Barrett, also screenwriter for *The Green Berets*). Eventually, Johnson's posse captures the Bishop gang in a Mexican village; but when *bandoleros* attack, the outlaws and Johnson's men join forces. In the ensuing battle most of the posse and all of the outlaws perish – including Dee and Mace. *Bandolero!* ends with Maria and Johnson heading back to Texas, the film's last image the graves of the Bishops, divided by war but united in death. Law and order, a 1968 election issue, triumphed in McLaglen's 1968 Western. There is no place for exuberant freebooters in Johnson's America, either July's or Lyndon's.

Bandolero! grossed $5,500,000, actually raking in $200,000 more than *The Wild Bunch* would gross in chronicling the bloody demise of another Bishop gang a year later.[43] The theme of Americans burying their differences and closing ranks to stave off a lethal foreign threat had a long pedigree. Yet the star teaming, the Mexican setting, the tragic motif of time running out for the two brothers and, of course, the stylized violence all establish *Bandolero!* as a paradigm mid-1960s Western. The plot resolution is acutely traditional – the outlaws die, the sheriff gets the girl. Yet the casting here certainly inverted audience expectations. Any unsuspecting Western buff glancing at the names and the order of billing (Stewart, Martin, Welch, Kennedy) on the way in would have happily put money on Stewart and Martin surviving and long-time screen heavy Kennedy biting the dust. Thus *Bandolero!* continually subverts conventions by casting two of the era's most congenial stars as desperadoes, then investing these villains with both charisma and sympathy, in contrast to the stolid sheriff. Finally, with the audience now rooting for Mace and Dee, *Bandolero!* kills them off.

Beneath the "sheriff gets the girl" resolution, the ending is unremittingly bleak. Clearly, Maria does not love Johnson. Clearly, she never will. It is impossible to believe these two will live happily ever after together. The film's true message and its inadvertent historic irony lie in that final close-up of the brothers' graves, side by side. In American cinema, the family has frequently been represented as the nation in microcosm. As such, *Bandolero!* ends with the death of the American family and, by extension, the death of the American Dream. Critics discerned no special merit in *Bandolero! TIME* observed: "the giddyap! gets mired in a lot of giddy yapping".[44] The great irony here lies in the timing of *Bandolero!*'s release. It was reviewed in *The Hollywood Reporter* on Monday June 3 1968 and in *Variety* on Wednesday June 5 1968. On the day between those reviews, Senator Robert Kennedy had won the Democratic primary in California, and Sirhan Sirhan had taken aim. *Bandolero!* did not merely, as did many Westerns, reflect events in American society. Its bleak ending, with two brothers buried in a makeshift cemetery in Mexico, anticipated the grim reality of Arlington, where another pair of brothers would lie buried – and how, for millions, one particular American dream truly was over.

Less than three weeks after the killing of Robert Kennedy, lamenting the national love affair with guns, *TIME* proclaimed: "All too widely, the country is regarded as a blood-drenched, continent-wide shooting range[.] ... The image, of course, is wildly overblown, but America's own mythmakers are largely to blame. In U.S. folklore, nothing has been more romanticized than guns and the larger-than-life men who wielded them. From the nation's beginnings, in fact and fiction, the gun has been provider and protector."[45] Yet as the 1960s drew to a close the gun and the genre which glorified it retained their allure for many Americans. The nation had been sickened by the events of that troubled decade, but neither on the streets nor on the screens was the intensity of violence about to abate. Indeed, within the Western in particular, one stunning, audacious film exploded with the rawest, most graphic violence yet seen in a mainstream American film, shocking both moviegoers and critics as it rejoiced in its own blood-bath.

CHAPTER 8

Receding Frontiers, Narrowing Options: *The Wild Bunch* and the Western in Richard Nixon's America

As the 1960s drew to a close, Americans could retain little of the optimism with which they had greeted that decade. Concepts of special national destiny had become redundant in the welter of assassinations, race riots and the entire extravagant folly of Vietnam. In the decade which saw three of liberal America's foremost spokesmen gunned down, the accession of Richard Nixon perhaps assumed an aura of banal inevitability. Lofty rhetoric and idealistic striving had all come to nothing. The 1960s had begun as an era abundant in hope and promise, only to end with Richard Nixon, the *bête noire* of American liberals, ostensibly the ultimate political victor.

In retrospect, 1960s America now appears heavily coated in Manichaean mythology. John Kennedy is cast as the great white hope, the latter-day Lincoln who would assuredly have reshaped America as a Utopia of interracial harmony while sidestepping the quagmire of Vietnam; Lyndon Johnson is the vulgar usurper who embroiled his country in that tragic, divisive and utterly wasteful conflict; and Richard Nixon is the agent of darkness, vanquished by the great white hope at the dawn of a happy age, thereafter biding his time in surly exile, girding himself for his return and the triumph of reactionary malevolence. So goes the legend. No matter that Kennedy was largely a slick, image-conscious foreign policy adventurer who had rated Civil Rights relatively low on his list of political priorities. No matter that Johnson wanted to make great headway in Civil Rights, but instead got sidetracked in Vietnam. The shots fired in Dallas have sanctified the legend forever.

As of January 1969, the dark side of the legend sat in the White House. Richard Nixon was in himself a rather colourless man who nevertheless prompted intemperate political passions. Revered by conservatives as the embodiment of Middle America's aspirations, he had been vehemently reviled by liberals as an unscrupulous and inherently mendacious witch-hunter ever since the Alger Hiss case catapulted him to nationwide prominence in 1949. Beneath the gloss of 1968's "New Nixon", his detractors claimed, lurked a crooked, vindictive, power-hungry charlatan. Watergate would only confirm such eager, cherished suspicions.

Middle America's most unprepossessing statesman, Nixon was essentially ill-suited to preside over U.S. society during the late 1960s and early 1970s. In this era of continual cultural fragmentation, particularly generational polarization, Nixon's presence in the White House may have seemed like a cruel joke. A stolid patriarch in the age of permissiveness, Richard Nixon was resolutely out of touch and out of sympathy with the most vocal and most visible sectors of American youth: the anti-war activists, the hippies, the celebrants of sex, drugs and rock and roll.

By the late 1960s, the counterculture had made significant inroads on American cinema fare. Films such as *Easy Rider, Bob & Carol & Ted & Alice* and *Alice's Restaurant* (all 1969) defied traditional American sensibilities, but unalloyed adherence to tradition was no longer a viable priority in Hollywood. Movies naturally remained geared toward profitability and, in pursuit of that paramount objective, remained responsive to any subtle shifts in American culture. At *operational* level, the fortunes of movie theatres fluctuated during the Nixon years. In 1969, there were 9,800 four-wall cinemas and 3,700 drive-ins; during the next four years four-wall cinemas gradually rose to 10,900 while drive-ins consistently numbered 3,800, but by 1974 these figures had fallen to 9,600 and 3,500 respectively.[1] Weekly attendance also fluctuated, from eighteen million in 1969 down to sixteen million in 1971 then back up to nineteen million by 1974, while movie admission prices rose from one dollar forty-two cents to one dollar eighty-seven over the same period.[2] Yet for the film *industry* these were boom years. After a sharp decline from 1956 to 1962 and a gradual resurgence since 1963, box office receipts skyrocketed from $1,099,000,000 in 1969 to $1,909,000,000 in 1974.[3] This was not simply a consequence of inflation; in the Nixon era moviegoing's slice of consumer, recreation and spectator expenditure grew from 0.19% to 0.28%, from 3% to 4.1%, and from 48.6% to 54% respectively.[4]

Although Western television series on air declined sharply from twelve to seven between 1969 and 1974, the cinema Western held its own, rising from twenty movies in 1969 to twenty-five in 1972, dropping to sixteen in 1973 and thirteen in 1974.[5] Of these, by far the most significant year for the Western was 1969. Alongside 1939 (year of *Stagecoach* and the beginning of the prewar epic cycle which, together, established the genre's respectability) and 1962 (the end-of-the-frontier melodramas), 1969 ranked as one of the Western's most important years ever. Yet, while the significance of those earlier years each lay in a distinctive thematic and temporal *convergence*, 1969 Westerns were striking in their stylistic *divergence*. The genre had, at heart, become schizophrenic.

Undisputed champion of the traditional Western, John Wayne weighed in with an Oscar-winning role in Henry Hathaway's *True Grit* (Paramount) and Andrew V. McLaglen's *The Undefeated* (20th Century-Fox), scripted by James Lee Barrett (*The Green Berets*, *Bandolero!*). *True Grit* was in no way innovative; it was simply far superior to Wayne's other vehicles of recent years, and it proved he was a first-rate actor. Too often during the 1960s, the Duke had settled for a poor script, the ballast of another big name as co-star, and reliance on his own star construct as "John Wayne". His co-stars in *True Grit* (Glen Campbell and Kim Darby) were not box office draws, but Marguerite Roberts wrote an exciting, literate screenplay based on Charles Portis's tale of a young girl who hires a boozy one-eyed lawman to track her father's murderer, and audiences responded enthusiastically. *True Grit* grossed $14,300,000 on its release; after inflation-adjustment in 1981 it ranked as the thirteenth most successful Western of all time.[6]

The Undefeated was a modest success, grossing $4,000,000, and the film was essentially strong on star teaming (Wayne and Rock Hudson) but undermined by a lacklustre narrative.[7] Set immediately after the Civil War, *The Undefeated* focused on two separate groups of Americans in Mexico: ex-Union colonel Wayne and his friends, herding three thousand horses for the French-backed Maximilian regime, and ex-Confederate colonel Hudson's family and followers, intent on building new lives outside the United States. Hudson's Southerners are captured by Juaristas, who will execute them unless Wayne and his men hand over their horses for the revolutionary cause. Wayne complies, leading to an altercation with French lancers (shades of *Major Dundee*). The film ends with another allusion to *Major Dundee* as the two groups, now merged as one, return to American soil: mirroring the beginning of Dundee's quest, a cowboy plays "Dixie" on the harmonica, then "The Battle Hymn of the Republic" and, finally, "Yankee Doodle" – one tune they can all heartily endorse.

The Undefeated replicated *Bandolero!*'s production team – not only

McLaglen as director and Barrett as screenwriter, but also Robert L. Jacks as producer and the initial story source, Stanley L. Hough. Like *Bandolero!*, *The Undefeated* stressed the need for Americans to bury outworn differences when confronted by foreign adversaries. This time, the heroes survive. As in *Two Flags West* (1950), *The Searchers*, *Run of the Arrow* (1957), *Major Dundee* and, still to appear, Clint Eastwood's *The Outlaw Josey Wales* (1976), unreconstructed Southerners must reconcile themselves to their identity as Americans. James Lee Barrett's script for *The Green Berets* was in effect a John Wayne Western set in Vietnam. Ironically, *The Undefeated* was a Vietnam drama recast as a Wayne Western. One scene has him warn his men: "We got Maximilian on one hand and Juarez on the other and bandits in between. N'on top o' that we're Americans in Mexico, takin' a cavy o' horses to a very unpopular government."[8] Even the ending subtly foreshadows the outcome of the Vietnam conflict: Wayne has no choice but to bow to the Juaristas' demand. There is no total victory for America. *The Hollywood Reporter* noted: "It just may be Wayne's only pro-revolution western."[9]

True Grit and *The Undefeated* were principally celebrations of John Wayne's indestructibility as the superhuman Westerner, unwithered by age. Other veterans of the genre enriched their repertoire by emphasizing their own mortality. A decade after *Warlock*, Henry Fonda and Richard Widmark wrought variations on their roles in Dmytryk's classic. In Sergio Leone's *Once Upon a Time in the West* (Paramount, 1968), Fonda was again a super-fast gunfighter aware that the onset of civilization means the end of his way of life. Yet here he is not a basically decent man but a cold-blooded killer who, in the film's most shocking scene, guns down a small boy. At picture's end Fonda bites the dust, outdrawn by Charles Bronson avenging his brother. "Allen Smithee"'s *Death of a Gunfighter* (Universal, 1969) pitted lawman Widmark against the greed, hypocrisy and corruption of his own citizenry.[10] As in *Warlock*, Widmark's relationship with the townsfolk is adversarial; here the reason is not an outlaw past but his moss-back approach to law enforcement. To a town anticipating an economic bonanza at the dawn of the twentieth century, he is a civic embarrassment, compounded by his affair with the local madam (echoing Gannon's involvement with Lily in *Warlock*). This time, the madam is a Black woman (Lena Horne). When Widmark marries her, it is as though Gary Cooper's beleaguered marshal in *High Noon* had chosen Katy Jurado's worldly Mexican madam rather than wed Grace Kelly's virginal Quaker. *Death of a Gunfighter*, with its long shots of the lawman alone on the street, purposely evokes *High Noon* and, furthermore, develops that scenario to its most treacherous conclusion:

here the townsmen actually assassinate the old throwback on the dusty Main Street. Modern America has murdered its archaic conscience, and an entire society stands guilty.

White America's guilt was also highlighted in that year's *Tell Them Willie Boy Is Here* (Universal), directed by longtime blacklist victim Abraham Polonsky, the saga of a Paiute Indian (Robert Blake) pursued by a white deputy (Robert Redford) in 1909. Polonsky was clearly exalting his own status as outcast, now reworked within a Western framework. He even asserted that *Willie Boy* "isn't a movie about Indians. It's about me."[11] Moreover, beyond the genre, the image of the cowboy came under fire in 1969. John Schlesinger's *Midnight Cowboy* was a modern drama, in which a naïve young Texan arrives in New York hoping to make his name and fortune servicing bored society matrons. The grimy reality of the metropolis does not match the country boy's dream. Instead, just as his only friend in the city had warned him, his cowboy garb renders him prey to the homosexual underworld.

The two most significant Westerns in 1969 were, like *Death of a Gunfighter* and *Tell Them Willie Boy Is Here*, set in the early years of the twentieth century. The significance of George Roy Hill's *Butch Cassidy and the Sundance Kid* (20th Century-Fox), however, lies primarily in its phenomenal commercial success: *Butch* grossed $29,200,000 on release and, following inflation-adjustment in 1981, was the second biggest Western money maker of all time, ranking behind only *Duel in the Sun*.[12] William Goldman's screenplay fused a mythic aura with stylized comedy. Butch (Paul Newman) and Sundance (Robert Redford) resemble Tom Sawyer and Huckleberry Finn grown up and gone south in a glib, joky movie which recast its outlaw heroes as hapless hipsters. The film's light-hearted iconoclasm and good-humoured cynicism caught the mood of late 1960s America. Yet, in a time of ever-growing disaffection over the pervasive influence of corporate power structures and the seemingly interminable involvement in Vietnam, *Butch* romanticized its renunciation of modern America with cool, laid-back irreverence rather than with blood-soaked fervour. Butch and Sundance are essentially innocents abroad, thoroughly appealing rogues who, realizing that American banks and trains are becoming progressively harder to rob, decide to light out for the territory (in their case, Bolivia). However, instead of easy pickings, they find a poor, barren country – and also a language barrier. Right down to the final sepia freeze-frame which mollifies the impact of their deaths, gunned down by the Bolivian army, *Butch Cassidy and the Sundance Kid* is above all a sophisticated comedy of errors in a genre normally given to broad and bucolic humour.

Teaming top male stars in Westerns had been an established practice since the 1950s. In 1968, while reviewing *5 Card Stud* for the *New York Times*, Vincent Canby christened the trend "*La Ronde*, Western-style" but concluded "Buddy System Westerns are somehow basically soft".[13] Yet these were showcases for the older male stars (John Wayne, James Stewart, Henry Fonda, Kirk Douglas, Robert Mitchum, Richard Widmark, Dean Martin and Rock Hudson). *Butch* was not so much a continuation of this trend as the first major "buddy movie" featuring younger American stars – which just *happened* to be a Western. Admittedly, Newman was already a formidable screen presence by 1969. Then only forty-four, he was effectively the grand old man of the new spate of "buddy movies", which ranged far beyond the Western. In truth, *Butch* was more a premature 1970s movie than a summation of the Western in the 1960s. Thematically, it purported to look back. Stylistically, it was contemporary with a vengeance, even down to some truly deplorable scat singing on the soundtrack. As an outlaw fantasy, *Butch* has more in common with *Bonnie and Clyde* and *Easy Rider* than with other Westerns of that era. Butch and Sundance regret their narrowing horizons, but the narrative is only superficially elegiac, ultimately sidestepping tragedy – and we laugh with them even as they die.

Despite *Butch*'s enormous box office success, reviews were mixed. The *Motion Picture Herald* rated it "Excellent", noting: "the film has an offbeat quality that will particularly appeal to the youthful audiences that make up the majority of today's patronage. ... [T]he film has, along with Sam Peckinpah's *The Wild Bunch*, the distinction of giving the western a new lease on life (albeit ... in a much different direction)."[14] While *Variety*'s notice was favourable, its reviewer had detected one subtext which probably was not even intended when he observed: "Butch is an affable, almost gay, individual."[15] Yet later, Joan Mellen's *Big Bad Wolves* (1977) contended *Butch* was indeed a thinly disguised homosexual love story.[16] "*Sundance* Beams With Joy: A Great & Profitable Film", proclaimed *The Hollywood Reporter*, which likened the film's opening to *Citizen Kane* and its conclusion to *The 400 Blows*.[17] However, the same modish cineliteracy which *The Hollywood Reporter* found charming irked *New York Times* critic Vincent Canby, who astutely judged *Butch* a derivative confection, its roots in *Jules and Jim* and *Bonnie and Clyde*: "it might have been very funny if you'd never seen a movie before. However, it is not an original and the movie experience one brings to *Butch Cassidy* diminishes it."[18] He predicted *Butch* would "make a fortune in the mass market with those movie patrons who don't give much of a damn".[19] *TIME* was equally unimpressed, but couched its objections in middlebrow instead of highbrow terms: "Every character, every scene, is marred by the film's double view, which oscillates between sympathy and farce. ... Newman and Robert Redford are afflicted with cinematic schizophrenia. One moment they are sinewy, battered remnants of a discarded tradition. The next they are low comedians whose chaffing relationship – and dialogue – could have been lifted from a Batman and Robin episode."[20] Pauline Kael, in her *New Yorker* review, deemed it "a facetious Western", concluding: "*Butch Cassidy* will probably be a hit[.] ... Yet, hit or no, I think what this picture represents is finished. Butch and Sundance will probably be fine for a TV series, which is what I mean by finished."[21]

Kael was half right. *Butch* was a trendsetting "buddy film" rather than a trendsetting Western, though it did provide the basis for a Western television series, Universal's *Alias Smith and Jones*, broadcast in the early 1970s. Yet, if *Butch*'s style initially seems overly frivolous, it is also covertly critical of America's political and corporate Establishment. When Butch and his gang rob the Union Pacific Flyer, they are temporarily obstructed by a devoted company employee. Butch asks him if he believes the unseen railroad tycoon, E. H. Harriman, would get killed for *him*. Later, when Butch and Sundance are pursued by Harriman's unyielding "Superposse", the duo's plaintive query, "Who *are* those guys?", is actually a quasi-paranoid rumination on the faceless wielders of real power in modern America.[22] Where did these men come from, how did they become so powerful and, ultimately, do they truly represent legitimate authority?

Furthermore, by fleeing to Bolivia, Butch and Sundance not only refuse to adapt to the increasing corporatism of American society, but their deaths serve to warn against adventurism in an alien culture Americans were ill-equipped to comprehend. As innocents abroad, nonconformists, dropouts and casualties of military violence, Butch and Sundance were clearly ideal icons for America's counterculture in the late 1960s.

One scene features a friendly sheriff (Jeff Corey) telling the pair: "You shoulda let yourself get killed a long time ago while you had the chance. ... It's *over*! Don't you get that? Your times is over, and you're gonna die bloody! And all you can do is choose where."[23] It is a powerful speech, almost too powerful for the general tone of *Butch*. Yet it would have belonged utterly and perfectly in the most significant Western of 1969, and of the entire decade – Sam Peckinpah's *The Wild Bunch* (Warner Brothers–Seven Arts).

Earlier, I demonstrated that *Stagecoach* had quickly become accepted as the paradigm of the genre on its release in 1939. In scrutinizing the 1950s I mentioned that *High Noon* and *Shane* were, during that decade, generally adjudged the finest of all Western films, but critical consensus has since eclipsed these in favour of *The Searchers*. I have already rebuked the concept of a "best-ever Western"; nonetheless, the construct persists. So it is as an observer rather than as partisan that I predict *The Wild Bunch* is next in line for this exalted fallacy.

Superficially, Peckinpah's film has much in common with its contemporary, *Butch Cassidy and the Sundance Kid*, even down to the fact that in reality Cassidy's gang was known as "The Wild Bunch". Both films focus on American outlaws who have outlived their time, opening with these outlaws absorbed into "history" by rudimentary media (Butch and Sundance by a silent film, the Bunch by the credit sequences freezing into a semblance of old newsprint). Each begins with the central character reluctantly recognizing banks are no longer easy to rob. Each features not only a train hold-up, but a railroad-sponsored posse who track the outlaws relentlessly, prompting their flight south of the border. Even the names of the railroad tycoons are startlingly similar: Harriman (unseen) in *Butch*, Harrigan (Albert Dekker) in *The Wild Bunch*. Each features a lyrical, idyllic interlude, affording the protagonists brief respite from their ultimately fatal odysseys. Each film stresses the outlaws' incongruity in the twentieth century by foregrounding the artifacts of modern technology, though *Butch* is content to linger on the seductive charms of the bicycle while *The Wild Bunch* pithily targets the railroad's corruptive influence and the destructive impact of airplanes, the automobile and, most lethally, the machine gun. Finally, each film ends with the outlaws massively outnumbered by foreign soldiers but going down fighting regardless.

While the two films shared many narrative similarities and a mutual distrust of America's corporate power structure, they were worlds apart in temper and tone. *Butch* was essentially a "G"-rated idealization of the outlaw myth. *The Wild Bunch* was, by contrast, the most shattering and most savage vision of the West ever put on screen.

The Wild Bunch begins with a group of soldiers riding into the Texan border town of Starbuck. On the outskirts of town, a band of children torture scorpions among a horde of red ants. Inside Starbuck, an outdoor temperance meeting is in session. Atop the building opposite the bank, the haggard Deke Thornton (Robert Ryan) is in reluctant command of a "posse" composed of the most odious frontier trash. These groups are introduced as the opening credits freeze on the screen, the tension building to a crescendo till the soldiers enter the bank and, suddenly, we realize they are not soldiers at all. They seize the banker and a teller, holding them at gunpoint as their leader snarls, "If they move – kill 'em!" and the screen freezes on the face of the normally genial William Holden and the credit "Directed by Sam Peckinpah".[24]

This opening alone inverts all the standard expectations of the genre. We are in a world in which children, traditionally symbols of innocence, are crueller than the venomous scorpions they torment. Children have a choice; it is in the scorpion's nature to be virulent. Yet perhaps these children do not fully comprehend how vicious their game is: the secondary members of the Bunch are billed against the children's gleeful faces; the actors playing the sources of truest evil (Emilio Fernandez as the brutal Mexican warlord Mapache, Strother Martin and L. Q. Jones as the scummiest of Thornton's bounty hunters, Dekker as railroad magnate Harrigan) are billed against the ants warring with the scorpions. Once the "soldiers" enter the bank, within twenty seconds Peckinpah stuns his audience with three daring, brilliant strokes. First, by posing his outlaws in uniform and then exposing them as lawless thugs, he has raised the spectre of America's military complex – and, by implication, American government policy – chiefly to shatter reverence for it. When *real* U.S. soldiers appear later in the film, Peckinpah depicts them as callow and incompetent. Secondly, he subverts Hollywood convention and audience expectations by casting his top-billed star, usually an amiable, clean-cut, All-American type whom we would expect to be the hero, as a ruthless criminal willing to murder indiscriminately. Yet Peckinpah also subverts narrative convention, because Holden's Pike Bishop *is* the hero. Finally, by juxtaposing Pike's infamous instruction with his own screen credit, Sam Peckinpah firmly and forever identifies himself as the high priest of cinematic violence.

He wastes no time in justifying this reputation. When Pike and his gang discover the bounty hunters lying in ambush, they resolve to shoot their way out. In the most shocking scene of carnage yet featured in a major American film, children watch, fascinated, as Starbuck's temperance marchers are butchered in the crossfire. Only a few of the Bunch survive the shoot-out, and as they flee town the children end their grotesque game by covering the scorpions and the ants with burning straw. A few minutes later the children will run down the street, mimicking the massacre. Their chants of "bang! bang!" are at first still heard on the soundtrack as we see one of the escaping outlaws fall from his horse. He had been shot in the face in Starbuck, and now Pike puts him out of his misery with a single bullet. Pike's gang cross the border into Mexico, with Thornton's rag-tag posse in pursuit.

Thornton was once Pike's closest friend and his partner in crime. Through Pike's error of judgement, Thornton was captured while Pike himself escaped. He only agreed to lead Harrigan's posse because he dreads the prospect of returning to the Yuma penitentiary, where he was cruelly tortured. Thornton despises his new cohorts, human dregs who looted the corpses of outlaws and townsfolk alike in the aftermath of the Starbuck massacre. Later he will tell them, "We're after *men*, and I wish to God I was with them".[25] Manichaean morality is this film's first fatality, and Peckinpah conjures up a world in which agents of law and order are even more reprehensible than the badmen they pursue, and a gang of unregenerate killers are the only heroes we have.

In total, only six of the Bunch are left: Pike; his faithful lieutenant, Dutch Engstrom (Ernest Borgnine), who wants to be the friend to Pike that Thornton was; two brutish brothers, Lyle (Warren Oates) and Tector Gorch (Ben Johnson); a youthful Mexican, Angel (Jaime Sanchez); and old Freddy Sykes (Edmond O'Brien), now too decrepit to take part in robberies but still in for a share of the plunder. When the others rendezvous with Sykes to divide their spoils from Starbuck, they discover they have been duped. All they have netted are sackfuls of washers.

Like Butch Cassidy, Pike realizes trains and banks are no longer a sure route to riches. "We gotta start thinkin' beyond our guns," he declares, "those days are closin' fast."[26]

Yet it is not simply a matter of changing times and narrowing opportunities. These men have squandered their lives wallowing in violence, and violence is their *raison d'être* (inescapably, it is also the film's). Without their enormous propensity for violence, they would be nothing. If they forsake the only line of work they know, they *will* be nothing, as one early exchange makes clear:

PIKE: This was gonna be my last. Ain't gettin' around any better. I'd like to make one good score and back off.
DUTCH: Back off to *what?*[27]

It is the same problem as confronted Gregory Peck in *The Gunfighter*, Henry Fonda in *Warlock*, Yul Brynner, Steve McQueen and friends in *The Magnificent Seven*, and Randolph Scott and Joel McCrea in Peckinpah's own *Ride the High Country* – but it has seldom been articulated so succinctly and so starkly.

The Bunch enjoy a brief respite from their murderous trade in Angel's village, an oasis of gentleness in this most savage of worlds, where they are literally serenaded as heroes. Yet this village, too, has been cursed with violence. The warlord Mapache has raided the village, killing Angel's father and six others. Angel is further aggrieved when he learns that Teresa (Sonia Amelio), the woman he loves, has willingly gone off to become Mapache's whore. Eve has fled this Eden to consort with the serpent.

Much of *The Wild Bunch*'s raw power stems from Peckinpah's uncompromising assault on Hollywood's conventions. He does not settle for inverting the clichés of the genre and the medium. Rather, Peckinpah is intent on shattering the entire framework of clichés and candy-coated myths in which movies customarily traffic as a prettified alternative to life. Not for Peckinpah the traditional Madonna/Magdalene dichotomy; *The Wild Bunch*, like life itself, is far more complex. Teresa is infused with elements of both Madonna and Magdalene, as is evident when the village elder tells Pike: "To him, Teresa was like a goddess, to be worshipped from afar. Mapache knew she was a mango, ripe and waiting."[28] Up to the late 1960s American movies – and certainly Westerns – were, in their romanticism, ill-equipped to grapple with the attraction of many women to a psychopathic personality. Yet that is precisely what Peckinpah infers here, again starkly, again succinctly. Equally noteworthy is Pike's stern reaction to Angel's fury: "Either you learn to live with it, or we'll leave you here."[29] No kindly, John Wayne-style cracker-barrel paternalism. No older, wiser gunfighter subtly protecting a young hothead against his own worst instincts, as Yul Brynner does for Horst Buchholz throughout *The Magnificent Seven*. If Angel allows personal anguish to interfere with his professional competence, then Pike has no further use for him.

Angel agrees to go with the Bunch to Mapache's stronghold, Agua Verde, where Pike plans to sell their extra horses to the dictator. In contrast to the simple joy of Angel's villagers, the people of Agua Verde are cowed. They live in squalor while Mapache rules in luxury, riding in a beautiful red automobile, surrounded by vicious henchmen, compliant women and his German military advisers. The Bunch enter Mapache's courtyard, scene of an almost permanent fiesta. Again with remarkable economy, Peckinpah illustrates a fundamental division between mercenary instincts and revolutionary sympathies within the Bunch:

DUTCH: Hey, I'm down to about twenty in silver.
PIKE: With the way the *generalissimo*'s cleaned out this part o' the country, you're gonna have a lot to spare.

DUTCH: Ahhh – *generalissimo*, hell! He's just another bandit grabbin' all he can for himself.

PIKE: Like some others I could mention? [*He and the Gorches laugh*].

DUTCH: Not so's you'd know it, Mr. Bishop. We ain't nothin' like him. We don't *hang* nobody. I hope someday these people here kick him and the rest o' that scum like him right into their graves.

ANGEL: We will – if it takes forever.[30]

Suddenly, Teresa appears. Angel speaks to her, but Pike restrains him as she leaves to make her way to Mapache. Teresa laughs mockingly at Angel as she canoodles with Mapache. Angel leaps to his feet and shoots Teresa off Mapache's lap. Powerless to stop him, the Bunch look on in horror. Then Pike grabs Angel while Tector punches him. As Mapache's troops descend on them, demanding to know why Angel tried to kill him, Pike must quickly explain Angel had aimed at the girl, having gone crazy with jealousy after seeing her with Mapache. Only by massaging the tyrant's massive ego does Pike avoid a slaughter. Teresa's death is actually a dry run for the climactic holocaust, which will begin with another sudden, shocking killing the Bunch, as by-standers, cannot prevent. Each of these killings is followed by a moment of immense tension, with the gang a hair's-breadth away from annihilation.

When Pike assures Mapache's German adviser, "We share very few sentiments with our government", a deal is struck: Mapache hires the Bunch, at $10,000, to hijack a U.S. army shipment of rifles.[31] Angel is disgusted at the prospect of furnishing Mapache with guns to oppress his people further. Unlike Horst Buchholz's Chico in *The Magnificent Seven*, Angel is fiercely proud of his Mexican identity. Another deal is struck: he will forego his share of the money if he can siphon off one case of rifles for his village.

The Bunch rob the train, thwarting the inexperienced troops guarding the rifles – and also thwarting Thornton's posse. In the ensuing mayhem, one of the bounty hunters kills a soldier. This recklessness puts Thornton beyond the law once again. Now he has no choice but to ride deeper into Mexico in pursuit of Pike. Meanwhile, the Bunch have been surprised by the stealthy mountain guerrillas allied with Angel's village. Clad and armed like the pillaging murderers of *Bandolero!*, they have come for their case of rifles. Before handing the rest to Mapache, Pike forestalls any double-cross by devising a piecemeal trade-off. He makes Mapache a gift of a machine gun they stole along with the rifles. Yet when Dutch and Angel deliver the last batch of rifles, Mapache orders

Angel seized. Teresa's father has told him about the rifles for the village.[32] Dutch has no option but to feign indifference and ride out, leaving Angel alone to face Mapache's wrath. He tells Pike and the Gorches that Angel never betrayed their complicity in giving guns to his village: "He played his string right out to the end!"[33] Pike admits the odds are insuperable but, when they see Sykes ambushed and wounded by Thornton's men, he decides to evade his pursuers by returning to Agua Verde.

As Pike, Dutch and the Gorches ride into Mapache's stronghold, they see Angel tethered to Mapache's automobile, dragged savagely in the dust as children scamper after him and one boy sits astride him. After a futile attempt to buy Angel back the Bunch indulge in one last bout of debauchery, then stride back to Mapache's courtyard to demand Angel's release. Initially, Mapache seems about to comply with this demand as he lifts the tortured, shredded wreckage of Angel to his feet, brings him toward his friends and cuts his bonds. Suddenly comes the most shocking moment in the history of the Western as Mapache yanks Angel's head back, drawing his knife swiftly along his throat. Horrified, Pike and Dutch instantly blast the warlord into the dirt. One of Mapache's officers nervously puts his hands up. The courtyard is enveloped in tense silence. The Bunch crouch, guns cocked, poised for the massacre, but there are no takers. Dutch giggles maniacally. Pike turns, straightens up, sees the principal German military adviser clad in a ceremonial uniform identical to Mapache's. Pike raises his pistol in cold disgust and shoots him dead. All hell breaks loose. The Bunch perish in the apocalyptic carnage, taking most of Mapache's army with them. Pike himself is shot by a woman, then by a small boy.

Shortly after the blood-letting, Thornton's posse arrives. The loathsome bounty hunters immediately set about looting the bodies. Thornton gently takes Pike's gun and sits forlornly by a wall as the bounty hunters load up the corpses of the Bunch. He tells them he is not returning to Texas. He remains sitting by the wall as the others ride off. Vultures perch atop bodies and peasants begin to leave the now desolate village (an image reminiscent of dispossessed peasants traversing the Vietnamese countryside). A dust storm rages, and Thornton can hear shots in the distance. He smiles with quiet satisfaction, realizing the bounty hunters have just been picked off. Still he remains by the wall. Eventually, riders approach, led by Sykes and the elder from Angel's village. Pike's two oldest friends are now face to face. Thornton has every reason to believe Sykes will kill him. Instead, *The Wild Bunch* surprises its audiences one last time:

SYKES: Didn't expect to find *you* here.
THORNTON: Why not? I sent 'em back. That's all I said I'd do.
SYKES: They didn't get very far.
THORNTON: I figured.
SYKES: What are your plans?
THORNTON: Drift around down here. Try to stay outa jail.
SYKES: Well, me and the boys here, heh, we got some work to do. You
  wanna come along? Ain't like it used to be but, eh, it'll do.[34]

Thornton grins, laughs quietly. Sykes laughs raucously. The last of the
old-time outlaws are reconciled and reinvigorated as they ride off together with the mountain guerrillas who had rescued Sykes. Suddenly,
we see Pike, Dutch, the Gorches and Angel, all laughing, as if giving
these survivors' last hurrah their blessing from Valhalla. Above all, it is
a *happy* ending.

The *Wild Bunch* was only moderately successful at the box office,
grossing $5,300,000.[35] Yet Peckinpah's film ignited a critical furore un-
precedented in the genre. The *Kansas City Star* deplored "the negative
effect of savagery carried beyond the level of horror to the level of
numbing surfeit".[36] *New York*'s Judith Crist reproved "the bloodiest and
most sickening display of slaughter that I can ever recall in a theatrical
film, and quotes attributed to Mr. Holden that this sort of ultra-violence
is a healthy purgative for viewers is just about as sick".[37] The *Manhattan
Tribune* declared the film's violence at heart "a cherished, sensually
pleasurable exercise in cinematic masturbation".[38] However, the *New York
Morning Telegraph* opined: "with all its brutality and sheer revulsion, *The
Wild Bunch* may have opened up a new form of screen violence, one that
may eventually prove much more beneficial in the end than what we've
been objecting to up to now".[39]

Other critics were forthright and fulsome in their praise. "Worth ten
times the puff ethical theses of films like, say, *Judgment at Nuremberg*",
Penelope Gilliatt asserted in *The New Yorker*.[40] The *Motion Picture Herald*
rated *The Wild Bunch* as "Excellent", but zeroed in on the film's savagery
as its major fascination: "there has seldom been a picture in which a
sense of cynicism and contempt for all mankind has been so pungently
conveyed right away. ... Blood is everywhere, and the moment of death
is oftentimes caught in slow-motion for emphasis. It is like being a
horrified yet spellbound spectator of an incredibly cruel and senseless
war. Upon leaving the theatre one would not be surprised to find blood
on the floor and the walls."[41] *The New Republic*'s Stanley Kauffmann
hailed it as the best Western since Marlon Brando's *One-Eyed Jacks*

(1961), astutely observing: "The violence *is* the film. Those who have complained that there's too much of it might as well complain that there's too much punching in a prizefight. ... [Peckinpah] likes killing and he does it very well."[42] Vincent Canby of the *New York Times* was an ardent champion: "very beautiful and the first truly interesting American-made Western in years. ... *The Wild Bunch* takes the basic element of the Western movie myth, which once defined a simple, morally comprehensible world, and by bending them turns them into symbols of futility and aimless corruption. ... All personal relationships in the movie seem somehow perverted in odd mixtures of noble senti-mentality, greed and lust. ... The ideals of masculine comradeship are exaggerated and transformed into neuroses. ... It's a fascinating movie and, I think I should add, when I came out of it, I didn't feel like shooting, knifing or otherwise maiming any of Broadway's often hostile pedestrians."[43] Canby's further insight, ten days later, drew an intriguing parallel between the Bunch and a rogue from America's recent past: "In a way – and this, I'm sure, was not in Peckinpah's mind – they are a little like the late Senator Joseph McCarthy: they're rather clever in carrying out short-range objectives, but they have no larger strategy".[44] Later that month, when four scenes were trimmed from *The Wild Bunch*, Canby wrote an extensive article lamenting three of the four revisions.[45]

TIME was equally laudatory, noting that Peckinpah's heroes "are eminently fallible, their deeds frequently inglorious. They are legends both because and in spite of themselves. *The Wild Bunch* is Peckinpah's most complex inquiry into the metamorphosis of man into myth. Not incidentally, it is also a raucous, violent, powerful feat of American film making."[46] Furthermore, *TIME* quoted Peckinpah's stated motivation for his extravagantly bloody display: "killing is no fun. I was trying to show what the hell it's like to get shot."[47] Yet *Variety* considered the plot "regulation stuff" and suggested the movie actually tended to sag some-what after its electrifying opening sequence.[48] *The Hollywood Reporter* termed the violence of *The Wild Bunch* "at once compelling and repelling" and spoke of the "squalid beauty" of the Mexican locations as filmed by the movie's cinematographer, Lucien Ballard.[49]

Squalid beauty. No phrase sums up the appeal, the nature and the essence of *The Wild Bunch* more precisely. A masterwork of intricate subtlety, it is also an epic of seething contradictions. Ugly *and* beautiful, vicious *and* moral, misanthropic *and* brimming with humanity, structured *and* chaotic, crude *and* sophisticated, controlled *and* hysterical, a stark affirmation of life *and* a voluptuously romantic paean to violent death – *The Wild Bunch* is a film of extremes, vast and complex enough to incorporate many opposite extremes. Above all, however, *The Wild Bunch* is a celebration of violence.

The film's reputation and its niche in cinema history rest entirely on its violence. Without all that blood exploding off the screen, alternately captivating and sickening moviegoers, what we have is another well-made, well-acted Western expertly combining two of the genre's most popular 1960s scenarios: the outmoded Westerner's last, doomed rearguard action against the onslaughts of time and civilization, and American adventurers in Mexico. Both these roads had already been well-travelled by 1969. Violence is *The Wild Bunch*'s *raison d'être*. Peckinpah's rationale for this gory indulgence may have been sincere, but it was also self-serving. We do not choose to linger on things we do not love. Significantly, critics have frequently chosen overtly sexual language to describe the film's presentation of blood-letting: voluptuous, erotic, pornographic, orgiastic, orgasmic.

It is certainly the last of these. Everything in the film has been building steadily, relentlessly to an unstoppable and truly explosive climax, in which the Bunch experience the most joyous release of all. Warren Oates's Lyle screams with ecstasy while firing the machine gun as bullets tear through his body; it recalls nothing so much as another Peckinpah stalwart, Slim Pickens, gleefully whooping his way to atomic oblivion astride a nuclear bomb in Stanley Kubrick's *Dr. Strangelove* (1964). In total, this final battle is the most explicitly orgasmic death sequence in the American cinema since James Cagney's demise in Raoul Walsh's *White Heat* (1949). However, if death in *The Wild Bunch* is ultimately orgasmic, in two cases violent death is an inversion of the sexual act. When Angel shoots Teresa, this is the spurned lover's last substitute for penetration. Even more disquieting is the manner in which Peckinpah presents the act. Angel is so distraught, Teresa's laughter so cruelly mocking, that it seems we are meant to conclude Angel has been provoked beyond endurance. Not only has Eve mated with the serpent; Eve has *become* the serpent. The second "sexual" killing occurs when Pike bursts into a room during the apocalyptic shoot-out. A Mexican woman is there, but Pike discounts her as a danger. She shoots him in the back, and he turns and blasts her with his shotgun. Again, this suggests a substitute for penetration. Immediately before the showdown Pike had been in a young whore's room, and his wordless, weary melancholy in that scene implied impotence as much as regret for his destructive life and the realization that now he has nothing left to do but die. In that context, Pike's killing of the back-shooting woman strongly resembles a curative and an orgasmic resolution of his anguish.

Pike's use of weapons during the massacre suggests a specifically phallic escalation of warfare. He begins with a pistol, switches to a pump-action shotgun, and finally graduates to the machine gun, with which he sets off a devastating explosion just before his own death. The killing of the woman in the room also denotes a political mentality akin to the My Lai holocaust: there are no friendlies, no neutrals, no civilians; there are only targets.

The Wild Bunch is inherently misogynous. Granted, to expect a rounded, major female characterization in this narrative is to ask for another film altogether, but here women are depicted as just one more source of treachery in a hostile world. Pike's mistake brings his own death closer. Even Dutch, perhaps the most moral of the Bunch, thinks nothing of seizing a woman to shield himself during the climactic slaughter. Peckinpah never reproaches his heroes for the violence they inflict on women. In effect, he says: these men are desperate killers and this is precisely how they would act under such circumstances. Chivalry and civilization become irrelevant here. Judging from the film's portrayal of children – torturing scorpions and Angel, playing among the corpses at Starbuck, participating in the carnage at Agua Verde – we may presume innocence is long dead. The future already bears seeds of degeneration. By traditional definitions of either American society or Hollywood Westerns, there are no virtues, no values in *The Wild Bunch*. It represents the apotheosis of nihilism.

Fundamental shifts in the temper of 1960s Westerns dealing with adventurers in Mexico chart the loss of American idealism in that decade. The 1960s began with the altruistic crusade of *The Magnificent Seven*, progressed to the cool cynicism of *The Professionals*, and culminated in the sour yet strangely joyous nihilism of *The Wild Bunch*. Yet underlying each is a similar, albeit selective code of honour clearly illustrated in the following exchanges.

From *The Magnificent Seven* (Yul Brynner as Chris, James Coburn as Britt, Steve McQueen as Vin and Brad Dexter as Harry):

BRITT: D'you wanna go?

HARRY: Well, there comes a time to turn Mother's picture to the wall and get out. The village will be no worse off than it was before we came.

CHRIS: You forget one thing: we took a contract.

VIN: Not the kind any court would enforce.

CHRIS: That's just the kind you've gotta keep.[50]

From *The Professionals* (Burt Lancaster as Dolworth, Lee Marvin as Fardan):

DOLWORTH: Amigo, three days' ride from Coyote Pass there's another graveyard, with one big difference. Instead o' dead heroes, they buried gold bullion. Two million dollars in Spanish gold, melted down into big beautiful bars, and waitin' for us with open arms. And we don't have to fight Raza to get it.

FARDAN: That couldn't be the reason you took this job?

DOLWORTH: Can you think of a better reason?

FARDAN: Our word. We gave our word to bring the woman back.

DOLWORTH: My word to Grant ain't worth a plug nickel.

FARDAN: You gave your word to *me*.[51]

From *The Wild Bunch*:

DUTCH: Damn that Deke Thornton to hell!

PIKE: What would you do in his place? He gave his word.

DUTCH: Gave his word to a railroad.

PIKE: *It's his word!*

DUTCH: *That ain't what counts! It's who you give it to!*[52]

Giving one's word, a moral code to live and die by – these themes are central to Sam Peckinpah's Westerns. *Ride the High Country*, *Major Dundee*, *The Wild Bunch* and *Pat Garrett & Billy the Kid* (Metro-Goldwyn-Mayer, 1973) all focus on two men, once best friends, now divided by time and circumstances. Each film eulogizes a die-hard who must do precisely that. The Westerner who refuses to compromise his self-styled concept of integrity must perish, while the man who can adapt to changing social or political realities survives – though, in Pat Garrett's case, only temporarily. Thus Sam Peckinpah is steeped in *Liebestod*, for he repeatedly kills those jaded romantic idealists whom he loves most. Peckinpah's heart, like John Ford's in *The Man Who Shot Liberty Valance*, is with the valiant but doomed hero, not the pragmatist who knows how to survive in a society which has devalued heroic individualism.

The gulf between the former friends widens progressively in film after film. In *Ride the High Country*, Steve Judd and Gil Westrum stride out to meet the Hammond brothers head-on, their own differences as good as resolved. In *Major Dundee*, however, Dundee and Tyreen are about to duel when they are compelled to join forces for the climactic skirmish with French lancers. In *The Wild Bunch*, Deke Thornton observes much of the massacre at Agua Verde through binoculars. There is no reunion just before the glorious last stand – but, curiously, *halfway through the carnage*, Thornton and his posse gallop frantically toward Agua Verde. Why? To help the Bunch? Thornton might; his posse would not. To ensure they retrieve the bodies of the Bunch? The low-life posse certainly would, but such motivation is far beneath Thornton. No explanation is ever given. In *Pat Garrett & Billy the Kid*, of course, the gulf is widest of all: Garrett (James Coburn) kills Billy (Kris Kristofferson).

Yet in *The Wild Bunch* there is, at least, a reconciliation of sorts. Thornton takes Pike's six-gun not as a trophy but as a fraternal memento, a relic of the old West and the days when they rode together. It is significant that Thornton takes the six-gun and not the modern, Army regulation pistol with which Pike shot Mapache; that weapon postdated their partnership and would have no emotional resonance for Thornton. When old Sykes invites him to join the guerrillas' war effort, Thornton's soft smile is partly one of blessed disbelief: he has been forgiven his transgression.

As for the Bunch, their deaths are the supreme achievement of their lives. They are not purposely aiding the grass-roots revolution. Their eradication of Mapache, like Ringo shooting the Plummers in *Stagecoach*, is only *incidentally* beneficial to society. The Bunch kill him – and contrive grandiose suicides – for their own sake. If this blood-drenched ending is partly a caution on American hubris in Vietnam, it is also a vigorous celebration of sensual death, a black hymn of triumph over the petty oppressions of regulated society. Where else could these men go? Angel's village is an Arcadian aberration in a corrupt universe of Starbucks and Agua Verdes, themselves intriguingly descended from *Stagecoach*'s nightmare communities of Tonto and Lordsburg in repressive puritanism and depravity respectively. What else could these men do? We cannot imagine them adjusting to the bureaucratic stringencies of modern life. That, too, is *their* triumph. Westerns had for decades glamorized a leathery hero on horseback, unfettered by mortgage payments, work deadlines, tax returns, traffic jams, smog, and an endless glut of family responsibilities. The limitless horizon had long been a major aspect of the genre's appeal. No matter the lives moviegoers led, the vicarious daydream of unrestricted freedom persisted. If Westerns had acted as a safety valve for twentieth-century man, as Frederick Jackson Turner suggested the frontier itself had done in the nineteenth century, then *The Wild Bunch* blasted that valve away forever. Even bloody, glorious death was preferable to punching clocks. Soured romanticism was better than no romanticism at all.

The myth of America had soured along with the romanticism. By the 1970s, filmic representations of the frontier past as a splendid pageant were no longer viable or credible. Television created instant history and, since the murder of John Kennedy, the nation's commonly shared past had largely been shaped and determined by the one-eyed tyrant in the parlour. In essence, murky reality had caught up with, outdistanced and ultimately supplanted Hollywood's roseate paeans to national progress. In the wake of Dallas, Watts, Newark, My Lai, Chicago and all the other chapters in the 1960s' dire chronicle of killings, riots and the endless conflict in Vietnam, a movie like *How the West Was Won* would have been inconceivable, whereas the savagery of *The Wild Bunch* was emblematic of modern America.

The Wild Bunch mirrored the pre-existing level of violence in American society, but worse was to come. A few weeks after the film's release, Charles Manson and his followers struck. Manson's vision of America's future was even bloodier than Sam Peckinpah's vision of America's past. It is a tragic fact that society is unable to legislate effectively against loners with a grievance or a "vision"; however, institutionalized violence implies an element of societal culpability, and the bombing of Cambodia and the subsequent shooting of students at Kent State University and Jackson State College in 1970, forty-three dead in the Attica prison revolt of 1971 and the saturation bombing of Hanoi in 1972 all accentuated the ascendancy of officially sanctioned violence as a response to political confrontations.

On screen as in society, violence remained a controversial yet integral component of modern American culture. During the years of Nixon's presidency, the floodgates of permissiveness were flung wide open. Moviegoers were deluged with depictions of every aspect of sexuality and ever more disturbing displays of violence, the latter including Peckinpah's own *Straw Dogs*, Stanley Kubrick's *A Clockwork Orange*, Roman Polanski's *Macbeth* and Ken Russell's *The Devils* (all 1971). Significantly, those films were all set in Britain; only the first two had American directors, and only *Straw Dogs* had an American as protagonist. Although these films were not commentaries on American society or national identity, each demonstrated the growing centrality of violence within early 1970s cinema. The era's most incisive exploration of violence in a specifically American context was Francis Ford Coppola's *The Godfather* (1972), which ingeniously criticized institutionalized brutality by presenting the Mafia as inextricably linked to the nation's political and financial power structures.

Yet the Western had already excoriated this institutionalization of violence in two films made in 1970, each reflecting the atrocity at My Lai: Ralph Nelson's *Soldier Blue* and Arthur Penn's *Little Big Man*. Both condemned the American military on the frontier as surely as *Butch Cassidy* and *The Wild Bunch* had eulogized outlaw defiance of corporate power. Again, one film was essentially humorous in tone while the other was notorious due to its shockingly violent content. *Little Big Man* was the *Butch Cassidy* of the pair, an expansive comic epic chronicling the misadventures of a young white man (Dustin Hoffman) raised by the Cheyenne, its My Lai equivalent a reconstruction of the Washita massacre of 1868. The violence here was the rough edge audiences had to accept along with the film's lighter moments, and *Little Big Man* was hugely profitable, grossing $15,000,000 and ranking as the eleventh most successful Western film after inflation-adjustment in 1981.[53] The film's moral centre was the hero's adoptive grandfather, the magnificently quirky Old Lodge Skins, portrayed by the Canadian Salish Indian Chief Dan George, who explains the white butchery of women and children by saying, "They do not seem to know where the centre of the earth is".[54] The July 23 1971 issue of *Pravda* was far less gentle in its rationalization, extolling the film for exposing "the enormous crimes against mankind that have marked the path of capitalism from the beginning of our days", and proclaiming the Washita massacre sequence reminiscent of "what was done by the Hitler barbarians and in our day is carried out by the American military in Indochina".[55]

Little Big Man depicted Cheyenne life as a countercultural idyll. Old Lodge Skins is a wise fool attuned to mystic dreams and in total harmony with nature; Little Big Man indulges in a polygamous and semi-incestuous marathon with his Indian wife's three sisters; and an effeminate homosexual named Little Horse is valued by the Cheyennes, not persecuted (his likely fate in white frontier society). *Soldier Blue*, too, leans toward idyll in the wilderness romance of Candice Bergen and Peter Strauss, but this interlude is in stark contrast to the film's cardinal *raison d'être*. Its parallel to the killings at My Lai was the Sand Creek massacre of 1864. While the carnage which climaxed *The Wild Bunch* was electrifying, *Soldier Blue*'s was sickening. Decapitations, mutilations, rapes, mass execution of women and children – all abound in a grotesque orgy which ends with the soldiers whooping delightedly as they dance around the Indian camp waving severed limbs and heads; here the military are the true savages.

Soldier Blue was intentionally controversial, but *Variety*'s reviewer adopted an inherently conservative stance, predicting that the image of the cavalry trampling over the American flag just prior to the massacre would "upset a lot of people", and terming Sand Creek an "allegedly historical incident".[56] In the *New York Times*, however, Dotson Rader's verdict was one of lavish praise for *Soldier Blue* and fervent condemnation of the American past:

> There are hundreds of historically verifiable atrocities committed by American troops against subject Indian nations, perhaps thousands more lost to history. ... Ralph Nelson ... said he made *Soldier Blue* in the light of Vietnam and Songmy. The same army. Different victims. ... *Soldier Blue* must be numbered among the most significant, the most brutal and liberating, the most honest American films ever made. It is a movie of great art and courage, and ... it attempts to confront and break with the indecent complicity of the American film industry in a racist falsification of history; to destroy at last the phony myth of Cowboys and Indians, Good Guys and Bad Guys, which Hollywood has gleefully been embellishing and profiting from for half a century.
>
> ... For an American to see *Soldier Blue* is to experience, I imagine, something comparable to what a German, a "good German" of decent sensibility, experienced when he witnessed the extermination camps opened after World War II.
>
> ... Sand Creek ... was a forerunner in a line of American-directed massacres running from before the Civil War ... through Dresden and Hiroshima into Vietnam. ...
>
> I think we need to face our violence more openly within its historical context; we need to face it as it was and is if we are ever to overcome it. ... *Soldier Blue*, in its shattering violence, for a moment snaps the deceitful armor of white "history" and lets blood run through. It is painful to witness. But it is necessary.[57]

That same year, Dee Brown's book *Bury My Heart at Wounded Knee* chronicled white America's genocidal campaign against the Indian Nations.[58] Thus in print and on screen, the myth of benevolent conquest was now being comprehensively debunked. By the early 1970s, the Western had become the stamping ground of revisionists. Although the genre itself retained considerable appeal for film-makers, triumphalism now lay dead in the dust. In the 1970s Westerns no longer romanticized the wide open spaces but instead mourned the bleak futility – and often fatality – of the prosaic frontier experience; thus the prairie becomes just a shade *too* crowded for the luckless heroes of Sam Peckinpah's *The Ballad of Cable Hogue* and William A. Fraker's *Monte Walsh* (both 1970), Blake Edwards's *Wild Rovers*, Robert Altman's over-praised *McCabe & Mrs. Miller* and Peter Fonda's *The Hired Hand* (all 1971) and Dick Richards's *The Culpepper Cattle Co.* (1972).

Women also fared poorly in this deglamorized West. Frontier wives

Verna Bloom and Jane Alexander were widowed at the close of *The Hired Hand* and Lamont Johnson's *A Gunfight* (also 1971) respectively. Prostitutes played by Stella Stevens and Julie Christie were similarly bereaved in *The Ballad of Cable Hogue* and *McCabe & Mrs. Miller*, the latter sinking into an opium-induced trance. Jeanne Moreau's prostitute in *Monte Walsh* died of tuberculosis; and Victoria Principal perished in childbirth in John Huston's *The Life and Times of Judge Roy Bean* (1972). *Stagecoach*'s good-hearted prostitute was rewarded with a home, marriage and security, but for the prostitutes of early 1970s Westerns this was no longer a viable alternative; and even if it were, the plot resolutions of *The Hired Hand* and *A Gunfight* implied the reality would probably not have matched the dream.

In the wake of *The Wild Bunch*'s savagely pejorative vision of children, several early 1970s Westerns detailed the loss of innocence as teenage and preadolescent boys became involved in bloodshed or robbery or both in *The Culpepper Cattle Co.*, Mark Rydell's elegiac *The Cowboys*, Robert Benton's *Bad Company* and Gary Nelson's *Santee* (all 1972), Andrew V. McLaglen's *Cahill: United States Marshal* and Ted Kotcheff's *Billy Two Hats* (both 1973), and Richard Fleischer's *The Spikes Gang* (1974).

Crooked capitalists marginalized legendary outlaws all the way into the grave in *The Life and Times of Judge Roy Bean* and Peckinpah's *Pat Garrett & Billy the Kid* (1973). At the end of *Stagecoach* the corrupt banker, Gatewood, had been exposed and arrested. Yet now, in the age of Nixon and Watergate, Gatewood had triumphed. America was no longer the domain of the heroic, mythic Westerner; finally, America was *his*.

Thus, although Westerns were still being made in the early 1970s, the genre's dominant ideology had become unremittingly bleak. As if reinforcing a sense of merely living on borrowed time, major stars confronted their own mortality by biting the dust on screen with increasing frequency. Among the fatalities were Kirk Douglas in Joseph L. Mankiewicz's *There Was a Crooked Man ...* (1970) and *A Gunfight*; William Holden in *Wild Rovers*; Burt Lancaster in Robert Aldrich's *Ulzana's Raid* (1972), yet another gory cavalry and Indians epic, whose subtext of internecine racial warfare was conceivably, in the wake of Attica, as much about race-related strife in America as about the war in Vietnam; Paul Newman's eponymous hero in *The Life and Times of Judge Roy Bean*; Dean Martin in George Seaton's *Showdown* (1972); Gregory Peck in *Billy Two Hats*; and Lee Marvin in *The Spikes Gang*. After *The Wild Bunch* and *Soldier Blue*, however, the most shocking moment of violence in the Nixon era Western was the most iconoclastic: in *The Cowboys*, a verminous villain brutally guns down, of all people, John Wayne. It is as though the Statue of Liberty had suddenly been toppled. More than any other, this moment marked the demise of the heroic Westerner.

American omnipotence, the Western's lasting centrality and the image of John Wayne's indestructibility had all been shattered during Richard Nixon's presidency. On February 25 1974 Pauline Kael proclaimed in *The New Yorker*: "A few more Westerns may still straggle in, but the Western is dead."[59] Now, as the United States stood poised on the eve of its Bicentennial, all that remained for the genre were fragments of legend.

CHAPTER 9

Legends Revisited, Legends Revised in "Bicentennial Westerns": *Buffalo Bill and the Indians, The Outlaw Josey Wales* and *The Shootist*

A MERICANS believe in renewal. From the promise of virgin land which enticed the earliest settlers to *become* Americans to the birth of the Republic, from the hard-won nation forged out of the Civil War to the lure of the frontier, from the Protestant work ethic to the Progressive reformers, from Hollywood's cosy mythology to an electoral process which demands a new national vision every four years, the United States has traditionally treasured the second chance and the brighter future. In truth, America's national emblem might more appositely be the phoenix than the eagle. Never had Americans needed this fervent belief in renewal more than in 1976.

In little more than a decade, the world's most prosperous, most powerful and most technologically advanced nation endured a massive upsurge in violence and an accompanying breakdown of the political infrastructure. One president had been murdered, another vilified as a megalomaniac and the killer of children, a third damned as a criminal and driven from office by his own paranoia and mendacity. The true significance of Watergate lay in its outcome: the Constitution prevailed as an instrument of republican virtue in the face of imperial arrogance, stressing that not even the president of the United States was above the law. Yet at the time it was another psychic crisis which, hard on the heels of the assassinations, urban riots and the war in Vietnam, only lent more credence to the claim that America had become a morally debased society. The Vietnam War was finally over, at long last lost. The United States had put men on the moon but could not bend a tiny, third-rate Third World country to its will. To the Left, this hubris was scandalous. To the Right, this failure was ludicrous. To both, the war in Vietnam was a tragedy from which, two decades later, the United States has not wholly recovered. While fifty-eight thousand American lives were being squandered in an unwinnable war, the domestic fabric of society suffered continual erosion as violent crime, narcotics and hard-core pornography acquired higher visibility within contemporary American culture.

The Bicentennial celebrations were therefore as much about what America could be again as about past glories, and as much about hope and myth as about history. Yet on the two hundredth anniversary of the Declaration of Independence, America's most potent and most resilient national myth was limping toward the sunset. In the two decades since 1976, the genre has twitched sporadically; if not dead, the Western is certainly comatose.

The Western's last hour before this long hiatus was one of its finest. Twenty-six Westerns were produced in 1976, hardly suggestive of a genre in decline; but the following year there would only be seven, and after 1974 television Western series had dropped from seven to four for 1975–1977, declining still further thereafter.[1] In 1976, 10,000 four-wall and 3,500 drive-in cinemas were in operation in the United States, the former rising to 16,800 by 1986, the latter declining to 1,000 by 1990.[2] A weekly average of eighteen million went to the movies in 1976, paying an average admission fee of two dollars thirteen cents; thirty-seven years before, when *Stagecoach* was released, over three times that number had flocked to cinemas for one-ninth of that price.[3] Box office receipts for 1976 totalled $1,994,000,000 – a drop from 1975's $2,115,000,000, but they have skyrocketed (with only minor temporary setbacks) ever since, totalling $5,023,000,000 in 1990.[4] The 1976 box office receipts account for 0.27%, 4.1% and 53.6% of consumer, recreation and spectator expenditures respectively.[5] Cinema has been the great global entertainment and the great art form of the twentieth century, and the world will always need it – because enthralment has become a necessity of life rather than a luxury. It is an ancient yet urgent requirement of the human condition: when all else fails there are, at worst, bread and circuses; there are, at best, myths and legends.

Three Westerns of 1976 were explicitly concerned with myth and legend, and it is appropriate that they should be the last gasp of the genre's golden age. Like the deaths of John Adams and Thomas Jefferson on July 4 1826, exactly fifty years after the Declaration of Independence, the Western's demise occurred at precisely the right moment. In the summer of 1976 theme and time converged perfectly as these discourses on the essence of frontier legends commingled with the national celebrations and then were gone, leaving the United States to face its prosaic third century largely bereft of its most cherished "foundation myth".

Bread and circuses, myths and legends. The first of the "Bicentennial Westerns" under scrutiny here is as much about a "circus" as about a legend. In effect, Robert Altman's *Buffalo Bill and the Indians or Sitting Bull's History Lesson* (United Artists) asserted the legend-making process *was* a circus. Set in 1885, the film focuses on the acquisition of Chief Sitting Bull (Frank Kaquitts) as a star attraction in Buffalo Bill's Wild West Show. Essentially a satirical treatise on the nature of legend, of stardom, of confected and glamorized history and of the marriage between celebrity and the American political process, Altman's *Buffalo Bill* has very little in the way of a traditionally structured plot. Buffalo Bill Cody (Paul Newman) is a vainglorious, hypocritical, impotent, drunken racist, his broad grin at times verging on the demonic. When Sitting Bull arrives at Bill's encampment, Cody and most of his entourage mistakenly assume one huge, muscular Indian is the Chief (and, in any other Western, he would be). Yet this figure is William Halsey (Will Sampson), not so much Sitting Bull's interpreter as his spokesman; the Chief himself is a small, shrivelled man who will endure Cody's taunts and fruitless efforts to degrade him with stoic dignity and mystic silence. Through Halsey, the Chief demands that Buffalo Bill's troupe re-enact the butchery of Sioux women and children at Killdeer Mountain. Cody's anger flares and he fires them, ordering them out of his encampment. As a consequence of this, sharpshooter Annie Oakley (Geraldine Chaplin) resolves to quit Cody's show in sympathy with Sitting Bull. Cody comes to talk her out of leaving:

CODY: Why are ya – sittin' in t'middle like this? What did Bull ever do for you?
ANNIE: He wanted to show the truth to the people. Why can't you accept that just once?
CODY: Because I got a better sense o' *history* than that![6]

Halsey has relayed Sitting Bull's definition of history as "nothing more than disrespect for the dead".[7] In the film's moral framework, Sitting Bull is correct – the *History Lesson* of the title is one Sitting Bull delivers, not one he learns. Yet Cody has grasped a more pertinent truth. His "better sense o' history" is a highly attuned perception of what nineteenth-century America's mostly white, Anglo-Saxon paying public will *accept* as history. Cody is symbol and product of a culture in which legend has been propagated as gospel; he no longer knows or cares about the difference. However, he is not merely concerned with preserving the integrity of a jealously guarded myth. There is genuine meanness in this man, clearly displayed just before Sitting Bull is first exhibited to an audience, as Cody informs the Chief's spokesman, "Halsey! You can tell Bull he's finally gonna discover what the show-business is all about. He'll come back in here and get down on his *knees* to me to do the Custer act. Bull's gonna suffer a worse defeat than Custer ever did. Custer could die. Bull's just gonna get humiliated."[8] Cody relishes this prospect; but he is to be disappointed. Sitting Bull rides out into the arena alone and the crowd begins to boo and jeer, much to Cody's amusement and Annie's chagrin. Yet Bull remains mounted in the centre of the arena – proud, stoic, silent, dignified. Suddenly, the crowd breaks into cheers and applause. If anyone is humiliated, it is Cody. To emphasize his failure and humiliation and the huge gap between public image and private self, the very next scene features Cody gingerly apologizing to a visiting opera singer for his impotence with her the night before.

Cody cannot conquer Sitting Bull's spirit. The Sioux chief has no interest in Cody's circus extravaganza. He only agreed to join Buffalo Bill's show due to a dream which revealed that President Grover Cleveland (Pat McCormick) would come there. Sure enough, Cleveland and his new bride visit while on honeymoon, and Cody stages an unprecedented evening show. For once, Sitting Bull actively participates, endearing himself to the president. Yet when he and Halsey arrive uninvited at a post-performance reception and attempt to make a simple request on behalf of their people, Cleveland fobs them off with political double-talk and never actually *hears* what the request is. Cody congratulates Cleveland on his manoeuvre, remarking, "You see, the difference between a President and a chief in a situation like this – the President always knows enough to retaliate before it's his turn."[9] Cleveland, in turn, pays tribute to Cody: "You know – it's a man like that that made this country what it is today."[10] This mutual admiration infers American political and popular culture are each dominated by inherently fatuous idols giving credence to one another's legends as well as their own.

Later, news reaches Cody's encampment that Sitting Bull has been killed by police at Standing Rock (this happened in 1890, but the film does not suggest an ellipsis of five years). Cody awakes to find the Chief's ghostly apparition in his quarters. Cody tells the spectre: "You ain't even the right image. ... Halsey's got all the brains – 'cept Halsey, he don't mean a word he says, which is why he sounds so real. ... God meant for me to be white, and it ain't easy. I got people with no lives. They're livin' through me. ... Custer was a star. Oh, he was a good man. ... He gave the Indians reason to be famous. ... You see, in a hundred years, I'm still gonna be Buffalo Bill – Star! And you're gonna be 'the Injun'."[11] If Cody is right about how white America will long remember these protagonists, he is also right about Halsey. The film ends with the "Custer act" which Cody had originally designed for Sitting Bull. This "act" was, historically, entitled "First Scalp for Custer". In revenge for the Little Big Horn massacre, Cody fights hand-to-hand with Chief Sitting Bull, effortlessly "killing" him. Cody thus presents himself as Custer's avenger in combat with a man he did not even recognize as Sitting Bull at film's beginning. Then, he thought Halsey was Sitting Bull. Now, Halsey *is*. He plays the role of Sitting Bull for Buffalo Bill's re-enactment of a fight which never took place. Here the legend is accepted as fact, and only the legend will be printed. Halsey has thus compromised himself as Sitting Bull never could: he manages to survive within white America by "dying" for its entertainment. So the triumph of mythic America is complete, a denouement Altman deplores even as he depicts it. Cody's "sense o' history" has displaced the true past, and the film ends with a close-up of his elated, brilliant, demonic grin.

Although he exposed the dark underside of a crowd-pleasing Western spectacle, Altman had certainly not produced a crowd-pleasing Western. *Buffalo Bill and the Indians* fared poorly at the box office, with critical reaction also largely negative. *Variety* savaged the film, proclaiming it "a puerile satire ... silly when it's not cynical, distasteful throughout[.] ... Paul Newman has rarely been seen so badly. ... Rarely has so much manpower produced such ludicrous effluvium. ... Considering the many more serious legends which might be treated, this all seems like a cowardly copout – it's easy to tap dance on the graves of dead persons. ... Coming down hard on this film is like using nuclear devices to blow up an outhouse. Suffice it to say that technical production competence is wasted on self-destructive pretentiousness."[12] Stanley Kauffmann's review for *The New Republic* was equally uncompromising: "Altman is an ideological fashion-monger. He exploits established anti-Establishment modes. He relies on predecessors to stake out and illuminate the ground, then he rides in like a black-humor Buffalo Bill expecting the cheers of a hip gallery for his safely satirical derring-do. ... But when he tries to sweep all of national character and destiny into a continental bear hug, he ends up with his hands full of the merely smart-aleck. ... The best scene in the film is the one in which the murdered Sitting Bull appears to Buffalo Bill[.] ... It's the one moment of poetry in a film that assumes it's flying with sardonic poetry all the way but that mostly is fussy and flat."[13] In the *New York Times*, Vincent Canby termed it "a sometimes self-indulgent, confused, ambitious movie that is often very funny and always fascinating. ... [Paul Newman's Buffalo Bill] can't easily be held accountable for having seized the opportunities open to him. He's the American way. ... The film that Mr. Altman has made is even more about theater-as-life and about the making of legends (matinee idols, movie stars and Presidents) than it is about genocide. ... The film is virtually formless[.] ... In place of narrative drive it relies on the momentum created by its visual spectacle, its prodigal way with ideas, its wit and its enthusiasm for the lunatic business of making movies. Mr. Altman makes movies the way other men go on binges – with an abandon that sometimes gets the better of him – and which should be preserved and protected."[14] Ironically, this notice was published exactly one hundred years after the Battle of the Little Big Horn.

Canby's review was much kinder than Stanley Kauffmann's or *Variety*'s, but *Buffalo Bill*'s foremost champion was probably Arthur Knight of *The Hollywood Reporter*: "a wondrously riotous movie ... fascinating inter-mix of fact and fantasy, of myth and reality, of debunkery and warm admiration. ... It's an extraordinary movie, encompassing ... the entire panorama of the West. ... While I found all of this enormously satisfying, I must confess that I repeatedly wondered about its impact on the so-called average audience. ... I can only hope that they will admire it as much as I do. The Western is an enormously resilient form, but never has that resilience been tested quite so much as in this movie. Altman uses it audaciously to comment upon minorities – black, red and female; but on a far deeper level, he is calling into question our need – and love – for mythic heroes. ... *Buffalo Bill and the Indians* isn't really a movie. It's a ... joyous sunburst of a happening, with a serious underside. I trust that neither aspect will be ignored."[15]

Buffalo Bill and the Indians might have been a huge money-spinner were it a quirky, expansive comic epic in the style of *Little Big Man*. Instead, it was a talky drama confined to the Wild West Show arena, Cody's encampment and, otherwise, indoor sets, its theatrical origins very much in evidence. The film's dialogue was frequently literate and supremely witty – but it was an essentially sour wit, characterized by Cody's indignant complaint, "It's harder bein' a star than an Injun".[16] Yet, on their own, sharp one-liners are seldom enough to constitute a classic. Significantly, several of the major characters have their own distinctive speech patterns. Cody's is a magnificent mixture of profundity and banality ("Remember, son – the last thing that a man wants to do is the last thing he does").[17] Sitting Bull's unique speech pattern is his dignified silence; President Cleveland's is diplomatic flannel; Cody's publicist, Major John Burke (Kevin McCarthy), luxuriates in bombast while his producer and business partner, Nate Salsbury (Joel Grey), mangles the English language with his affected, contorted corporate-speak; and, best of all, the man who made Cody a legend, Ned Buntline (Burt Lancaster) sits in a saloon on the fringe of Cody's camp and punctuates the drama with grandiose aphorisms ("Bill, any youngster like yourself who figures to set the world on fire best not forget where he got the matches").[18]

When Burt Lancaster became a first-rank star the world lost a superb character actor. His Buntline is the elder statesman of frontier lore and, alongside Sitting Bull, the moral centre of the film. Though not as morally pristine as the Chief, Buntline is honest enough to acknowledge his own complicity in creating a myth which has long since turned ugly. Unlike Cody, at least Buntline can still distinguish fabrication from reality, gleefully referring to the very concept of a Wild West show as "just dreamin' out loud".[19] Again, however, Cody's grasp of marketable pageantry takes precedence over literal truth:

BUNTLINE: You ain't changed, Bill.
CODY: I ain't supposed to. That's why people pay to see me.
BUNTLINE: Well! This has been the most soberin' experience I've ever had. Damn near a religious awakening. Buffalo Bill! The thrill o' my life to have invented you.[20]

Buffalo Bill and the Indians is eminently quotable, but it is also an extremely self-conscious Western, utterly devoid of the action which had been a traditional mainstay of the genre. By contrast, Clint Eastwood's *The Outlaw Josey Wales* (Warner Brothers) was chock-full of violent incidents. Yet it was much more than just another slam-bang Eastwood fantasy.

Paul Newman's performances in Westerns have been varied and his contribution to the genre has been much under-rated. Along with the disparate outcasts he has played for director Martin Ritt in *Hud* (1963), *The Outrage* (1964) and *Hombre* (1966), Paul Newman has starred as four frontier legends: Billy the Kid in Arthur Penn's *The Left-Handed Gun* (1958), Butch Cassidy, Judge Roy Bean and Buffalo Bill. No two roles were similar; in each film Newman delivered a highly individualized performance. In both quality and range, this is a very impressive track record for an actor who is not considered a major *Western* star. Clint Eastwood, on the other hand, has in fact been over-praised for *his* contribution to the genre, which is more quantitative than qualitative.

After seven years as the second lead of CBS–TV's *Rawhide* (1959–1966), Eastwood shot to international stardom as the unshaven, laconic, thoroughly mercenary killer of Sergio Leone's *Fistful of Dollars* (1964), *For a Few Dollars More* (1965) and *The Good, the Bad and the Ugly* (1966). The Italian-made *Dollar* films were innovative and entertaining, crudely reworking many of the Western's mythic components without specific national/ideological subtexts. Their dominant ideology was no more than amoral self-interest, their principal appeal heavily stylized, comic-book violence. As movies, they were tremendous fun; but, aside from Lee Van Cleef's dignified Colonel Mortimer in *For a Few Dollars More*, these narratives have no sentiment – and no heart. In most of his Westerns Eastwood has made infinitesimal adjustments to his character in Leone's trilogy, combining his monolithic star image and a one-dimensional acting style with a nihilistic *Weltanschauung*. Several of his self-directed star vehicles have successfully disguised minimalism as superficial and/or pretentious mysticism (*High Plains Drifter* (1972) and *Pale Rider* (1985) are especially guilty of this), with several critics subsequently lapsing into paroxysms of adulation. Even his Oscar-winning *Unforgiven* (1992) is little more than a very competently made Western, and certainly not in the same league as many of the greats made during the 1950s and 1960s – which were seldom nominated for Academy Awards. Eastwood is a major film-maker, and some of his most recent efforts are abrim with enormous poignancy and sensitivity (*A Perfect World* (1993) and *The Bridges of Madison County* (1995)). As regards the Western, however, Eastwood helped bastardize the genre, thus aiding its eventual demise. His "Man With No Name" persona helped to take the heart out of the Western.

All credit to Eastwood, then, for *The Outlaw Josey Wales*, which puts some of that heart back. He plays the title role, a peaceful Missouri farmer whose wife and son are butchered when Kansas Redlegs led by Captain Terrill (Bill McKinney) burn his property during the Civil War. Josey joins up with Confederate guerrillas led by "Bloody Bill" Anderson (John Russell). At the war's end, Anderson is dead; one of his riders, Fletcher (John Vernon) brings news of the Union's offer of amnesty. They will be free to return to their homes unhampered if they will just ride into a nearby Union camp and swear loyalty to the United States.

Only one of the guerrillas holds out: Josey. Although he does not explain why, the inference is clearly that he will not forgive the Union (and by extension America) for the death of his wife and son. Yet he advises a young Rebel, Jamie (Sam Bottoms), to go along with the others. Jamie idolizes him, but Josey is a loner, not an ideological crusader. His continued renegade status is a private choice made for personal reasons. From a hillside, Josey watches his companions surrender to the Union troops commanded by Terrill; but treachery is afoot. The Northerners machine-gun the guerrillas. Josey gallops into the camp, killing as many Union soldiers as possible. He and Jamie escape, but the youth has been badly wounded, shot in the back by Terrill. Terrill's Redlegs set off in pursuit, reluctantly accompanied by Fletcher, who, like Robert Ryan's Deke Thornton in *The Wild Bunch*, has been coerced into tracking his former friend. Fletcher is basically a decent man who had no inkling of a double-cross when he prompted the other guerrillas to seek amnesty, but Terrill is a bloodthirsty fanatic who epitomizes the military mind gone mad in the unchecked exercise of power. Even his name is a clue to his arrogance, for Terrill was also the name of Charles Bickford's self-righteous Major in *The Big Country*. Yet in his dogged pursuit and quasi-puritanical zeal, this Terrill is even more reminiscent of another Major – Amos Charles Dundee:

TERRILL: We've got him now. We'll get these two first, then we'll get the others.
FLETCHER: What others? Wales and the kid are the last ones.
TERRILL: Oh, no. Texas is full of Rebels. *Lots* of work to do down in Texas.
FLETCHER: We get Josey Wales and it ends.
TERRILL: Doin' right ain't got no end.[21]

Jamie dies of his wounds, but Josey soon acquires another travelling companion – a quirky old Cherokee named Lone Watie (Chief Dan George, in effect reprising his role in *Little Big Man*). When we first see Lone Watie, he is dressed in a top hat and frock coat, the "white" diplomatic attire which he wore to Washington to negotiate with the federal government before the Civil War. When he throws in with Josey, he burns this hat and coat as a symbolic reassertion of his own renegade status. He also recounts his own experience of white America's perfidy – whether Josey wants to hear it or not. *Buffalo Bill*'s Sitting Bull uses silence to indicate his contempt for white America's mistreatment of his people, whereas Lone Watie never shuts up. Like Walter Brennan in *Red River*, Lone Watie is the garrulous sidekick whose amusing chatter underscores the hero's natural reticence ("I didn't surrender, neither; but, eh, they took my horse and made *him* surrender. They have him pullin' a wagon up in Kansas, I'll bet").[22]

The Outlaw Josey Wales is an expansive, episodic epic which begins as an odyssey of resistance and revenge but ultimately becomes a reaffirmation of community. Josey dispatches a wide variety of villains on his travels, but he spends as much time restoring life to lost souls as he spends dispensing death. He finds himself at the head of a motley band of travellers, most notably a disgraced young Navajo woman who is handy with a gun and even more loquacious than Lone Watie, and two Kansan women whom Josey rescues after their menfolk have been murdered by Comancheros. Eventually, they all reach the Edenic Texas ranch to which the Kansan pioneers had been heading before they were bushwhacked. Yet even in this paradise, danger lurks. Comanche chief Ten Bears (Will Sampson, *Buffalo Bill*'s Halsey) takes to the warpath in anger at being edged further off the map by the U.S. army. He prepares to launch an attack on the ranch Josey and his friends have made their home. Josey advises the others on how best to defend the ranch; then he rides out to meet Ten Bears and offers him an alternative to bloodshed:

JOSEY: You'll be Ten Bears?

TEN BEARS: I am Ten Bears.

JOSEY [*spits tobacco juice*]: I'm Josey Wales.

TEN BEARS: I have heard. You are the Grey Rider. You would not make peace with the bluecoats. *You* may go in peace.

JOSEY: I reckon not. I got nowhere to go.

TEN BEARS: Then you will die.

JOSEY [*nods*]: I came here to die with you – or live with you. Dyin' ain't so hard for men like you and me. It's livin' that's hard, when all you've ever cared about's been butchered or raped. Governments don't live together; people live together. From governments you don't always get a fair word or a fair fight. Well, I've come here to give you either one, or get either one from you. I came here like this so you'll know my word of death is true, and that my word of *life* is then true. The bear lives here, the wolf, the antelope, the Comanche – and so will we. Now, we'll only hunt what we need to live on, same as the Comanche does; and every spring when the grass turns green and the Comanche moves north, he can rest here in peace, butcher some of our cattle and jerk beef for the journey.

The sign of the Comanche – that will be on our lodge. That's my word of life.

TEN BEARS: And your word of death?

JOSEY: Here in my pistols, there in your rifles. I'm here for either one.

TEN BEARS: These things you say we will have, we already have.

JOSEY: That's true. I ain't promisin' you nothin' extra. I'm just givin' you life and you're givin' me life. And I'm sayin' that men can live together without butcherin' one another.

TEN BEARS: It's sad that governments are chiefed by the double-tongues. There is iron in your words of death for all Comanche to see – and so there is iron in your words of life. No signed paper can hold the iron. It must come from men. The words of Ten Bears carries the same iron of life and death. It is good that warriors such as we meet in the struggle of life – or death. It shall be life.[23]

Josey's speech is a filibuster by Eastwood's standards and has strong political overtones: environmentalism, coexistence, distrust of faceless power structures, and good faith based on individual honour. Further, Josey's "word of death" prefigures the 1980s nuclear concept of Mutual Assured Destruction. After Josey returns to the ranch, his friends hold an outdoor dance. Laura Lee (Sondra Locke), the younger Kansan woman, is in love with Josey, and asks him if they can play a song for him. The only song Josey can recall is "Rose of Alabama", which he once heard Jamie sing. By requesting this song, Josey is including his dead young friend in this new Eden. Eastwood's directorial touch is both deft and authoritative: the key here is subtlety rather than sentimentality. Josey and Laura become lovers, but Josey is still haunted by the violence of the past. Just as he prepares to leave the ranch, Terrill and his Redlegs catch up with him. However, Lone Watie and Josey's other friends spring to his aid, assuming the strategic positions Josey had taught them for their own defence against Ten Bears. This is no *High Noon*-style community which would wash its hands of the hero as soon as its own safety is no longer threatened. Even Laura's grandmother, whose son died for the Union, helps Josey against Terrill, setting personal friendship above an abstract cause. Josey's friends defeat the Redlegs, but Terrill escapes. Josey hunts Terrill down and kills him with his own sword, but he is also wounded. On his way back to the ranch Josey stops off at a neighbouring saloon. The people there are friends of his. When he enters, they address him as Mr. Wilson. They are busy recounting the details of a gunfight they witnessed in Mexico, in which the notorious desperado Josey Wales was killed. Their listeners are three men: two Texas Rangers, and Fletcher. This ploy of fabricating an infamous outlaw's death to let him live in peace thereafter was well-worn long before 1976 (*The Return of Frank James* (1940), *The Fastest Gun Alive* (1956) and, most ludicrously, Howard Hughes's *The Outlaw* (1943)). Here, however, it has especial significance. This saloon had been a wasteland in a withered community till Josey restored it with whiskey he took from the dead Comancheros. Echoing his agreement with Ten Bears, he had given them life; now his friends in the saloon give him life. The Texas Rangers clearly realize who Josey is, but they accept the pseudonym and consider their investigation closed. Fletcher keeps silent until the Rangers ride off, then tells Josey's friends that he doesn't believe their story. He says he thinks Josey is still alive. As Fletcher is speaking, Josey steps out into the street, readying himself for the last showdown. Yet, like the Blaisedell–Gannon face-off in *Warlock* and Sykes's confrontation with Deke Thornton at the end of *The Wild Bunch*, the expected blood-letting never comes. Fletcher surprises Josey:

FLETCHER: I think I'll go down to Mexico, to try to find him.
JOSEY: And then?
FLETCHER: He's got the first move. I owe him that. I think I'll try to
    tell him the war is over. [*Notices Josey is bleeding*] What do you say,
    Mr. Wilson?
JOSEY: I reckon so. I guess we all died a little in that damn war.[24]

As *The Wild Bunch* is essentially a celebration of death, so *The Outlaw Josey Wales* is fundamentally a celebration of life. *Josey Wales* was a popular success, grossing $12,800,000.[25] Critical reaction was mixed. In *The Hollywood Reporter*, Arthur Knight's notice was favourable, beginning with an appraisal of Eastwood's on-screen charisma: "As the Western loner, he tends to invoke 'a plague on both your houses', until forced to take a stand – invariably on the side of the weak and oppressed. He's all the 'good guys' of this nation's past 200 years rolled into one. And while we may on occasion deplore his methods, we definitely want him on our side. ... There is a positivism about *Josey Wales* that is really quite wonderful, especially today when we are never quite sure whom we should be rooting for. ... As director, Eastwood continues to grow in his mastery of the medium. This is a large-scale movie, and at no time is there any sense of faltering or indecision. ... At better than two hours, *The Outlaw Josey Wales* is that rarity – a long movie that doesn't seem too long. And that's a top credit for everyone concerned."[26]

Other reviewers were less enthusiastic. In *TIME*, Richard Schickel observed, "One man's classicism ... is another man's cliché", but also applauded Clint Eastwood's knack of "gaining sympathetic interest not so much through command as through insinuation. ... [H]e reminds us of a traditional American style of screen heroism – a moral man slow to rile but wonderfully skilled when he must finally enforce his conception of right and wrong. ... [H]e links us pleasingly, satisfyingly with our movie pasts, rekindles briefly a dying glow."[27] *Variety* was forthright in its condemnation of the film's violence: "Taking each slaughter set piece separately, the footage and editing are not especially offensive; it's the cumulative impact that really appalls[.] ... If each killing were instead to be a scene of sexual intercourse, the film would be super-X in calibre; but somehow murder – even good plot-motivated carnage (not here) – passes increasingly as mildly-rated 'entertainment'. ... A film can sometimes get away with borderline material if there is some strong motivation, but that's not the case here. ... It is nothing more than a prairie *Death Wish* in which the protagonist soon emerges more psychotic than wronged, despite the over-loaded backdrop of Civil War antagonisms, Indian repression and other cardboard excuses shoe-horned into the script."[28] In the *New York Times*, Richard Eder slated *Josey Wales* as "a soggy attempt at a post-Civil War western epic", concluding: "There seems to be a ghost of an attempt to assert the romantic individualism of the South against the cold expansionism of the North. Every Unionist is vicious and incompetent, whereas Wales, despite his spitting, is really a perfect gentleman. There is something cynical about this primitive one-sidedness[.] ... To the degree a movie asserts history, it should at least attempt to do it fairly."[29] Ten days later, Eder took another swipe at *Josey Wales*, calling it "long and thoroughly mediocre".[30]

The last line of *The Outlaw Josey Wales* – "I guess we all died a little in that damn war" – undoubtedly connects to the trauma of the Vietnam War, so recent and so bitter in American memory; and the new community Josey and friends forge in Texas is emblematic of the multicultural consensus steadily evolving in the United States in the wake of Vietnam.[31] The film has deep roots in recent American history and also in many earlier classic Westerns. Much of this I have outlined already but, in addition, *Josey Wales* owes some debt to Anthony Mann's *Bend of the River* (1952), in which an ex-border raider (James Stewart) is rehabilitated via defending a vulnerable pioneer community, and particularly to Samuel Fuller's *Run of the Arrow* (1957), with its un-reconstructed Confederate hero, quirky Indian sidekick and Yankee sadist. Like Rod Steiger's O'Meara in Fuller's film, Josey finds a new home and new family, and is completely purged of all hatred after killing the evil Northerner who has wrought so much needless destruction. Two of the most popular and impressive Westerns of the last twenty years – *The Outlaw Josey Wales* and Kevin Costner's *Dances With Wolves* (1990) – are hugely indebted to *Run of the Arrow*. *Josey Wales*, like *Run of the Arrow*, also overturns the *Two Flags West*/*Major Dundee* cliché of North and South burying their differences to fight Indians. Here the die-hard Confederate and the Indian are the natural allies; after all, their enemy is one and the same.

Yet, despite all of the above, the most significant single influence on *Josey Wales* is, a shade incongruously, John Ford. The old master had died in 1973, unrivalled poet of the genre. Even Ford's revisionist Westerns of the 1960s romanticized the frontier experience, whereas Eastwood had helped deromanticize the myth to the point of oblivion. However, Ford's films were essentially life-affirming, and so is *Josey Wales*. Josey is in fact a variation on John Wayne's Confederate outcast in Ford's *The Searchers*, but with potential for regeneration which Ethan Edwards never truly possessed. Josey is personally *aggrieved*, but Ethan is tortured by racial and sexual demons he can never vanquish. We could not imagine Ethan making peace with Scar as Josey does with Ten Bears. Yet there are other overtly Fordian allusions: when Josey and his companions reach the ranch, both the hymn on the soundtrack and the delight of these travellers evoke memories of *Wagon Master* (1950); the open-air dance is a rudimentary relative of *My Darling Clementine*'s famous outdoor church-dance sequence; and Josey's friends shoot at Terrill's Redlegs through crucifix-shaped holes in the doors and window-shutters, just as cavalrymen ward off Apaches in *Rio Grande*.

There is considerable irony in Eastwood using John Ford as a principal frame of reference in his 1976 film about a mythic gunfighter, for that same year, Eastwood's mentor, Don Siegel, directed Ford's most famous protégé in the tale of a legendary gunman dying of cancer. After this, the genre's greatest icon bowed out – and so, effectively, did the Hollywood Western.

The Shootist (Paramount) was a superb elegiac Western, as fine as *The Gunfighter* and *Ride the High Country*. It chronicled the last week in the life of John Bernard Books, notorious gunman (like Gregory Peck's Jimmy Ringo) and former lawman (like Joel McCrea's Steve Judd). Like those earlier films, *The Shootist* focused on a heroic Westerner who has outlived his time. Both his skill with guns and his fiercely individualistic integrity are irrelevant in 1901 Carson City. Books is a man of violence in a now mostly pacified civilization, a legend living out his last days surrounded by the mundane. *The Shootist* is about the death of the old West, once and for all. There will be no more "last stands" after this; this is *the* last, literally the edge of the sunset. *The Shootist* marks the passing of the last hero – and, in an increasingly regulated and implicitly feminized society – the last man truly worthy of the name. Most of all, *The Shootist* is about John Wayne.

The film opens with a potted history of Books's background, accompanied by clips from previous Wayne classics: *Red River*, John Farrow's *Hondo* (1953), Howard Hawks's *Rio Bravo* (1959) and his *El Dorado* (1967). It is not so much instant identification of actor with character as an outright merger. With these few excerpts we are reminded that the Western has aged with Wayne. In *The Shootist*, we watch the genre die with him. There could be no more fitting elegy for the man or the genre. Wayne's own battle against cancer in the early 1960s had only added to his indestructible image. *Buffalo Bill and the Indians* had rebuked white America for burlesquing the Indian's tragedy. *The Outlaw Josey Wales* had romanticized regeneration in the aftermath of divisive national trauma. *The Shootist*, however, is primarily concerned with one particular American personality rather than with U.S. national identity. Never in the history of Hollywood has a film been more perfectly timed. The foremost star of the genre, the greatest box office draw in cinema history and the screen's most aggressive symbol of U.S. patriotism, John Wayne had become an American institution in his own right. His last film, reverent and self-referential, ended the Western's reign in the midst of the nation's Bicentennial celebrations. Yet in among all the fortuitous coincidences lurked an unwelcome one: John Wayne's own cancer was coming back.

Books arrives in Carson City to consult old acquaintance Dr. Hostetler (James Stewart), who confirms he has an advanced cancer. Even more than the last teaming of Wayne and Stewart, this is an old man's film. *The Man Who Shot Liberty Valance* is primarily about disillusion; *The Shootist* focuses on the last, hardest obstacle of all. We are back to Buffalo Bill's remark: "the last thing a man wants to do is the last thing he does". The scene in Hostetler's office is a masterpiece of restraint, entirely appropriate for an elegy obsessed with dignity. Books takes lodgings with a starchy local widow, Bond Rogers (Lauren Bacall), whose teenage son Gillom (Ron Howard) yearns to break free from the boredom of modern urban life. A basically decent youth, Gillom is trying to grow up too fast. When we first see him he is with the loutish Jay Cobb (Bill McKinney, Terrill in *Josey Wales*). Cobb is an irredeemable, swaggering punk akin to Skip Homeier's Hunt Bromley in *The Gunfighter*, whereas Gillom, like Ron Starr's Heck Longtree in *Ride the High Country*, truly just needs a finer role model. As Books holes up at the Rogers house, the vultures gather, among them a thoroughly obnoxious lawman (Harry Morgan) who gloats over Books's pain; an ex-lover (Sheree North) who wants to marry him so she can trade on his name; and a writer (Richard Lenz) who wants to immortalize him in lurid, blood-and-thunder prose. Of this last, Books snarls, "I'll not be remembered for a pack o' lies".[32] This is but one instance of Books's obsession with dignity. Just as he will not have his memory defiled by a scurrilous opportunist, Books ultimately cannot tolerate the prospect of degrading death. He decides to die quickly, with dignity, and rid the town of some local undesirables into the bargain. He arranges to have the loud-mouthed Cobb, an old enemy (Richard Boone) and a sure-shot gambler (Hugh O'Brian) meet him for a showdown in a cavernous saloon. Books kills his three opponents, but he is shotgunned in the back by the bartender. Gillom, who in the course of the film has come to idolize Books, enters just in time to witness this last killing. He picks up Books's gun and shoots the bartender, then tosses the gun far across the huge saloon. Gillom thus renounces the lure of violence. Books nods his approval, and dies content.

The *Shootist* grossed $5,987,000 at the North American box office.[33] As with the genre's other explorations of legend in 1976, critical response was mixed. In the September 11 1976 issue of *The New Republic*, Stanley Kauffmann observed: "Out of this view of the past that reflects the vantage point of the present, a touchingly elegaic [*sic*] film might have been made; but this script is absolutely awful."[34] In *The New Yorker*, Pauline Kael was even more acerbic: "Wayne attempts to go back and complete his Western legend, but it's always dangerous when a movie sets out to be a classic, and the director, Don Siegel, who has an enjoyably trashy talent, has been so paralyzed by his high intentions that he's made a piece of solemn, unenjoyable trash. ... In 1976, after the Western hero is dead, how can movies go on bringing us the message that he's dying? *The Shootist* digs him up to rebury him, and then has the gall to tell the story of how other people want to exploit him. Siegel has no real interest in the code; he's in his element when he stages the final shoot-out, but there's no rationale for it – no greed, no anger, and no moral drive."[35] *TIME*'s Jay Cocks wrote: "*The Shootist* is deliberately low-keyed and sometimes affecting. But it is hampered by a sentimental, overwrought script and, finally, by its own reserve. The movie keeps the rigid bearing of a kid trying to sit still at a wake."[36] *New York Times* reviewer Richard Eder noted: "None of the characters have any real precision, and after the first impact they wither. The attitude of Books to his own passing ... is quite unclear. Is the extinction of his own violent way of life something he accepts or resists? Mr. Siegel allows him to point both ways, and the ambiguity takes the bone out of the movie and it collapses."[37] In *The Hollywood Reporter*, Arthur Knight asserted: "Just when it seemed that the western was an endangered species, due for extinction because it had repeated itself too many times, Wayne and Siegel have managed to validate it once more. ... *The Shootist* tentatively raises the possibility that we may have lost more than we gained. It's a film to remember."[38] *Variety*'s review was positively exuberant: "*The Shootist* will stand as one of John Wayne's towering achievements, and his very best since *True Grit*. Don Siegel's terrific film is simply beautiful, and beautifully simple[.] ... Legitimate masculinity, not phony macho stuff, pervades the writing, action and direction. ... The entire film is in totally correct balance, artistically and technically[.] ... *The Shootist* is one of the great films of our time."[39]

John Wayne was not principally an actor. He was a star – the greatest Hollywood has ever produced. Yet when he *did* act, extending his range beyond his standard characterization, his finest performances all stressed some degree of vulnerability, and *The Shootist* followed in that distinguished tradition. His John Bernard Books is alternately gruff and gentle. Especially poignant are two statements to Bond Rogers: "I've been full of alone lately", and "I'm a dying man, scared of the dark."[40] Yet Books's most important relationship is with Gillom Rogers, to whom he articulates his personal code: "I won't be wronged, I won't be insulted, and I won't be laid a hand on. I don't do these things to other people, and I require the same from them."[41] As a mature Western star, one of John Wayne's most frequent postures had been as a moral exemplar for the younger generation. Gillom is the last in this long line of disciples.

Buffalo Bill and the Indians ends with Cody's fake triumph over Sitting Bull in the arena, *The Outlaw Josey Wales* with Josey riding back to Laura and his other friends as the fabric of post-Civil War America slowly begins to heal. So one legend continues his tawdry self-mythology; the second rides off into obscurity and contentment; but the third lies dead and bloody in an ornate saloon. *The Shootist* closes with Gillom returning home, townsman of a stiller town and citizen of a sadder world as the American flag waves listlessly on the street corner – and so it should. A vital era of American life has just ended. Gillom and his contemporaries must meet the challenges of the new century without the aid or continuing example of legendary heroes of old. In the same manner, the

American Republic must face its third century without the comfort and the inspiration of the Western. The myth is over. Now we are on our own.

The Shootist was John Wayne's last film, but it was not his final appearance on a screen. That came on April 9 1979, when he appeared on the stage of the Dorothy Chandler Pavilion in Los Angeles to give Michael Cimino's *The Deer Hunter* the Oscar for Best Picture of 1978. Ravaged by cancer, gaunt, skeletal, clearly dying, Wayne told the thunderously applauding audience that he planned to be around for a long time yet. It was more courageous than anything he had ever done in films, and it was heartbreaking. It was also something else.

In half a century on screen, it was the first and only time John Wayne had ever lied.

Conclusion

I N 1939, the year of *Stagecoach* and war in Europe, the concept of two-ocean security still shielded Americans from conflicts raging beyond their shores. After Hiroshima and Nagasaki, two-ocean security had irretrievably vanished; so, after Vietnam, had American invincibility. Yet America has a third ocean, one which no foreign power can ever cross or conquer. It is the Ocean of Dreams.

For close to four decades, the Western was the most potent of these dreams. Now, however, the genre is virtually as outmoded as two-ocean security, each of which had roots in a once dominant ideology predicated on belief in exceptional national destiny. Ironically, as the Western ceased to be a vital force in American cinema, the most impressive genre artifacts of the late 1970s were two openly celebratory television mini-series. *How the West Was Won* (pilot *The MacAhans* (1976), series 1977–1979) was loosely based on the 1962 Cinerama epic of the same name, starring James Arness, the small screen's John Wayne, as a grizzled, unfailingly benevolent mountain man at the head of a hardy pioneer family. Its content was a traditional blend of action and sentiment, its style folksy and expansive. Far more ambitious was *Centennial* (1978), the twelve-part epic based on James A. Michener's monumental novel. *Centennial* ran nineteen-and-a-half hours and spanned more than two hundred years as it chronicled the history of a Colorado town. Although vehemently condemning the butchery of Indians by a racist cavalry officer (Richard Crenna) and emphasizing the multicultural composition of the frontier, *Centennial* skilfully absorbed its revisionist components within a larger framework of consensus ideology. In essence, *Centennial* acknowledged disgraceful episodes from the nation's past while asserting that, overall, America's history still merited celebration. Awesome in scope and magnificent in execution, *Centennial* has no critical reputation in the manner of the Afro-American epic *Roots* (1977), which may have more to do with its partially conservative representation of America's past than with its inherent high quality.

In 1980, the very year Americans elected as president a man who traded on his association with the Western, the genre took another blow. Moviemakers who believed the time was ripe for a revival of the Western had their hopes dashed when three films flopped at the box office. Walter Hill's *The Long Riders*, yet another Jesse James movie, was gimmicky (four sets of brothers portrayed four sets of brothers) and derivative (of *The Wild Bunch* – as was Hill's 1987 modern Western *Extreme Prejudice*). William Wiard's *Tom Horn*, played by a dying Steve McQueen, was unremittingly bleak. Most significant of all was the disaster which befell Michael Cimino's *Heaven's Gate*, an ambitious epic reconstruction of the 1892 Johnson County War. The film was an overlong, prodigiously indulgent mix of variable performances, lyrical beauty and stupefying banality which not only crippled any prospect of a major revival of the Western but wrecked its releasing studio, United Artists, in the process.[1] *Heaven's Gate*, like *Centennial*, stressed the multi-ethnic nature of the nineteenth-century West, even featuring immigrants speaking in their native language. Yet *Centennial* essentially advanced the melting-pot interpretation of America, *Heaven's Gate* the salad bowl. *Centennial*'s immigrant heroes were highly individualized characters, resourceful, entrepreneurial and of preponderantly Northern European stock, while *Heaven's Gate*'s immigrants were an undifferentiated mass of proletarian Eastern Europeans. The genre had habitually marginalized issues of class to the point of invisibility. Moviegoers who enjoyed Westerns did not go to them with expectations of a quasi-Marxist discourse, while the genre was anathema to many of those who would be ideologically responsive to such a theme. Instead of embracing diametrically opposite political impulses and doubling the box office gross, *Heaven's Gate* fell between two stools and bombed abysmally.

The Hollywood Western had no solid resonance in the era of Ronald Reagan, and this was more appropriate than might first seem apparent. I have already indicated in the Introduction to this book that Ronald Reagan's status as a cowboy star was, in truth, tenuous. He was neither much of a cowboy nor, in movie terms, much of a star. If Reagan had not subsequently entered national politics and capitalized on the image of the leathery Westerner there, today he would be about as well-remembered as Wayne Morris. Excluding a couple of early lightweight comedies with superficial links to the genre, Ronald Reagan appeared in a grand total of six big-screen Westerns; he was top-billed in only two. Paul Newman has made (and *starred*) in more Westerns than Reagan but, if Newman had run for president, no one would have referred to him as a cowboy star. The point is not merely that Ronald Reagan subjugated reality to a Hollywood-confected myth but that, artfully, he supplanted his personal "mythic" past, grounded in actuality, with another version he preferred more. Bearing in mind both this and the build-up of America's massive deficit during Reagan's presidency, it is fitting that the one genre (or, more accurately, trans-generic theme) which skyrocketed in the 1980s was the "displacement movie". By this I mean narratives, usually comedies, in which the protagonists undergo a change of identity, time and/or space. To cite but two examples, comedies where the central characters masquerade as the opposite sex (*Victor/Victoria*, *Tootsie* (both 1982)) or travel back through time (*Back to the Future* (1985), *Peggy Sue Got Married* (1986)) are displacement movies. These films were enjoyable on their own terms, but their fundamental appeal lay in implausible fantasies of escape from self and from society. Granted, such films were mostly lightweight; but in the Reagan era, the lightweight movies tended to be the box office heavyweights. Thus running away from reality became a central theme of American cinema during the Reagan years. Westerns certainly contained elements of escapism and fantasy – but theirs was a fantasy rooted in time and place, a fantasy of responsibility or of destiny or of tragedy rather than one of farce. Whether overtly or obliquely, the Western was keyed to America's past, and not a past which time machines could alter. The final part of the *Back to the Future* trilogy (1990) sends its heroes back through time to the old West, but that does not make the movie a Western – merely a movie *monkeying around* with the Western. The "displacement movie" is popular with the twelve to twenty-four age bracket which constitutes a majority of modern cinema audiences, a generation enthralled by special effects (which Westerns cannot provide), a reputedly ahistorical generation largely steeped in televisual culture, and one which has grown up without the Western. Little wonder that the great deluge of the 1950s and 1960s is now no more than a sporadic trickle.

The next loudly trumpeted revival of the genre was in 1985, but two films do not a resurrection make. Lawrence Kasdan's *Silverado* was an enjoyable, spirited, action-packed adventure, stylish in its own right yet replete with touches of homage to classic Westerns of the past. Clint Eastwood's *Pale Rider* was not so much homage as plagiarism. Within the first few minutes it became clear that the film was no more than a remake – not a reworking, but a remake – of *Shane*, featuring miners rather than farmers, and with the community's saviour now Eastwood's mystical (and possibly reincarnated) persona from *High Plains Drifter* (1972), hardly a fascinating creation from the outset. After his superb

The Outlaw Josey Wales, Eastwood had returned to the genre in 1985 with no more than second-hand dross. The finest big-screen "Westerns" of the 1980s were actually Philip Kaufman's magisterial, romantic, panoramic paean to America in space, *The Right Stuff* (1983), and Brian De Palma's splendidly mythic film version of *The Untouchables* (1987), in which Kevin Costner's Eliot Ness effectively ran the gamut of movie Wyatt Earps, starting as an idealistic lawman akin to Henry Fonda in *My Darling Clementine*, becoming buddy to Sean Connery's Irish cop in the style of Burt Lancaster to Kirk Douglas in *Gunfight at the O.K. Corral* (but without *Gunfight*'s homosexual subtext) and ending as a cold-blooded killer similar to James Garner in *Hour of the Gun*.

Toward the end of a decade in the doldrums, when it seemed as though the genre proper had no more wonders to offer, there appeared the most remarkable Western since *The Wild Bunch*. In my case studies I have twice refuted the conceited notion of a "best-ever Western". I remain convinced that such a title can only ever be awarded as a matter of personal taste, not one of academic objectivity. So, if I may be forgiven for offering my own wholly subjective assessment, I would nominate as the most magnificent of all Westerns not a cinema release, but the 1988 television mini-series, *Lonesome Dove*.

Directed by Australian Simon Wincer, from Larry McMurtry's Pulitzer Prize-winning novel, *Lonesome Dove* is an epic saga of men who leave a dying community to embark on the greatest of odysseys. Robert Duvall and Tommy Lee Jones portray two ageing former Texas Rangers, bored with their lives in Lonesome Dove, a South Texan backwater at the ragged edge of nowhere. The duo are morally upright men, but they steal a herd of cattle which they then drive north to Montana, planning to set up as cattle barons in as yet unsettled territory. Admittedly, this sounds as if the protagonists from *Ride the High Country* had wandered into the script of *Red River*, and along the way there are also minor homages to *The Searchers*, *Rio Bravo* and *The Outlaw Josey Wales*; one secondary character is a sheriff with precisely the same name as George Kennedy's lawman in *Bandolero!* Yet, above all, *Lonesome Dove* is an original work of dazzling scope, true emotion, passion and depth, in six hours as much psychological as physical epic – and never more so than in the relationship between the two central characters. Augustus McCrae (Duvall) and Woodrow F. Call (Jones) have lived cheek by jowl for so long that they have, in effect, become the same man (they have a virtually identical code of ethics). Yet, in another sense, they represent warring halves of the American and, indeed, the human psyche. McCrae is a hedonist and free spirit; Call is a puritan with capitalist aspirations. Although each regrets the passing of the old days, only one will survive when they reach their last frontier in Montana. The supreme irony of *Lonesome Dove* is that McCrae, who lives life to the full, sees himself, in slightly delusory terms, as an unappreciated heroic legend. Yet it will be the unimaginative Woodrow Call who ultimately becomes the true legend, while remaining largely inadequate as a human being.

Cinema Westerns since the late 1980s have been of variable quality. Two have even won Best Picture Oscars. Throughout the golden age of the Hollywood Western from 1939 to 1976, no film in the genre had won this award. The only previous Western to win the coveted statuette had been Wesley Ruggles's *Cimarron* of 1931 (disastrously remade by Anthony Mann in 1960). Yet in the early 1990s, two actors lifted Best Picture and Best Director awards, Kevin Costner for *Dances With Wolves* (1990), and Clint Eastwood for *Unforgiven* (1992). *Dances With Wolves* was an epic reworking of themes previously covered in *Broken Arrow*, *Run of the Arrow* and *Little Big Man* but also a film of majestic sweep and lyricism. The story of an army lieutenant (Costner) who is assigned to an isolated frontier outpost but gradually becomes assimilated within the Sioux nation, this was the chronicle of one man's odyssey of self-discovery and self-fulfilment – but with a conservative message at the core of its countercultural idyll. In those earlier films, James Stewart, Rod Steiger and Dustin Hoffman had each married Indian women, an integral part of their assimilation within the larger Indian society. *Dances With Wolves* sidestepped miscegenation by conveniently having a white woman (Mary McDonnell) as a ready-made romantic interest living among the Sioux. Thus, at heart, *Dances With Wolves* was not so much a repudiation of WASP America as, in George Bush's "kinder, gentler" society, a hymn to an attractive alternative (and ecologically harmonious) culture in which nice young WASP couples may find a home. *Unforgiven*, by contrast, was a dark, savage tale about a reformed killer (Eastwood) who sets out to avenge the mutilation of two prostitutes and ends by ridding a town of its corrupt, sadistic lawman (Gene Hackman). With much contemplation of the nature and psychology of violence, it was a vast improvement on Eastwood's last entry in the genre – up until the showdown, which degenerated into the same old *High Plains Drifter/Pale Rider* nonsense about the man who cannot be killed, as several villains blast away at Eastwood, in full view and at point-blank range, but he still walks away without a scratch.

Other major early 1990s Westerns included two new versions of the Wyatt Earp saga, George P. Cosmatos's superior *Tombstone* (1993), starring Kurt Russell, and Lawrence Kasdan's ambitious but overlong *Wyatt Earp* (1994), yet another purposeful attempt to mythologize Kevin Costner. Yet so far, possibly the finest 1990s film set far back in the American past was, in truth, at the edge of the genre: the four-hour reconstruction of a vital Civil War battle in Ronald F. Maxwell's magnificent *Gettysburg* (1993). A sizeable number of lesser Westerns have appeared in the 1990s but in qualitative terms the Western's best hope for the future would appear to be the occasional, superbly crafted epic. *Centennial*, *Lonesome Dove*, *Dances With Wolves*, *Tombstone* and *Gettysburg* all demonstrate the Western can still captivate if approached with ambition, with intelligence, with integrity and with respect.

However, as a central force in the culture of contemporary American society, the Western is never coming back. It strikes me that the genre in fact ran a course parallel to human life, with the difference that its birth and death cannot be exactly determined, whereas specific crucial areas of human experience which are frequently gradual and ongoing can, in the Hollywood Western, be pinpointed meticulously: onset of maturity (*Stagecoach*); increase of sexual awareness (*The Outlaw*); first full-blown sexual experience (*Duel in the Sun*); work (*Red River*); approach of middle age (*The Gunfighter*); assumption of greater responsibility (*High Noon*); disillusionment and midlife crisis (*The Man Who Shot Liberty Valance*, *Ride the High Country*); and intimations of mortality (most notably *The Wild Bunch* and *The Shootist*). Thus the genre's life cycle has now run its course.

There is no need to reiterate in copious detail the myriad of reasons for the Western's demise. The ugly reality of ever-increasing violence in modern American society helped puncture the appeal of a genre which sanctified gunplay, and moviegoers could take little comfort from John Wayne making Western towns safe for the American future if they were themselves afraid of being mugged on the way home (one example of how the cop movie might fulfil a modern societal need which Westerns could not).

The waning of American power in the world, especially with regard to the Vietnam débâcle, made mockery of long-cherished national concepts of invincibility and righteousness, and the Western was a casualty of the accompanying cultural fallout.

Television had, during the years of the Western's primacy, saturated American homes with small-screen frontier sagas. In this respect, the genre eventually became too commonplace and, frankly, too traditionalist – too old-hat – to fascinate the younger generation *en masse*. In the space age, youngsters were now more apt to respond to science-fiction adventures than the lore of the old West. The omnipresence of television Westerns, I suggested in my Introduction, finally familiarized the genre to the point of ennui and derision. Moreover, disenchantment with America's role in Vietnam and fundamental socio-political shifts in American culture doomed television Western series as much as their big-screen counterparts.[2]

Those fundamental shifts were major factors in the genre's demise. They also constitute a primary reason why the Western will never – *can never* – regain its former pre-eminence. The United States of the post-Bicentennial era is not the land the Western celebrated. America is not the nation it once was, and it never will be that nation again. Overall, the genre posited a socially homogenous ideal, with white male in-dividualists at its pinnacle. Disparate minority groups have in the last three decades become more vocal and more visible in asserting their own particular American identities, and these are antithetical to the dominant ideology of the Western. Once multiculturalism is empowered within a society it is there to stay. The Western might occasionally incorporate modern political themes as subplots but, in all probability, could not lastingly accommodate feminism, Black rights and gay rights as crucial issues within the genre. As with the quasi-Marxism of *Heaven's Gate*, such an innovation would alienate the traditionalists and likely still fail to entice droves of the multicultural campaigners to take a second look at a genre which has historically marginalized their causes out of existence. In return, multiculturalism has marginalized the West-ern. If, as a consequence, the white male middle-class American has gone on the defensive, then Michael Douglas's frustrated white-collar worker on the rampage in Joel Schumacher's urban rage thriller *Falling Down* (1992) is the 1990s equivalent of his father's cowboy on the run from modern civilization in *Lonely Are the Brave* thirty years earlier.

Certainly, the Western has been supplanted in genre terms by the police thriller, the road movie and the science-fiction epic. Suffice it to state here that the cop movie is natural successor to the community Western, while the road movie is the heir of the odyssey Western, and the science-fiction epic by and large has much the same appeal (and for much the same reasons) as those "displacement movies" I discussed earlier. As in the community Westerns of the 1950s, cop movies may ultimately judge society the true villain, though here the fault lies not with cowardly or self-interested citizens but with a haywire judicial system which gives reprehensible criminals the benefit of the doubt. Don Siegel's *Dirty Harry* (1971) is, above all, urban America's moral equivalent of *High Noon*, straight down to the cop (Clint Eastwood) throwing his badge away at the end. Road movies tend to favour outlaws over lawmen, romanticizing outcasts who find their souls by defying societal restrictions. Ridley Scott's marvellous *Thelma & Louise* (1991) effectively reprises the end of *Butch Cassidy and the Sundance Kid*, freezing on the movie's heroines in the second before their romantic deaths become too bloody for comfort. Science-fiction epics address a mythic and either global or intergalactic future as surely as the Western addressed a specifically American mythic past; so, in a sense, the science-fiction genre flourishes not merely as a successor to the Western but as a repudiation of its overt nationalism and its explicit temporality, *Independence Day* (1996) notwithstanding.

In two decades of the Western's relative quiescence, film-makers have increasingly turned to other areas of the American past which were long neglected during the genre's supremacy. A few were searing attacks on the U.S. corporate power structure for abuses of race (Milos Forman's *Ragtime* (1981)) or class (John Sayles's "socialist Western" *Matewan* (1987)). While these films were anything but celebratory, American cinema is on the whole still wedded to concepts of myth to explain and advance national identity. Clearly the Western no longer qualifies, at least to modern cinema audiences, as a viable foundation myth. American culture therefore requires a new foundation myth from the nation's history. One is already at hand. Modern America's most potent myth is born from its most recent turmoil.

Vietnam has killed the Western twice. The first time, the war in Vietnam debilitated the cinematic myth of the West. The second killing is still an ongoing process: the cinematic myth of the Vietnam experience is gradually supplanting the Western as America's most resonant historical moment.

This mythic exchange of the West for Vietnam is not just a case of new frontiers for old, nor of Western movies in jungle clothing, as in John Wayne's *The Green Berets*. The Vietnam era has the same vital cultural components as the end of the Civil War and the end of World War II: the violence of war; conflict with a non-Caucasian people; domestic racial problems; growing corporate influence; the returning veterans' need to reconcile themselves to society; and the political ramifications of the death of a beloved president.

In the sensitive climate of Cold War America, film-makers encoded these components in narratives set after 1865. Today's film-makers are bolder. Political sensibilities have changed. The crusty, militaristic patriotism of John Ford is long gone. In the 1990s, cinema's primary chronicler of American identity is no celebrant. The unctuous liberalism of Oliver

Stone owes more to Stanley Kramer than to Ford. Again, America has moved on. Allegory is no longer necessary – and in all probability, no longer profitable. Now Hollywood offers America its history and its identity through the prism of the 1960s instead of the 1860s. Robert Zemeckis's *Forrest Gump* (1994) is *Little Big Man* for the baby-boomers, but the most significant illustration of the mythic power of the 1960s is Clint Eastwood's 1993 film, *A Perfect World*. Eastwood stars as a Texas lawman in pursuit of a genial outlaw, played by Kevin Costner. Given stars and the plot, it sounds like a Western; yet it is set in Texas of 1963, shortly before John Kennedy's fateful trip – the last time "a perfect world" was possible, according to the most potent myth of late twentieth-century America.

Film has been the great popular art form of a century which the United States has dominated. As the century approaches its end, American cinema will continue to forge resonant national myths for the Republic and the world beyond. Yet the Western, America's gift to the world, may only survive in palsied form, if at all. Seventeen years after his death, John Wayne remains one of the most revered of national heroes, both for the image of America which he projected to the world and for his valiant last battle against cancer. There are public monuments to John Wayne in the United States, but the fact that the Western has not really survived him is perhaps the greatest one of all.

The new national myth is of another America. The Vietnam veteran has replaced the itinerant gunfighter as the heroic stranger at the heart of modern America's movie narratives. For a cinema-going public with little interest in the past, a generation is far enough back. So, appropriately, the cultural components of the 1960s and 1970s are used to explain the only America, the only "mythic" history, the only national identity the twelve to twenty-four age group of moviegoers can relate to: their own. This is not as self-centred as it sounds. To them, this *is* history. It is their point of departure. Vietnam was their fathers' war, Camelot the mythic golden age before the Fall, and the gunfire in Dallas the moment Eden was forever denied; and they are not at all offended that, earlier that morning in Fort Worth, John Fitzgerald Kennedy had disdained to wear a stetson.

Notes

Introduction

1. William Manchester, *The Glory and the Dream: A Narrative History of America, 1932–1972* (Michael Joseph, London, 1975), p. 643; John Griggs, *The Films of Gregory Peck* (Columbus Books, London, 1988), p. 155.

2. Frederick Jackson Turner, "The Significance of the Frontier in American History" (1893), reprinted in Ray Allen Billington (ed.), *Frontier and Section: Selected Essays of Frederick Jackson Turner* (Prentice-Hall, Englewood Cliffs, 1961), p. 62.

3. See Henry Nash Smith, *Virgin Land: The American West as Symbol and Myth* (Harvard University Press, Cambridge, [1950] 1978), *passim*; Richard Slotkin, *Regeneration Through Violence: The Mythology of the American Frontier, 1600–1860* (Wesleyan University Press, Middletown [1973] 1987), *passim*; and Richard Slotkin, *The Fatal Environment: The Myth of the Frontier in the Age of Industrialization, 1800–1890* (Harper Collins, New York, [1985] 1994), *passim*.

4. Garry Wills, *Reagan's America: Innocents at Home* (Heinemann, London, 1988), p. 174.

5. *Dodge City* (Warner Brothers, 1939), directed by Michael Curtiz, screenplay by Robert Buckner.

6. On women in Westerns, see, e.g., Philip French, *Westerns: Aspects of a Movie Genre* (Secker & Warburg, London, 1973), pp. 62–9; Will Wright, *Six Guns and Society: A Structural Study of the Western* (University of California Press, Berkeley, [1975] 1977), pp. 41–5, 84, 165–6; David Thomson, "Saloon Sirens and Prairie Roses", in Ann Lloyd (ed.), *The Movie*, Vol. 10 (Orbis, London, 1982), pp. 2350–53; Sandra Kay Schackel, "Women in Western Films: The Civilizer, the Saloon Singer, and Their Modern Sister", in Archie P. McDonald (ed.), *Shooting Stars: Heroes and Heroines of Western Film* (Indiana University Press, Bloomington, 1987), pp. 196–217; Jon Tuska, *The American West in Film: Critical Approaches to the Western* (University of Nebraska Press, Lincoln, [1985] 1988), pp. 223–35; Pam Cook's essay on women in Edward Buscombe (ed.), *The BFI Companion to the Western* (André Deutsch/BFI, London, 1988), pp. 240–43; and Jane Tompkins, *West of Everything: The Inner Life of Westerns* (Oxford University Press, London, 1992), pp. 47–67.

7. On Indians in Westerns, see, e.g., French, *op. cit.*, pp. 76–93; John H. Lenihan, *Showdown: Confronting Modern America in the Western Film* (University of Illinois Press, Urbana, [1980] 1985), pp. 25–32, 38–51, 57–83; Tuska, *op. cit.*, pp. 52, 54–61, 72, 79, 86–8, 96, 102–3, 105, 111–12, 113, 120; Hartmut Lutz's essay on Indians in Buscombe, *op. cit.*, pp. 155–9; and Tompkins, *op. cit.*, pp. 7–10.

8. On Blacks in Westerns, see, e.g., French, *op. cit.*, pp. 94–9; Lenihan, *op. cit.*,

pp. 56, 84–6; Wayne Michael Sarf, *God Bless You, Buffalo Bill: A Layman's Guide to History and the Western Film* (Fairleigh Dickinson University Press, New York, 1983), pp. 224–9; and Jim Pines's essay on Blacks in Buscombe, *op. cit.*, pp. 68–71.

9. William L. O'Neill, *American High: The Years of Confidence, 1945–1960* (Macmillan, New York, 1986), p. 7.

10. Turner, *loc. cit.*

11. See David Pirie (ed.), *Anatomy of the Movies* (Windward, London, 1981), p. 208.

12. See also the brief discussion of the literary tradition of journey narratives in Kim Newman, *Wild West Movies: Or How the West Was Found, Won, Lost, Lied About, Filmed and Forgotten* (Bloomsbury, London, 1990), p. 48.

13. On Mann, see André Bazin, "The Evolution of the Western", in his *What is Cinema?: Vol. II*, translated by Hugh Gray (University of California Press, Berkeley, 1971), p. 156; J. H. Fenwick and Jonathan Green-Armytage, "Now You See It: Landscape and Anthony Mann", in *Sight and Sound: The International Film Quarterly*, Autumn 1965, Vol. 34 No. 4 (British Film Institute, London, 1965), pp. 186–9; Jim Kitses, *Horizons West: Anthony Mann, Budd Boetticher, Sam Peckinpah: Studies of Authorship within the Western* (Thames & Hudson, London, 1969), pp. 29–87; Julian Petley, "Mann of the West", in Lloyd, *op. cit.*, Vol. 5 Chapter 53 (1981), pp. 1046–8; and Tuska, *op. cit.*, pp. 85–100.

On Boetticher, see Kitses, *op. cit.*, pp. 89–137; Richard T. Jameson, "The Ranown Cycle", in Lloyd, *op. cit.*, Vol. 5 Chapter 53, pp. 1054–5; and Tuska, *op. cit.*, pp. 101–14.

14. See Wright, *op. cit.*, pp. 15, 32–59, 130–53; and Herbert L. Jacobson, "Cowboy, Pioneer and American Soldier", in *Sight and Sound*, April–June 1953, Vol. 22 No. 4, pp. 189–90.

15. See, e.g., Fenwick and Green-Armytage, *op. cit.*, pp. 188–9; and Kitses, *op. cit.*, pp. 33, 66, 68–72.

16. David Potter, "American Individualism in the Twentieth Century" (1963), reprinted in Rupert Wilkinson (ed.), *American Social Character: Modern Interpretations from the '40s to the present* (HarperCollins, New York, 1992), pp. 161–2.

17. *The Man Who Shot Liberty Valance* (Paramount, 1962), directed by John Ford, screenplay by James Warner Bellah and Willis Goldbeck, based on the story by Dorothy M. Johnson.

18. *The Life and Times of Judge Roy Bean* (National General Pictures, 1972), directed by John Huston, screenplay by John Milius.

19. André Bazin, "The Western", in his *What is Cinema?: Vol. II*, pp. 141, 143.

From here, this chapter mostly condenses my M.Phil. thesis's analysis of previous writings on the genre. For the full text, see "The Hollywood Western: A Bibliographical Evaluation", in Michael Coyne, *The Social Construction of American National Identity: The Role of the Hollywood Western, 1939–1962* (submitted at Lancaster University, England, 1994), pp. 20–53.

20. Bazin, "The Western", pp. 143, 147; and see John G. Cawelti, *The Six-Gun Mystique* (Bowling Green State University Popular Press, Bowling Green, [1970] 1984), pp. 83–4.

21. See, e.g., Kathryn C. Esselman, "From Camelot to Monument Valley", in Jack Nachbar (ed.), *Focus on the Western* (Prentice-Hall, Englewood Cliffs, 1974), pp. 9–18.

22. Cawelti, *op. cit.*, pp. 65–8.

23. See Andrew Sarris, *The American Cinema: Directors and Directions, 1929–1968* (E. P. Dutton, New York, 1968), *passim*; and Andrew Sarris, *The John Ford Movie Mystery* (Secker & Warburg, London, 1976), *passim*, but especially p. 160 in this context.

24. See Cawelti, *op. cit.*, pp. 10–21, 36–50, 58, 74, 85–91, 106–7, 110, 112; and Frederick Elkin, "The Psychological Appeal for Children of the Hollywood B Western", and Peter Homans, "Puritanism Revisited: An Analysis of the Contemporary Screen-Image Western", both in Nachbar, *op. cit.*, pp. 73–7 and 84–92 respectively.

25. Wright, *op. cit.*, p. 131, and pp. 130–84.

26. *Ibid.*, pp. 85–122; Wright's analysis of the "professional plot" is on pp. 164–84.

27. See Coyne, *op. cit.*, pp. 32–4.

28. French, *op. cit.*, p. 10; see also the revised edition of French (1977), p. 199, and French's review of Will Wright's *Six Guns and Society*, in *Sight and Sound*, Spring 1976, Vol. 45 No. 2, pp. 126–7.

29. See French, *Westerns* (1973), pp. 28–34.

30. Lenihan, *op. cit.*, p. 7.

31. Richard Slotkin, *Gunfighter Nation: The Myth of the Frontier in Twentieth-Century America* (HarperCollins, New York, [1992] 1993), *passim*.

32. *Ibid.*, pp. 288, 292, 315–16, 718 fn. 6.

1. Mirror for Prewar America

1. See Joel W. Finler, *The Hollywood Story* (Mandarin, London, 1992), p. 504.

2. *Ibid.*, p. 506.

3. With reference to the specific remit of this chapter, see also Richard Slotkin, *Gunfighter Nation: The Myth of the Frontier in Twentieth-Century America* (HarperCollins, New York, [1992] 1993), pp. 278–312.

4. Andrew Bergman, *We're in the Money: Depression America and Its Films* (New York University Press, New York, 1971), p. 88.

5. These figures are excerpted from Edward Buscombe (ed.), *The BFI Companion to the Western* (André Deutsch/BFI, London, 1988), Table 5 on p. 428, which includes a year by year breakdown of the major studios' production of Westerns in that era.

6. On this point, see also Andrew Sarris, *The John Ford Movie Mystery* (Secker & Warburg, London, 1976), p. 82.

7. *The Nation* (New York, 1939), June 3 1939, p. 654.

8. *New York Times*, February 7 1941, p. 23, reprinted in *The New York Times Film Reviews, 1913–1968: Vol. 3: 1939–1948* (New York Times & Arno Press, New York, 1970), p. 1768.

9. Ford admitted *Stagecoach*'s debt to *Boule de Suif* in a 1966 interview with Peter Bogdanovich, reprinted in the latter's *John Ford* (University of California Press, Berkeley, [1967] 1978), p. 69; Jon Tuska asserts Jean-Louis Rieupeyrout first identified *Stagecoach*'s thematic link to *The Outcasts of Poker Flat* in his *La Grande Aventure du Western* (Éditions du cerf, 1964), quoted in Tuska's *The American West in Film: Critical Approaches to the Western* (University of Nebraska Press, Lincoln, [1985] 1988), p. 50; Madonna/Magdalene contrasts often featured in nineteenth-century European literary classics (e.g., Charles Dickens's *Oliver Twist* (1838) and Victor Hugo's *Les Misérables* (1862)); and Sarris, *op. cit.*, accepts the possibility of literary debt "by osmosis", p. 81.

10. *New York Times*, March 3 1939, p. 21, reprinted in *The New York Times Film Reviews, Vol. 3: 1939–1948*, p. 1583.

11. See also reviews of *Stagecoach* in *The Hollywood Reporter*, February 3 1939, p. 3; *Variety*, February 8 1939, p. 17, reprinted in *Variety's Film Reviews, Vol. 6: 1938–1942* (R. R. Bowker, New York, 1983), pages unnumbered but reviews are printed chronologically; *Motion Picture Herald*, February 11 1939, p. 35; and *The Nation*, March 11 1939, p. 302.

12. Sarris, *op. cit.*, p. 81; by contrast, Joseph McBride and Michael Wilmington propose an over-fanciful allegorical interpretation in their *John Ford* (Secker & Warburg, London, 1974), p. 55.

13. See Edward Buscombe, *Stagecoach* (BFI Film Classics, British Film Institute, London, 1992), pp. 28–32.

14. *Stagecoach* (United Artists, 1939), directed by John Ford, screenplay by Dudley Nichols, based on the story "Stage to Lordsburg" by Ernest Haycox.

15. *Stagecoach* (film).

16. The benevolent conspiracy of father figures is a recurring subplot in Ford's films, from the silent *Three Bad Men* (1926) to subtle reworkings of this theme in *Fort Apache* (1948), *She Wore a Yellow Ribbon* (1949) and *The Sun Shines Bright* (1953).

17. *Stagecoach* (film).

18. See also John H. Lenihan, *Showdown: Confronting Modern America in the Western Film* (University of Illinois Press, Urbana, [1980] 1985), p. 23.

19. With its prohibitionist harpies, grasping capitalist and gangsterish Plummers, *Stagecoach* implicitly condemned American society of the 1920s as much as the 1930s.

20. See the *New York Times* reviews for: *Dodge City*, April 8 1939, p. 19; *Virginia City*, March 23 1940, p. 16; *The Westerner*, October 25 1940, p. 25; *Santa Fe Trail*, December 21 1940, p. 21; *Billy the Kid*, June 20 1941, p. 28; *The Return of Frank James*, August 10 1940, p. 16; *Brigham Young*, September 21 1940, p. 13; *Belle Starr*, November 1 1941, p. 20; *Union Pacific*, May 11 1939, p. 31; *Northwest Passage*, March 8 1940, p. 25; *North West Mounted Police*, November 7 1940, p. 33; and *They Died With Their Boots On*, November 21 1941, p. 23. All are reprinted in *The New York Times Film Reviews, Vol. 3: 1939–1948*, on pp. 1595, 1694, 1742, 1756, 1794, 1726, 1734, 1819–20, 1605–6, 1690, 1745–6 and 1825 respectively.

21. See David Pirie (ed.), *Anatomy of the Movies* (Windward, London, 1981), p. 208; and *New York Times, loc. cit.*

22. Randolph Scott's outlaw hero Vance Shaw in *Western Union* straddled these trends: he forsook his outlaw past in the name of national progress, but the film hewed to an "Establishment" line by killing him off and having Robert Young's Eastern fop avenge him. This plot resolution is identical to *Reap the Wild Wind*, DeMille's seafaring epic also from 1941, in which rugged John Wayne perishes and a dandified Ray Milland survives.

23. On *Jesse James*, see Lenihan, *op. cit.*, pp. 20, 92–3.

24. *Virginia City* (Warner Brothers, 1940), directed by Michael Curtiz, screenplay by Robert Buckner. Whether out west, on the high seas or in Sherwood Forest, Flynn's enemies in his films for Curtiz were essentially the same.

25. *North West Mounted Police* (Paramount, 1940), directed by Cecil B. DeMille, screenplay by Alan LeMay, Jesse Lasky, Jr. and C. Gardner Sullivan.

26. *The Westerner* (United Artists, 1940), directed by William Wyler, screenplay by Jo Swerling and Niven Busch, from the story by Stuart N. Lake.

27. *Variety*, November 19 1941, p. 9, reprinted in *Variety's Film Reviews, Vol. 6: 1938–1942*.

28. *They Died With Their Boots On* (Warner Brothers, 1941), directed by Raoul Walsh, screenplay by Wally Kline and Aeneas MacKenzie.

29. *Drums Along the Mohawk* is ambiguous insofar as its savage Iroquois are actually the pawns of British redcoats, but there is little evidence to support William K. Everson's contention, in his *The Hollywood Western: 90 Years of Cowboys and Indians, Train Robbers, Sheriffs and Gunslingers, and Assorted Heroes and Desperados* (Citadel Press, Secaucus, 1992), that the film was "made at that time to remind American audiences that they had once been at war with Britain, and that perhaps they should not advocate rushing to her defence", pp. 208–9; John E. O'Connor, "A Reaffirmation of American Ideals: *Drums Along the Mohawk* (1939)", in John E. O'Connor and Martin A. Jackson (eds), *American History/American Film: Interpreting the Hollywood Image* (Continuum, New York, [1979] 1991), actually cites documentary evidence to the contrary, p. 113.

30. *The Westerner*.

31. Quoted in Kim Newman, *Wild West Movies: Or How the West Was Found, Won, Lost, Lied About, Filmed and Forgotten* (Bloomsbury, London, 1990), p. 204.

2. Puritan Paradigms

1. Quoted in John Costello, *Love, Sex and War: Changing Values, 1939–1945* (Pan/Collins, London, 1986), p. 76.

2. *Ibid.*, p. 15.

3. Ford's darker postwar *Weltanschauung* took longer to develop fully on screen, but Capra's *It's A Wonderful Life* (1946), for example, presents a nightmarish "other world" at odds with the sunny prewar certainties of *You Can't Take It With You* (1937).

4. See Joel W. Finler, *The Hollywood Story* (Mandarin, London, 1992), p. 504.

5. *Ibid.*

6. *Ibid.*, pp. 506–7.

7. *Ibid.*, p. 506.

8. *TIME*, November 11 1946, p. 40; see also review of *Stagecoach* in *The Hollywood Reporter*, February 3 1939, p. 3.

9. *Motion Picture Herald Product Digest*, October 12 1946, p. 3249.

10. *New Movies*, January 1947, pp. 6–8, reprinted in Anthony Slide (ed.), *Selected Film Criticism, 1941–1950* (Scarecrow Press, Metuchen, 1983), pp. 170, 171.

11. *Ibid.*, reprinted in Slide, *op. cit.*, p. 172.

12. Bosley Crowther, "The 'Ten Best'", *New York Times*, December 29 1946, Section II, p. 1, reprinted in *The New York Times Film Reviews, 1913–1968: Vol. 3: 1939–1948* (New York Times & Arno Press, 1970), p. 2156; *New York Times*, December 4 1946, p. 44, reprinted in the same volume, p. 2149.

13. *Variety*, October 9 1946, p. 14, reprinted in *Variety's Film Reviews, Vol. 7: 1943–1948* (R. R. Bowker, New York, 1983), pages unnumbered but reviews are printed chronologically.

14. *Rob Wagner's Script*, November 1946, p. 10, reprinted in Slide, *op. cit.*, p. 169.

15. *The New Republic*, December 16 1946, pp. 836, 838.

16. *Duel in the Sun* went on general release in 1947, but was premièred at the very

end of 1946 to qualify for that year's Oscars. Ironically, it was not nominated for Best Picture.

17. Review of *Duel in the Sun* in *TIME*, March 17 1947, p. 39.

18. *Motion Picture Herald,* January 4 1947, p. 32, also in *Motion Picture Herald Product Digest,* January 11 1947, pp. 3409, 3410.

19. *New York Times,* May 8 1947, p. 30, reprinted in *The New York Times Film Reviews, Vol. 3: 1939–1948,* p. 2180.

20. *Rob Wagner's Script,* January 18 1947, pp. 14–15, reprinted in Slide, *op. cit.,* pp. 50, 51.

21. *Ibid.,* p. 15, reprinted in Slide, *op. cit.,* p. 52.

22. *Cue,* May 10 1947, p. 11, reprinted in Slide, *op. cit.,* p. 52.

23. *Variety,* January 1 1947, p. 14, reprinted in *Variety's Film Reviews, Vol. 7: 1943–1948.*

24. See also "Duel over *Duel*" in *TIME,* January 27 1947, pp. 34–5.

25. Quoted in Ronald Haver, *David O. Selznick's Hollywood* (Bonanza Books, New York, [1980] 1985), p. 366.

26. Quoted in Jon Tuska, *The Filming of the West* (Doubleday, Garden City, 1976), p. 506.

27. See Stuart N. Lake, *He Carried a Six-Shooter: The Biography of Wyatt Earp* (Peter Nevill, London, 1952) (original title: *Wyatt Earp, Frontier Marshal* [Houghton Mifflin, Boston, 1931]), much of it based on Earp's conversations with Lake.

28. Clanton cohorts Tom and Frank McLaury do not appear in *Clementine*, which Danny Peary suggests was partially due to Ford's reluctance to depict Irishmen as villains: see Peary's *Cult Movies 2: 50 More of the Classics, the Sleepers, the Weird, and the Wonderful* (Dell, New York, 1983), p. 107. For discrepancies between Ford's version and the facts of the gunfight, see Robert Lyons (ed.), *My Darling Clementine* (Rutgers University Press, New Brunswick, [1984] 1990), p. 5.

29. See Olga J. Martin, *Hollywood's Movie Commandments: A Handbook for Motion Picture Writers and Reviewers* (Arno Press & New York Times, New York, [1937] 1970), pp. 96, 97, 99, 178, 181–5.

30. Quoted in William R. Meyer, *The Making of the Great Westerns* (Arlington House, New Rochelle, 1979), p. 50.

31. *My Darling Clementine* (20th Century-Fox, 1946), directed by John Ford, screenplay by Samuel G. Engel and Winston Miller from story by Sam Hellman, based on a book by Stuart N. Lake.

32. *Ibid.*

33. On Ford's filmic treatment of Indians, see the following criticisms: review of *Rio Grande* in *TIME,* December 11 1950, p. 40; Robert Hatch's review of *The Searchers* in *The Nation* (New York, 1956), June 23 1956, p. 536; Hatch's review of *Sergeant Rutledge* in *The Nation,* June 11 1960, pp. 519–20; "Indian Exodus", review of *Cheyenne Autumn* in *TIME,* January 8 1965, p. 43; "No Ford in Our Future", Stanley Kauffmann's review of *Cheyenne Autumn* in *The New Republic,* January 23 1965, pp. 36–7; and the retrospective verdict on *Stagecoach* in Andrew Sarris, *The John Ford Movie Mystery* (Secker & Warburg, London, 1976), p. 82.

34. Ford's reminiscence, from The John Ford Papers at Lilly Library, Indiana University, quoted in Tag Gallagher, *John Ford: The Man and His Films* (University of California Press, Berkeley, 1986), p. 5.

35. Letter to Thomas (Tag) Gallagher, reprinted in Gallagher, *op. cit.,* p. 437.

36. See Niven Busch, *Duel in the Sun* (W. H. Allen, London, 1947), pp. 246, 256.

37. See Finler, *op. cit.*, p. 474, for *Duel*'s ranking as No. 2 grosser for the 1940s; David Pirie (ed.), *Anatomy of the Movies* (Windward, London, 1981), p. 208, for its inflation-adjusted status as the most commercially successful Western of all time; but see also David Thomson, *Showman: The Life of David O. Selznick* (Abacus, London, 1993), pp. 490–91, for a dissenting interpretation of *Duel*'s *actual* success, in terms of profit rather than box office receipts.

38. Review of *Duel in the Sun* in *TIME*, *loc. cit.*

39. Quoted in "Duel over *Duel*" in *TIME*, *loc. cit.*, p. 34.

40. Quoted in Thomson, *op. cit.*, p. 480.

41. Review of *Duel* in *TIME*, *loc. cit.*; see also "Duel over *Duel*", in *TIME*, *loc. cit.*, p. 34.

42. Review of *Duel* in *TIME*, *loc. cit.*, pp. 39–40.

43. *TIME*, February 24 1947, p. 40.

44. Review of *Duel* in *New York Times*, *loc. cit.*, reprinted in *The New York Times Film Reviews, Vol. 3: 1939–1948*, p. 2180.

45. *Duel in the Sun* (Selznick Releasing Organization, 1946), directed by King Vidor, screenplay by the producer, David O. Selznick, suggested by a novel by Niven Busch, adapted by Oliver H. P. Garrett.

46. *Ibid.* Cotten's delivery of this line is very indistinct, and conceivably he is saying: "Mother's learning never made Mother any happier". In either case, the ideological inference is the same.

47. *Ibid.*

48. Costello, *op. cit.*, p. 20.

49. See Pirie, *loc. cit.*

50. See Edward Buscombe (ed.), *The BFI Companion to the Western* (André Deutsch/BFI, London, 1988), Table 2, p. 426.

51. Review of *My Darling Clementine* in *TIME*, *loc. cit.*; review of *Rio Grande* in *TIME*, *loc. cit.*

52. Leo Lowenthal, "Biographies in Popular Magazines", in Paul F. Lazarsfeld and Frank Stanton (ed.), *Radio Research, 1942–1943* (Duell, Sloan & Pearce, New York, 1944), reprinted as "The Triumph of Mass Idols", in Lowenthal's *Literature, Popular Culture and Society* (Pacific Books, Palo Alto, 1961), pp. 109–40.

53. *Duel in the Sun.*

3. "The Lonely Crowd"

1. Intriguingly, *Colorado Territory* may owe some debt to Carol Reed's classic British thriller, *Odd Man Out* (1947). In both films the outlaw on the run is named McQueen; and in each, the girl who loves the doomed hero provokes his and her own death by opening fire as the pursuing lawmen close in on them.

2. *New York Times*, January 24 1948, p. 11, reprinted in *The New York Times Film Reviews, 1913–1968: Vol. 3: 1939–1948* (New York Times & Arno Press, New York, 1970), p. 2231.

3. In my last chapter I justified *Duel in the Sun*'s inclusion as a 1946 *production*, but the film went on general *release* in 1947, which is when it achieved success at the box office. For *Unconquered*'s commercial success ($5,300,000), see David Pirie (ed.), *Anatomy of the Movies* (Windward, London, 1981), p. 208. Joel W. Finler, *The Hollywood*

Story (Mandarin, London, 1992), cites *Unconquered* as fourteenth most successful movie in the North American rental market between 1941 and 1950, p. 474.

4. See Robert Parrish, *Growing Up in Hollywood* (Bodley Head, London, 1976), pp. 201–10; DeMille's proposal about directors compiling reports on co-workers is recounted on pp. 203–4.

5. Quite unwittingly, Bond lent himself to criticism of the witch-hunt by appearing as a heavy in several anti-McCarthy Westerns: see Gordon Douglas's *The Great Missouri Raid* (1951), Nicholas Ray's *Johnny Guitar* (1954) and Ray Milland's *A Man Alone* (1955).

6. *TIME*, October 27 1947, p. 48.

7. *New York Times*, October 11 1947, p. 11, reprinted in *The New York Times Film Reviews, Vol. 3: 1939–1948*, p. 2208.

8. *Unconquered* goes so far as to have one character dispatch a redskin and then mutter, "That's *one* good Indian" – in a tale set more than a century before General Sheridan's famous utterance: *Unconquered* (Paramount, 1947), directed by Cecil B. DeMille, screenplay by Charles Bennett, Frederic M. Frank and Jesse Lasky, Jr., from a novel by Neil H. Swanson.

9. Finler, *op. cit.*, p. 504.

10. *Ibid.*, p. 506.

11. See Edward Buscombe (ed.), *The BFI Companion to the Western* (André Deutsch/BFI, London, 1988), Table 2 on p. 426.

12. *Ibid.*, Table 4 on p. 427.

13. Quoted from "What's Wrong with the Movies", *TIME*, February 28 1949, p. 38.

14. Pirie, *loc. cit.*

15. Cobbett Steinberg, *Reel Facts: The Movie Book of Records* (Penguin, Harmondsworth, 1981), pp. 479–82; Pirie, *op. cit.*, pp. 108–11. For an early 1950s evaluation of John Wayne as a box office phenomenon, see "The Wages of Virtue", *TIME*, March 3 1952, pp. 32–4.

16. Quoted in Jon Tuska, *The American West in Film: Critical Approaches to the Western* (University of Nebraska Press, Lincoln, [1985] 1988), p. 65.

17. *Red River* (United Artists, 1948), directed and produced by Howard Hawks, screenplay by Borden Chase and Charles Schnee from the *Saturday Evening Post* story by Borden Chase.

18. Pirie, *op. cit.*, p. 208.

19. *New York Times*, October 1 1948, p. 31, reprinted in *The New York Times Film Reviews, Vol. 3: 1939–1948*, p. 2281.

20. *TIME*, October 11 1948, p. 36.

21. "Git Along", *The New Republic*, October 18 1948, p. 29.

22. *Motion Picture Herald Product Digest*, July 17 1948, p. 4241.

23. *Variety*, July 14 1948, p. 12, reprinted in *Variety's Film Reviews, Vol. 7: 1943–1948* (R. R. Bowker, New York, 1983), pages unnumbered but reviews are printed chronologically.

24. *Motion Picture Herald Product Digest*, *loc. cit.*

25. Review of *Red River* in *TIME*, *loc. cit.*

26. Review of *Red River* in the *New York Times*, *loc. cit.*

27. *Red River*.

28. *Ibid.*

29. David Riesman, with Nathan Glazer and Reuel Denny, *The Lonely Crowd: A Study of the Changing American Character* (Yale University Press, New Haven, [1950] 1989), *passim*.

30. *Ibid.*, especially pp. 9–25.

31. *Ibid.*, pp. xxix–xxx, lvi.

32. Peter Biskind, *Seeing Is Believing: How Hollywood Taught Us to Stop Worrying and Love the Fifties* (Pluto Press, London, [1983] 1984), p. 282.

33. *Red River*.

34. Will Wright, *Six Guns and Society: A Structural Study of the Western* (University of California Press, Berkeley, [1975] 1977), pp. 32–59, 130–53.

35. *Red River*.

36. Riesman, *op. cit.*, p. 9; p. 13 notes "a decline in sexual energy" in tradition-directed societies, and Groot is asexual. Riesman does not suggest the coexistence of White Anglo-Saxon tradition-directed types with *both* inner- and other-directed types in America, but Groot's character and unequivocal status as Dunson's underling conform to a tradition-directed profile.

37. *Ibid.*, pp. 24–5.

38. Biskind, *op. cit.*, pp. 40 fn., 41–2.

39. William H. Whyte, Jr., *The Organization Man* (Doubleday, Garden City, 1956), outlines a social type akin to York, p. 3: "the ones of our middle class who have left home, spiritually as well as physically, to take the vows of organization life, and ... who are the mind and soul of our great self-perpetuating institutions. Only a few are top managers or ever will be. ... But they are the dominant members of our society nonetheless. They have not joined together into a recognizable elite ... but it is from their ranks that are coming most of the first and second echelons of our leadership, and it is their values which will set the American temper".

40. *Fort Apache* (R-K-O, 1948), directed by John Ford, screenplay by Frank S. Nugent, suggested by the story "Massacre" by James Warner Bellah.

41. *Ibid.*

42. Pirie, *op. cit.*, p. 208.

43. *New York Times*, June 25 1948, p. 26, reprinted in *The New York Times Film Reviews, Vol. 3: 1939–1948*, p. 2263.

44. *Motion Picture Herald Product Digest*, March 13 1948, p. 4094.

45. *Variety*, March 10 1948, p. 10, reprinted in *Variety's Film Reviews, Vol. 7: 1943–1948*.

46. *The New Republic*, July 12 1948, pp. 29–30.

47. *TIME*, May 10 1948, p. 37.

48. *The Nation* (New York), July 24 1948, p. 109.

49. *Fort Apache*.

50. *Ibid.*

51. *Ibid.*

52. See Paul Blanshard, *American Freedom and Catholic Power* (Beacon Press, Boston, [1949] 1950), *passim*. This book first appeared as a series of articles in *The Nation* in 1948, contemporaneous with *Fort Apache*'s release.

53. "What's Wrong with the Movies", in *TIME, loc. cit.*

54. For texts of these speeches see, e.g., Tag Gallagher, *John Ford: The Man and His Films* (University of California Press, Berkeley, 1986), pp. 252–3.

55. Pirie, *op. cit.*, p. 208.

56. *The Hollywood Reporter*, July 27 1949, p. 3.

57. *Variety*, July 27 1949, p. 12, reprinted in *Variety's Film Reviews, Vol. 8: 1949–1953* (R. R. Bowker, New York, 1983).

58. *New York Times*, November 18 1949, p. 35, reprinted in *The New York Times Film Reviews, Vol. 4: 1949–1958* (New York Times & Arno Press, New York, 1970), p. 2376.

59. *She Wore a Yellow Ribbon* (R-K-O, 1949), directed by John Ford, screenplay by Frank Nugent and Laurence Stallings, story by James Warner Bellah.

60. John H. Lenihan, *Showdown: Confronting Modern America in the Western Film* (University of Illinois Press, Urbana, [1980] 1985), asserts *Rio Grande*'s border incursion plot was actually a Korean War film in cowboy garb, pp. 27–31. Jeffrey Richards, at the time unaware of Lenihan's thesis, imparted his similar conclusion to me in an interview on November 12 1990. Richard Slotkin has since developed an extensive interpretation of the contemporary relevance of Ford's cavalry trilogy in *Gunfighter Nation: The Myth of the Frontier in Twentieth-Century America* (HarperCollins, New York, [1992] 1993), pp. 328–43, 353–65.

61. Richard Hofstadter, *The American Political Tradition and the Men Who Made It* (Random House, New York, 1948), *passim*.

4. Dysfunctional Family Structures

1. *One Foot in Hell* was a 1960 film, but the plot centres on revenge against a selfish community, which was essentially a social construct of 1950s Westerns (e.g., *High Noon, The Proud Ones, The Tin Star*).

See the review of *Gunfight at the O.K. Corral* in *TIME*, June 17 1957, pp. 60, 62. Its stars were aware of the subtext; see Kirk Douglas, *The Ragman's Son: An Autobiography* (Pan, London, 1989), pp. 271–2, and "Burt Lancaster", interview (co-edited by Shirley Sealy) in Judith Crist, *Take 22: Moviemakers on Moviemaking* (Continuum, New York, [1984] 1991), p. 101.

2. Geoffrey Gorer, *The Americans: A Study in National Character* (Cresset Press, London, 1948), pp. 152–3, 155, 157.

3. David Pirie (ed.), *Anatomy of the Movies* (Windward, London, 1981), p. 208.

4. *Ibid.*

5. See Edward Buscombe (ed.), *The BFI Companion to the Western* (André Deutsch/ BFI, London, 1988), Table 2 on p. 426. R-K-O ceased production in 1957.

6. *Ibid.*, Table 4 on p. 427.

7. See Joel W. Finler, *The Hollywood Story* (Mandarin, London, 1992), pp. 506–7.

8. *Ibid.*, pp. 504–5.

9. *Ibid.*

10. Buscombe, *op. cit.*, Table 6 on p. 428. See "The Six-Gun Galahad", *TIME*, March 30 1959, p. 36.

11. *The Gunfighter* (20th Century-Fox, 1950), directed by Henry King, screenplay by William Bowers and William Sellers, from a story by William Bowers and André de Toth.

12. *Variety*, April 26 1950, p. 8, reprinted in *Variety's Film Reviews, Vol. 8: 1949–1953* (R. R. Bowker, New York, 1983), pages unnumbered but reviews are printed chronologically.

13. *New York Times*, June 24 1950, p. 7, reprinted in *The New York Times Film Reviews, 1913–1968: Vol. 4: 1949–1958* (New York Times & Arno Press, New York, 1970), p. 2432.

14. *TIME*, July 17 1950, p. 39.

15. Pirie, *loc. cit.*

16. *Shane* (Paramount, 1953), directed by George Stevens, screenplay by A. B. Guthrie, Jr., additional dialogue by Jack Sher, based on the novel by Jack Schaefer.

17. Pirie, *loc. cit.*

18. *The Hollywood Reporter*, April 13 1953, p. 3.

19. *Motion Picture Herald Product Digest*, April 18 1953, p. 1797.

20. *Variety*, April 15 1953, p. 6, reprinted in *Variety's Film Reviews, Vol. 8: 1949–1953*.

21. *TIME*, April 13 1953, p. 46.

22. *New York Times*, April 24 1953, p. 30, and December 27 1953, Section II, p. 3, reprinted in *The New York Times Film Reviews, Vol. 4: 1949–1958*, pp. 2688–9 and 2749 respectively.

23. "Shock Around the Clock", *TIME*, September 9 1957, p. 58.

24. Pirie, *loc. cit.*

25. *The Hollywood Reporter*, March 13 1956, p. 3.

26. *Motion Picture Herald*, March 17 1956, p. 16, also in *Motion Picture Herald Product Digest*, March 31 1956, p. 843.

27. *New York Times*, May 31 1956, p. 21, reprinted in *The New York Times Film Reviews, Vol. 4: 1949–1958*, p. 2929.

28. *Variety*, March 14 1956, p. 6, reprinted in *Variety's Film Reviews, Vol. 9: 1954–1958* (R. R. Bowker, New York, 1983).

29. *TIME*, June 25 1956, p. 59.

30. *The Nation* (New York, 1956), June 23 1956, p. 536.

31. *Motion Picture Herald Product Digest*, May 27 1961, p. 140.

32. *The Hollywood Reporter*, May 24 1961, p. 3; *Variety*, May 24 1961, p. 6, reprinted in *Variety's Film Reviews, Vol. 10: 1959–1963* (R. R. Bowker, New York, 1983).

33. *New York Times*, June 15 1961, p. 51, reprinted in *The New York Times Film Reviews, 1913–1968: Vol. 5: 1959–1968* (New York Times & Arno Press, New York, 1970), p. 3261.

34. *Shane*.

35. Quoted in Elaine Tyler May, *Homeward Bound: American Families in the Cold War Era* (HarperCollins, New York, 1988), p. 30.

36. See Michael Freedland, *Gregory Peck* (W. H. Allen, London, 1980), p. 102.

5. Politics and Codes of Masculinity

1. Eric F. Goldman, *The Crucial Decade – And After: America, 1945–1960* (Random House, New York, 1960), p. 260.

2. See, for example, Cobb's villainous patriarchs in *On the Waterfront* (1954), *Twelve Angry Men* (1957), *Party Girl*, *Man of the West* and *The Brothers Karamazov* (all 1958).

3. See Raymond Durgnat, "King Vidor: Part II", in *Film Comment*, September/October 1973, Vol. 9 No. 5 (Film Comment, Boston, 1973), p. 22; and also Raymond Durgnat and Scott Simmon, *King Vidor, American* (University of California Press, Berkeley, 1988), p. 255 fn.

4. *The Big Country* (United Artists, 1958), directed by William Wyler, screenplay by James R. Webb, Sy Bartlett and Robert Wilder, adaptation by Jessamyn West and Robert Wyler, from the novel by Donald Hamilton.

5. *Ibid.*

6. *Ibid.*

7. *Ibid.*

8. *Ibid.*

9. *Ibid.*

10. *Ibid.*

11. Another 1958 United Artists Western, Anthony Mann's *Man of the West*, featured a more sadistic variation on this scene, in which hero Gary Cooper humiliates brutish Jack Lord by beating and stripping him. Rather than accept defeat, Lord reaches for a gun, thus forcing his outlaw gang's deranged patriarch (Lee J. Cobb) to shoot *him*.

12. Ronald Bergan, *The United Artists Story* (Octopus, London, 1986), p. 185.

13. *TIME*, September 8 1958, p. 60.

14. *Variety*, August 13 1958, reprinted in *Variety's Film Reviews, Vol. 9: 1954–1958* (R. R. Bowker, New York, 1983), pages unnumbered but reviews are printed chronologically.

15. *Ibid.*

16. *The Hollywood Reporter*, August 8 1958, p. 3.

17. *Motion Picture Herald Product Digest*, August 16 1958, p. 945.

18. *New York Times*, October 2 1958, p. 44, reprinted in *The New York Times Film Reviews, Vol. 4: 1949–1958* (New York Times & Arno Press, New York, 1970), p. 3085.

19. Peter G. Baker's review in *Films and Filming*, February 1959, Vol. 5 No. 5 (London, 1959), p. 23.

20. Philip French, *Westerns: Aspects of a Movie Genre* (Secker & Warburg, London, 1973), p. 43.

21. John H. Lenihan, *Showdown: Confronting Modern America in the Western Film* (University of Illinois Press, Urbana, [1980] 1985), pp. 25 fn., 135.

22. Numerous texts erroneously refer to Fonda's character as "Blaisdell"; yet both Hall's novel and the Regulators' Wanted poster in the film spell his name "Blaise dell".

23. *Warlock* (20th Century-Fox, 1959), produced and directed by Edward Dmytryk, screenplay by Robert Alan Aurthur, based on the novel by Oakley Hall.

24. *Ibid.*

25. *Ibid.*

26. *Ibid.*

27. *Ibid.*

28. *New York Times*, May 1 1959, p. 34, reprinted in *The New York Times Film Reviews, Vol. 5: 1959–1968* (New York Times & Arno Press, New York, 1970), pp. 3123–4.

29. *Variety*, April 1 1959, reprinted in *Variety's Film Reviews, Vol. 10: 1959–1963* (R. R. Bowker, New York, 1983).

30. *Motion Picture Herald Product Digest*, April 4 1959, p. 212.

31. *The Hollywood Reporter*, April 1 1959, p. 3.

32. *TIME*, May 25 1959, p. 60.

33. Quoted in Frank D. McConnell, *The Spoken Seen: Film & the Romantic Imagination* (Johns Hopkins University Press, Baltimore, 1975), p. 147.

34. Peter John Dyer's review in *Films and Filming*, June 1959, Vol. 5 No. 9, pp. 22–3.

35. However, see McConnell, *op. cit.*, pp. 146–62; Phil Hardy, *The Aurum Film Encyclopedia: The Western* (Aurum Press, London, 1983), p. 271; Nicholas Anez, "Wyatt

Earp", in *Films in Review*, August/September 1990, Vol. XLI Nos 8/9 (National Board of Review of Motion Pictures, New York, 1990), pp. 404–6.

36. McConnell, *op. cit.*, p. 147.

37. Colin McArthur, *Underworld U.S.A.* (Secker & Warburg, London, 1972), p. 19.

38. See French, *op. cit.*, pp. 34–6.

39. *Warlock*.

40. *Ibid.*

6. "No More West to Win"

1. Quoted in Philip French, *Westerns: Aspects of a Movie Genre* (Secker & Warburg, London, 1973), p. 14. The five films were: Delmer Daves's *Broken Arrow*, Anthony Mann's *Devil's Doorway* and his *Winchester '73*, John Ford's *Wagon Master* and Henry King's *The Gunfighter*.

2. See Frederick Jackson Turner, "The Significance of the Frontier in American History" (1893), reprinted in Ray Allen Billington (ed.), *Frontier and Section: Selected Essays of Frederick Jackson Turner* (Prentice-Hall, Englewood Cliffs, 1961), pp. 37–62.

3. Edward Buscombe (ed.), *The BFI Companion to the Western* (André Deutsch/ BFI, London, 1988), Tables 1 and 2 on p. 426, Table 4 on p. 427, Table 6 on p. 428.

4. Joel W. Finler, *The Hollywood Story* (Mandarin, London, 1992), pp. 505, 507.

5. *Ibid.*, p. 507.

6. *The Man Who Shot Liberty Valance* (Paramount, 1962), directed by John Ford, screenplay by James Warner Bellah and Willis Goldbeck, based on the story by Dorothy M. Johnson.

7. *Ibid.*

8. *Variety*, April 11 1962, p. 6, reprinted in *Variety's Film Reviews, Vol. 10: 1959–1963* (R. R. Bowker, New York, 1983), pages unnumbered but reviews are printed chronologically; *New York Times*, May 24 1962, p. 9, reprinted in *The New York Times Film Reviews, 1913–1968: Vol. 5: 1959–1968* (New York Times & Arno Press, New York, 1970), p. 3325.

9. *Variety*, *loc. cit.*

10. *New York Times*, *loc. cit.*

11. *Motion Picture Herald Product Digest*, April 18 1962, p. 524.

12. *The Hollywood Reporter*, April 11 1962, p. 3.

13. John H. Lenihan, *Showdown: Confronting Modern America in the Western Film* (University of Illinois Press, Urbana, [1980] 1985), p. 159.

14. Richard Hofstadter, *Anti-Intellectualism in American Life* (Random House, New York, 1963), pp. 48–9.

15. *Lonely Are the Brave* (Universal, 1962), directed by David Miller, screenplay by Dalton Trumbo, based on the novel *Brave Cowboy* by Edward Abbey.

16. *Ibid.*

17. *Ibid.*

18. *New York Times*, June 28 1962, p. 21, reprinted in *The New York Times Film Reviews, Vol. 5: 1959–1968*, p. 3332.

19. *Variety*, May 2 1962, p. 6, reprinted in *Variety's Film Reviews, Vol. 10: 1959–1963*.

20. *Motion Picture Herald Product Digest*, May 9 1962, p. 548.

21. *The Hollywood Reporter*, May 3 1962, p. 3.

22. *TIME*, July 13 1962, p. 80 B.

23. *Ibid.*, p. 80 C.

24. McCrea appeared in a couple of films during the 1970s, but his career effectively ended with *Ride the High Country*.

25. *Ride the High Country* (Metro-Goldwyn-Mayer, 1962), directed by Sam Peckinpah, screenplay by N. B. Stone, Jr.

26. *New York Times*, June 21 1962, p. 26, reprinted in *The New York Times Film Reviews, Vol. 5: 1959–1968*, p. 3331.

27. *The Hollywood Reporter*, May 7 1962, p. 3.

28. *Motion Picture Herald Product Digest*, May 16 1962, p. 556.

29. *TIME*, July 13 1962, p. 80 B.

30. *Variety*, May 9 1962, p. 7, reprinted in *Variety's Film Reviews, Vol. 10: 1959–1963*.

31. Jack Nachbar, "Introduction", in Jack Nachbar (ed.), *Focus on the Western* (Prentice-Hall, Englewood Cliffs, 1974), p. 6.

32. See David Pirie (ed.), *Anatomy of the Movies* (Windward, London, 1981), p. 208.

33. *Motion Picture Herald Product Digest*, November 28 1962, p. 700.

34. *The Hollywood Reporter*, November 7 1962, p. 3.

35. *Variety*, November 7 1962, p. 6, reprinted in *Variety's Film Reviews, Vol. 10: 1959–1963*.

36. *The New Republic*, April 20 1963, p. 29.

37. *New York Times*, April 1 1963, p. 54, reprinted in *The New York Times Film Reviews, Vol. 5: 1959–1968*, p. 3378.

38. *TIME*, March 22 1963, p. 58.

7. The Vietnamization of the Western

1. Carl Bakal, *No Right to Bear Arms* (Paperback Library, New York, 1968), pp. 1, 5.

2. Joel W. Finler, *The Hollywood Story* (Mandarin, London, 1992), p. 505.

3. *Ibid.*, pp. 505, 507.

4. Edward Buscombe (ed.), *The BFI Companion to the Western* (André Deutsch/ BFI, London, 1988), Table 6 on p. 428.

5. *Ibid.*, Table 4 on p. 427; the tabulated breakdown between major studios' Westerns and independent productions goes up to 1967, but Table 1 on p. 426 lists the undifferentiated total for 1968 as sixteen.

6. *New York Times*, May 28 1964, p. 40, for *A Distant Trumpet*, and December 24 1964, p. 8, for *Cheyenne Autumn*, reprinted in *The New York Times Film Reviews, 1913–1968: Vol. 5: 1959–1968* (New York Times & Arno Press, New York, 1970), pp. 3467 and 3516 respectively.

7. "Indian Exodus", *TIME*, January 8 1965, p. 43.

8. "No Ford in Our Future", *The New Republic*, January 23 1965, pp. 36, 37.

9. *Cheyenne Autumn* (Warner Brothers, 1964), directed by John Ford, screenplay by James R. Webb, suggested by *Cheyenne Autumn* by Mari Sandoz. Jon Tuska exposes the fallacious mythic content of this scene in *The American West in Film: Critical Approaches to the Western* (University of Nebraska Press, Lincoln, [1985] 1988), pp. 6–7.

10. John Wayne's son was billed as "Pat" in *The Searchers* but as "Patrick" in *Cheyenne Autumn*.

11. David Pirie (ed.), *Anatomy of the Movies* (Windward, London, 1981), p. 208.

12. See also Richard Slotkin, *Gunfighter Nation: The Myth of the Frontier in Twentieth-*

Century America (HarperCollins, New York, [1992] 1993), pp. 405–638, 729–61 *passim*.

13. For a comprehensive account of *Major Dundee*'s production history, see David Weddle, *"If They Move .. Kill 'Em!": The Life and Times of Sam Peckinpah* (Grove Press, New York, 1994), pp. 229–44, 249–54.

14. See Charlton Heston (ed. by Hollis Alpert), *The Actor's Life: Journals, 1956–1976* (Allen Lane, London, 1979), entries for January 8 1964, p. 190, and for September 16 1964, p. 208.

15. *Major Dundee* (Columbia, 1965), directed by Sam Peckinpah, screenplay by Harry Julian Fink, Oscar Saul and Sam Peckinpah, story by Harry Julian Fink.

16. *Ibid.*

17. On *Dundee*'s cuts, see Jim Kitses, *Horizons West: Anthony Mann, Budd Boetticher, Sam Peckinpah: Studies of Authorship within the Western* (Thames & Hudson, London, 1969), pp. 139–40; and Paul Seydor, *Peckinpah: The Western Films* (University of Illinois Press, Urbana, 1980), pp. 52–3. On *Major Dundee*'s gross, see Weddle, *op. cit.*, p. 253.

18. *Motion Picture Herald Product Digest*, March 31 1965, p. 257.

19. "Arms and the Man", *The New Republic*, April 17 1965, p. 40.

20. *Ibid.*

21. *New York Times*, April 8 1965, p. 45, reprinted in *The New York Times Film Reviews, Vol. 5: 1959–1968*, pp. 3539–40.

22. "Unholy Western", *TIME*, April 16 1965, p. 7.

23. *Variety*, March 17 1965, reprinted in *Variety's Film Reviews, Vol. 11: 1964–1967* (R. R. Bowker, New York, 1983), pages unnumbered but reviews are printed chronologically.

24. *The Hollywood Reporter*, April 14 1965, p. 3.

25. *Major Dundee.*

26. *Ibid.*

27. *Ibid.*

28. Pirie, *loc. cit.*

29. *The Hollywood Reporter*, November 2 1966, p. 3.

30. *Variety*, November 2 1966, reprinted in *Variety's Film Reviews, Vol. 11: 1964–1967*.

31. *Motion Picture Herald Product Digest*, November 9 1966, p. 625.

32. Pauline Kael, *Kiss Kiss Bang Bang* (Calder & Boyars, London, 1970), p. 334.

33. "Four for the Raid", *TIME*, November 11 1966, p. 67.

34. *New York Times*, November 3 1966, p. 45, reprinted in *The New York Times Film Reviews, Vol. 5: 1959–1968*, p. 3644. A few weeks later, however, Crowther gave Brooks's film an honourable mention in his end-of-year appraisal, *ibid.*, December 25 1966, Section X, p. 1, reprinted in *ibid.*, p. 3655.

35. *The Professionals* (Columbia, 1966), written for the screen and directed by Richard Brooks, based on the novel *A Mule for the Marquesa* by Frank O'Rourke.

36. *Ibid.*

37. *Ibid.*

38. *Ibid.*

39. Publicity posters and end credits billed Lancaster first, followed by Marvin and Ryan. The film billed the Professionals as each appeared on screen: first Marvin, then Ryan, Strode – and, finally, Lancaster. In the end credits, Strode was billed fourth, after Ryan.

40. *Will Penny* (Paramount, 1967), written and directed by Tom Gries.

41. On *The Green Berets*, see, e.g., Gilbert Adair, *Hollywood's Vietnam: From The Green*

Berets to Full Metal Jacket (Heinemann, London, 1989), especially pp. 21–36; and Slotkin, *op. cit.*, pp. 520–33.

42. Reviewing *The Way West*, *TIME* also identified Kirk Douglas's character as a Moses figure, June 2 1967, p. 64.

43. See Phil Hardy, *The Aurum Film Encyclopedia: The Western* (Aurum Press, London, 1983), Appendix 1 on p. 364.

44. *TIME*, August 2 1968, p. 49.

45. "The Gun Under Fire", *TIME*, June 21 1968, p. 13.

8. Receding Frontiers, Narrowing Options

1. Joel W. Finler, *The Hollywood Story* (Mandarin, London, 1992), p. 505.

2. *Ibid.*

3. *Ibid.*, p. 507.

4. *Ibid.*

5. Edward Buscombe (ed.), *The BFI Companion to the Western* (André Deutsch/ BFI, London, 1988), Table 6 on p. 428, Table 1 on p. 426.

6. David Pirie (ed.), *Anatomy of the Movies* (Windward, London, 1981), p. 208.

7. Phil Hardy, *The Aurum Film Encyclopedia: The Western* (Aurum Press, London, 1983), Appendix 1 on p. 364.

8. *The Undefeated* (20th Century-Fox, 1969), directed by Andrew V. McLaglen, screenplay by James Lee Barrett, based on a story by Stanley L. Hough.

9. *The Hollywood Reporter*, September 30 1969, p. 3.

10. "Allen Smithee" is, rather notoriously, a pseudonym which obscures true directorial credit. *Death of a Gunfighter* began with Robert Totten at the helm. Following a difference between Totten and star Richard Widmark, Don Siegel took over.

11. Quoted in "The Exiles", *TIME*, December 19 1969, p. 53.

12. Pirie, *loc. cit.*

13. *New York Times*, August 1 1968, p. 24, reprinted in *The New York Times Film Reviews, 1913–1968: Vol. 5: 1959–1968* (New York Times & Arno Press, 1970), p. 3776.

14. *Motion Picture Herald Product Digest*, September 17 1969, p. 273.

15. *Variety*, September 10 1969, reprinted in *Variety's Film Reviews, Vol. 12: 1968–1970* (R. R. Bowker, New York, 1983), pages unnumbered but reviews are printed chronologically.

16. Joan Mellen, *Big Bad Wolves: Masculinity in the American Film* (Elm Tree Books, London, [1977] 1978), p. 286.

17. *The Hollywood Reporter*, September 10 1969, p. 3.

18. *New York Times*, October 5 1969, Section II, p. 1, reprinted in *The New York Times Film Reviews, 1969–1970* (New York Times & Arno Press, New York, 1971), p. 85.

19. *Ibid.*

20. "Double Vision", *TIME*, September 26 1969, p. 62.

21. "The Bottom of the Pit", reprinted in Pauline Kael, *Deeper Into Movies* (Calder & Boyars, London, [1973] 1975), pp. 6, 7.

22. *Butch Cassidy and the Sundance Kid* (20th Century-Fox, 1969), directed by George Roy Hill, written by William Goldman.

23. *Ibid.*

24. *The Wild Bunch* (Warner Brothers–Seven Arts, 1969), directed by Sam Peck-

inpah, screenplay by Walon Green and Sam Peckinpah, story by Walon Green and
Roy N. Sickner.

25. *Ibid.*

26. *Ibid.*

27. *Ibid.*

28. *Ibid.*

29. *Ibid.*

30. *Ibid.*

31. *Ibid.*

32. Paul Seydor, *Peckinpah: The Western Films* (University of Illinois Press, Urbana,
1980), p. 90, refers to reviewers who garble the plot by mistakenly attributing Angel's
betrayal to his own mother instead of Teresa's. This confusion stems from a remark
of Lyle's, in which the first word is not immediately clear; but what he actually says
is, "*Her* own momma turned him in" (emphasis mine). However, Mapache clearly
stated to Dutch that Teresa's *father* had informed on Angel.

33. *The Wild Bunch.*

34. *Ibid.*

35. Pirie, *loc. cit.*

36. Quoted in William R. Meyer, *The Making of the Great Westerns* (Arlington House,
New Rochelle, 1979), p. 405.

37. Quoted in Lawrence J. Quirk, *The Films of William Holden* (Citadel Press,
Secaucus, 1973), p. 238.

38. Quoted in Meyer, *op. cit.*, p. 406.

39. *Ibid.*, p. 405.

40. Quoted in Quirk, *loc. cit.*

41. *Motion Picture Herald Product Digest*, July 2 1969, p. 219.

42. Quoted in Quirk, *loc. cit.*

43. *New York Times*, June 26 1969, p. 45, reprinted in *The New York Times Film
Reviews, 1969-1970*, pp. 50-51.

44. *Ibid.*, July 6 1969, Section II, p. 1, reprinted in *ibid.*, p. 53.

45. *Ibid.*, July 20 1969, Section II, p. 1, reprinted in *ibid.*, pp. 55-6.

46. "Man and Myth", *TIME*, June 20 1969, p. 70.

47. *Ibid.*

48. *Variety*, June 18 1969, reprinted in *Variety's Film Reviews, Vol. 12: 1968-1970.*

49. *The Hollywood Reporter*, June 16 1969, p. 3.

50. *The Magnificent Seven* (United Artists, 1960), produced and directed by John
Sturges, screenplay by William Roberts, based on the Japanese film *Seven Samurai*,
Toho Company, Ltd.

51. *The Professionals* (Columbia, 1966), written for the screen and directed by
Richard Brooks, based on the novel *A Mule for the Marquesa* by Frank O'Rourke.

52. *The Wild Bunch.*

53. Pirie, *loc. cit.*

54. *Little Big Man* (National General Pictures, 1970), directed by Arthur Penn,
screenplay by Calder Willingham, based on the novel by Thomas Berger.

55. Quoted in *New York Times,* July 24 1971, p. 14, reprinted in *The New York Times
Film Reviews, 1971-1972* (New York Times & Arno Press, New York, 1973), p. 106.

56. *Variety*, August 12 1970, reprinted in *Variety's Film Reviews, Vol. 12: 1968-1970.*

57. *New York Times*, September 20 1970, Section II, p. 13, reprinted in *The New York
Times Film Reviews, 1969-1970*, pp. 218-19.

58. Dee Brown, *Bury My Heart at Wounded Knee: An Indian History of the American West* (Pan Books, London, [1970] 1975), *passim*.

59. "The Street Western", reprinted in Pauline Kael, *Reeling* (Marion Boyars, London, [1976] 1977), p. 283.

9. Legends Revisited, Legends Revised

1. See Edward Buscombe (ed.), *The BFI Companion to the Western* (André Deutsch/ BFI, London, 1988), Table 1 on p. 426, Table 6 on p. 428.

2. See Joel W. Finler, *The Hollywood Story* (Mandarin, London, 1992), p. 505.

3. *Ibid.*, pp. 504–5.

4. *Ibid.*, p. 507.

5. *Ibid.*

6. *Buffalo Bill and the Indians or Sitting Bull's History Lesson* (United Artists, 1976), produced and directed by Robert Altman, screen story and screenplay by Alan Rudolph and Robert Altman, suggested by the play *Indians* by Arthur Kopit.

7. *Ibid.*

8. *Ibid.*

9. *Ibid.*

10. *Ibid.*

11. *Ibid.*

12. *Variety*, June 30 1976, reprinted in *Variety's Film Reviews, Vol. 14: 1975–1979* (R. R. Bowker, New York, 1983), pages unnumbered but reviews are printed chronologically.

13. *The New Republic*, July 24 1976, reprinted in Stanley Kauffmann, *Before My Eyes: Film Criticism and Comment* (Da Capo Press, New York, 1980), pp. 39–40.

14. *New York Times*, June 25 1976, Section C p. 8, reprinted in *The New York Times Film Reviews, 1975–1976* (New York Times & Arno Press, New York, 1977), pp. 225–6.

15. *The Hollywood Reporter*, June 24 1976, pp. 2, 6.

16. *Buffalo Bill and the Indians*.

17. *Ibid.*

18. *Ibid.*

19. *Ibid.*

20. *Ibid.*

21. *The Outlaw Josey Wales* (Warner Brothers, 1976), directed by Clint Eastwood, screenplay by Phil Kaufman and Sonia Chernus, from the book *Gone To Texas* by Forrest Carter.

22. *Ibid.*

23. *Ibid.*

24. *Ibid.*

25. David Pirie (ed.), *Anatomy of the Movies* (Windward, London, 1981), p. 208.

26. *The Hollywood Reporter*, June 29 1976, pp. 3, 31.

27. "Classic Heroism", *TIME*, August 2 1976, p. 4.

28. *Variety*, June 30 1976, reprinted in *Variety's Film Reviews, Vol. 14: 1975–1979*.

29. *New York Times*, August 5 1976, p. 26, reprinted in *The New York Times Film Reviews, 1975–1976*, p. 238.

30. "Film View: There's a Great Deal More to Acting Than Making Faces", *ibid.*, August 15 1976, Section II, p. 13, reprinted *ibid.*, p. 241.

31. See also Philip French, *Westerns: Aspects of a Movie Genre* (Secker & Warburg, London, rev. edn, 1977), pp. 172–3; and Richard Slotkin, *Gunfighter Nation: The Myth of the Frontier in Twentieth-Century America* (HarperCollins, New York, [1992] 1993), pp. 632–3.

32. *The Shootist* (Paramount, 1976), directed by Don Siegel, screenplay by Miles Hood Swarthout and Scott Hale, based on the novel by Glendon Swarthout.

33. Phil Hardy, *The Aurum Film Encyclopedia: The Western* (Aurum Press, London, 1983), Appendix 1 on p. 364.

34. *The New Republic*, September 11 1976, reprinted in Kauffmann, *op. cit.*, p. 238.

35. "Notes on Evolving Heroes, Morals, Audiences", reprinted in Pauline Kael, *When the Lights Go Down* (Marion Boyars, London, 1980), p. 197.

36. "Dying in the Saddle", *TIME*, August 30 1976, p. 5.

37. *New York Times*, August 12 1976, p. 38, reprinted in *The New York Times Film Reviews, 1975–1976*, p. 241.

38. *The Hollywood Reporter*, July 23 1976, p. 4.

39. *Variety*, July 28 1976, reprinted in *Variety's Film Reviews, Vol. 14: 1975–1979*.

40. *The Shootist*.

41. *Ibid.*

Conclusion

1. For a full account of this film's catastrophic history, see Steven Bach, *Final Cut: Dreams and Disaster in the Making of Heaven's Gate* (Faber & Faber, London, [1985] 1986), *passim*.

2. See J. Fred MacDonald, *Who Shot the Sheriff?: The Rise and Fall of the Television Western* (Praeger, New York, 1987), pp. 87–131.

Filmography

Prefatory note

Preparation for this study required saturation viewing, and in the course of my research I have viewed around three hundred and ninety items, then streamlined the following lists to a total of two hundred and eighty-five feature films. The first list cites those Westerns which formulated a major part of this study, plus directors and production companies; the second list similarly details all major and some minor "A" Westerns released between 1930 and 1980 which I viewed for the study. Though my time-frame has been 1939–1976, since my text constantly refers to a 1981 table of Western box office hits, it makes sense to include all films seen which may be covered by this tabulation and exclude those released thereafter. Some major Westerns within my time-frame are omitted from the list, either because I could not view them *while engaged on research* or because, in very few instances, I have never managed to see them at all.

Also excluded are several comedy and musical Westerns, most Spaghetti Westerns, "B" and Disney movies, and all films, star profiles, documentaries and mini-series made for television.

The lists have been organized chronologically overall, and alphabetically within each year, with studio names abbreviated thus:

Allied Artists	AA
Columbia	Col.
Metro-Goldwyn-Mayer	MGM
National General	NG
Paramount	Para.
Republic	Rep.
R-K-O Radio	RKO
20th Century-Fox	Fox
United Artists	UA
Universal	Univ.
Warner Brothers	WB

Westerns forming the principal focus of analysis, 1939–1976

1939   *Stagecoach* (John Ford, UA)
1946   *Duel in the Sun* (King Vidor, Selznick Releasing Organization)
       My Darling Clementine (John Ford, Fox)
1948   *Fort Apache* (John Ford, RKO)
       Red River (Howard Hawks, UA)
1949   *She Wore a Yellow Ribbon* (John Ford, RKO)
1950   *The Gunfighter* (Henry King, Fox)
1953   *Shane* (George Stevens, Para.)
1956   *The Searchers* (John Ford, WB)
1958   *The Big Country* (William Wyler, UA)
1959   *Warlock* (Edward Dmytryk, Fox)
1961   *The Last Sunset* (Robert Aldrich, Univ.)
1962   *How the West Was Won* (John Ford, George Marshall, Henry Hathaway,
          MGM–Cinerama)
       Lonely Are the Brave (David Miller, Univ.)
       The Man Who Shot Liberty Valance (John Ford, Para.)
       Ride the High Country (Sam Peckinpah, MGM)
1964   *Cheyenne Autumn* (John Ford, WB)
1965   *Major Dundee* (Sam Peckinpah, Col.)
1966   *The Professionals* (Richard Brooks, Col.)
1968   *Bandolero!* (Andrew V. McLaglen, Fox)
1969   *Butch Cassidy and the Sundance Kid* (George Roy Hill, Fox)
       The Wild Bunch (Sam Peckinpah, WB–Seven Arts)
1976   *Buffalo Bill and the Indians or Sitting Bull's History Lesson* (Robert Altman,
          UA)
       The Outlaw Josey Wales (Clint Eastwood, WB)
       The Shootist (Don Siegel, Para.)

Other Westerns viewed

1930   *The Big Trail* (Raoul Walsh, Fox)
       Billy the Kid (King Vidor, MGM)
1931   *Cimarron* (Wesley Ruggles, RKO)
1936   *The Plainsman* (Cecil B. DeMille, Para.)
1939   *Allegheny Uprising* (William Seiter, RKO)
       Destry Rides Again (George Marshall, Univ.)
       Dodge City (Michael Curtiz, WB)
       Drums Along the Mohawk (John Ford, Fox)
       Jesse James (Henry King, Fox)
       Union Pacific (Cecil B. DeMille, Para.)
1940   *Brigham Young - Frontiersman* (Henry Hathaway, Fox)

Dark Command (Raoul Walsh, Rep.)
North West Mounted Police (Cecil B. DeMille, Para.)
Northwest Passage (King Vidor, MGM)
The Return of Frank James (Fritz Lang, Fox)
Santa Fe Trail (Michael Curtiz, WB)
Virginia City (Michael Curtiz, WB)
The Westerner (William Wyler, UA)

1941   *Billy the Kid* (David Miller, MGM)
Honky Tonk (Jack Conway, MGM)
They Died With Their Boots On (Raoul Walsh, WB)
Western Union (Fritz Lang, Fox)

1942   *The Spoilers* (Ray Enright, Univ.)

1943   *The Outlaw* (Howard Hughes, UA/RKO)
The Ox-Bow Incident (William A. Wellman, Fox)
Tall in the Saddle (Edwin L. Marin, RKO)

1944   *Buffalo Bill* (William A. Wellman, Fox)

1945   *Along Came Jones* (Stuart Heisler, RKO)
San Antonio (David Butler, WB)

1946   *Canyon Passage* (Jacques Tourneur, Univ.)

1947   *Angel and the Badman* (James Edward Grant, Rep.)
Pursued (Raoul Walsh, WB)
Ramrod (André de Toth, UA)
Unconquered (Cecil B. DeMille, Para.)

1948   *Blood on the Moon* (Robert Wise, RKO)
Four Faces West (Alfred E. Green, UA)
The Man from Colorado (Henry Levin, Col.)
Silver River (Raoul Walsh, WB)
Station West (Sidney Lanfield, RKO)
Three Godfathers (John Ford, MGM)
The Treasure of the Sierra Madre (John Huston, WB)
Yellow Sky (William A. Wellman, Fox)

1949   *Colorado Territory* (Raoul Walsh, WB)

1950   *Ambush* (Sam Wood, MGM)
Broken Arrow (Delmer Daves, Fox)
Dallas (Stuart Heisler, WB)
Devil's Doorway (Anthony Mann, MGM)
The Furies (Anthony Mann, Para.)
The Kid from Texas (Kurt Neumann, Univ.)
Rio Grande (John Ford, Rep.)
Two Flags West (Robert Wise, Fox)
Wagon Master (John Ford, RKO)
Winchester '73 (Anthony Mann, Univ.)

1951   *Across the Wide Missouri* (William A. Wellman, MGM)
The Great Missouri Raid (Gordon Douglas, Para.)

Only the Valiant (Gordon Douglas, WB)
Rawhide (Henry Hathaway, Fox)
The Red Badge of Courage (John Huston, MGM)
Red Mountain (William Dieterle, Para.)
Vengeance Valley (Richard Thorpe, MGM)

1952   *Bend of the River* (Anthony Mann, Univ.)
The Big Sky (Howard Hawks, RKO)
The Big Trees (Felix Feist, WB)
Duel at Silver Creek (Don Siegel, Univ.)
The Half-Breed (Stuart Gilmore, RKO)
High Noon (Fred Zinnemann, UA)
Lone Star (Vincent Sherman, MGM)
Rancho Notorious (Fritz Lang, RKO)
Springfield Rifle (André de Toth, WB)

1953   *Arrowhead* (Charles Marquis Warren, Para.)
The Charge at Feather River (Gordon Douglas, WB)
Devil's Canyon (Alfred Werker, RKO)
Escape from Fort Bravo (John Sturges, MGM)
Gun Fury (Raoul Walsh, Col.)
Hondo (John Farrow, WB)
Law and Order (Nathan Juran, Univ.)
The Naked Spur (Anthony Mann, MGM)
Pony Express (Jerry Hopper, Para.)

1954   *Apache* (Robert Aldrich, UA)
The Boy from Oklahoma (Michael Curtiz, WB)
Broken Lance (Edward Dmytryk, Fox)
Cattle Queen of Montana (Allan Dwan, RKO)
Drum Beat (Delmer Daves, WB)
Drums Across the River (Nathan Juran, Univ.)
Johnny Guitar (Nicholas Ray, Rep.)
Ride Clear of Diablo (Jesse Hibbs, Univ.)
Silver Lode (Allan Dwan, RKO)
Taza, Son of Cochise (Douglas Sirk, Univ.)
Vera Cruz (Robert Aldrich, UA)

1955   *At Gunpoint* (Alfred Werker, AA)
Bad Day at Black Rock (John Sturges, MGM)
The Far Country (Anthony Mann, Univ.)
The Indian Fighter (André de Toth, UA)
The Kentuckian (Burt Lancaster, UA)
The Last Command (Frank Lloyd, Rep.)
A Man Alone (Ray Milland, Rep.)
The Man from Laramie (Anthony Mann, Col.)
Man Without a Star (King Vidor, Univ.)
Man With the Gun (Richard Wilson, UA)

Run for Cover (Nicholas Ray, Para.)
The Tall Men (Raoul Walsh, Fox)
Tennessee's Partner (Allan Dwan, RKO)
The Violent Men (Rudolph Mate, Col.)
White Feather (Robert D. Webb, Fox)
Wichita (Jacques Tourneur, AA)

1956   *The Burning Hills* (Stuart Heisler, WB)
Dakota Incident (Lewis R. Foster, Rep.)
The Fastest Gun Alive (Russell Rouse, MGM)
Friendly Persuasion (William Wyler, AA)
Giant (George Stevens, WB)
Great Day in the Morning (Jacques Tourneur, RKO)
Jubal (Delmer Daves, Col.)
The King and Four Queens (Raoul Walsh, UA)
The Last Hunt (Richard Brooks, MGM)
The Last Wagon (Delmer Daves, Fox)
The Oklahoman (Francis D. Lyon, AA)
The Proud Ones (Robert D. Webb, Fox)
7th Cavalry (Joseph H. Lewis, Col.)
Tension at Table Rock (Charles Marquis Warren, RKO)
Tribute to a Bad Man (Robert Wise, MGM)
Walk the Proud Land (Jesse Hibbs, Univ.)

1957   *The Big Land* (Gordon Douglas, WB)
Dragoon Wells Massacre (Harold Schuster, AA)
Forty Guns (Samuel Fuller, Fox)
Gunfight at the O.K. Corral (John Sturges, Para.)
Gun Glory (Roy Rowland, MGM)
The Halliday Brand (Joseph H. Lewis, UA)
The Lonely Man (Henry Levin, Para.)
Night Passage (James Neilson, Univ.)
The Restless Breed (Allan Dwan, Fox)
Revolt at Fort Laramie (Lesley Selander, UA)
Run of the Arrow (Samuel Fuller, RKO)
The Tall T (Budd Boetticher, Col.)
3:10 to Yuma (Delmer Daves, Col.)
The Tin Star (Anthony Mann, Para.)
The True Story of Jesse James (Nicholas Ray, Fox)

1958   *The Bravados* (Henry King, Fox)
Buchanan Rides Alone (Budd Boetticher, Col.)
Cattle Empire (Charles Marquis Warren, Fox)
Fort Dobbs (Gordon Douglas, WB)
Fort Massacre (Joseph M. Newman, UA)
The Law and Jake Wade (John Sturges, MGM)
Man of the West (Anthony Mann, UA)

The Proud Rebel (Michael Curtiz, MGM)
Saddle the Wind (Robert Parrish, MGM)
The Sheepman (George Marshall, MGM)
Terror in a Texas Town (Joseph H. Lewis, UA)

1959 *Day of the Outlaw* (André de Toth, UA)
The Hanging Tree (Delmer Daves, WB)
The Horse Soldiers (John Ford, UA)
Last Train from Gun Hill (John Sturges, Para.)
Ride Lonesome (Budd Boetticher, Col.)
Rio Bravo (Howard Hawks, WB)
Westbound (Budd Boetticher, WB)
Yellowstone Kelly (Gordon Douglas, WB)

1960 *The Alamo* (John Wayne, UA)
Cimarron (Anthony Mann, MGM)
Comanche Station (Budd Boetticher, Col.)
The Magnificent Seven (John Sturges, UA)
North to Alaska (Henry Hathaway, Fox)
Sergeant Rutledge (John Ford, WB)
The Unforgiven (John Huston, UA)

1961 *The Comancheros* (Michael Curtiz, Fox)
The Misfits (John Huston, UA)
One-Eyed Jacks (Marlon Brando, Para.)
Posse from Hell (Herbert Coleman, Univ.)
Two Rode Together (John Ford, Col.)

1963 *Hud* (Martin Ritt, Para.)
McLintock! (Andrew V. McLaglen, UA)

1964 *A Distant Trumpet* (Raoul Walsh, WB)
Fistful of Dollars (Sergio Leone, UA)
Rio Conchos (Gordon Douglas, Fox)

1965 *Apache Uprising* (R. G. Springsteen, Para.)
Cat Ballou (Elliot Silverstein, Col.)
For a Few Dollars More (Sergio Leone, UA)
The Glory Guys (Arnold Laven, UA)
The Hallelujah Trail (John Sturges, UA)
The Rounders (Burt Kennedy, MGM)
Shenandoah (Andrew V. McLaglen, Univ.)
The Sons of Katie Elder (Henry Hathaway, Para.)

1966 *Alvarez Kelly* (Edward Dmytryk, Col.)
The Appaloosa (Sidney J. Furie, Univ.)
A Big Hand for the Little Lady (Fielder Cook, WB)
Duel at Diablo (Ralph Nelson, UA)
The Good, the Bad and the Ugly (Sergio Leone, UA)
Hombre (Martin Ritt, Fox)
Nevada Smith (Henry Hathaway, Para.)

The Rare Breed (Andrew V. McLaglen, Univ.)
Return of the Seven (Burt Kennedy, UA)
Stagecoach (Gordon Douglas, Fox)

1967   *The Ballad of Josie* (Andrew V. McLaglen, Univ.)
El Dorado (Howard Hawks, Para.)
40 Guns to Apache Pass (William Witney, Col.)
Hostile Guns (R. G. Springsteen, Para.)
Hour of the Gun (John Sturges, UA)
The War Wagon (Burt Kennedy, Univ.)
The Way West (Andrew V. McLaglen, UA)
Welcome to Hard Times (Burt Kennedy, MGM)
Will Penny (Tom Gries, Para.)

1968   *Custer of the West* (Robert Siodmak, Security Pictures)
Firecreek (Vincent McEveety, WB)
5 Card Stud (Henry Hathaway, Para.)
Guns of the Magnificent Seven (Paul Wendkos, UA)
Hang 'Em High (Ted Post, UA)
Once Upon a Time in the West (Sergio Leone, Para.)
The Scalphunters (Sydney Pollack, UA)
Shalako (Edward Dmytryk, WB)
The Stalking Moon (Robert Mulligan, NG)
Villa Rides! (Buzz Kulik, Para.)

1969   *Death of a Gunfighter* ("Allen Smithee", Univ.)
The Good Guys and the Bad Guys (Burt Kennedy, WB)
Mackenna's Gold (J. Lee Thompson, Col.)
Sam Whiskey (Arnold Laven, UA)
True Grit (Henry Hathaway, Para.)
The Undefeated (Andrew V. McLaglen, Fox)
Young Billy Young (Burt Kennedy, UA)

1970   *The Ballad of Cable Hogue* (Sam Peckinpah, WB)
The Cheyenne Social Club (Gene Kelly, NG)
Chisum (Andrew V. McLaglen, WB)
Little Big Man (Arthur Penn, NG)
Monte Walsh (William A. Fraker, NG)
Rio Lobo (Howard Hawks, NG)
Soldier Blue (Ralph Nelson, Avco–Embassy)
There Was a Crooked Man ... (Joseph L. Mankiewicz, WB)
Two Mules for Sister Sara (Don Siegel, Univ.)

1971   *Big Jake* (George Sherman, NG)
A Gunfight (Lamont Johnson, Para.)
Hannie Caulder (Burt Kennedy, Tigon British)
The Hired Hand (Peter Fonda, Univ.)
The Hunting Party (Don Medford, UA)
Lawman (Michael Winner, UA)

McCabe & Mrs. Miller (Robert Altman, WB)
Wild Rovers (Blake Edwards, MGM)
1972   *Bad Company* (Robert Benton, Para.)
The Cowboys (Mark Rydell, WB)
The Culpepper Cattle Co. (Dick Richards, Fox)
The Great Northfield Minnesota Raid (Philip Kaufman, Univ.)
High Plains Drifter (Clint Eastwood, Univ.)
Jeremiah Johnson (Sydney Pollack, WB)
Joe Kidd (John Sturges, Univ.)
Junior Bonner (Sam Peckinpah, ABC Pictures)
The Life and Times of Judge Roy Bean (John Huston, NG)
Santee (Gary Nelson, Vagabond)
Showdown (George Seaton, Univ.)
Ulzana's Raid (Robert Aldrich, Univ.)
1973   *Billy Two Hats* (Ted Kotcheff, UA)
Cahill: United States Marshal (Andrew V. McLaglen, WB)
Pat Garrett & Billy the Kid (Sam Peckinpah, MGM)
The Train Robbers (Burt Kennedy, WB)
1975   *Bite the Bullet* (Richard Brooks, Col.)
From Noon Till Three (Frank D. Gilroy, UA)
Posse (Kirk Douglas, Para.)
Rooster Cogburn (Stuart Millar, Univ.)
1976   *The Last Hard Men* (Andrew V. McLaglen, Fox.)
1978   *China 9, Liberty 37* (Monte Hellman, CEA–ASPA)
Eagle's Wing (Anthony Harvey, Rank)
1979   *The Mountain Men* (Richard Lang, Col.)
1980   *Heaven's Gate* (Michael Cimino, UA)
The Long Riders (Walter Hill, UA)
Tom Horn (William Wiard, WB)

Bibliography

Primary sources

Contemporary reviews in:

The Hollywood Reporter   1939: Vols 50, 54; 1949: Vol. 105; 1950: Vols 108, 111; 1952: Vol. 119; 1953: Vol. 123; 1956: Vol. 138; 1958: Vol. 151; 1959: Vols 154, 155; 1960: Vols 159, 162; 1961: Vol. 165; 1962: Vols 169, 170, 172; 1964: Vol. 182; 1965: Vols 184, 185; 1966: Vol. 193; 1967: Vol. 195; 1968: Vol. 201; 1969: Vols 206, 207; 1970: Vol. 212; 1976: Vol. 242

Motion Picture Herald (including *Product Digest*)   1939: Vols 134, 137; 1946: Vol. 165; 1947: Vol. 166; 1948: Vols 170, 173; 1950: Vols 179, 181; 1952: Vol. 187; 1953: Vol. 191; 1956: Vol. 202; 1958: Vol. 212; 1959: Vols 214, 215; 1960: Vols 219, 221; 1961: Vol. 223; 1962: Vols 227, 228; 1964: Vol. 232; 1965: Vols 233, 234; 1966: Vol. 236; 1967: Vol. 237; 1968: Vol. 238; 1969: Vol. 239; 1970: Vol. 240; 1971: Vol. 241

The Nation (New York)   1939: Vol. 148; 1945: Vol. 160; 1948: Vol. 167; 1950: Vol. 171; 1952: Vol. 176; 1956: Vol. 182; 1960: Vol. 190; 1965: Vol. 201

The New Republic   1939: Vol. 101; 1946: Vol. 115; 1948: Vol. 119; 1950: Vol. 123; 1954: Vol. 131; 1960: Vol. 142; 1963: Vol. 148; 1965: Vol. 152

New York Times, 1939–1976, reviews reprinted in:

The New York Times Film Reviews, 1913–1968   Vol. 3: 1939–1948; Vol. 4: 1949–1958; Vol. 5: 1959–1968 (all New York Times & Arno Press, New York, 1970)

The New York Times Film Reviews, 1969–1970; *1971–1972*; *1973–1974*; *1975–1976* (all New York Times & Arno Press, New York, 1971, 1973, 1975 and 1977 respectively)

TIME, 1946–1976: Vols 47–108

Variety, 1939–1976, reprinted in:

Variety's Film Reviews   Vol. 6: 1938–1942; Vol. 7: 1943–1948; Vol. 8: 1949–1953; Vol. 9: 1954–1958; Vol. 10: 1959–1963; Vol. 11: 1964–1967; Vol. 12: 1968–1970; Vol. 13: 1971–1974; Vol. 14: 1975–1979 (all R. R. Bowker, New York, 1983)

Other contemporary film reviews

Peter G. Baker, review of *The Big Country*, *Films and Filming*, February 1959, Vol. 5 No. 5 (London, 1959), p. 23.

Peter G. Baker, review of *How the West Was Won*, *Films and Filming*, December 1962, Vol. 9 No. 3, pp. 41–2.

John Cutts, review of *The Alamo*, *Films and Filming*, December 1960, Vol. 7 No. 3, pp. 32–3.

John Cutts, review of *Guns in the Afternoon* (U.K. title for *Ride the High Country*), *Films and Filming*, June 1962, Vol. 8 No. 9, p. 38.

Peter John Dyer, review of *Warlock*, *Films and Filming*, June 1959, Vol. 5 No. 9, pp. 22–3.

John Gillett, review of *How the West Was Won*, *Sight and Sound: The International Film Quarterly* (British Film Institute, London, 1962), Winter 1962–1963, Vol. 32 No. 1, p. 41.

Gordon Gow, review of *The Man Who Shot Liberty Valance*, *Films and Filming*, June 1962, Vol. 8 No. 9, p. 33.

DuPre Jones, review of *The Man Who Shot Liberty Valance* and *Guns in the Afternoon*, *Sight and Sound*, Summer 1962, Vol. 31 No. 3, p. 146.

Richard Whitehall, review of *The Magnificent Seven*, *Films and Filming*, April 1961, Vol. 7 No. 7, p. 26.

Richard Whitehall, review of *Lonely Are the Brave*, *Films and Filming*, June 1962, Vol. 8 No. 9, p. 34.

Richard Whitehall, review of *Hud*, *Films and Filming*, June 1963, Vol. 9 No. 9, p. 26.

Related contemporary articles, etc.

Jan Aghed, "*Pat Garrett and Billy the Kid*", *Sight and Sound*, Spring 1973, Vol. 42 No. 2, pp. 64–9.

Nigel Andrews, "Sam Peckinpah: the Survivor and the Individual", *Sight and Sound*, Spring 1973, Vol. 42 No. 2, pp. 69–74.

Eric Bentley, "The Political Theatre of John Wayne" (1972), reprinted in John Tulloch (ed.), *Conflict and Control in the Cinema: A Reader in Film and Society* (Macmillan, South Melbourne, 1977), pp. 291–6.

Pat Dowell, review of Kim Newman's *Wild West Movies*, Richard Slotkin's *Gunfighter Nation* and Jane Tompkins' *West of Everything* in *CINEASTE*, Vol. 20 No. 3 (New York, 1994), pp. 65–7.

Philip French, review of Will Wright's *Six Guns and Society* in *Sight and Sound*, Spring 1976, Vol. 45 No. 2, pp. 126–7.

Herbert L. Jacobson, "Cowboy, Pioneer and American Soldier", *Sight and Sound*, April–June 1953, Vol. 22 No. 4, pp. 189–90.

Editors of *LIFE* Magazine, "How the West Was Won", six-part weekly series in *LIFE*, April 6 1959–May 11 1959.

Colin McArthur, "The Real Presence", *Sight and Sound*, Summer 1967, Vol. 36 No. 3, pp. 141–3.

Colin McArthur, "Sam Peckinpah's West", *Sight and Sound*, Autumn 1967, Vol. 36 No. 4, pp. 180–183.

Douglas McVay, "The Five Worlds of John Ford", *Films and Filming*, June 1962, Vol. 8 No. 9, pp. 14–17, 53.

Janey Place, "Structured Cowboys", review of Will Wright's *Six Guns and Society* in

JUMP CUT: A Review of Contemporary Cinema, August 1978, No. 18 (JUMP CUT Associates, Berkeley & Chicago, 1978), pp. 26–8.

John Sturges, "How the West Was Lost!", *Films and Filming*, December 1962, Vol. 9 No. 3, pp. 9–10.

Variety, "All-Time Boxoffice Champs", Sixty-fifth *Variety* Anniversary, January 6 1971, pp. 12, 34, 36.

Richard Whitehall, "Talking with Sam Peckinpah", *Sight and Sound*, Autumn 1969, Vol. 38 No. 4, pp. 172–5.

Secondary sources

Books

Gilbert Adair, *Hollywood's Vietnam: From The Green Berets to Full Metal Jacket* (Heinemann, London, 1989).

Lawrence Alloway, *Violent America: The Movies 1946–1964* (Museum of Modern Art, New York, 1971).

Lindsay Anderson, *About John Ford* (Plexus, London, 1981).

Geoff Andrew, *The Films of Nicholas Ray: The Poet of Nightfall* (Charles Letts, London, 1991).

Richard J. Anobile (ed.), *Stagecoach* (Darien House, New York, 1975).

Steven Bach, *Final Cut: Dreams and Disasters in the Making of Heaven's Gate* (Faber & Faber, London, [1985] 1986).

Carl Bakal, *No Right to Bear Arms* (Paperback Library, New York, 1968).

Carroll Baker, *Baby Doll: An Autobiography* (W. H. Allen, London, 1984).

James L. Baughman, *The Republic of Mass Culture: Journalism, Filmmaking, and Broadcasting in America since 1941* (Johns Hopkins University Press, Baltimore, 1992).

John F. Bauman and Thomas H. Coode, *In the Eye of the Great Depression: New Deal Reporters and the Agony of the American People* (Northern Illinois University Press, DeKalb, 1988).

John Baxter, *The Cinema of John Ford* (A. Zwemmer, London, 1971).

John Baxter, *Sixty Years of Hollywood* (A. S. Barnes, South Brunswick, 1973).

William Bayer, *The Great Movies* (Hamlyn, London, 1973).

André Bazin, *What is Cinema? Vol. II*, translated by Hugh Gray (University of California Press, Berkeley, 1971).

Ronald Bergan, *The United Artists Story* (Octopus, London, 1986).

Andrew Bergman, *We're in the Money: Depression America and Its Films* (New York University Press, New York, 1971).

Peter Biskind, *Seeing Is Believing: How Hollywood Taught Us To Stop Worrying and Love the Fifties* (Pluto Press, London, [1983] 1984).

Paul Blanshard, *American Freedom and Catholic Power* (Beacon Press, Boston, [1949] 1950).

Michael Bliss (ed.), *Doing It Right: The Best Criticism on Sam Peckinpah's The Wild Bunch* (Southern Illinois University Press, Carbondale, 1994).

Peter Bogdanovich, *John Ford* (University of California Press, Berkeley, [1967] 1978).

Peter Bogdanovich, *Picture Shows* (George Allen & Unwin, London, 1975).

Donald Bogle, *Toms, Coons, Mulattoes, Mammies & Bucks: An Interpretive History of Blacks in American Films* (Bantam, New York, 1974).

Leo Braudy, *The World in a Frame: What We See in Films* (Anchor Press/Doubleday, Garden City, 1976).

Douglas Brode, *The Films of the Fifties: Sunset Boulevard to On The Beach* (Citadel Press, Secaucus, 1976).

Douglas Brode, *The Films of the Sixties* (Citadel Press, Secaucus, 1980).

Dee Brown, *Bury My Heart at Wounded Knee: An Indian History of the American West* (Pan Books, London, [1970] 1975).

Julie Burchill, *Girls on Film* (Virgin Books, London, 1986).

Niven Busch, *Duel in the Sun* (W. H. Allen, London, 1947).

Edward Buscombe (ed.), *The BFI Companion to the Western* (André Deutsch/BFI, London, 1988).

Edward Buscombe, *Stagecoach* (BFI Film Classics, British Film Institute, London, 1992).

Terence Butler, *Crucified Heroes: The Films of Sam Peckinpah* (Gordon Fraser, London, 1979).

Jenni Calder, *There Must Be a Lone Ranger* (Hamish Hamilton, London, 1974).

Kingsley Canham, *The Hollywood Professionals, Vol. 1: Michael Curtiz, Raoul Walsh, Henry Hathaway* (A. S. Barnes, New York, 1973).

John Carroll, *Humanism: The Wreck of Western Culture* (HarperCollins, 1993).

Paul A. Carter, *Another Part of the Fifties* (Columbia University Press, New York, 1983).

John M. Cassidy, *Civil War Cinema: A Pictorial History of Hollywood and the War Between the States* (Pictorial Histories, Missoula, 1990).

John Caughie (ed.), *Theories of Authorship: A Reader* (Routledge, London, 1990).

John G. Cawelti, *The Six-Gun Mystique* (Bowling Green State University Popular Press, Bowling Green, [1970] 1984).

William H. Chafe, *The Unfinished Journey: America since World War II* (Oxford University Press, New York, 1986).

Terry Christensen, *Reel Politics: American Political Movies From Birth of a Nation to Platoon* (Basil Blackwell, London, 1987).

Pam Cook (ed.), *The Cinema Book* (British Film Institute, London, 1992).

John Costello, *Love, Sex and War: Changing Values, 1939–1945* (Pan/Collins, London, 1986).

Peter Cowie, *Seventy Years of Cinema* (Castle Books, New York, 1969).

Peter Cowie (ed.), *Hollywood 1920–1970* (A. S. Barnes, New York, 1977), comprising: David Robinson, *Hollywood in the Twenties* (1968); John Baxter, *Hollywood in the Thirties* (1968); Charles Higham and Joel Greenberg, *Hollywood in the Forties* (1968); Gordon Gow, *Hollywood in the Fifties* (1971); John Baxter, *Hollywood in the Sixties* (1972).

Michael Coyne, *The Social Construction of American National Identity: The Role of the*

Hollywood Western, 1939–1962 (M.Phil. thesis, submitted at Lancaster University, England, 1994).

George F. Custen, *Bio/Pics: How Hollywood Constructed Public History* (Rutgers University Press, New Brunswick, 1992).

Philip Davies and Brian Neve (eds), *Cinema, Politics and Society in America* (Manchester University Press, Manchester, 1981).

Robert Murray Davis, *Playing Cowboys: Low Culture and High Art in the Western* (University of Oklahoma Press, Norman, 1992).

Brian W. Dippie, *Custer's Last Stand: The Anatomy of an American Myth* (University of Nebraska Press, Lincoln, [1976] 1994).

Linda Dittmar and Gene Michaud (eds), *From Hanoi to Hollywood: The Vietnam War in American Film* (Rutgers University Press, New Brunswick, 1990).

Kirk Douglas, *The Ragman's Son: An Autobiography* (Pan, London, 1989).

Nancy Dowd and David Shepard, *A Directors' Guild of America Oral History: King Vidor* (Directors' Guild of America & Scarecrow Press, Metuchen, 1988).

Raymond Durgnat, *Eros in the Cinema* (Calder & Boyars, London, 1966).

Raymond Durgnat, *Films and Feelings* (Faber & Faber, London, 1967).

Raymond Durgnat and Scott Simmon, *King Vidor, American* (University of California Press, Berkeley, 1988).

John Douglas Eames, *The MGM Story* (Octopus, London, 1977).

John Douglas Eames, *The Paramount Story* (Octopus, London, 1985).

Anne Edwards, *Early Reagan: The Rise of an American Hero* (Hodder & Stoughton, London, 1988).

Anne Edwards, *Shirley Temple: American Princess* (Fontana/Collins, London, 1989).

Gabe Essoe and Raymond Lee, *DeMille: The Man and His Pictures* (Castle Books, New York, 1970).

William K. Everson, *The Hollywood Western: 90 Years of Cowboys and Indians, Train Robbers, Sheriffs and Gunslingers and Assorted Heroes and Desperados* (Citadel Press, Secaucus, 1992).

Allen Eyles, *John Wayne* (A. S. Barnes, South Brunswick, 1979).

George N. Fenin and William K. Everson, *The Western: From Silents to the Seventies*, rev. edn (Penguin, New York, 1978).

Leslie A. Fiedler, *Love and Death in the American Novel* (Penguin, Harmondsworth, 1984).

Joel W. Finler, *The Movie Directors Story* (Octopus, London, 1985).

Joel W. Finler, *The Hollywood Story* (Mandarin, London, 1992).

Frances Fitzgerald, *America Revised: History Schoolbooks in the Twentieth Century* (Random House, New York, 1980).

Dan Ford, *The Unquiet Man: The Life of John Ford* (William Kimber, London, [1979] 1982).

Jib Fowles, *Starstruck: Celebrity Performers and the American Public* (Smithsonian Institution Press, Washington D.C., 1992).

John Fraser, *America and the Patterns of Chivalry* (Cambridge University Press, Cambridge, 1982).

Christopher Frayling, *Spaghetti Westerns: Cowboys and Europeans from Karl May to Sergio Leone* (Routledge & Kegan Paul, London, 1981).

Michael Freedland, *Gregory Peck* (W. H. Allen, London, 1980).

Brandon French, *On the Verge of Revolt: Women in American Films of the Fifties* (Frederick Ungar, New York, 1973).

Philip French, *Westerns: Aspects of a Movie Genre* (Secker & Warburg, London, 1973; and rev. edn, 1977).

Ralph E. Friar and Natasha A. Friar, *The Only Good Indian…: The Hollywood Gospel* (Drama Book Specialists, New York, 1972).

Otto Friedrich, *City of Nets: A Portrait of Hollywood in the 1940s* (Headline, London, 1988).

Neal Gabler, *An Empire of Their Own: How the Jews Invented Hollywood* (Anchor Books/Doubleday, New York, 1989).

J. K. Galbraith, *The Affluent Society* (Penguin, Harmondsworth, 1963).

Tag Gallagher, *John Ford: The Man and His Films* (University of California Press, Berkeley, 1986).

Brian Garfield, *Western Films: A Complete Guide* (Da Capo Press, New York, 1982).

James Gilbert, *Another Chance: Postwar America 1945–1985* (Wadsworth, Belmont, 1986).

Eric F. Goldman, *The Crucial Decade – And After: America, 1945–1960* (Random House, New York, 1960).

William Goldman, *Adventures in the Screen Trade: A Personal View of Hollywood and Screenwriting* (Little, Brown & Co., London, [1983] 1994).

Geoffrey Gorer, *The Americans: A Study in National Character* (Cresset Press, London, 1948).

John Griggs, *The Films of Gregory Peck* (Columbus Books, London, 1988).

Hans Habe, *Anatomy of Hatred: The Wounded Land*, translated by Ewan Butler (George G. Harrap, London, 1964).

Oakley Hall, *Warlock* (Pan Books, London, [1958] 1961).

John R. Hamilton (photographs) and John Calvin Batchelor (text), *Thunder in the Dust: Great Shots from the Western Movies* (Aurum Press, London, 1987).

Patricia King Hanson and Stephen L. Hanson, *Film Review Index, Vol. 1: 1882–1949; Vol. 2: 1950–1985* (Oryx Press, Phoenix, 1986; 1987).

Phil Hardy, *The Aurum Film Encyclopedia: The Western* (Aurum Press, London, 1983).

Michael Harrington, *The Other America: Poverty in the United States* (Penguin, Harmondsworth, [1962] 1963).

Molly Haskell, *From Reverence to Rape: The Treatment of Women in the Movies*, 2nd edn (University of Chicago Press, Chicago, 1987).

Ronald Haver, *David O. Selznick's Hollywood* (Bonanza Books, New York, [1980] 1985).

M. J. Heale, *American Anticommunism: Combating the Enemy Within 1830–1970* (Johns Hopkins University Press, Baltimore, 1990).

Steven Heller (ed.), *Jules Feiffer's America: From Eisenhower to Reagan* (Penguin, New York, 1982).

Charlton Heston (ed. by Hollis Alpert), *The Actor's Life: Journals, 1956–1976* (Allen Lane, London, 1979).

Foster Hirsch, *The Hollywood Epic* (A. S. Barnes, South Brunswick, 1978).

Clive Hirschhorn, *The Warner Bros. Story* (Octopus, London, 1979).

Clive Hirschhorn, *The Universal Story* (Octopus, London, 1986).

Clive Hirschhorn, *The Columbia Story* (Octopus, London, 1989).

Godfrey Hodgson, *America In Our Time* (Random House, New York, 1978).

Richard Hofstadter, *The American Political Tradition and the Men Who Made It* (Random House, New York, 1948).

Richard Hofstadter, *Anti-Intellectualism in American Life* (Random House, New York, 1963).

Richard Hofstadter, *The Paranoid Style in American Politics and Other Essays* (Jonathan Cape, London, 1966).

Jay Hyams, *The Life and Times of the Western Movie* (Gallery Books, New York, 1983).

Richard B. Jewell with Vernon Harbin, *The RKO Story* (Octopus, London, 1983).

Pauline Kael, *Kiss Kiss Bang Bang* (Calder & Boyars, London, 1970).

Pauline Kael, *Deeper Into Movies* (Calder & Boyars, London, [1973] 1975).

Pauline Kael, *Reeling* (Marion Boyars, London, [1976] 1977).

Pauline Kael, *When the Lights Go Down* (Marion Boyars, London, 1980).

Pauline Kael, *5001 Nights at the Movies* (Zenith, London, 1984).

Stanley Kauffmann, *Before My Eyes: Film Criticism and Comment* (Da Capo Press, New York, 1980).

Eddie Dorman Kay, *Box Office Greats: The Most Popular Movies of the Last 50 years* (Tiger Books International, London, 1990).

Michael Kerbel, *Henry Fonda* (Pyramid, New York, 1975).

Jim Kitses, *Horizons West: Anthony Mann, Budd Boetticher, Sam Peckinpah: Studies of Authorship within the Western* (Thames & Hudson, London, 1969).

Philip B. Kunhardt, Jr. (ed.), *LIFE: The First Fifty Years 1936–1986* (Little, Brown & Co./Hutchinson, Boston, 1986).

Mort Künstler (paintings) and Henry Steele Commager (text), *The American Spirit: The Paintings of Mort Künstler* (Rutledge Hill Press, Nashville, 1986).

Stuart N. Lake, *He Carried a Six-Shooter: The Biography of Wyatt Earp* (Peter Nevill, London, [1931] 1952).

John H. Lenihan, *Showdown: Confronting Modern America in the Western Film* (University of Illinois Press, Urbana [1980] 1985).

Emmanuel Levy, *John Wayne: Prophet of the American Way of Life* (Scarecrow Press, Metuchen, 1988).

George Lipsitz, *Time Passages: Collective Memory and American Popular Culture* (University of Minnesota Press, Minneapolis, 1990).

Ann Lloyd (ed.), *The Movie* (13 vols) (Orbis, London, 1979–1983).

David Lowenthal, *The Past is a Foreign Country* (Cambridge University Press, Cambridge, 1985).

Christopher Lyon (ed.), *The International Dictionary of Films and Filmmakers, Vol. 1: Films* (Firethorn Press, London, 1986).

Christopher Lyon (ed.), *The International Dictionary of Films and Filmmakers, Vol. 2: Directors/Filmmakers* (Firethorn Press, London, 1986).

Robert Lyons (ed.), *My Darling Clementine* (Rutgers University Press, New Brunswick, [1984] 1990).

Frank N. Magill (ed.), *Magill's Survey of Cinema: English Language Films*, 1st Series – 4 vols; 2nd Series – 6 vols (Salem Press, Englewood Cliffs, 1980; 1981).

Charles J. Maland, *American Visions: The Films of Chaplin, Ford, Capra, and Welles, 1936–1941* (Arno Press, New York, 1977).

Richard Maltby, *Harmless Entertainment: Hollywood and the Ideology of Consensus* (Scarecrow Press, Metuchen, 1983).

William Manchester, *The Glory and the Dream: A Narrative History of America, 1932–1972* (Michael Joseph, London, 1975).

Michael T. Marsden, John G. Nachbar and Sam L. Grogg, Jr., *Movies as Artifacts: Cultural Criticism of Popular Film* (Nelson-Hall, Chicago, 1982).

Olga J. Martin, *Hollywood's Movie Commandments: A Handbook for Motion Picture Writers and Reviewers* (Arno Press & New York Times, New York, 1970).

Elaine Tyler May, *Homeward Bound: American Families in the Cold War Era* (Harper Collins, New York, 1988).

Lary May (ed.), *Recasting America: Culture and Politics in the Age of Cold War* (University of Chicago Press, Chicago, 1989).

Colin McArthur, *Underworld U.S.A.* (Secker & Warburg, London, 1972).

Joseph McBride, *Hawks on Hawks* (University of California Press, Berkeley, 1982).

Joseph McBride and Michael Wilmington, *John Ford* (Secker & Warburg, London, 1974).

Graham McCann, *Rebel Males: Clift, Brando and Dean* (Hamish Hamilton, London, 1991).

Frank D. McConnell, *The Spoken Seen: Film & the Romantic Imagination* (Johns Hopkins University Press, Baltimore, 1975).

J. Fred MacDonald, *Who Shot the Sheriff?: The Rise and Fall of the Television Western* (Praeger, New York, 1987).

Archie P. McDonald (ed.), *Shooting Stars: Heroes and Heroines of Western Film* (Indiana University Press, Bloomington, 1987).

Richard D. McGhee, *John Wayne: Actor, Artist, Hero* (McFarland, Jefferson, 1990).

Michael Medved, *Hollywood vs. America: Popular Culture and the War on Traditional Values* (HarperCollins, New York, 1992).

Joan Mellen, *Big Bad Wolves: Masculinity in the Americam Film* (Elm Tree Books, London, [1977] 1978).

William R. Meyer, *The Making of the Great Westerns* (Arlington House, New Rochelle, New York, 1979).

Tom Milne (ed.), *Time Out Film Guide*, 3rd edn (Penguin, London, 1993).

Mike Munn, *The Stories Behind the Scenes of the Great Film Epics* (Argus Books, Watford, 1982).

Michael Munn, *Charlton Heston: A Biography* (Robson Books, London, 1986).

Gunnar Myrdal, with Richard M. E. Sterner and Arnold Rose, *An American Dilemma: The Negro Problem and Modern Democracy* (Harper & Row, New York, [1944] 1962).

Jack Nachbar (ed.), *Focus on the Western* (Prentice-Hall, Englewood Cliffs, 1974).

John G. Nachbar, *Western Films: An Annotated Critical Bibliography* (Garland, New York, 1975).

Jay Robert Nash, *Murder, America: Homicide in the United States from the Revolution to the Present* (Harrap, London, [1980] 1981).

Victor S. Navasky, *Naming Names* (Viking Press, New York, 1980).

Kim Newman, *Wild West Movies: Or How the West Was Found, Won, Lost, Lied About, Filmed and Forgotten* (Bloomsbury, London, 1990).

John E. O'Connor and Martin A. Jackson (eds), *American History/American Film: Interpreting the Hollywood Image* (Continuum, New York, [1979] 1991).

William L. O'Neill, *American High: The Years of Confidence, 1945–1960* (Macmillan, New York, 1986).

James Robert Parish and Michael R. Pitts, *The Great Western Pictures* (Scarecrow Press, Metuchen, 1976).

James Robert Parish and Don E. Stanke, *The All-Americans* (Rainbow Books, Carlstadt, 1978).

Robert Parrish, *Growing Up in Hollywood* (Bodley Head, London, 1976).

Danny Peary, *Cult Movies: A Hundred Ways to Find the Reel Thing* (Vermilion, London, 1982).

Danny Peary, *Cult Movies 2: 50 More of the Classics, the Sleepers, the Weird, and the Wonderful* (Dell, New York, 1983).

Danny Peary (ed.), *Close-Ups: The Movie Star Book: Intimate Profiles of Movie Stars by Their Costars, Directors, Screenwriters, and Friends* (Simon & Schuster, London, 1988).

Danny Peary, *Cult Movies 3: 50 More of the Classics, the Sleepers, the Weird, and the Wonderful* (Sidgwick & Jackson, London, 1989).

Danny Peary, *Alternative Oscars: One Critic's Defiant Choices for Best Picture, Actor, and Actress – from 1927 to the Present* (Simon & Schuster, London, 1993).

Richard H. Pells, *The Liberal Mind in a Conservative Age: American Intellectuals in the 1940s and 1950s*, 2nd edn (Wesleyan University Press, Middletown, 1989).

Ralph Barton Perry, *Puritanism and Democracy* (Vanguard Press, New York, 1944).

Lee Pfeiffer, *The John Wayne Scrapbook* (Citadel Press, Secaucus 1989).

Roy Pickard, *The Hollywood Studios* (Frederick Muller, London, 1978).

David Pirie (ed.), *Anatomy of the Movies* (Windward, London, 1981).

Michael R. Pitts, *Hollywood and American History: A Filmography of over 250 Motion Pictures Depicting U.S. History* (McFarland, Jefferson, 1984).

J. A. Place, *The Western Films of John Ford* (Citadel Press, Secaucus, 1974).

J. A. Place, *The Non-Western Films of John Ford* (Citadel Press, Secaucus, 1979).

Richard Polenberg, *One Nation Divisible: Class, Race, and Ethnicity in the United States since 1938* (Penguin, London, [1980] 1988).

Dilys Powell (ed. by George Perry), *The Golden Screen: Fifty Years of Films* (Pavilion Books/Michael Joseph, London, 1989).

Lawrence J. Quirk, *The Films of William Holden* (Citadel Press, Secaucus, 1973).

Richard L. Rapson, *American Yearnings: Love, Money, and Endless Possibility* (University Press of America, Lanham, 1988).

Robert B. Ray, *A Certain Tendency of the Hollywood Cinema, 1930–1980* (Princeton University Press, Princeton, 1985).

Charles A. Reich, *The Greening of America* (Penguin, Middlesex, [1970] 1972).

Jeffrey Richards, *Visions of Yesterday* (Routledge & Kegan Paul, London, 1973).

Jeffrey Richards and Anthony Aldgate, *Best of British: Cinema and Society, 1930–1970* (Basil Blackwell, Oxford, 1983).

David Riesman, with Nathan Glazer and Reuel Denney, *The Lonely Crowd: A Study of the Changing American Character* (Yale University Press, New Haven, [1950] 1989).

Randy Roberts and James S. Olson, *John Wayne: American* (Free Press, New York, 1995).

Bernard Rosenberg and David Manning White (eds), *Mass Culture: The Popular Arts in America* (Collier-Macmillan, London, 1957).

Richard Roud (ed.), *Cinema: A Critical Dictionary: The Major Film-Makers* (2 vols) (Nationwide/Martin Secker & Warburg, London, 1980).

John Carlos Rowe and Rick Berg (eds), *The Vietnam War and American Culture* (Columbia University Press, New York, 1991).

Wayne Michael Sarf, *God Bless You, Buffalo Bill: A Layman's Guide to History and the Western Film* (Fairleigh Dickinson University Press, New York, 1983).

Andrew Sarris, *The American Cinema: Directors and Directions, 1929–1968* (E. P. Dutton, New York, 1968).

Andrew Sarris (ed.), *Hollywood Voices: Interviews with Film Directors* (Secker & Warburg, London, 1971).

Andrew Sarris, *The John Ford Movie Mystery* (Secker & Warburg, London, 1976).

William W. Savage, Jr., *The Cowboy Hero: Image in American History and Culture* (University of Oklahoma Press, Norman, 1986).

Thomas Schatz, *Hollywood Genres: Formulas, Filmmaking, and the Studio System* (Random House, New York, 1981).

Arthur M. Schlesinger, Jr. (ed.), *The Almanac of American History* (G. P. Putnam's Sons, New York, 1983).

Ted Sennett, *Great Hollywood Westerns* (Harry N. Abrams, Inc., New York, [1990] 1992).

Paul Seydor, *Peckinpah: The Western Films* (University of Illinois Press, Urbana, 1980).

Donald Shepherd and Robert Slatzer with Dave Grayson, *Duke: The Life and Times of John Wayne* (Weidenfeld & Nicolson, London, 1986).

Andrew Sinclair, *John Ford* (George Allen & Unwin, London, 1979).

Robert Sklar, *Movie-Made America: A Cultural History of American Movies* (Chappell, London, 1978).

Arlene Skolnick, *Embattled Paradise: American Family in an Age of Uncertainty* (Harper Collins, New York, 1991).

Anthony Slide (ed.), *Selected Film Criticism, 1941–1950* (Scarecrow Press, Metuchen, 1983).

Richard Slotkin, *Regeneration Through Violence: The Mythology of the American Frontier, 1600–1860* (Wesleyan University Press, Middletown, [1973] 1987).

Richard Slotkin, *The Fatal Environment: The Myth of the Frontier in the Age of Industrialization, 1800–1890* (HarperCollins, New York, [1985] 1994).

Richard Slotkin, *Gunfighter Nation: The Myth of the Frontier in Twentieth-Century America* (HarperCollins, New York, [1992] 1993).

Henry Nash Smith, *Virgin Land: The American West as Symbol and Myth* (Harvard University Press, Cambridge, [1950] 1978).

Donald Spoto, *Camerado: Hollywood and the American Man* (New American Library, New York, 1978).

Cobbett Steinberg, *Reel Facts: The Movie Book of Records* (Penguin, Harmondsworth, 1981).

Peter Stowell, *John Ford* (Twayne, Boston, 1986).

Larry Swindell, *The Last Hero: A Biography of Gary Cooper* (Robson Books, London, 1987).

Tony Thomas, *The Films of Kirk Douglas* (Citadel Press, Secaucus, 1972).

Tony Thomas, *The Films of the Forties* (Citadel Press, Secaucus, 1975).

Tony Thomas, *Gregory Peck* (Pyramid, New York, 1977).

Tony Thomas, *Hollywood and the American Image* (Arlington House. Westport, 1981).

Tony Thomas, *The West That Never Was: Hollywood's Vision of the Cowboys and Gunfighters* (Citadel Press, Secaucus, 1989).

Tony Thomas and Aubrey Solomon, *The Films of 20th Century Fox* (Citadel Press, Secaucus, 1985).

Frank Thompson, *Alamo Movies* (Old Mill Books, East Berlin, P.A., 1991).

David Thomson, *Showman: The Life of David O. Selznick* (Abacus, London, 1993).

Jane Tompkins, *West of Everything: The Inner Life of Westerns* (Oxford University Press, New York, 1992).

Jon Tuska, *The Filming of the West* (Doubleday, Garden City, 1976).

Jon Tuska, *The American West in Film: Critical Approaches to the Western* (University of Nebraska Press, Lincoln, [1985] 1988).

Wiley Lee Umphlett, *Mythmakers of the Americam Dream: The Nostalgic Vision in Popular Culture* (Bucknell University Press, Lewisburg, 1983).

Gore Vidal, *On Our Own Now* (Panther Books, St Albans, 1976).

Gore Vidal, *Armageddon?: Essays 1983–1987* (Grafton Books, London, 1989).

King Vidor, *A Tree is a Tree* (Longman, Green, London, 1954).

James Vinson (ed.), *The International Dictionary of Films and Filmmakers, Vol. 3: Actors and Actresses* (Macmillan, London, 1988).

Alexander Walker, *Stardom: The Hollywood Phenomenon* (Michael Joseph, London, 1970).

Duncan Webster, *Looka Yonder!: The Imaginary America of Populist Culture* (Routledge, London, 1988).

Dixon Wecter, *The Hero in America: A Chronicle of Hero-Worship* (University of Michigan Press, Ann Arbor, [1941] 1966).

David Weddle, *"If They Move ... Kill 'Em!": The Life and Times of Sam Peckinpah* (Grove Press, New York, 1994).

Stephen J. Whitfield, *The Culture of the Cold War* (Johns Hopkins University Press, Baltimore, 1991).

William H. Whyte, Jr., *The Organization Man* (Doubleday-Anchor, Garden City, 1956).

Mason Wiley and Damien Bona, *Inside Oscar: The Unofficial History of the Academy Awards* (Ballantine Books, New York, 1987).

Rupert Wilkinson, *American Tough: The Tough-Guy Tradition and American Character* (Greenwood Press, Westport, 1984).

Rupert Wilkinson (ed.), *American Social Character: Modern Interpretations from the '40s to the present* (HarperCollins, New York, 1992).

Gary Wills, *Reagan's America: Innocents at Home* (Heinemann, London, 1988).

Peter Wollen, *Signs and Meanings in the Cinema* (Thames & Hudson, London, 1970).

Robin Wood, *Howard Hawks* (British Film Institute, London, 1983).

Will Wright, *Six Guns and Society: A Structural Study of the Western* (University of California Press, Berkeley, [1975] 1977).

David Zinman, *Fifty Grand Movies of the 1960s and 1970s* (Crown Publishers, New York, 1986).

Fred Zinnemann, *An Autobiography* (Bloomsbury, London, 1992).

Maurice Zolotow, *John Wayne: Shooting Star* (W. H. Allen, London, 1974).

Articles/magazines

Nicholas Anez, "Wyatt Earp" in *Films in Review*, June/July and August/September 1990, Vol. XLI Nos 6–7 and 8–9 (National Board of Review of Motion Pictures, New York, 1990), pp. 323–33 and pp. 395–406 respectively.

Gerald Clarke, "1939: Twelve Months of Magic", in *TIME*, March 27 1989, pp. 38–40.

Gerald Cockshott, "The Curious Cult of John Ford", in *The Film Society Magazine*, December 1954, No. 2 (Federation of Film Societies, London, 1954), pp. 8–10, 31.

Edward Countryman, "John Ford's *Drums Along The Mohawk*: The Making of an American Myth", in Susan Porter Benson, Stephen Brier and Roy Rosenzweig (eds), *Presenting the Past: Essays on History and the Public* (Temple University Press, Philadelphia, 1986), pp. 87–102, 377.

David F. Coursen, "John Ford's Wilderness: *The Man Who Shot Liberty Valance*", in *Sight and Sound: International Film Quarterly*, Autumn 1978, Vol. 47 No. 4 (British Film Institute, London, 1978), pp. 237–41.

Judith Crist, "Burt Lancaster", interview (co-edited by Shirley Sealy), in Judith Crist, *Take 22: Moviemakers on Moviemaking*, (Continuum, New York, [1984] 1991), pp. 69–101.

Raymond Durgnat, "King Vidor", in *Film Comment*, July/August and September/October 1973, Vol. 9 Nos 4 and 5 (Film Comment, Boston, 1973), pp. 10–49 and pp. 16–51 respectively.

Raymond Durgnat, "Will Western Heroes Ride Back Out of the Sunset?", in *The Movie Scene*, Vol. 1 No. 4, May 1985 (Robud Productions, Surrey, 1985), pp. 30–31.

Kirk Ellis, "On the Warpath: John Ford and the Indians", in *Journal of Popular Film & Television*, Summer 1980, Vol. VIII No. 2 (Heldref Publications, Washington D.C., 1980), pp. 34–41.

William K. Everson, "1939: A Retrospective Reappraisal", in *Films in Review*, August/ September 1990, Vol. XLI No. 8/9 (National Board of Review of Motion Pictures, New York, 1990), pp. 407–13.

J. H. Fenwick and Jonathan Green-Armytage, "Now You See It: Landscape and Anthony Mann", in *Sight and Sound*, Autumn 1965, Vol. 34 No. 4, pp. 186–9.

Paul Gray, "Whose America?", in *TIME*, July 8 1991, pp. 22–7.

Reynold Humphries, "The Function of Mexico in Peckinpah's Films", in *JUMP CUT: A Review of Contemporary Cinema*, August 1978, No. 18 (JUMP CUT Associates, Berkeley & Chicago, 1978), pp. 17–20.

Paul Andrew Hutton "'Correct in Every Detail': General Custer in Hollywood", in Paul Andrew Hutton (ed.), *The Custer Reader* (University of Nebraska Press, Lincoln, 1992), pp. 488–524.

Greg Kimble, "*How The West Was Won* – in Cinerama", in *American Cinematographer: International Journal of Film and Video Production Techniques*, October 1983, Vol. 64 No. 10 (A.S.C. Holding Corp., Hollywood, 1983), pp. 46–50, 89–99.

Leo Lowenthal, "The Triumph of Mass Idols" (1944), reprinted in Leo Lowenthal *Literature, Popular Culture and Society* (Pacific Books, Palo Alto, 1961), pp. 109–40.

Henry R. Luce, "The American Century", in *LIFE*, February 17 1941, reprinted in *LIFE* Editors, *Great Readings from LIFE: A Treasury of the Best Stories and Articles Chosen by the Editors* (Jonathan Cape, London, 1962), pp. 173–88.

John E. Mann and A. L. Wise, "In Praise of John Ford", in *The Film Society Magazine*, February 1955, No. 3, pp. 25–6.

Roland Marchand, "Visions of Classlessness, Quests for Dominion: American Popular Culture, 1945–1960", in Robert Hamlett Bremner and Gary W. Reichard (eds), *Reshaping America: Society and Institutions, 1945–1960* (Ohio State University Press, Columbus, 1982), pp. 163–90.

Colin McArthur, "The Roots of the Western", in *Cinema*, All American issue, October 1969, No. 4 (Cambridge, England, 1969), pp. 11–13.

Gabriel Miller, "*Shane* Redux: *The Shootist* and the Western Dilemma", in *Journal of Popular Film & Television*, Summer 1983, Vol. 11 No. 2, pp. 66–77.

Lance Morrow, "Rediscovering America", in *TIME*, July 7 1980, pp. 26–31.

Laura Mulvey, "Afterthoughts on 'Visual Pleasure and Narrative Cinema' inspired by King Vidor's *Duel in the Sun* (1946)", in Laura Mulvey, *Visual and Other Pleasures* (Macmillan Press, London, 1989), pp. 29–38.

William S. Pechter, "John Ford: A Persistence of Vision", reprinted in Leo Braudy and Morris Dickstein (eds), *Great Film Directors: A Critical Anthology* (Oxford University Press, New York, 1978), pp. 344–56.

Jeffrey Richards, "John Ford and the American National Myth", in Keith Stringer, Alexander Grant and Claus Bjorn (eds), *Social and Political Identities in Western History* (Akademisk Vorlag, Copenhagen, 1994), pp. 244–66.

Arthur Schlesinger, Jr., "The Cult of Ethnicity, Good and Bad", in *TIME*, July 8 1991, p. 28.

Scott Simmon, "The Kid Hangs Tough", in *The Movie Scene*, May 1985, Vol. 1 No. 4, pp. 33–5.

Scott Simmon, "How We Lost The West", in *The Movie Scene*, June 1985, Vol. 1 No. 5 (Robud Productions, Surrey, 1985), pp. 31–3.

Andrew Sinclair, "The Man on Horseback: The Seven Faces of John Wayne", in *Sight and Sound*, Autumn 1979, Vol. 48 No. 4, pp. 232–5.

Stephen Tatum, "The Western Film Critic as Shootist", in *Journal of Popular Film and Television*, Fall 1983, Vol. 11 No. 3, pp. 114–21.

Frank Thompson, "*The Alamo*: Wayne's Reel Heroes", in *American Cinematographer*, July 1990, Vol. 71 No. 7, pp. 34–40.

David Thomson, "All Along the River", in *Sight and Sound*, Winter 1976–77, Vol. 46 No. 1, pp. 9–13.

Frederick Jackson Turner, "The Significance of the Frontier in American History" (1893), reprinted in Ray Allen Billington (ed.), *Frontier and Section: Selected Essays of Frederick Jackson Turner* (Prentice-Hall, Englewood Cliffs, 1961), pp. 37–62.

Mike Wallington, "Auteur & Genre: The Westerns of Delmer Daves", in *Cinema*, All American issue, October 1969, No. 4, pp. 6–9.

Wide Angle, John Ford issue (ed. by Peter Lehman), 1978, Vol. 2 No. 4 (Ohio University Press, Athens, 1978), pp. 2–61.

Martin M. Winkler, "Tragic Features in John Ford's *The Searchers*", in Martin M. Winkler (ed.), *Classics and Cinema* (Bucknell University Press, Lewisburg, 1991), pp. 185–208.

Index

Alamo, The, 105, 137
Aldrich, Robert, 12, 71, 79, 125, 133, 164
Altman, Robert, 163, 168, 170, 171
Alvarez Kelly, 99, 125
Americans, The: A Study in National Character (book), 70
American Political Tradition, The (book), 64
American West in Film, The (book), 4–5
Angel and the Badman, 43
Anti-Intellectualism in American Life (book), 109–10
Apache, 71
Arness, James, 184
Arrowhead, 67, 70, 71, 130, 137
Arthur, Jean, 74
Aurthur, Robert Alan, 98, 100

Bacall, Lauren, 180
Bad Day at Black Rock, 76, 103
Bakal, Carl, 120
Baker, Carroll, 87
Ballad of Cable Hogue, The, 163, 164
Bandolero!, 126, 138–40, 144, 145, 153, 187
Barrett, James Lee, 139, 144, 145
Barrymore, Lionel, 36, 55
Bazin, André, 8
Bedford Incident, The, 127
Bellamy, Ralph, 132, 134, 135
Bergen, Candice, 162
Berger, Senta, 129
Bergman, Andrew, 17
Bickford, Charles, 87, 92, 174
Big Bad Wolves (book), 147
Big Country, The, 1, 46, 76, 83, 86–94, 102, 104, 137, 174
Big Trail, The, 17, 51
Billy the Kid (1941), 18, 23, 24, 27–8
Biskind, Peter, 57, 58
Blanshard, Paul, 62
Boetticher, Budd, 6, 10, 67, 68
Bogart, Humphrey, 27

Bond, Ward, 50, 59, 61
Boone, Richard, 181
Borgnine, Ernest, 151
Brando, Marlon, 55, 100, 155
Bravados, The, 62
Brennan, Walter, 27, 37, 52, 57, 58, 174
Brigham Young – Frontiersman, 18, 23–4, 25, 26, 27
Broken Arrow (1950), 46, 69–70, 71, 188
Brooks, Richard, 67, 125, 126, 132, 133, 135
Brown, Dee, 163
Brynner, Yul, 136, 151, 152, 158
Buffalo Bill (1944), 29, 69
Buffalo Bill and the Indians or Sitting Bull's History Lesson, 6, 168–72, 174, 175, 180, 182
Bury My Heart at Wounded Knee (book), 163
Busch, Niven, 41, 48
Butch Cassidy and the Sundance Kid, 25, 74, 126, 146–8, 149, 162, 191

Cardinale, Claudia, 132, 134
Carey, Harry, 46
Carey, Harry, Jr., 63
Carradine, John, 22, 39
Cat Ballou, 124, 132
Cawelti, John G., 9, 10
Centennial (TV series), 184, 185, 189
Cheyenne Autumn, 40, 51, 123–4
Churchill, Berton, 20
Cimarron (1931), 17, 188
Clift, Montgomery, 52, 54, 55, 56, 87
Clinton, Bill, 2
Cobb, Lee J., 86, 118
Coburn, James, 130, 158, 160
Cohn, Roy, 101
Colorado Territory, 48
Connors, Chuck, 87
Cooper, Gary, 27, 29, 49, 50, 55, 57, 67, 69, 102, 136, 145

234

Corey, Jeff, 148
Costner, Kevin, 179, 187, 188, 189, 192
Cotten, Joseph, 36, 55, 56, 79, 87
Cowboys, The, 52, 137, 164
Culpepper Cattle Co., The, 163, 164
Curtiz, Michael, 4, 20, 23, 26
Custer, George, 6, 24, 28, 40, 59, 60, 63, 64, 123, 131, 170

Dances With Wolves, 6, 179, 188, 189
Dark Command, 18, 23, 27
Darnell, Linda, 38, 43
Da Silva, Howard, 49, 50
Daves, Delmer, 10, 46, 67, 69, 103
Death of a Gunfighter, 145-6
DeMille, Cecil B., 19, 23, 27, 36, 40, 49, 50, 117
Devil's Doorway, 46, 69-70, 71
de Wilde, Brandon, 74, 110
Dirksen, Everett, 37
Dirty Harry, 190-1
Distant Trumpet, A, 123
Dmytryk, Edward, 6, 67, 94, 94, 98, 99-101, 125, 145
Dodge City, 4, 6, 18, 20, 23, 24, 25, 26, 46, 69
Douglas, Kirk, 4, 67, 76, 78-9, 80, 94, 110-11, 136, 137, 138, 147, 164, 187
Downs, Cathy, 34
Drake, Tom, 95
Dru, Joanne, 53, 63
Drums Along the Mohawk, 18, 23, 25, 26, 28, 50
Duel at Diablo, 125, 135-6
Duel in the Sun, 4, 35-7, 39, 41-5, 46, 47, 48, 49, 52, 53, 55, 70, 73, 85, 86, 87, 93, 103, 133, 137, 146, 189
Dulles, John Foster, 85
Durgnat, Raymond, 87
Duvall, Robert, 187

Earp, Wyatt, 6, 23, 34, 35, 37, 38, 39, 62, 72, 94, 101, 126, 187, 188
Eastwood, Clint, 125, 145, 172, 173, 176, 177, 178, 179, 186-7, 188, 190, 192
Eisenhower, Dwight D., 1, 55, 68, 84, 85, 92, 105, 109
El Dorado, 103, 126, 137, 180

Falling Down, 190
Fastest Gun Alive, The, 177
Fistful of Dollars, 173
Flynn, Errol, 4, 23, 24, 25, 26, 28, 46, 69

Fonda, Henry, 25, 26, 34, 35, 39, 40, 52, 55, 58-9, 94, 98, 100, 101, 102, 103, 117, 130, 136, 138, 145, 147, 151, 187
For a Few Dollars More, 173
Ford, Glenn, 67, 136
Ford, John, 3, 4, 6, 9-10, 15, 18, 19, 20, 22, 26, 33, 34, 35, 37-8, 39-41, 44, 48, 51, 52, 60, 62, 63, 64, 66, 70, 76, 77, 78, 82, 88, 94, 99, 101, 103, 107, 108, 112, 116, 123, 124, 125, 127, 129, 130, 135, 159, 179, 191, 192
Foreman, Carl, 68-9, 99
Fort Apache, 40, 46, 51, 52, 55, 58-62, 63, 64, 65, 66, 69, 124, 130, 131
French, Philip, 12, 13, 93, 106
Fuller, Samuel, 71, 178
Furies, The, 48, 87

Garner, James, 103, 187
George, Chief Dan, 162, 174
Gettysburg, 189
Giant, 55, 86
Gish, Lillian, 36
Glory Guys, The, 126, 131
Goddard, Paulette, 49, 50
Godfather, The, 161
Goldman, William, 146
Goldwater, Barry, 1, 12, 121, 138
Gomez, Marie, 133
Gone With the Wind, 16, 35, 42, 44
Good, the Bad and the Ugly, The, 173
Gorer, Geoffrey, 70, 81
Grapes of Wrath, The, 26, 40, 59
Green Berets, The, 137, 138, 139, 144, 145, 191
Gries, Tom, 125, 126, 136
Gunfight, A, 164
Gunfight at the O.K. Corral, 67, 68, 76, 94, 102, 187
Gunfighter, The, 4, 13, 14, 67, 69, 72-4, 75, 80-3, 86, 102, 103, 136, 151, 179, 180, 189
Gunfighter Nation (book), 14
Guns in the Afternoon (see *Ride the High Country*)

Hackett, Joan, 137
Hackman, Gene, 188
Hall, Oakley, 94, 98, 100
Harris, Richard, 127, 129, 130
Hartley, Mariette, 113
Hathaway, Henry, 10, 23, 103, 116, 125, 138, 144

Hawks, Howard, 4, 10, 52, 53, 54, 56, 57, 67, 87, 94, 99, 103, 126, 137, 180
Heaven's Gate, 42, 185, 190
Heflin, Van, 74
Heston, Charlton, 67, 87, 89, 94, 125, 126, 127, 129, 130, 136, 137, 138
High Noon, 1, 2, 3, 22, 68–9, 73, 75, 76, 99, 102, 103, 145, 148, 176, 189, 190
High Plains Drifter, 173, 186, 188
Hill, George Roy, 126, 146
Hired Hand, The, 163, 164
Hiss, Alger, 64, 143
Ho Chi Minh, 134
Hoffman, Dustin, 162, 188
Hofstadter, Richard, 64, 109–10
Holden, William, 67, 94, 125, 136, 150, 155, 164
Holliday, John H. ("Doc"), 38, 94
Hombre, 136, 172
Homeier, Skip, 72, 180
Hondo, 180
Horne, Lena, 145
Horse Soldiers, The, 94
Horton, Mildred MacAffee, 32
Hour of the Gun, 103, 126, 187
Howard, Ron, 180
How the West Was Won (film), 6, 12, 13, 42, 43, 115–19, 122, 132, 161, 184
How the West Was Won (TV series), 184
Hud, 55, 110, 172
Hudson, Rock, 79, 80, 144, 147
Hughes, Howard, 30, 42, 177
Hunter, Jeffrey, 77
Huston, John, 8, 33, 48, 49, 110, 164
Huston, Walter, 43, 87

Invitation to a Gunfighter, 136
Ives, Burl, 87, 92

Jesse James (1939), 18, 20, 23, 25, 26, 46
Johnny Guitar, 4, 46, 69, 99
Johnson, Ben, 63, 151
Johnson, Lyndon B., 1, 12, 108, 121, 122, 139, 142
Jones, Jennifer, 4, 35–6, 42, 43, 85
Jones, Tommy Lee, 187
Jordan, Dorothy, 77
Journey to Shiloh, 132
Jurado, Katy, 145

Kasdan, Lawrence, 186, 189
Kazan, Elia, 100
Kelly, Grace, 145

Kennedy, George, 139, 140, 187
Kennedy, John F., 1, 2, 12, 105, 108–9, 120, 121, 123, 142, 161, 192
Kennedy, Robert F., 120, 125, 138, 140
King, Henry, 4, 18, 62, 72, 86
King, Martin Luther, 120, 125, 138
Kristofferson, Kris, 160

Ladd, Alan, 67, 74, 76
Lake, Stuart N., 37
Lancaster, Burt, 67, 71, 94, 102, 132, 133, 134, 135, 136, 159, 164, 172, 187
Lang, Fritz, 19
Last Hunt, The, 67
Last Sunset, The, 12, 67, 79–82, 94, 110
Last Train from Gun Hill, 69
Last Wagon, The, 67
Law and Jake Wade, The, 67
Left-Handed Gun, The, 55, 67, 68, 172
Lenihan, John H., 13, 26, 93, 108
Leone, Sergio, 25, 101, 125, 145, 173
Life and Times of Judge Roy Bean, The, 8, 164
Lincoln, Abraham, 25, 40, 105, 123, 142
Little Big Man, 162, 171, 174, 188, 192
Locke, Sondra, 176
Lonely Are the Brave, 4, 5, 110–12, 114, 115, 118, 190
Lonely Crowd, The (book), 56–7, 58
Lonesome Dove (TV series), 187–8, 189
Long Riders, The, 185
Lowenthal, Leo, 47
Lynley, Carol, 79

MacAhans, The (TV pilot), 184
MacArthur, Douglas, 101
Magnificent Seven, The, 105, 126, 132, 134, 151, 152, 153, 158
Major Dundee, 126–31, 132, 135, 137, 138, 144, 145, 159, 174, 179
Malone, Dorothy, 79, 95, 103
Manchurian Candidate, The, 119
Man from Colorado, The, 67
Man from Laramie, The, 125
Man in the Gray Flannel Suit, The, 85–6, 93
Mankiewicz, Joseph L., 49, 164
Mann, Anthony, 6, 7, 10, 46, 48, 67, 68, 69, 87, 101, 117, 125, 178, 188
Manson, Charles, 122, 161
Man Who Shot Liberty Valance, The, 6, 8, 46, 88, 102, 107–9, 112, 114, 115, 118, 119, 123, 135, 137, 159, 180, 189

Man Without a Star, 110
Marshall, George, 116
Martin, Dean, 67, 94, 130, 136, 137, 138, 139, 140, 147, 164
Marvin, Lee, 107, 124, 132, 133, 134, 159, 164
Matthau, Walter, 110
Mature, Victor, 37
Mayo, Virginia, 48
McArthur, Colin, 99
McCarthy, Joseph, 2, 49, 68, 69, 84, 99, 101, 156
McConnell, Frank D., 99
McCrea, Joel, 24, 25, 48, 55, 67, 69, 112, 136, 151, 179
McKinney, Bill, 173, 180
McLaglen, Andrew V., 126, 131, 138, 139, 144, 145, 164
McLaglen, Victor, 59, 63
McMurtry, Larry, 187
McQueen, Steve, 125, 151, 158, 185
Mellen, Joan, 147
Meyer, Emile, 74
Michaels, Dolores, 94, 103
Michener, James A., 184
Midnight Cowboy, 146
Miles, Vera, 107
Miller, David, 4, 27, 110
Mineo, Sal, 124
Misfits, The, 110
Mitchell, Millard, 72
Mitchell, Thomas, 19
Mitchum, Robert, 48, 103, 137, 138, 147
Monte Walsh, 163, 164
Moreau, Jeanne, 164
Moross, Jerome, 91
My Darling Clementine, 34–5, 36, 37–41, 42, 43, 45, 46, 48, 52, 59, 60, 62, 69, 70, 73, 101, 103, 136, 179, 187

Nachbar, Jack, 115
Nelson, Ralph, 125, 162, 163
Nevada Smith, 125
Newman, Paul, 55, 67, 110, 136, 146, 147, 148, 164, 168, 170, 171, 172–3, 185
Nixon, Richard M., 1, 142–3, 161, 164, 165
North, Sheree, 181
North West Mounted Police, 18, 24, 27
Northwest Passage, 18, 23, 24, 25, 26, 28, 47, 50

Oates, Warren, 151, 157

O'Brian, Hugh, 181
O'Brien, Edmond, 107, 151
Once Upon a Time in the West, 25, 101, 145
One-Eyed Jacks, 55, 155
100 Rifles, 126, 136
O'Neill, William L., 5
On the Waterfront, 100
Oswald, Lee Harvey, 120
Outlaw, The, 29, 30, 42, 177, 189
Outlaw Josey Wales, The, 6, 145, 172, 173–9, 180, 182, 187
Ox-Bow Incident, The, 29, 30, 59, 101

Palance, Jack, 74, 132, 133, 134
Pale Rider, 173, 186–7, 188
Pat Garrett & Billy the Kid, 159, 160, 164
Peck, Gregory, 36, 42, 72, 73, 76, 83, 85–6, 87, 88, 89, 92, 93, 94, 102, 117, 136, 151, 164, 179
Peckinpah, Sam, 5, 6, 10, 25, 73, 74, 112, 126, 127, 128, 129, 130, 132, 136, 147, 148, 149, 150, 151, 152, 155, 156, 157, 158, 159, 161, 163, 164
Penn, Arthur, 55, 67, 125, 162, 172
Peppard, George, 116, 118, 132
Perfect World, A, 173, 192
Pleasence, Donald, 125
Poitier, Sidney, 135–6
Polonsky, Abraham, 145
Potter, David, 7
Power, Tyrone, 23, 46
Professionals, The, 126, 132–5, 158, 159
Proud Ones, The, 68, 69
Pursued, 48, 67

Quiet Man, The, 76
Quigley, Martin, 37
Quinn, Anthony, 67, 94, 98

Rankin, John, 37
Rawhide (TV series), 173
Ray, Nicholas, 4, 46, 68, 69, 99
Reagan, Ronald, 1–2, 185–6
Redford, Robert, 146, 148
Red River, 4, 46, 52–8, 63, 66, 87, 175, 180, 187, 189
Return of Frank James, The, 18, 23, 24, 25, 177
Reynolds, Debbie, 116
Ride the High Country (a.k.a. *Guns in the Afternoon*), 6, 73, 112–14, 115, 118, 136, 137, 151, 159, 179, 181, 187, 189
Riesman, David, 56–7, 58, 59

Right Stuff, The, 187
Rio Bravo, 67, 94, 103, 130, 137, 180, 187
Rio Grande, 46, 60, 62, 64, 70, 131, 179
Ritt, Martin, 55, 110, 136, 172
Robinson, Edward G., 123
Rowlands, Gena, 110
Roosevelt, Franklin D., 20, 46
Run of the Arrow, 71, 145, 178–9, 188
Ryan, Robert, 25, 132, 133, 134, 135, 149, 174
Rydell, Mark, 52, 164

Sampson, Will, 168, 175
Santa Fe Trail, 18, 23, 24, 27
Sarris, Andrew, 9, 19
Scalphunters, The, 136
Scott, Randolph, 6, 24, 55, 67, 112, 136, 151
Searchers, The, 4, 14, 39, 40, 52, 67, 68, 71, 73, 76–8, 80–2, 123, 124, 125, 145, 148, 179, 187
Seeing Is Believing (book), 57
Selznick, David O., 35, 36, 37, 42, 43, 48
Sergeant Rutledge, 99, 124, 135
Shane, 6, 12, 13, 14, 46, 67, 69, 73, 74–6, 77, 80–2, 86, 91, 102, 124, 133, 148, 186
Shenandoah, 131–2, 138
She Wore a Yellow Ribbon, 52, 56, 60, 62, 63–5, 66, 67, 124, 131
Shootist, The, 6, 73, 179–83, 189
Showdown (book), 13
Siegel, Don, 73, 103, 179, 181, 182, 190
Silverado, 186
Simmons, Jean, 88, 93
Sirhan, Sirhan B., 140
Six-Gun Mystique, The (book), 10
Six Guns and Society (book), 10–11, 12, 13, 57
Slotkin, Richard, 14
Soldier Blue, 162–3, 164
Stagecoach, 3, 5, 15, 18–22, 23, 24, 25, 26, 30, 34, 35, 39, 41, 46, 51, 52, 66, 73, 88, 132, 144, 148, 160, 164, 167, 184, 189
Stanwyck, Barbara, 87
Starr, Ron, 113, 181
Steiger, Rod, 71, 178, 188
Stevens, George, 6, 33, 55, 74, 75, 86
Stewart, James, 1, 6, 7, 55, 67, 103, 107, 108, 117, 123, 125, 136, 138, 139, 140, 147, 178, 180, 188
Stone, Oliver, 191–2

Strauss, Peter, 162
Strode, Woody, 132, 133, 135
Sturges, John, 10, 67, 69, 76, 94, 103, 105, 123, 126, 132
Suber, Howard, 29

Tall T, The, 68
Taylor, Robert, 67
Tell Them Willie Boy Is Here, 146
Temple, Shirley, 59, 60
Thelma & Louise, 191
They Died With Their Boots On, 18, 20, 23, 24, 28, 45, 69, 123
3:10 to Yuma, 67, 69, 103
Thurmond, Strom, 59
Tin Star, The, 68, 69, 101
Tombstone, 188, 189
Tom Horn, 185
Tracy, Spencer, 76, 116, 117, 118
Treasure of the Sierra Madre, The, 48, 49
Trevor, Claire, 19
True Grit, 103, 137, 144, 145, 182
Trumbo, Dalton, 80, 110
Turner, Frederick Jackson, 2, 6, 73, 106, 115, 160
Tuska, Jon, 4–5
Two Flags West, 67, 145, 179
Two Rode Together, 82, 103, 124

Ulzana's Raid, 164
Unconquered, 49–50, 52
Undefeated, The, 126, 144–5
Unforgiven (1992), 6, 173, 188
Union Pacific, 18, 19, 20, 23, 24, 25, 26
Untouchables, The, 187

Van Cleef, Lee, 173
Vernon, John, 173
Vidor, King, 4, 24, 35, 47, 70, 86, 87, 110
Virginia City, 18, 24, 25, 26–7, 28

Wagon Master, 136, 179
Wallach, Eli, 118
Walsh, Raoul, 10, 24, 48, 51, 67, 69, 123, 157
Warlock, 6, 12, 46, 67, 68, 83, 94–103, 104, 125, 130, 138, 145, 151, 177
Wayne, John, 1, 2, 4, 12, 19, 22, 24, 39, 40, 46, 51, 52, 53, 55, 56, 58–9, 60, 63, 67, 69, 71, 76, 77, 78, 87, 94, 103, 105, 107, 108, 116, 121, 125, 135, 136, 137–8, 144, 145, 147, 152, 164–5, 179, 180, 181, 182, 183, 184, 189, 191, 192

Wayne, Patrick (Pat), 123, 124
Way West, The, 138
Welch, Raquel, 139, 140
Wellman, William A., 30, 69, 101
Westerner, The, 18, 23, 24, 25, 27, 29, 57
Westerns (book), 12–13
Western Union, 18, 19, 23, 24, 25, 28
Widmark, Richard, 67, 94, 95, 98, 100,
    103, 117, 118, 125, 127, 136, 138, 145,
    147
Wild Bunch, The, 5, 25, 29, 74, 126, 127,
    132, 134, 139, 147, 148–60, 161, 162,
    164, 174, 177, 185, 187, 189

Will Penny, 125, 136–7
Wills, Garry, 4
Wincer, Simon, 187
Wood, Natalie, 77
Wright, Will, 7, 10–11, 12, 13, 57
Wyatt Earp, 189
Wyler, William, 1, 27, 57, 76, 86, 92, 93

Yellow Sky, 49
Young Mr. Lincoln, 16, 59, 101

Zanuck, Darryl F., 73
Zinnemann, Fred, 3, 68, 99